Linguistische Arbeiten 395

Herausgegeben von Hans Altmann, Peter Blumenthal, Herbert E. Brekle, Gerhard Helbig, Hans Jürgen Heringer, Heinz Vater und Richard Wiese

George Broderick

Language Death in the Isle of Man

An investigation into the decline
and extinction of Manx Gaelic
as a community language in the Isle of Man

Max Niemeyer Verlag
Tübingen 1999

To the People of Man

Die Deutsche Bibliothek – CIP-Einheitsaufnahme

Broderick, George: Language death in the Isle of Man : an investigation into the decline and extinction of Manx Gaelic as a community language in the Isle of Man / George Broderick. – Tübingen : Niemeyer, 1999
  (Linguistische Arbeiten ; 395)

ISBN 3-484-30395-6   ISSN 0344-6727

Contents

Acknowledgements

In connection with this work I would like to extend my thanks and appreciation to the following who have made possible this undertaking:

To the Deutsche Forschungsgemeinschaft, Bonn, for substantial funding over a period of two years to enable this work to be carried out.

To Prof. Dr. P. Sture Ureland, Seminar für Allgemeine Linguistik der Universität Mannheim, for making available facilities to ensure the completion of this project, together with providing every encouragement and guidance and offering the benefit of his expertise in the field of language contact and language death.

To Rev. Robert L. Thomson, former Reader in Celtic Studies, University of Leeds, now of the Isle of Man, for helpful discussion and criticism in the preparation of this work, particularly in the formal linguistic section (Section 4).

To Prof. Dr. Georg Bossong, Romanisches Seminar der Universität Zürich, Prof. Dr. Dr. Bernhard D. Haage, Institut für Germanistik der Universität Mannheim, Prof. Dr. Máirtín Ó Murchú, Dublin Institute for Advanced Studies, and again to Prof. Dr. P. Sture Ureland, Seminar für Allgemeine Linguistik der Universität Mannheim, for additional comment and suggestions in preparing this work for publication.

To Ann Harrison, former Librarian Archivist at the Manx Museum, to Roger Sims, present Librarian Archivist at the Manx Museum, and to Yvonne Cresswell, Assistant Keeper: Social History, Manx Museum, for bringing to my attention additional documentation relevant to the sociolinguistic section (Section 2), and to the Library staff at the Manx Museum for their generous help and assistance in providing access to the documentary material.

To Anne Fevang, Sandefjord, and Lars Anders Ruden, Roa, Norway, for their transcription of the original Norwegian text of Marstrander's diary, and to Knut Janson, Dublin, for his translation of the text (see Appendix A).

To colleagues in the Isle of Man and elsewhere who had contact with the old native Manx speakers for the benefit of their knowledge concerning them.

To Marc Koschel, Seminar für Allgemeine Linguistik der Universität Mannheim, for drawing the graphics for Figure 8.

To all these I would like to extend my sincerest thanks and gratitude for their encouragement and support. Any mistakes that remain are my own.

George Broderick,
Seminar für Allgemeine Linguistik
der Universität Mannheim,
January 1999.

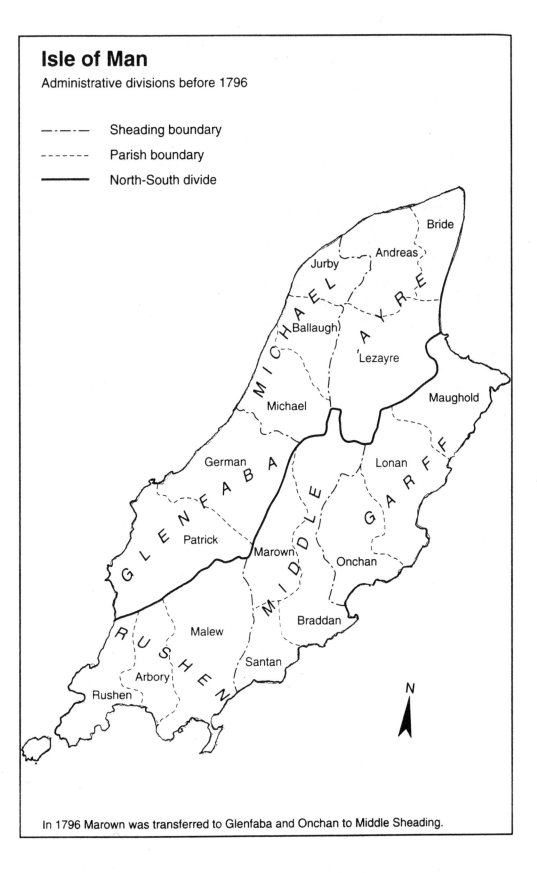

Isle of Man

Administrative divisions before 1796

— · — · — Sheading boundary

— — — — — Parish boundary

————— North-South divide

Bride

Andreas

Jurby

MICHAEL

Ballaugh

AYRE

Lezayre

Maughold

Michael

German

GLENFABA

Lonan

GARFF

MIDDLE

Patrick

Marown

Onchan

Malew

Braddan

RUSHEN

Santan

Arbory

Rushen

N

In 1796 Marown was transferred to Glenfaba and Onchan to Middle Sheading.

Preface

This work is a continuation of *A Handbook of Late Spoken Manx*, a work in three volumes dealing with the Manx of the last native speakers (cf. Broderick 1984a, 1986). These volumes essentially contain the raw material which makes the present work possible. The main theme of this book is language death, using Manx Gaelic as an example. Manx presents itself here perhaps as a prime example of language death, since we are here dealing with a language in its own right (though it lies closely to both Irish and Scottish Gaelic), and not a dialect, as in the case of East Sutherland Gaelic (cf. Dorian 1981). In this work I have attempted to combine both the sociohistorical and sociolinguistic, as well as the formal linguistic situations affecting Manx Gaelic to set the entire process in context with its component parts.

Finally, I include a short excursus on the Manx language revival movement in Man, since this activity was taking place at the same time Manx was in its death throes. In addition, it throws some light on attitudes at various times of the revival process towards Manx. In that respect it could be argued that language revival is a facet of language death, since if a language is in full bloom and vigour, such as German or English, any revivalist activity is surely unnecessary?

It is hoped that this work contributes to a better understanding of the phenomenon of language death.

G.B.

List of Abbreviations
common abbreviations not included

a/acc. - accusative.
Adj. - adjective.
Adv. - adverb.
Affirm. - affirmative (form of verb).
AL - Abandoned Language (language which is dying out - here Manx Gaelic).
Art. - definite article.
BBCS - Bulletin of the Board of Celtic Studies, Cardiff: University of Wales Press.
BUPS - Bulletin of the Ulster Place-Names Society, Series 2, Belfast.
C. - Cregeen's Manx Dictionary (1835).
Christian 1983 - see below.
CM - Classical Manx (defined in Section 4.1.).
CMS - Centre for Manx Studies (University of Liverpool), Douglas.
Conj. - conjunction.
Cop. - copula.
Craine 1974 - see below.
d/dat. - dative.
Dem.adj. - demonstrative adjective.
Dem.pn. - demonstrative pronoun.
Dep. - dependent (form of verb).
DGKS - Deutsche Gesellschaft für Keltische Studien (1936-45).
Diary - see Marstrander 1929-33b.
DIAS - Dublin Institute for Advanced Studies.
DIL - Dictionary of the Irish Language (RIA Contributions 1913-76).
Don. - Donegal (Irish).
ecl. - eclipsed, eclipsis (sse also Nas.).
EF - Edward Faragher *Reminiscences* (cf. Broderick 1981b).
EM - Early Manx (defined in Section 4.1.).
ESG - East Sutherland Gaelic; cf. Dorian 1981 esp.
Excerpts - Excerpts (about the Isle of Man) from (mainly British) Journals; cf. Cubbon 1939: 1307-16.
Exclam. - exclamation.
f./fem. - feminine.
fc. - forthcoming.
fn. - footnote.
G - Gaelic (here Irish, Scottish Gaelic).
g/gen. genitive.
GB - George Broderick.
GEM - Glossary of Early Manx (cf. Thomson 1954-57).
Ger. - German.
HE - Hiberno-English.
HLSM - Handbook of Late Spoken Manx (cf. Broderick 1984a & 1986).
IBS - Innsbrucker Beiträge zur Sprachwissenschaft.
IFC - Irish Folklore Commission (Dublin).
IJSL - International Journal of the Sociology of Language, The Hague: Mouton.
Indef.pn. - indefinite pronoun.
Indep. - independent (form of verb).
Inflec. - inflected.
Interrog. - interrogative.
IOMNHAS - Isle of Man Natural History and Antiquarian Society (Proc.), Douglas.
JMM - Journal of the Manx Museum, Douglas (1924-80).
L. - Latin.

LD - Language Decay: Pathological language disintegration.
len. - lenited, lenition.
LM - Late Manx (defined in Section 4.1.).
LP - Language Replacement (= Comnplete Shift): Total replacement of AL by TL (possibly TL/AL substratum, i.e. an AL-influenced variety (dialect) of TL).
LSM - Late Spoken Manx (of the last native speakers).
LSS - Linguistic Survey of Scotland (University of Edinburgh).
LT - Language Transmission: Deliberate direct passing on of a language from one generation to the next.
LTS - Language Transmission Strategies: The whole array of techniques used by adults to assist their children in first language acquisition - motherese, repetitions, exercise games, corrections, word-discussion, metacommunications, etc.
M - Marstrander.
m./masc. - masculine.
MFLS - Manx Folklife Survey MM.
MH - Mona's Herald (Douglas 1833-1975); newspaper.
MIr. - Middle Irish.
MM - Manx Museum.
ModIr. - Modern Irish.
MPNS - Manx Place-Name Survey (1988-).
MS - Manx Sun (Douglas 1826-1906); newspaper.
MTT - Manx Tape Transcriptions (of sound recordings of Manx native speakers) - GB.
Mx. - Manx Gaelic.
MxE. - Manx English.
N - (Manx native speaker informant from the) North of Man; (in morphological script) noun.
NP - noun phrase.
n/nom. nominative.
nas. - nasalised, nasalisation (see also Ecl.).
Neg. negative particle.
non-len. - non-lenited.
NTS - Norsk Tidsskrift for Sprogvidenskap, Oslo 1928-1972 (1972-78 Norwegian Journal of Linguistics, 1978- Nordic Journal of Linguistics).
Num. - numeral.
Ó Danchair 1981 - see below.
OFS - Older Fluent Speaker(s); cf. Dorian 1981.
OIr. - Old Irish.
PB - Phillips' Mx. trans. of Anglican Book of Common Prayer (cf. Moore & Rhŷs 1893-94).
pc. - personal communication.
Pers.N - personal name.
PL - Primary Language, with higher degree of lexical, grammatical, and pragmatic competence.
pl. - plural.
PLS - Primary Language Shift: Shift from AL as Primary to TL as Primary and from TL as Secondary to AL as Secondary.
Pn. - pronoun.
PN - place-name.
PNIM - Place-Names of the Isle of Man (cf. Broderick 1994, 1995, 1997).
Poss.part. - possessive particle.
Prep. - preposition.
Prep.part. - prepositional particle.
Prep.pn. - prepositional pronoun.
Q - question form of.
Reduction - Removal of significant/essential/functionally necessary parts of the language.Rel. - relative form of verb.
RIA - Royal Irish Academy (Dublin).
RLT - Robert L. Thomson.

S - (Manx native speaker informant from the) South of Man.
SbV - substantive verb ('be').
ScG. - Scottish Gaelic.
sg. - singular.
SGS - Scottish Gaelic Studies, Aberdeen.
SILL - Studies in Irish Language and Literature (Dept. of Celtic, the Queen's University of Belfast), Belfast.
Simplification - Removal of linguistic complexities.
Skt. - Sanskrit.
SL - Secondary Language, with lower degree of lexical, grammatical, and pragmatic competence.
SPCK - Society for Promoting Christian Knowledge.
SS - Semi-speaker: Member of the post-Language Transmission break generation with imperfect knowledge of AL.
TGSI - Transactions of the Gaelic Society of Inverness, Inverness.
TL - Target Language (dominant language which is continued - here English).
TS - Terminal Speaker: Last generation speaker.
Vcond. - verb conditional (tense).
VbN/vn. - verb-noun.
Vfut. verb future.
Vimp. - verb imperative.
Vinf. - verb infinitive.
Voc. - vocative case.
Vppp. - verb past participle passive.
Vpres. - verb present.
Vpret. - verb preterite.
W - Welsh.
YCG - Yn Cheshaght Ghailckagh ('the Manx Language Society'), Douglas.
YFS - Young Fluent Speaker(s); cf. Dorian 1981.
ZCP - Zeitschrift für celtische Philologie, Halle/Tübingen: Niemeyer.

Information from the following interviews has been used in this study:
- 7 July 1974, Ballaugh, Isle of Man.
  interview with Mr. Chalse C. Craine (d. 1979), Mywllin Squeen, Ballaugh, Isle of Man. Similar information was also gleaned from Mr. Craine again in the summer of 1977.
- 27 May 1981, Dublin, Ireland.
  interview with Dr. Caoimhín Ó Danchair, Dept. of Irish Folklore, University College Dublin, Dublin, Ireland.
- Summer 1983, Ramsey, Isle of Man.
  interview with Mr. Edward Christian (1907-1996), 'Abertay', Walpole Road, Ramsey, Isle of Man, and on subsequent occasions till 1996.
These interviews will be referred to as Craine 1974, Ó Danchair 1981, and Christian 1983 respectively.

1. Language Death

1.1. Language death as a world-wide phenomenon

Language death as a field of study has become the main preoccupation of a number of linguists over the past twenty years or so, during which time this aspect has developed into a branch of linguistics in its own right. Though somewhat macabre in formulation, the notion of 'language death' would adequately describe the endpoint of a sociolinguistic development affecting minority languages in competition with a dominant language or languages, during which process the cultural traditions attached to the dying language and the sociocultural and perhaps the ethnic distinctiveness of the group that speaks it may perish together with it. Yet this phenomenon is not uncommon. We have seen during the course of history even within the European and adjacent spheres the disappearance of such languages as Sumerian, Hittite, Old Egyptian, Latin, Etruscan, Iberian, Continental Celtic, Gothic, etc. However, alone in the last 500 years or so it is reckoned that about half the known languages of the world have disappeared due to colonisation and expansion by larger ethnic units over a myriad of smaller ethnic units, the formation of national states, the development of transport technology and communications, etc, whereby even the remotest corners of the world are now reachable and penetrable. As a result many more languages are in danger of becoming extinct before long. The process seems unstoppable. The following list may give some idea as to the extent of the phenomenon throughout the world (cf. Dorian 1989, Robins & Uhlenbeck 1991, Krauss 1992). It is by no means exhaustive[1]:

Africa: *Eastern Africa*: in Sudan, Ethiopia, Uganda, Kenya, Tanzania, Ruanda, Burundi; numerous Nilo-Saharan languages, some Afro-Asiatic, and some Niger-Kordofanian languages. See also Dimmendaal (1989).
Egypt: Nubian.
America: *Canada*: Ontario Cayuga, Welland French, Cape Breton Scottish Gaelic, Newfoundland French.
El Salvador: Pipil, Cacaopera, Salvadoran Lenca.
Guatemala: Jumaytepeque Xinca, Yupiltepeque Xinca, Guazacapan, Chiquimulilla Xinca.
Honduras: Honduran Lenca, Jicaque Yoro.
Mexico: Ocuilteco, Malinche-region Mexicano, Chiapanec, South-eastern Tzeltal, Chicomuceltec, Tuxtla Chico Mam.
USA: Gros Ventre (Montana), Pennsylvania and Kansas German, Oklahoma Cayuga, Cupeño, Norwegian (in N & S Dakota, Minnesota, Iowa, Illinois). For Canada and the USA together of the 187 languages reckoned to be spoken some 149 are endangered (cf. Krauss 1992: 5).

---

[1] The distribution of the world's languages is uneven. Of the estimated total of 6000 the Americas together have ca. 900 (15%), Europe and the Middle East together ca. 275 (4%). The other 81% are to be found In Africa (ca. 1900) and in Asia and the Pacific (ca. 3000) (cf. Krauss 1992: 5).

For Central America (including Mexico) only ca. 50 of the c. 300 indigenous languages are endangered (cf. Krauss 1992: 5).

For the situation in South America, cf. Adelaar 1991. Of the 400 or so languages spoken in South America some 110 (or 27%) are regarded as being moribund (cf. Krauss 1992: 5).

Asia:*Thailand*: Ugong.

In Asia and the Pacific some 3000 languages are known to be spoken, some 10% of which are known to be 'nearly extinct', though the condition of 40% of the above 3000 is inadequately known (Krauss 1992: 6). In the Russian Federation 45 of the 65 indigenous languages, or 70%, are now believed to be moribund, while for the former Soviet Union the figure is reckoned to be 50% (Krauss 1992: 5).

Australasia: *Australia*: Dyirbal (cf. Schmidt 1985), Warlpiri;

The Pacific Region and Papua New Guinea: Tok Pisin (cf. Mühlhäusler 1982, 1996).

In Australia of the ca. 250 aboriginal languages spoken some 90% are now regarded as moribund, most near extinction. The so-called 'English-speaking world' has seemingly the highest documented rate of destruction, approaching now 90% (cf. Krauss 1992: 5).

Europe: *Austria*: Oberwart Hungarian.

British Isles: Irish, Scottish Gaelic.

Bulgaria: Mandrìtsa Albanian.

Former Yugoslavia: Arbanasi Albanian, Gusi Albanian, Tetovo Albanian, Dibrë/Dibra Albanian, Aromân/Vlašk.

France: Breton, Alsatian.

Greece: Aromân/Koutsovlahiká, Arvanítika Albanian, Màndres Albanian.

Italy: Resian (Slovene), Arbresh (Albanian).

Sweden: Swedish Estonian.

Switzerland: Surmeir Romansch.

One of the first to use 'language death' as a linguistic term and metaphor is Dressler (1972a/b) and, as he put it (Dressler 1981: 5):

> language death may include such an extinction of a minority language due to language shift, physical liquidation (genocide) of all speakers of a language or brutally enforced assimilation to a majority language (linguacide) or rapid extinction of a language without intermediate bilingualism (multilingualism) (Dressler 1981: 5).

But usually language death is understood to be the final phase of the decay of linguistic structure a minority language undergoes on the way to language shift (Dressler & Wodak-Leodolter 1977a, Dorian 1981, Dressler 1981). For the purposes of this study Language Death will be taken to be that as it is now generally understood in the latter sense.

1.2. General studies on language death

The available literature on language death reveals that the phenomenon is dealt with from differing standpoints: 1. primarily socio-economic with little or no linguistic input (e.g. Hindley 1984, 1990), 2. formal linguistic descriptions with little or no attention paid to the sociolinguistic status of the language under investigation (cf. Broderick 1984–86). In order to understand the entire process both a sociolinguistic and a formal linguistic approach is necessary.

In the context of European minority languages extensive material covering such matters as economic factors, their underlying historical causes, linguistic and sociolinguistic details in different phases of linguistic decline and contraction, and speech behaviour of different types of imperfect speakers just prior to language extinction is found only in two known cases: 1. East Sutherland Gaelic (Dorian 1973-1981b), and 2. Arvanítika (Sasse 1991 and forthcoming), though these works properly speaking concern themselves with dialect death, not language death, since other dialects of the languages concerned are still spoken. A longitudinal study covering the development within a single self-contained community, e.g. a village, over a stretch of time has been made of Italo-Albanian (cf. Breu 1991). Outside Europe two works which come to mind in the context of language death are Hill and Hill on Nahuatl (Mexico) and Schmidt on Dyirbal (Australia).

1.3. Studies in language death concerning Insular Celtic

In the sphere of the Insular Celtic languages so far only Scottish Gaelic in the context of language death has been the subject of minute analysis both from a formal linguistic and sociolinguistic standpoint (see §1.2. above, and below). However, the apparent threat of 'language death' in Insular Celtic, especially in Goidelic, prompted a series of monographs on various dialects through the course of the 20th century, in some cases earlier, mainly in Ireland and Scotland, and to a much lesser degree in Wales and Brittany. Although such monographs really belong in the realm of phonology, nevertheless in our context they are included here. Excepting works on the various literatures of the Insular Celtic languages, most works of a linguistic nature deal almost exclusively with various aspects of the languages themselves, whether in their earlier or modern phases, and as such lie outwith the scope of this study. However, in the context of language death the following could be included:

Scottish Gaelic: *formal linguistic*: Dorian 1973, 1976, 1977a, 1978a-c, 1980b; MacAulay 1982a/b;

dialectal: Borgstrøm 1937 (Barra), 1940 (Outer Hebrides), 1941 (Skye & Ross-shire); Gleasure 1987 (general); Holmer 1938 (Argyllshire), 1942 (Rathlin), 1957 (Arran), 1962b (Kintyre); MacAulay 1978 (Berneray, Lewis); Macbain 1894 (Badenoch); Maclennan 1966 (South Uist); Ó Dochartaigh 1976 (Rathlin); Ó Murchú 1989a (East Perthshire); Oftedal 1956 & 1969 (Leurbost, Lewis); Robertson 1897 (Arran), 1900 (Perthshire), 1901-03 (Sutherland); Ternes 1973 (Applecross, Ross-shire); Wagner 1969 (mainly Hebridean); Watson 1974 (N. E. Ross-shire), 1986 (Easter Ross);

sociolinguistic: Dorian 1977b, 1978a, 1981-89; Durkacz 1983; MacAulay 1982; MacKinnon 1977-1993; Withers 1984.

Irish: *dialectal*: Breatnach 1947 (Ring, Co. Waterford); de Bhaldraithe 1945, 1953 (Cois Fhairrge, Co. Galway); de Búrca 1958 (Tourmakeady, Co. Mayo); Finck 1899 (Aran Islands, Co. Galway); Hamilton 1974 (Tory Island, Co. Donegal); Holmer 1940 (Glens of Antrim), 1962a, 1965 (Co. Clare); Hughes 1952 (Aran Islands, Co. Galway); Lucas 1979 (Ros Goill,

Co. Donegal); Mac an Fhailigh 1968 (Erris, Co. Mayo); Ó Baoill 1979 (Donegal); Ó Cuív 1944 (West Muskerry, Co. Cork), 1951 (Ir. dial. in general); Ó Dochartaigh 1987 (Ulster); O'Rahilly 1932 (Ir/ScG/Mx. in general); Quiggin 1906 (Meenawannia, Co. Donegal); Sjoestadt 1931 / Sjoestadt-Jonval 1938 (Kerry), Sommerfelt 1922, 1965 (Torr, Co. Donegal), 1929 (South Armagh); Stenson & Ó Ciardha 1986, 1987 (Ráth Cairn, Co. Meath); Stockman 1974 (Achill Island, Co. Mayo); Wagner 1958-69 (all known Ir. dial.), 1959 (Teelin, Co. Donegal); Watson 1984, 1987 (Antrim).

sociolinguistic: Akutagawa 1987; Breatnach 1956; Coiste Comhairleach Pleanála 1988; Commins 1988; Ó Cuív 1969; Fennell 1980, 1981; FitzGerald 1984; Ó Murchú 1985, 1993.

Manx: *formal linguistic*: Broderick 1991 and this volume;

dialectal: Broderick 1986; Jackson 1955; Thomson 1976, Wagner 1969;

sociolinguistic: Broderick 1991 and this volume; Hindley 1984, König 1996.

Welsh: *dialectal*: Darlington 1900 (Mid-Wales); Fynes-Clinton 1913 (Bangor district); Sommerfelt 1925 (Cyfeiliog); Thomas, A. R. 1973 (general); Thomas, C. H, 1993 (Nantgarw);

sociolinguistic: Jones 1981; Lewis 1978; Pryce 1978.

Cornish: *formal linguistic*: Wakelyn 1975;

sociolinguistic: Pool 1982.

Breton: *dialectal*: Jackson 1960 (Plougrescant), McKenna 1988 (Guémené-sur-Scorff); Sommerfelt 1920 (Saint-Pol-de-Léon), Ternes 1970 (L'île de Groix), Timm 1984 (Carhaislen);

sociolinguistic: Berger 1988; Dressler 1972a/b, 1981, 1982; Dressler and Wodak-Leodolter 1977; Timm 1980; Vetter 1997.

For an overview of the terminal stages in dying Goidelic dialects cf. Stockman 1988, and for a sociolinguistic overview of the Celtic languages in general see also Greene 1981.

1.4. Models of language death

As noted above, the study of language death as a branch of linguistics is relatively recent, and theories or models to deal with this phenomenon are now being constructed. The most recent is that of Hans-Jürgen Sasse (Sasse 1992a), where he postulates a schema based on the works of Nancy Dorian for East Sutherland Gaelic, Scotland (Dorian 1973-89), of Lukas Tsitsipis on Arvanítika, a peripheral Albanian dialect in central western Greece (Tsitsipis 1981), and Sasse's own on Arvanítika (Sasse 1991 & forthcoming). This schema will be looked at more closely below.

In the context of the Insular Celtic languages the term 'language death' has been applied by Dressler (1977, 1981) and by Dorian (1973-1981) in circumstances which reflect the processes of decline and decay in the dialects of Breton and Scottish Gaelic discussed by them. Dressler (1981: 5) regards language death "as the final state of the decay of linguistic structure a minority language undergoes on the way to total language shift". In the case of Manx the 'state of language decay' could properly be applied to the Late Manx period (late 19th, 20th-cents.) where the evidence for this period is based (except for the Faragher material, cf.

Broderick (1981-82)), exclusively on the material collected from the native speakers (cf. HLSM/I: xv-xxxii, HLSM/III: xi-xxxvi).

In her work on East Sutherland Gaelic Dorian (Dorian 1981: 117ff.) distinguishes between three sorts of speaker: 1. Older Fluent Speakers (OFS), 2. Younger Fluent Speakers (YFS), and 3. Semi-Speakers (SS) (i.e. not "fully proficient" speakers Dorian (1981: 119)), though Dressler (Dressler 1981: 6) regarded Dorian's choice of terminology for the first two categories as "infelicitous", as it suggests an overall age difference which he believes she does not intend. In dealing with Breton Dressler (Dressler 1981: 6-7) distinguishes five categories of speaker:

I. Healthy speakers corresponding to Dorian's OFSs;

II. Weaker speakers, approximately corresponding to Dorian's YFSs, but with reductions in their nominal inflection due to shrinkage of lexicon;

III. Preterminal speakers who exhibit "reductions and generalizations";

IV. Better terminal speakers who exhibit "even more reductions and generalizations";

V. Worse terminal speakers who "have a severely reduced lexicon and a still more reduced nominal inflection system".

However, neither of the above systems is entirely suitable for the Manx situation. Both Dorian and Dressler were able to interview *living* speakers of varying degrees of competence. In the case of Manx all the recorded material exists either in phonetic script (cf. Marstrander 1929-33a, Jackson 1955, Wagner 1969) or on a series of sound-recordings (see Section 3.5. below) from people who are long since dead. At the time I came to deal with the material (in 1979/80) all the native speakers of Manx had passed on. However, I met the last native speaker Ned Maddrell (1877-1974) on one occasion (namely, when he was recorded by the Linguistic Survey of Scotland in August 1972; cf. Section 3.5.3.7. below), as well as the semi-speaker Ewan Christian (1907-1985) of Peel (August 1972) and on later occasions until 1983. In addition to recordings made by LSS in 1972 I made my own recordings of Christian both on tape and in phonetic script (1978-83). Having dealt with the available native Manx speech material I would place most of the speakers roughly in Dressler's categories II to V; some were better than others. Christian's Manx, however, though it made clear that he had had contact with native Manx speech, was in its formulation somewhat literary and stilted, as though he had studied the Bible (he admitted in 1972 he in fact had), and in this respect leaned more towards that of the Manx language enthusiasts of the 1930s. His grammar was at times shaky, suggesting imperfection of study rather than loss of fluency (see also Section 3.5.3.7. & 3.6.9-10. below).

The floruits of the earlier speakers range from ca.1840-1935, and of the later - the last dozen or so - from ca.1860-1974. The period of language shift in Man extends essentially from ca.1840- ca.1880, and by 1900 the shift was, with perhaps the exception of Cregneash where Manx allegedly lingered on till ca.1910, to all intents and purposes complete. The 'later' native speakers were reared in Manx, either from their parents or grandparents (or great aunt in the case of Ned Maddrell, the last native speaker), at a time when Manx outside their immediate community was passing rapidly into extinction, if not already extinct. For communication outside their community English was necessary and came to be their ordinary means of discourse till their deaths (except in the presence of enthusiasts when they were pressed to resuscitate their knowledge of Manx for the purposes of the Revival).

Such speakers can for our purposes here be regarded as Terminal Speakers (Dressler's categories II-V, as noted above), in so far as they are the last native speakers reared with Manx as their first language (with perhaps the exception of Ned Maddrell who apparently knew some English before he learned Manx) and by all accounts had full command of it, though in later years owing to lack of use of their Manx they had forgotten much of it. In such circumstances they could be regarded as Rusty Speakers, as understood by Menn (Menn 1989)[2]. Some of the speakers themselves were conscious that their Manx was not as good as it was or could be, as evidenced by the following comment from Ned Maddrell:

> Ta cooinaghtyn aym tra va mee abyl loayrt yn Gaelg cha mie as y Baarle, ny share na'n Baarle neesht, agh cha nel mee son...lurg mee faagail Creneash as goll magh ayns y teihll cha row mee clashtyn monney Gaelg as ren eh bunnys faagail mee, as neayr's ren mee cheet er y thalloo reesht ta paart jeh er cheet rhym as ta mee abyl jannoo bit beg, agh cha nel mee jannoo eh cha mie as b'are lhiam
> ('I remember when I was able to speak Manx as well as English - better than English - too, but I'm not able...after I left Cregneash and went out into the world I wasn't hearing any Manx and it almost left me, and since I came back again some of it has come to me and I can do a wee bit, but I'm not doing it as well as I'd like to') (HLSM/I: 362-63).

Also Mrs. Sage Kinvig (1870-1962), the last woman native Manx speaker, relates how her husband (John Dan Kinvig) told here that her Manx was 'scrappy':

> Ren yn dooiney aym's gra dy vel mee jannoo brooillagh jeh ('my husband said that I make crumbs of it, I am scrappy with it (Manx)') (HLSM/II: 48 s.v. *brooillagh*).

From personal enquiry with those concerned, this approach by enthusiasts first took place in the mid-1930s as a result of Marstrander's visits to Man 1929-1933 (cf. Marstrander 1929-33a/b). The tape recordings made between 1948 and 1972 of the last native speakers (Section 3.5.) record their efforts at remembering the Manx of their youth.

The degree of fluency varies, and inhibitions could perhaps be attributed more to the presence of the microphone and recording machine than any short-comings on their part. A cursory glance at the material (collected between 1909 and 1972) makes clear that it is fairly homogenous, though the presence and influence of anglicisation, particularly in the syntax and sentence structure (cf. Section 4 below), is especially noticeable in the speech of the later Terminal Speakers. In most cases, however, Manx had ceased to be the everyday language since the period of youth, and in some instances a lapse of some 60 years had taken place before the language was brought back to mind. Even Marstrander commented that his best speaker Thomas Christian of Ramsey (1851-1930) "was a long time without practice at speaking the language" (Diary: 53-54).

It has been shown (Thomson 1969a: 194-201; Broderick 1991: 65-81) that Manx nominal inflection, for example, had reached a stage of relative simplicity before the era of the last native speakers, and any 'lapses' in grammar, etc, could in part be due more to imperfect memory in later life than to imperfect learning in infancy or youth. Nevertheless, their Manx does exhibit features of 'linguistic decay'. In no case had any of the last native speakers passed Manx on to his/her children, even if most, if not all, took great pride in the language, since they realised that to 'get on' in life English was essential. The position of Manx would fit the description as expressed by Dorian (Dorian 1981: 106, n. 24) that "a group undergoes a long period during which its language is actively devalued, while speakers of that language

---

[2]   i.e. not semi-speakers, as all are believed to have been full native speakers of Manx from the cradle.

are penalised socially and economically, before members of the group see fit to withhold that language from their own children" (cf. Section 2).

In presenting his schema Sasse (Sasse 1992a: 9-19) observes three types of phenomena which he regards as relevant to the study of language death:

1. The *External Setting* (ES) whereby extra-linguistic factors, such as cultural, sociolinguistic, ethnohistorical, economic, etc, create pressure (whether political, or whatever) in a given speech community, which forces that community to give up its language. It is this setting which triggers off the process ending in language death (*ibid.*: 9-10).

2. *Speech Behaviour* (SB), namely, the regular use of variables whereby different languages in multilingual settings, or different styles or registers of one language are used in various domains or situations (*ibid.*: 10).

3. *Structural Consequences* (SC) are the formal linguistic phenomena, i.e. changes in the phonology, morphology, syntax, and lexicon of the language threatened by extinction. Structural impoverishment and so-called 'bastardisation' (or 'going to pot' as it is called in Man) may help accelerate the process of language death in the final stage (*ibid.*: 10).

As the political and social conditions are primary, ES phenomena must therefore have an impact on SB. Attitudes towards languages and styles of language, Sasse (*ibid.*: 10) adds,

> develop on the basis of political, social and economic pressure, and this pressure in turn develops on the basis of the historical situation in which a speech community finds itself. Endangered languages remain functionally intact and are not recgarded as 'deviant' until they reach the terminal stage of extinction (Sasse 1992a: 10).

For his framework for Language Death Sasse has taken the situation of East Sutherland Gaelic (Dorian 1973-1989) and Arvanítika (Tsitsipis 1981, Sasse 1991 and forthcoming) as his models, since both have been investigated in great detail both from a sociolinguistic and formal linguistic standpoint. This framework Sasse (1992a: 11-19) calls his GAM (Gaelic-Arvanítika-Model). This model is essentially adopted in this study, but with some slight modification to reflect the situation of Manx and is referred to here as GAMM (Gaelic-Arvanítika-Manx-Model).

The present state of research into language death shows that the interrelation of the three aspects as outlined above is one of chain reaction: *External Setting* phenomena induce a certain kind of *Speech Behaviour*, which in turns results in certain *Structural Consequences* in the dying language, i.e. the extra-linguistic factors appear first; this sets off a change in speech behaviour due to or as a reaction to the former. Finally structural changes emerge as a result of the change in speech behaviour. The first appearance of the factors in each case would be phased-displaced and would operate continually throughout the entire process. The following diagram would show this:

Figure 1: *Sociolinguistic displacement leading to language death* (after Sasse 1992a: 13):

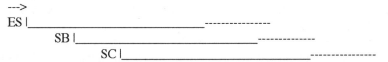

Every case of language death is embedded in a bilingual situation which involves two languages, one which is dying out and one which which continues. The language given up is usually referred to as the *Abandoned Language* (henceforth AL), in our case Manx Gaelic, and the language acquired is called the *Target Language* (TL), in our case English. The story begins when a substantial portion of a bilingual speech community shows simultaneous, or near simultaneous shift in their primary language (PL), from AL to TL and a consequent shift in their secondary language (SL) from TL to AL, i.e. (in our case) the Primary Language (Manx) at first takes precedence over the Target Language (English), then in the process of language shift the Target Language (English) takes precedence over the former Primary Language, i.e. the Abandoned Language (Manx). This process Sasse (1992a: 13) calls *Primary Language Shift* (PLS). Sasse continues:

> How is primary language shift initiated? It is triggered by the decision of [members of] a speech community to cease to transmit their language to their descendants. The result is an interruption in *language transmission* (LT) (Sasse 1992a: 13).

Language transmission is the deliberate passing on of a language from one generation to the next. The process by which this is achieved is known as *Language Transmission Strategy* (LTS), which, as Ingram (1989: 127) shows, seems to be partly intuitive and partly community-specific (traditional), and which involves a specific way in which mothers (or language-transmitting agents) talk to their children, the so-called *motherese* (cf. Kaye 1980), as well as repetitions, exercise games, corrections, and other types of metacommunications, e.g. discussions about word-meaning, and a strong tendency to assist and encourage children in their own efforts to improve their linguistics skills. LTS is therefore essential to language acquisition.

Interruption in language transmission to the next generation can be motivated by several considerations, e.g. restrictive language policy, economic reasons, etc. However, studies in language death situations so far available to us, as Sasse (*ibid.*: 13-14) points out, indicate one common factor, viz. the presence of socio-economic and/or sociopsychological pressures which move the members of an economically weaker or minority speech community to give up its language. This happens very often as a result of negative language attitude which leads to doubts about the usefulness of language loyalty. The attitude towards AL may not be entirely negative, i.e. the language is valued for one reason, but rejected for another - its serves as a badge of group identity, but is given up because it is regarded as useless; in the Manx case *cha jean oo cosney ping lesh y Ghailck* 'you will not earn a penny with the Manx' was the cry from many a Manxman during the last and this century.

Uneven distribution of languages in a bi- or multilingual situation always results, so Sasse (*ibid.*: 14), in complementary distribution of domains, which consequently leads to lexical loss or failure of lexical development in domains where the dominant language is favoured. Due to the restriction of domains, collective bilingualism increases, because the speakers are forced to learn the dominant language in order to use it in domains where the recessive language cannot be used (cf. Dressler - Wodak-Leodolter 1977, Hill 1978, Tsitsipis 1981). This may increase interference and simplification (e.g. loss of complex morphophonemic systems, loss of allophonic variation, etc), but AL nevertheless still remains a functionally intact language.

However, once the decision to abandon AL has been taken and language transmission ceases, the situation changes radically. The former primary language AL (Manx) becomes secondary and begins to show serious symptoms of imperfection, and due to a lack of LTS the only source of AL data for the infant is what he occasionally hears in his environment. In addition, in a situation where most, if not all, domains have been taken over by TL, AL is simply no longer used in a number of important speech styles (e.g. narrative, formal, etc).

From a sociolinguistic standpoint the restrictive use of AL has a feedback on the speaker's sociopsychological evaluation as well as on that of the rising generation, and contributes to a negative attitude towards AL (cf. also Dressler 1982: 324ff).

It is at this point, so Sasse (1992a: 15), that we enter the phase of 'language death'. This is characterised by a process called *Language Decay* (LD). Language decay is defined as the serious linguistic disintegration typical of the speech of the so-called *Semi-Speakers* (SS), i.e. that speaker generation which results from the interruption of language transmission and acquires an imperfect knowledge of AL due to a lack of LTS in that language.

> Their morphology is extremely defective, they lose important grammatical categories such as tense, aspect, mood, even if these categories are present in T[L]. Their speech often shows a pidgin-like simplification of syntax and a strong insecurity in the mapping of forms and functions. They are hardly able to master the phonological distinctions of A[L] and show extreme variation in their pronunciation (Sasse 1992a: 15).

In the process of language decay two symptoms are discernible: *simplification* and *reduction*. *Simplification* is the loss of external complexity and involves readjustments in substance (but essentially the language remains intact), while *Reduction* is the loss of essentials in both form and substance and results in defectivity, disintegration and heavy expression deficit. The first, so Sasse (*ibid.*: 16), can occur in normal language contact situations involving the transfer of substantial material, of patterns, and of category distiction, and can always be explained as the imitation by the first language of some linguistic trait or traits of the second. However in the second, in the case of Language Decay, we are not dealing with imitation or borrowing or transfer in any sense, but with downright loss leading to substantial deficit.

An example of this is *negative borrowing*, a morphosyntactic borrowing process connected with any situation of intensive language contact, whereby a category is lost in the first language because of its absence in the model language. However, this 'loss' can be compensated by functionally equivalent means of expression which imitate the morphosyntactic pattern of the model language, while in language decay no compensation takes place at all and results in functional defectivity.

> What remains of the A language in the phase of decay is not a language in the sense properly understood (a structured code), but an amorphous mass of words and word forms, stereotype sentences and phrases, formulaic expressions, idioms and proverbs, which are learned in "chunks", whose forms are imperfectly known and whose functions are poorly understood. When used in actual conversation, these linguistic fossils are put together in some random linear order without fixed syntactic rules [...]. Semi-speakers often remember an amazing amount of vocabulary, but may get totally lost with morphology and syntax [...]. In spite of their being normal full speakers of T[L], they suffer from the awareness of their linguistic deficiency in A[L], especially as long as A[L] is still represented in their environment by a sufficient number of full speakers. This creates a kind of collective language-pathological situation which can be overcome by the acceleration of language death. Many semi-speakers avoid speaking a language in which they cannot easily express themselves and which they conceive of as a bastardised, pidginised non-language (the typical attitude of a semi-speaker: 'X is not a language') (Sasse 1992a: 17).

At what point is a language regarded as dead? Was Manx a dead language when Heinrich Wagner and Kenneth Jackson interviewed its last speaker Ned Maddrell in 1950, or did it die when Ned Maddrell died (1974)? Was Hebrew a dead language before its revival in the form of Ivrith, or did it never die? Did Manx never die? Perhaps the answer can only be given from case to case. In linguistic terms (cf. Sasse *ibid.*: 59-80) the final point of language death is the cessation of regular communication in that language.

> A dead language may leave residues of various kinds. It may continue as a ritual language, as a secret language, as a professional jargon, etc. It may leave a codified version, which in turn can be used for ritual or other purposes. It may finally leave a substratum influence (especially lexically) in the dialect of T[L] which the former speech community of A[L] continues to speak (Sasse 1992a: 18).

In the case of Manx this has left a substratum mainly of lexical, but also of phonological and syntactic traces in Manx-English, that dialect of English spoken in Man by the older generation of native-born Manx men and women (cf. Barry 1984, Broderick 1997b).

Furtherresearch work into Manx English is now being undertaken by the University of Mannheim and Centre for Manx Studies, Douglas.

An overview of GAMM is found below in Figure 2.

Figure 2: *A framework of language death in the Isle of Man* (after Sasse 1992a: 19)

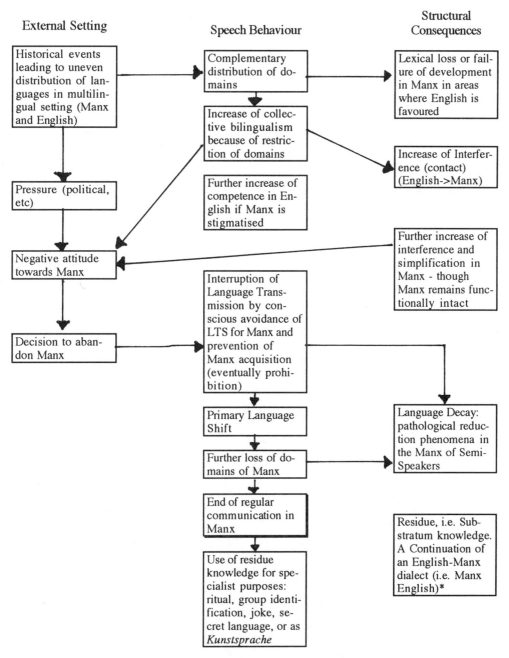

External Setting   **Speech Behaviour**   **Structural Consequences**

Historical events leading to uneven distribution of languages in multilingual setting (Manx and English)

Complementary distribution of domains

Lexical loss or failure of development in Manx in areas where English is favoured

Increase of collective bilingualism because of restriction of domains

Increase of Interference (contact) (English->Manx)

Pressure (political, etc)

Further increase of competence in English if Manx is stigmatised

Negative attitude towards Manx

Further increase of interference and simplification in Manx - though Manx remains functionally intact

Interruption of Language Transmission by conscious avoidance of LTS for Manx and prevention of Manx acquisition (eventually prohibition)

Decision to abandon Manx

Primary Language Shift

Language Decay: pathological reduction phenomena in the Manx of Semi-Speakers

Further loss of domains of Manx

End of regular communication in Manx

Residue, i.e. Substratum knowledge. A Continuation of an English-Manx dialect (i.e. Manx English)*

Use of residue knowledge for specialist purposes: ritual, group identification, joke, secret language, or as *Kunstsprache*

---

* A form of English spoken in Man would have come into being long before the decline of Manx from English speakers residing mainly in the towns, particularly from ca.1800 onwards (see Section 3), and would have run parallel with Manx gradually outliving it. Manx English is at present spoken by the native Manx populace, particularly in the farming community.

2. The Sociolinguistic Situation of Manx

cha jean oo cosney ping lesh y Ghailck
'you will not earn a penny with the Manx'
Oral Tradition 1880s.

2.1. Sociohistorical developments

So far as is known, the only work done on the latter stages of Manx are by Hindley and Broderick. Hindley (1984) portrays a concise and precise picture of the sociolinguistic situation which lead to the decline and death of Manx Gaelic as a community language in Man. Broderick, however, has concentrated on the latter stages of the language from a formal linguistic standpoint in his three-volume *Handbook* (Broderick 1984-86). In addition he has presented the sociolinguistic position in general terms together with a formal linguistic description, concentrating mainly on the nominal system in so far as the simplification of case, number and gender marking is concerned, and has shown that such simplification was in all likelihood due to internal development, rather than any aspect of language death creeping in from outside (Broderick 1991: 65-81). It is the intention here to go into some detail into the formal linguistic situation regarding aspects of contact that led to language decay and death in Manx Gaelic (cf. Section 4). But first the sociolinguistic situation will be presented to set the process of language death in the context of the GAMM framework (cf. Section 1.4.).

The arrival of Goidelic or Gaelic speech in Man seems to have taken place ca. 500 AD[1] and it eventually ousted a British language spoken there.[2] The early history of Goidelic in Man is obscure, but it survived four centuries of Scandinavian presence (9th-cent. to 1266).[3] From 1289 to 1334 Man was contended for in Scottish-English rivalries, and from 1334 to 1405 it was held by several Anglo-Norman magnates from the English king and retained the title 'King of Man'. From 1405 to 1736 Man found itself in the possession of the Stanley lords of Knowsley (near Liverpool), after 1485 'Earls of Derby' and from 1521 (if not before) styled 'Lords of Man'. From 1736 to 1765 Man was in the hands of the anglicised Dukes of Atholl.[4]

---

[1]   An early testimony for this is the bilingual Ogam (Goidelic) and Latin Knock y Doonee Stone (CIIC 500; Andreas 9:5(-) end of 5th/first quarter of 6th cent. AD). The Latin inscription indicates the probable presence of British speech in Man at that time (cf. Jackson 1953: 173 note). The earliest Ogam inscribed stones in Man range in date from 5th-7th cent. AD (pers. comm. Dr. Ross Trench-Jellicoe 05.03. 1987).

[2]   In addition to the Knock y Doonee (Latin) inscr. there is the (now lost) place-name *Hentre* (cf. W. *Hendref* 'old farm, stead', Mx. *shenn valley*, G. *sean bhaile*) recorded in the *Limites* appended (ca.1280) to the Chronicles of Man (cf. Broderick 1995: (f.53r.)) as plausible evidence for British speech having once existed in Man.

[3]   For an outline of the difference of opinion as to the language(s) spoken in Man during the Scandinavian period, cf. Gelling 1970, 1971.

[4]   In 1765 the manorial rights of the Duke of Atholl, the then Lord of Man, were bought out by the British government on behalf of the British Crown, though the final sum was not settled till 1828. The British Crown felt it had the right to revest in itself the suzerainty of Man in 1765, as in 1406 the English Crown, as it was then, had vested the suzerainty of Man in the Stanley

Though there appears to have been a Gaelic bardic tradition in Man[5] supported by a native Gaelic speaking aristocracy before and during the existence of the Manx kingdom of the Isles (ca.960-1266), this is unlikely to have continued under a non-Gaelic speaking overlordship from the beginning of the 14th century, if not before. Though the language of administration from that time would also have been non-Gaelic, it was nevertheless found necessary, for example, for Bishop John Phillips (1604-1633) to translate the Anglican Book of Common Prayer into Manx ca.1610 (in ms, but not printed till 1894; see Moore & Rhys 1893-94) and for Bible translations (published 1748-75; last edition of complete Bible 1819, of New Testament 1825) and a Manx version of the Prayer Book (1765, last published 1842) to be made. These facts make it clear that up until the latter date at least the bulk of the ordinary Manx people spoke Manx, or at any rate felt more at home in that language.

In 1726, the first date for which we have population figures (see Appendix C), the population of Man was no more than ca.14,000, the four towns being thus populated: Castletown (capital till 1869) 785, Douglas (capital from 1869 to present) 810, Peel 475, Ramsey 460. The Manx gentry were also able to understand and speak Manx, as Gibson admits.[6] The language of government and law (English) would not have affected the everyday lives of the ordinary people very much at that time, since they would have dealt through intermediaries, e.g. native judges, administrators, etc, who would have spoken Manx.

2.2. General factors of language shift in Man

2.2.1. The first measures of Anglicisation

So far as is known, the first determined effort to bring in English in a systematic way to the ordinary Manx people was made by Bishop Isaac Barrow (1663-1671). Barrow's appointment in that year followed the restoration of the Stanley lordship after the collapse of the 'Commonwealth'. Cromwell's forces, it will be remembered, were introduced into Man in 1651 (though it is known they would have come anyway) through the agency of William Christian (*Illiam Dhone*), Receiver-General and head of the Manx militia, as an act of 'rebellion' against the then Earl of Derby.[7] As his supporters were the Manx people who spoke Manx, that language seems to have been looked upon by Derby and his supporters as

---

family of Knowsley. To this day the British Government on behalf of the British Crown regards itself as being responsible for "good government", as it puts it, in the Isle of Man. For details cf. Moore 1900.

[5] The existence of an Early Modern Irish poem by a visiting Irish poet in praise of King Reginald of Man and the Isles (1188-1226) dated ca.1200 suggests that such a tradition was receiving official patronage in Man at that time (cf. Ó Cuív 1957: 283-301).

[6] Gibson (1695: col. 1063; quoted after Price 1984: 73): "their Gentry are very courteous and affable, and are more than willing to discourse with one in English than their own language". As Price commented (p. 73 note) they could not, of course, have done otherwise, except to speak Manx with other Gaelic speakers.

[7] For details of this see Moore (1900: 266-75, 376-82), and of the ballad see Broderick (1982b: 105-23).

identifiable with 'rebellion' and its speakers viewed with suspicion. In addition, as the state of the Anglican Church in Man (the Established Church) was considered by Barrow as leaving a lot to be desired,[8] the introduction of English was to form part of his 'improvement scheme'. He had apparently found on his arrival that the Manx clergy (almost all native Manx) extemporised from the English versions of the scriptures before their Manx congregations, and considered that a lack of knowledge of English among the Manx populace was preventing an adequate understanding and appreciation of the scriptures. There was, however, Phillips' translation of the Prayer Book (ca.1610, see above), but which was evidently unknown to Barrow.[9]

Instead of providing the scriptures in Manx (through which the people would have understood them better), as was later to be the case (see below), Barrow, in line with the thinking of his time, resolved to impose English on the Manx population through a parish school system (Clamp 1988c: 185-98). For those Manx children who would aspire to 'higher learning' a grammar school was established in Castletown in 1676. In 1668 an Academic Fund

---

[8]   For details of the 'Barrovian Design' see Clamp (1988a: 10-21). Barrow apparently found on his arrival in Man that the local clergy were poorly paid, and to make a living had to resort to keeping ale houses.

[9]   Moore/Rhys 1894. Phillips' version, made ca.1610, exists in one extant ms. only Manx Museum MS.3 & 4 (in two vols.) dated ca.1630. Thomson (1969: 182) plausibly argues that this ms, rather than having been one of a number of copies distributed to the clergy for use in the church, may have been a fair copy for the press, but due to the probable high costs of printing for as so few copies would have been needed, it never saw the light of day until 1893-94 (Manx Soc. XXXII & XXXIII) when its production then was purely for scholarly purposes. Yet it was evidently Phillips' intention that his translation be printed, for in a letter from him to the Earl of Salisbury (responsbible for matters in Man during the brief period of English suzerainty 1607-10) concerning a number of other matters also, Phillips argues:

> [...] That whereas I, with my clergy did this year purpose to have perused the Mannish Book of Common Prayer by me translated, so with one uniform consent to have made it ready for the printing, for the comfort of that poor church, if your Honr. would think meet to give allowance thereof [...] (Letter 01.02.1610/11 Phillips to Salisbury quoted after Moore & Rhys 1893-94: xi).

However, his efforts were rejected. In a letter of reply to Phillips made by the then Governor of Man, John Ireland, in February 1610/11 who had the clergy look at it, Ireland commented:

> The two Viccars General (Sr. Wm. Norres and Sr. Wm. Crowe) were asked by the Lieutennante whether they saw or knew of the Book of Common Prayer said to have been translated into the Mansche speech; they answered that they have seen the Book translated by the new Bishop of Sodor [Phillips] into Mannish. And Sr. Wm. Norres for his part further answereth that he could not read the same Book perfectly but here and there a word. And Sr. Wm. Crowe for his part answereth that having the same Book a day or two before he could upon deliberate perusall thereof read some part upon it, and doth verily think that few else of the clergy can read the same Book for that it is spelled with vowels wherewith non of them are acquainted. And the said Viccars being further asked whether they purposed with the Bishop to peruse the said Book to th' entent the same might be made ready for the printing, they replyed saying they were not therewith acquainted by the Bishop at any time since he was Bishop, and therefore did not, nor could not propose any such thing (Letter Feb. 1610/11 John Ireland to John Phillips quoted after Moore & Rhys 1893-94: xii).

The pertinent comment here that the clergy at the time (ca.1610) had difficulty in reading Phillips' orthography because suggests that they had seen Manx in another orthography (perhaps a forerunner of that in use today), examples of which have so far not materialised, though the tone of the above letter suggests that the Vicars General were luke-warm about the whole idea for reasons other than those given.

was set up with a view to enabling deserving students to proceed to a university (Dublin or Oxford) for a term of five years in order to enter the ministry . Matters were to be so arranged that they would be obliged to return to Man for their employment. The upshot of this was the acquisition of Ballagilley and Hango Hill farms (the latter acquired through confiscation; cf. Stenning 1956: 122-45), the revenues from which would service the fund for setting up a grammar school. This materialised only in 1833 in the form of King William's College (Clamp 1988a: 15).[10]

Barrow's scheme met with limited success, until it was revamped by Bishop Thomas Wilson (1698-1755) at the start of the 18th century. Wilson's policy, pursued with vigour, of enjoining all Manx parents under penalty of fines to send their children to school to learn English formed part of his greater scheme to create a theocratic state. Inevitably the Church under Wilson came into conflict with the civil power in Man, and in 1722 Wilson and his two Vicars-General (John Curghey, vicar of Braddan, and William Walker) were committed to prison for some two months at Castle Rushen. The supremacy of the State over the Church resulted in the decline of Wilson's education system, and by 1736 it was in virtual collapse (cf. Clamp 1988c: 185-98).

2.2.2. The language policy of the Anglican Church in Man

In spite of Wilson's pro English language stance, he nevertheless realised that the scrip-tures would have to be made available in Manx simply because the bulk of the people (in Wilson's view more than two-thirds)[11] could not understand English. In 1707 he had printed bilingually his *Principles and Duties of Christianity*, known in Manx as *Coyrle Sodjey* 'further advice' (the first book in Manx to be printed) and during their sojourn in gaol Wilson and his Vicars-General set about organising the translation into Manx of St. Matthew's Gospel. This translation is credited to Dr. William Walker, one of the Vicars-General and a Manxman (d.1729), but it came into print only in 1748 (by. John Oliver, London, printer to the Society for Promoting Christian Knowledge (SPCK)) at Wilson's expense. Wilson also encouraged the translation of the Anglican Prayer Book in Manx which came out in 1765

---

[10] In this regard Archibald Cregeen, compiler of a Manx dictionary (cf. Cregeen 1835), hoped that the establishment of this college would not neglect 'the cultivation of the vernacular tongue' (Cregeen 1834: Preface). He added:

> The establishment of a *professorship* [Cregeen's italics] for that specific object [i.e. for the cultivation of Manx] would be highly desirable, - such an arrangement would be in perfect unison with the pious and benevolent design of *the Founder of the Academic Fund* [Cregeen's italics], whose primary object appears to have been to prepare candidates for the *Holy Ministry* [Cregeen's italics] in the Isle of Man, and thus promote the highest and best interests of the country (Cregeen 1834: Preface).

However, it was not to be.

[11] cf. James Wilks 1777 (in Moore 1887: 179). In his history, written in the early 18th century, Bishop Wilson states (in a chapter on the clergy):

> The clergy are generally natives, and, indeed, it cannot well be otherwise, none else being qualified to preach and administer the sacraments in the Manx Language; for English is not understood by two-thirds at least of the Island, though there is an English school in every parish, so hard is it to change the language of a whole country (quoted after Kneen 1931: 8).

(Thomson 1979: ii), even though he knew of Phillips' translation of ca.1610. However, as Robert Thomson reminds me, the English version of the Prayer Book was throughout changed in 1662 from what Phillips used to conform with the Bible version of 1611 (Authorised Version). This then required a complete new translation of the Manx version, except for the Psalms which were left unaltered in English and only slightly revised in Manx.

However, it is due to his successor Bishop Mark Hildesley (1755-1772), also an Englishman, that we owe the main drive to having the full Bible translated into Manx and published 1763-73.[12] It was also during his episcopate that Manx became the language of education for the first time. Having recognised the absurdity of children being taught in a language most of them did not understand, he provided teaching materials in Manx and urged the clergy to do their best to improve the use and practice of that language. The result was that, whereas only three parishes were using Manx as the language of instruction in 1757, by 1766 children in all parishes in the Island except one were being taught the Catechism and prayers through the medium of Manx. This remarkable turn-around made clear Bishop Hildesley's support for the ordinary Manx people and their language, in spite of resentment in anglicised circles in Castletown and Douglas who were in favour of teaching through English (cf. Bird [1991]: 86-87, König 1996: 13).

However, this situation was to be short-lived. After Hildesley's death in 1772 support by the Anglican Church for the continued use of Manx in schools evaporated, and by 1782 a visitation revealed that only five schools retained Manx as the language of instruction. Although Manx was reintroduced, albeit in the Island's Sunday Schools (though see below), during the 1820s as a means of enabling Manx children to read the scriptures their own language (Bird [1991]: 217), the weight in favour of English from the Church was too over-

---

[12] For details on the history of the Manx Bible translation and its publication see Thomson (1979: Intro.). Hildesley seemingly felt some responsibility towards the Manx language and was disapproving of the attitude of those who wanted it to disappear. In 1761 he wrote the following circular to the Manx clergy:

Whereas I find some doubts have arisen among some of the clergy concerning the sense in which they are to observe my late injunctions to instruct the people in a language they best understand. I here think fit more explicitly to declare my meaning to be not that every sermon preached in the Country Churches should be in the Manx tongue, but that the Sundays thro-out the year in the English and the Manx shall be proportioned to the capacities and talents of the Congregation, for each respectively as near as the Minister can be able to compute from his knowledge or enquiry. This I take to be righteous, and the excess either way, if considerable, both cruel and unjust, and for which I might appeal to the conscience of any equitable person whatever, that does not think that respect of persons, in spiritual dispensations, is to be had according to the temporal possessions or stations they hold in the external appearances of this world. Mark Sodor and Man. Oct. 2. 1761. (Moore 1887: 99).

A little later, ca. autumn 1763, Hildesley wrote the following to Rev. Philip Moore, general editor of the Manx Bible translation.

I presume your Douglas assistant will be disposed to breathe a little northern air among his relations on this side, at the ensuing holidays [Christmas 1763], and then he will be at hand to try his voice at Lezayre. Has he made a Manks sermon yet? If he has not, 'tis fit he should; unless he is one of those geniuses of the South, who think the cultivation of that language *unnecessary*. If I were not fraught with full conviction of its utility, and with resolution to pursue my undertaking, what with the coolness of its reception by some, and the actual disapprobation of it by others, I should be so discouraged as to give it up. This, I believe, is the only country in the world, that is ashamed of, and even inclined to extirpate, if it could, its own native tongue (Butler 1799: 449-501).

whelming to sustain a Manx teaching policy from that quarter. In 1825 Bishop Murray, an apparent opponent of the Manx language (though see *Manks Advertiser* 10.01.1822 in §2.3.1. below), informed the SPCK (hitherto a main provider of religious material in Manx for the Island; another being the Sunday School Society of London) in a letter that:

> there is no longer any necessity for impressions of the Bible and the Book of Common Prayer in the Manks Tongue; but that in the English Tongue they are much wanted, and sought after with great avidity (quoted after Bird [1991]: 218).

In addition he advised the SPCK that the teaching of Manx Gaelic had been prohibited by an Act of Westminster (which was not the case), and was thereby successful in achieving SPCK withdrawal at any rate for the Manx language (Bird [1991]: 87-88, 217-218, König 1996: 21-22).

However, this line of thinking, inherited from Barrow's time, permeated the 19th century. Even Manx dictionary compilers had to justify their efforts by arguing (even if they did not believe it themselves) that a promotion of Gaelic would ultimately lead to its demise and to the advance of English, a knowledge of which, they argued, would alleviate poverty and ignorance brought on its speakers by a knowledge of Gaelic. Kelly, for instance, in the Introduction to his dictionary (originally intended for his Triglot Dictionary and written in 1805 but not published till 1866 with his Manx-English Dictionary) (cf. Section 2.2.2.)), was vigorous in the promotion of this argument:

> It has long been the policy of France to render her language universal, and she has acquired more influence by its becoming the court language of Europe than even by her arms in the field. Had a similar policy been extended by this country [England] to Ireland; - had books been printed in Gaelic, and Gaelic schools established in those parts of Ireland where Gaelic is the vulgar tongue, the people would have acquired learning by using the English alphabet, - they would have read English before they could read Irish, by reading Irish through an English medium, - they would have understood English before they had learnt Irish, - such a portion at least of English as would beyond a doubt have enabled them by reading and conversation to have diminished, if not altogether to have removed, the deplorable ignorance, poverty and bigotry under which they have so long laboured. Had the beneficed clergy likewise been qualified by a knowledge of the language spoken by their parishioners - had they been obliged to preach, - had they been obliged to pray in Gaelic, many of the evils which have befallen Ireland might have been avoided, and those with which it is at present threatened most probably prevented. It is true that in process of time this cultivation of the Gaelic language will destroy the language itself, as a living language; but it will have produced the knowledge of a better [language], and will descend to posterity by means of the press in a more perfect state, than if it should be found only in the conversation of unlettered individuals. There would be no more cause for regret, then, that it was not a living language, than there is at present, that the Hebrew, Greek, and Latin are no longer such.
>
> By the publication of Gaelic books, and the more particularly by the clergy being obliged to understand, and to use the Gaelic language, the Roman Catholic faith was entirely superseded in Man. Of thirty thousand inhabitants, there is not to be found one native who is a Roman Catholic, nor a single dissenter from the Established Church of England [Kelly seems to have forgotten the Methodists here whose influence by this time was not insignificant]. The same wisdom exercised by the rulers of the Church of Scotland, has produced similar effects in the Highlands. By their clergy being obliged to use the Gaelic language in the Highland parishes, the national and political prejudices [i.e. support for the Jacobite cause], which formerly existed so strongly there, are entirely removed, and the knowledge of the English language, in consequence of the publication of the Gaelic Scriptures and Gaelic books, is everywhere gaining ground. And when there shall be one national language [i.e. English], then only will the union of the empire be completely established (Kelly 1805: Introduction).

Similarly Cregeen writing in June 1834:

> I am well aware that the utility of the following work will be variously appreciated by my brother Manksmen. Some will be disposed to deride the endeavour to restore vigour to a decaying language. Those who reckon the extirpation of Manx a necessary step towards that general extension of the English, which they deem essential to the interest of the Isle of Man, will condemn every effort which seems likely to retard its extinction.
>
> But those will think otherwise who consider that there are thousands of the natives of the Island that can at present receive no useful knowledge whatever, except through the medium of the Manks language; they will judge from experience, as well as from the nature of the case, that no work of this description will hinder the progress of the English, but in fact have the contrary effect. (Cregeen 1834: Introduction).

The logic of the above arguments, especially those of Kelly, may baffle belief today, and no doubt many people then (including probably the dictionary compilers themselves) would have regarded them as 'window-dressing'. But we have to remember that Kelly and Cregeen were writing shortly after the 1798 rebellion in Ireland which challenged English rule and that of the Protestant ascendancy in that country, and that a promotion of Gaelic could be seen as a political gesture against English (and Protestant) interests.[13] Hence the argument (in its thesis contradictory) that a promotion of Gaelic would secure the future for Protestantism (as in Scotland) and enhance the dissemination and understanding of English.

The advent of Methodism into Man during the 1770s took advantage of Anglican Church hostility (and apparent arrogance) towards Manx to promote the use of that language as a medium of converting the people, and in that way, in spite of contradictory comments on the Manx language by Wesley himself,[14] Methodism gained considerable ground from the established Anglican Church.[15]

---

[13] The English authorities would see the Gaelic language as a sort of *Zündschnur* against their interests and would therefore fear it. The use of Gaelic culture (including language) in the service of nationalism as a *Zündschnur zum Sprengstoff* against British interests was promoted by Celticist Rudolf Thurneysen in a lecture in 1915 and by linguist and Celticist Leo Weisgerber in an article in 1941 (Weisgerber 1941) in their support for the Irish cause (cf. Simon 1982: 40-41, Lerchenmüller 1997: 148-51).

[14] In a letter dated 1783 to one of his preachers in Man Wesley exhorted him:
> if you would learn the Manx language I would commend you (Telford 1931/ VII: 178).

However, six years later, in 1789, in a communication to another of his preachers, George Holder, Wesley admonished:
> I exceedingly disapprove of your publishing anything in the Manx language. On the contrary, we should do everything in our power to abolish it from the earth, and persuade every member of our Society to learn and talk English. This would be much hindered by providing them [the Manx] with hymns in their own language (Telford 1931/VIII: 189).

Neverthless, his ministers in Man saw the situation more realistically and went ahead in 1795 (and again in 1799) with their publication in Manx of Methodist and other hymns in English (cf. Cubbon 1939: 792-93).

[15] The Methodists also actively supported the old Manx tradition of the *Oie'll Voirrey* (/i:l 'veri/) at which carvals (comprising an extensive corpus of some 20-25,000 lines of original Manx verse, mostly on religious themes arranged in a series of songs averaging some 35 stanzas in length) would be sung, initially in the parish churches, then in the course of the 19th century in the Methodist chapels on Christmas Eve, i.e. Oie'll Voirrey. *Oie'll Voirrey*, G. **oidhche fhéille a' bheiridh* 'eve of the feast of the nativity', i.e. G. *breth* (Mx. *breh*) replaced in this sense by 'regular' verb-noun *beireadh*, g. *-idh*, cf. Mx. *berraghtyn* (**beireachtain*) in the sense of 'over-take'.

Nevertheless, in the early 19th century there were moves by private religious organisations (and organisations having close connections with the Anglican Church), and the Methodists themselves, to cater for the education of the Manx populace through the medium of Manx, especially in the Holy Scriptures. One society that was prominent in this activity was the Sunday School Society of London. According to Bird ([1991]: 215-18), the Sunday School idea was first started by properous newspaper owner Robert Raikes in Gloucester ca.1785 and the first known Sunday School in Man opened in a room in Mucclesgate, Douglas (opposite the present bus station), in 1786. In Man it was the Methodists who evidently developed this idea, opening schools in Douglas and Castletown, though of short duration. However, the first lasting Sunday School in Man seems to have been that of Rev. Hugh Stowell, former master of the Douglas Grammar School and Rector of Ballaugh, set up in Lonan parish (of which he was now vicar) on 27.03.1808, holding the teaching in the parish church (?in Manx, cf. Stowell 1808), with himself and his family as instructors. A flurry of Sunday Schools then opened, mostly under the auspices of the Methodists, and a return in 1818 put the number of Sunday Schools at thirty three, with 187 teachers and 2390 pupils. A further ten schools were opened in 1819, bringing the number of pupils to 3477. The material used in the schools (copies of the New Testament and spelling books) were from 1809 onwards supplied by the Sunday School Society of London.

In 1821 this society sent over a supply of spelling books, but for the first ime in Manx. The reasoning was explained in a notice in the *Manks Advertiser* for 05.07.1821 as follows:

> It seemed most desirable that the Inhabitants should be taught to read their vernacular tongue, which had not been taught to any of the children attending schools, nor for a very long period (if indeed ever in the schools), a primer or spelling book in Manx, having never before been printed. The rich boon was considered a real acquisition, as hereby many children would become enabled to read the Holy Scriptures to their parents in the only language which they understood (*Manks Advertiser* 05.07.1821 quoted after Bird [1991]: 217).

Shortly after the Liverpool Tract Society followed this up with a printing at their own expense of 4000 copies each of 'James Covey' and 'Poor Joseph' in Manx, while the Bristol Church of England Tract Society had printed 2000 copies of *Cooney dy gheddyn aarloo son baase ny yn Chreestee er lhiabbee dy hingys* ('help to prepare for death, or the Christian on a bed of sickness'). In 17 Sunday Schools some 400 children began learning Manx, and by 1821 this number had risen to 612 (Bird [1991]: 217).

Another society prominent in this field was the *Manks Society for promoting the Education of the Inhabitants of the Isle of Man, through the the medium of their own Language*. Taking its cue from *The Society for the Support of Gaelic Schools* (i.e. in Scotland) and *The Irish Society for promoting the Education of the Native Irish, through the medium of their own Language*, the Manks Society was set up in 1821 and established a number of schools. In an "address" in the *Manks Advertiser* for 22.11. 1821 the above Manks Society made clear its intentions. Its aim was definitely not to support the Manx language, but merely to use it

---

The *Oie'll Voirrey* tradition has a certain similarity with the Welsh *Plygain* (< L. *Pullicantium*; cf. Fisher 1929: 308-16). From personal enquiry it seems that Oie'll Voirreys in Manx are remembered as late as the 1920s, but mostly in English, and in English exclusively till the Second World War. The last reputed carval singer in Manx was Will Wade of Orrisdale, Michael, who died in 1948. Oie'll Voirreys are still held today in Man, but as occasions of Manx entertainment, and not necessarily on Christmas Eve.

as a means to promote Protestantism in Man via religious tracts translated from English, since the majority of the Manx people simply did not understand that language:

> That every individual should be furnished with the means of reading the Holy Scriptures, in the language which he best understands, appears to be an acknowledged principle amongst all Protestants. The command of the Saviour of the world to "search the scriptures" implies the necessity of communicating the ability to search them. This ability, in the present age of benevolence, has been communicated to multitudes. The Report of *"The Society for the Support of Gaelic Schools"* and of *"The Irish Society for promoting the Education of the Native Irish, through the medium of their own Language"*[editor's italics], fully prove what can be done, and what has been done for the accomplishment of this important end by the establishment of circulating Schools.
>
> The arguments which have been so ably adduced by those Societies to evince the necessity and utility of their efforts, apply with equal force to the meridian of the Isle of Man. When it is known, that there are from fifteen to twenty thousand of the inhabitants who are incapable of receiving religious instruction in any other language than the Manks, and when it is considered that a large proportion of that number are unable to read, who does not perceive the necessity of making vigorous efforts to teach them to read their vernacular tongue?
>
> It is, by no means, the design of the Society to perpetuate the Manks language, or in the smallest degree to impede the progress of the English tongue amongst the inhabitants of the Island, but simply to teach both children and adults to read their Bible in the only language which they fully comprehend. [...] (*Manks Advertiser* 22.11.1821).

The "address" then aks for financial contributions. In a notice in the *Manks Advertiser* for 26.12.1822 (running till 09.01.1823) the same society presents further details about itself and its activities in the interests of its own credibility and gives a list of twenty subscribers, the main ones being the Sunday School Society, London (whose donation of £25.0.0 is "to be applied solely in aid of Sunday Schools" (see below)), the Bristol Church of England Tract Society £10.0.0 "to print Translations of their tracts", and the Religious Trust Society, London, £5.0.0 for the same purpose. The rest are private individuals mainly from the Man and Ireland, with one or two from Liverpool and London (*Manks Advertiser* 26.12.1822). The Manks Society declares as its object

> [...] to teach the Inhabitants to read the sacred Scriptures, in their Native Tongue. The Affairs of the Society, are managed by a Committee of Twelve, Members of the Church of England, who meet on the first Monday in the Month in Douglas. The Society has met with a considerable degree of Encouragement within the past Year. They have given grants of 428 Manks Spelling Books, 189 Watt's Divine Songs, and printed 7,500 Religious Tracts in Manks. They have established Nine Evening Schools, wherein 480 Persons have been instructed, and assisted Ten Sunday Schools [...] (*Manks Advertiser* 26.12.1822).

For details of the activities of other similar societies, e.g. the 'Religious Tract Society", the 'Teetotal Society of Kirk Andreas' and the 'Prayer-book and Homily Society', etc, see Cubbon (1939: 783-88).

It is difficult to ascertain how successful these various societies and Sunday Schools were and how good a standard of teaching was achieved in them before the Education Act of 1872 (see §2.2.3. below). The fact that a number of tracts continued to be printed and reprinted till as late as 1872 that we know of (e.g. *Yn Jeirkagh Meshtyllagh* ('the drunken beggar') by John Quirk, Carnagreie, Patrick; cf. Cubbon 1939: 786) is testimony to the necessity of having material printed in Manx till that date at any rate.

Nevertheless, the view that Manx was associated with backwardness and moral laxity was beginning to gain ground in the 1820s (cf. Letters in Appendix B), and the activities of

22

Bishop Muray (as noted above) did not help. In addition, as we have already seen (§2.2.1.) and will see below (§2.2.4.), other considerations began to usher in the advance of English speech in Man.

2.2.3. The language policy of secular authorities

After the virtual collapse of Wilson's 'cure' (as his education proposals were termed) for the Manx (Clamp 1998c: 198), English schooling in Man thereafter was never set on a firm footing until Man came fully within the English education ambit in 1858. In 1872 the Manx authorities adopted the English Elementary Education Act of 1870 which provided for compulsory schooling from 5-13 years. Though the medium of tuition was to be English this was not compulsorily laid down in the Act. The only subject made compulsory under the Act was religious education. However, though there was nothing in the Act providing against the teaching of Manx, in practical terms the Act facilitated the dissemination of English in Man. However, by the time the Act came into being Manx was in an advanced state of demise, and any hostile intent towards Manx abetted by the 1872 Act was in reality ineffectual (cf. Bird 1995: 1-43).[16]

In addition, the parents of immigrant children, who had only English, demanded the teaching of English as a means of advancement in life, and given that Man was now being drawn more and more into an English-speaking world through commerce and tourism, etc, this attitude gained ground at the expense of Manx. The children of Manx-English families would be predominantly English-speaking, as would those of all Manx families in the course of time (Hindley 1984: 15-17, 26, 32). However, even as late as the 1870/80s there were still a number of Manx families who brought up their children in Manx, and whose children had no English until they went to school. In some cases the school had difficulty in getting the children to learn English. For example, John Tom Kaighin, one of the last native Manx speakers recorded here by the Manx Museum's folklife survey ca. 1950, tells the story of the difficulty he had learning English at school:

> Tra ren mee goll dy schoill va mee bunnys hoght vleeaney (*sic*) as va mee toiggal Gailck foddee share na va mee toiggal Baarle, as ren ad goll dy gynsaghey mee son dy gra...'nane' - *they were saying 'one'* a[s] va mish gra 'nane', as *they were saying 'two'* a[s] va mee gra 'jees', as ren ad gra *'three'* as ren mee gra 'strass' (*sic*), as v'ad gra...*'four'* as va mee gra 'kiare', as ren ad goll dys y mainshter dy geddyn yn fer shoh, 'Cha jarg mee gynsaghey, cha jarg mee gynsaghey, t'eh loayrt Gailck [...].
> ('when I was going to school I was almost eight years old, and I was understanding Manx far better than I was understanding English, and they went to teach me for to say 'one' - they were saying 'one' and I was saying *nane*, and they were saying 'two' and I was saying *jees*, and they said 'three' and I said *strass* [i.e. *tree*], and they were saying 'four' and I was saying *kiare*, and they went to the master to get this one (sorted) [and said], 'I cannot teach him, I cannot teach him, he's talking Manx...') (MM Tape 22, HLSM/I: 286-87).

---

[16] Nevertheless, children were allegedly actively discouraged from speaking Manx at school by means of a 'knot' or 'tally' passed from one child to another till the close of school, when the last recipient would be punished (see also Letter 3 in Appendix B and §2.3.2. below).

From the late 19th century to the present day the Manx education system has largely followed that of England and Wales, including the recent decision to shadow the English / Welsh 'National Curriculum' without making any provision for the teaching of Manx Gaelic. The present programme of teaching Manx in the Island's schools (cf. Section 5) is conducted outwith this curriculum (cf. König 1996: 23).

2.2.4. Socio-economic causes of language shift

2.2.4.1. Trade

The decline of Manx results not so much from rigorous action against it from within, but from a changing set of circumstances emanating from without. Until the mid-18th century Man had little contact with the outside world. Given its small population and resources external trade and contact could hardly have been all that great anyway, and English was therefore unnecessary to people outside the small towns, where it was spoken alongside Manx without displacing it. There was little incentive or reason for outsiders to come to Man, and so everyday contact between town and country areas was therefore important and Manx would need to be used. The impetus in the direction of English came ca. early/mid-18th century, largely as a result of the 'running trade' from which many Manx people profitted (cf. Hindley 1984: 18).

Because of restrictive English (British from 1707) trading practices Manx seamen reacted by adopting smuggling into England, Scotland, and Ireland of such commodities as wines, spirits, tea, tobacco, obtained principally from France, Spain, Portugal, Norway, and Sweden, as a major industry. The practice was not smuggling into Man, but out of it, since duty on the above was paid in Man at the (low) Manx rate. However, the 'running trade' or 'trade', as it was known in Man, also attracted English and Scottish merchants to the Island and stimulated the Manx ports, particularly Douglas, and with it brought new ideas, capital, and an increase in the use of English.

In 1765 the British government stepped in and through an Act of Revestment[17] bought out the manorial rights of the Duke of Atholl, the then Lord of Man, thus transfering sovereignty to the British Crown, thereby attempting to suppress 'smuggling' by direct rule.[18] This meant in effect that the Island's finances were controlled by the British; they paid

---

[17] For details of English rule in Man as a result of Revestment in 1765 till ca.1800, see Dolley (1977: 207-45). This transference of sovereignty was felt by many Manxmen to have been an act of gross injustice - Revestment being known in Man at the time as *Yn Chialg Vooar* 'the great deception' - because they were operating within their own laws, and it was not their fault if the British were losing money hand over fist as a result of their own trading restrictions. However, the whole issue was evidently conducted in a clandestine manner, due largely, it seems, to the presence of not insignificant numbers of English and Scottish operators in the Island, which caused the British authorities to see matters differently (cf. Kinvig 1975: 120-22). It is interesting to note that, though the 'trade' lasted ca.100 years, very little about it has come down into Manx folklore, probably because of the covert way in which it was conducted (cf. Killip 1975: 143-55). After Revestment oral tradition has it that many Manx families left Man to continue the 'trade' elsewhere, notably in Orkney.

[18] The 'trade' evidently continued in some form till after 1800, cf. HLSM/I: 256-59.

24

the costs of Man's administration and kept the rest in London. A direct result of this was an onset of poverty through loss of earnings from the 'trade' and the ensuing depression resulted in emigration, for which Manx was useless, and the administration of direct rule enhanced the status of English. The contacts with the outside world, particularly during the latter period of the 'trade' (about 100 years) and the depression that followed Revestment forced Manxmen to emigrate (cf. Carlisle 1813, Campbell 1885-86, Hindley 1984).[19]

In addition, during the course of the 19th century a number of changes and developments militated against Manx:

2.2.4.2. Migration

Immigration into the Island particularly from north-west England ca.1790-ca.1814 (Moore 1900: 575) of people on low fixed incomes. The settlement was not restricted to the towns. In the north of Man there was significant settlement from southern Scotland (Campbell 1885-86: 177). In 1813 Carlisle commented that the Island was "a place of considerable resort for strangers" (quoted after Hindley 1984: 28). This immigration, especially in the towns, formed the basis of the Manx (Methodist) bourgeoisie.

A second period of depression, this time after the Napoleonic Wars, but especially from ca.1825-ca.1837, resulted in mass emigration, particularly from northern and western areas, to Liverpool, Manchester, but mostly to America where Ohio was the main destination (Moore 1900: 930-31, Birch 1964: 20, 79). Additional 'peaks' in emigration occurred also in the 1830s due to a depression in the fishing (a vital industry for local labour), in the 1840s (potato famine), and in the 1860s resulting from commonland reorganisation which would have affected many squatter-farmers (Birch 1964: 79-80, 119, 136-37; Hindley 1984: 29).

2.2.4.3. Communications

The increase in the Island's population during the course of the 19th century concentrated largely on the towns where English had become established. By 1881 26,394 out of a population of 53,558 (cf. 1881 Census in Appendix C) were living in the four towns of Douglas, Castletown, Ramsey, and Peel. The first 'modern' roads of 1750-1800 brought closer links between town and country areas.

The arrival of the first steamer at Douglas in 1819 was to revolutionise the Island's economy, for it heralded the onset of tourism (see below). This was enhanced by the establishment of regular steamer services, especially from 1830 (when the Isle of Man Steam Packet Co. Ltd. was founded) between Man and Liverpool, Whitehaven, and the Clyde. The opening of the Liverpool and Manchester Railway in 1830 facilitated sea travel to Man from Liverpool for the rising middle classes of the Lancashire industrial towns (Hindley 1984: 28).

---

[19] Such emigration would also include those English and Scottish merchants engaged in the 'trade' who lived for the most part in the towns and who would have spoken English.

2.2.4.4. Tourism

From 1830-50 some 20-30,000 visitors a year came to Man's shores, when the Island's population was ca.40-50,000. By ca.1870 the number of visitors rose to ca.60,000 per year, and by the 1890s to over 250,000 per year. Though most would find entertainment (then as now) in and around Douglas, the building of the steam and electric railways (between 1873 and 1898) facilitated access to remoter areas. The penetration of the innermost parts of the Island by visitors and the immigration of additional personnel to service the tourist industry meant that a knowledge of English was essential everywhere during the 3-4 months (June-September) of the tourist season.[20] But that in itself did not make Manx redundant.

2.2.4.5. Agriculture and mining

The rise of utilitarianism in the 19th century resulted in loss of vernacular in many western European countries, and affected Man in a similar way. The Manx rural economy was transformed by improved agricultural methods and ideas from outside and by the opportunities of an expanded market due to tourism.

The expansion of the mining industry ca.1870 at Laxey and Foxdale resulted in the importation of specialised labour from Cornwall to service the industry. The localisation of mining, essentially in those two areas, would not have contributed much to the decline of Manx outside those areas, nor would the fishing industry have done (also in full swing at that time), staffed as it was by a local Manx labour force.The serious decline to both these industries by ca.1890, however, and the resultant emigration would have had little linguistic impact, as Manx by then had receded considerably. Nevertheless, the new social and economic improvements brought about the abandonment of obsolete means of production and of a means of communication associated with it. It was this 'utilitarian spirit of modern times', as A. W. Moore put it (cf. Hindley 1984: 26) that persuaded parents not to pass Manx on to their children. As Charles Loch, writing in 1946, put it:

> A generation or two ago, as in Scotland and Ireland, it was thought among the old people that a knowledge of Manx was a handicap to a child's progress in the world. There was also a strange[21] inferiority complex which gave the impression that Gaelic was the language of the ignorant, the humble and the servants, whereas English was the language of the educated and superior classes. Many cases have occurred of native speakers who pretended that they knew no Gaelic, and parents in the Island have refused to let their children learn Manx, and have spoken it together only when they did not wish their children to understand what they were saying (Loch 1946: 5; see also note 30).

---

[20] The high number of visitors began to decrease dramatically during the 1960s when cheap package travel to warmer climes became affordable to many English families. At present Man attracts some 120,000 visitors each summer, many of whom - including some 12-15,000 Germans - come for the TT and Manx Grand Prix motor-cycle races held in May/June and August respectively (cf. also König 1996: 18, note 22).

[21] Not really since this accorded with the facts - RLT, GB.

2.2.4.6. Increased mobility

The onset of the 20th century saw the increase in internal and external mobility, particularly the establishment of regular air services to the Island after the Second World War. In addition the coming of the motor-car within easy financial reach of many ordinary people facilitated access to remoter areas (Hindley 1984: 30-31).

2.3. Contemporary opinions on the position of Manx during the 19th and 20th centuries

2.3.1. Contemporary opinion during the 19th century

In spite of the above developments Manx did not disappear overnight.[22] Comments on Manx during the 19th century from Carlisle (1813), Bullock (1816), Lewis (1831), Cumming (1848, 1861), and Rosser (1849) make it clear that anglicisation first took place in the towns (Peel a little later due to its strong contacts with the fishing industry), then the spread of bilingualism into the country areas via the children, and lastly the retention of Manx in everyday use in the mountain areas and in districts well away from the main ports, e.g. in the north-west. In 1859 Gill (1859: v) lamented the passing of Manx from the law-courts, churches and schools.

> The decline of the spoken Manx, within the memory of the present generation, has been marked. The language is no longer heard in our courts of law, either from the bench or the bar, and seldom from the witness-box [...]. In our churches the language was used by many of the present generation of clergy three Sundays in the month. It was afterwards restricted to every other Sunday, and is now entirely discontinued in most of the churches. In the schools throughout the Island the Manx has ceased to be taught; and the introduction of the Government system of education has done much to displace the language. It is rarely now heard in conversation, except among the peasantry. It is a doomed language, - an iceberg floating into southern latitudes (Gill 1859: v; also quoted after Price 1984: 77, König 1996: 15).

In 1872 the Vicar of St. Mark's, Malew, and collector of Manx traditional songs Rev. J. T. Clarke noted:

> Ta ard-reiltee Vannin noi'n Ghailck. Ta shirveishee yn Ghoo jeh dy-chooilley chredjue noi eck. Ta aegid troggit seose nish ny s'meehushtee jeh chengey ny mayrey na va maase y vagheragh cliaghtey ve (quoted after Kneen 1931: 14)
> ('the rulers of Man are against the Manx. Servants of all religions are against it. The young are brought up now more ignorant of the mother tongue than the cattle of the field ever used to be').

---

[22] Manx newspapers (in English), such as the *Manx Mercury* (1792-?1801), *Manks Advertiser* (1801-1845), *The Manx Sun* (1821-1906)(for other titles see Cubbon 1939: 1337), etc, whose news was largely culled from English newspapers (though some would contain some news about the Isle of Man), were set up to serve the needs of a growing English-speaking population (of non-Manx as well as Manx) in the island. Material in Manx is occasionally found; see note 25.

Bearing in mind that talking to one's domestic or farm animals is a means of keeping a language alive, Clarke added:

> [...] Ta cooinaghtyn aympene, ayns laghyn m'aegid, dy re ayns Gailck va shin ooilley loayrt rish nyn gabbil as nyn ollagh. Eer ny moddee hene mannagh loayragh shin roo ayns Gailck, cha jinnagh ad cloh dooin - agh jeeaghyn my-geayrt y moo, goaill yn yindys s'moo 'sy theihll c'red va shin laccal ad 'yannoo dooin. Cha row ny moddee voghtey hene toiggal Baarle, son she Gailck ooilley v'oc, as cha row ad goaill nearey jee noadyr
> ('I well remember in my young days that it was Manx we were all talking to our horses and to our cattle. Even the dogs themselves, if we didn't speak to them in Manx, they wouldn't heed us - but look all around them and wonder what on earth we were wanting them to do. The poor dogs themselves couldn't understand English, for they only had Manx, and they were not ashamed of it either') (quoted after Kneen 1931: 14).

Jenner (1875: 21) noted the gradual decline in the number of services in Manx per month in the churches, from three Sundays a month "in many parishes" at the beginning of the 19th century to only one service a month in one parish (Arbory) at the time of writing.

2.3.1.1. Comment in Manx newspapers and other periodicals during the 19th century

A cursory glance at Manx newspapers and other publications (in English) during the course of the 19th century makes interesting reading:

2.3.1.1.1. *THE MONTHLY MAGAZINE* (1801) "The Present State of the Isle of Man". In: *Excerpts* I: 26:

> Almost every Manksman can speak English; their accent is very like that of Ireland, and they may easily be mistaken for Hibernians, by those who have not attended closely to the niceties of pronunciation. Little Manks music is to be met with. There are a few original airs which have much of the wildness of the Irish. To these are sometimes sung ballads in the Manx language (*The Monthly Magazine* 1801. Excerpts I: 26, quoted after Speers 1997: 253).

Given the comment we have below from others and from Jenner's survey, that every Manxman could speak English in 1801 is perhaps somewhat exaggerated. The commentator was in all likelihood referring to the Manx people living in the towns.

2.3.1.1.2. *MANKS ADVERTISER* 13.12.1821: Letter (in Manx) from 'Manninagh Dooie' criticising a letter (also in Manx) from a certain Robin Briw published in an earlier issue (which has not survived) advocating the retention of Manx. The letter of 13.12.21 advocates the non-retention of Manx. It is significant to note here that 'Manninagh Dooie's' letter is in fact in Manx. Had it been in English, he could have been accused of being anti-Manx language because he could not speak or write Manx. He writes it in (good) Manx to show that he knows what he is talking about, but nevertheless prefers to place his loyalty with English. Full text given in Appendix B.

2.3.1.1.3. *MANKS ADVERTISER* 10.01.1822: Letter to the editor in support of a resolution by the then bishop (George Murray) not:

to admit in future any candidate for the Manks Church, even to Deacon's orders, before he has acquired a complete knowledge of the Manks language [...][because][...] the Manks language, owing to a certain peculiarity belonging to itself, is perfectly understood by the most ordinary capacity to be found in an assembly of Manksmen (*Manks Advertiser* 10.01.1822).[23]

The above is in stark contrast to Murray's alleged attitude towards Manx only a few years later (ca. 1825) when he apparently persuaded the SPCK not to send any more Bibles, etc, in Manx (cf. §2.2.2. above).

The same paper for 11.04.1837 also carries details of a 'Bill to prevent the Introduction of Clergymen who are not fully conversant with the Manx language to Parish livings within the Island'.

2.3.1.1.4. *MANKS ADVERTISER* 06.06.-04.07.1822: Heated correspondence for and against the retention of Manx. One of the best examples of contempt and hostility towards Manx in the early 19th century is a letter to the editor of the *Manks Advertiser*, from 'A Native' written 26 May 1822 and published 6 June 1822. He takes the view that "Mankind ought to improve, and not remain in their pristine barbarism" and continues:

> What better is the gibberish called Manx than an uncouth mouthful of coarse (*sic*) savage expressions, as distant from any degree of civilized sound as that of the Kamskatcadales (*sic*) is from the classic beauty of one of the orations which grace the first orators of the British senate? Such a jargon is Manx [...] (*Manks Advertiser* 06.06.1822; full text in Appendix B).

The writer then appeals to the 'learned of the country' to

> Abolish the Manx [...]. Allow no one, not even one of your servants or neighbours to speak one word of Manx; and thus, by degrees annihilate it" (*Manks Advertiser* 06.06.1822).

In spite of its hostile stance I cannot help thinking that the exaggerated tone of the letter is machiavellian in intent (a not uncommon trait among Manxmen, i.e. that the writer was in fact in favour of Manx!) designed to elicit a decisive response in that respect. If this is the case then he succeeded (cf.letter 13.06.1822 next).

Nevertheless, it mirrors a hostility and arrogant attitude towards Manx evidently prevalent at the time among the 'learned of the country'[24] which may also have included recent lower middle class immigrants from Lancashire (see letter of 07.07.1824 below).

---

[23] The same letter also comments on the inadequacy of the Manx of some of the clergy, arguing that they study the dead languages sufficiently, but not the living ones necessary for their parish work.

[24] Nevertheless, Manx was evidently held in esteem by native speakers in the Manx establishment, as is shown by comment from Lt. Mark Cubbon (later Sir Mark Cubbon, Governor of Mysore in India (cf. Moore 1900: 643 note), in a letter home to his father 24.07.1805 from his army camp at Madras:

> I have lost the greatest part of my Manx and will expect you will send me through Mrs [James] Wilks some Manx Books, and all the old Ballads you can collect with a Bible and Prayer Book. I never got the one Mrs Wilks brought out [...]. I however feel such an Amor for my mother tongue that I am not willing to forget it entirely and a Book or two would always recall it to my memory (MM.MS.MD436).

2.3.1.1.5. *MANKS ADVERTISER* 13.06.1822. A reply to the foregoing.

> Your correspondent, A Native, deserves to be thrashed, for writing such stuff, and you are not
> much better for taking it in your paper. He is an enemy to this Isle [...]. If you put the manx
> down, our nation will be no longer manx - it will be english or scotch or irish - it will be
> mungrel at least.[...]. It is true enough, when a man gets rich his words goes farther than when
> he was poor [...] but it will never buy sense [...]. And what common sense is there in speaking
> to a people in a language which they do not understand [...] (*Manks Advertiser* 13.06.1822;
> full text in Appendix B).

The letter makes clear that at that time there were many people in the Island who could not
understand English.

2.3.1.1.6. *MANKS ADVERTISER* 25.07.1822: Notice of a speech delivered by Rev. Hugh
Stowell (the elder, 1768-1835) at the annual meeting of the Peel Ladies' Bible Association
on the need for more Bibles in Manx.

2.3.1.1.7. *MANKS ADVERTISER* 01.01.1824: English and Manx text of a bill for the
commutation of tithes. The editorial (p. 3) gives as the reason for printing the Manx text:

> that they [the Manx speaking population] may the more comprehend the purport of them [the
> proposals]. It is a remarkable fact, that although the Manks dialect or Gailc is gradually falling
> into disuse, the generality of *the people* [editor's italics] continue to speak it, and love to hear
> it - more particularly when it concerns their more intimate interest (*Manks Advertiser*
> 01.01.1824).[25]

2.3.1.1.8. *MANX PATRIOT* 07.07.1824: Letter to the editor supporting the notion of national pride, and castigates those who wish to force the Manx people to learn another language, rather than be taught it. He adds:

> I am a Manxman, and we Manxmen are often doomed to hear with patience the worst epithets
> bestowed upon us, without daring to resent the insult in any way [...].We are blown up and bul-
> lied on all sides for want of knowledge and information, and our native language is ridiculed by
> those who cannot comprehend or understand it (*Manx Patriot* 07.07.1824; full text in Ap-
> pendix B).

Except for comments above made by Hildesley concerning anti-Manx language attitudes (see
note 13) and leaving aside the comments in the above letter of 1822 (which, as noted, seems
machiavellian in tone), this is the earliest known reference to alleged open hostility towards
Manx from non-Manx speakers.

2.3.1.1.9. *MANKS ADVERTISER* 01.01.1833 (also in *MANX SUN* 01.01.1833): Letter
from Rev. Robert Brown of Kirk Braddan, that as he could not recollect during his time in
Douglas that a sick person whom he visited could not converse with him in English, he does
not consider a knowledge of Manx absolutely necessary for a minister at St. Barnabas's
(Douglas), provided he prevails on neighbouring clergymen to perform the Manx services for

---

[25] For scattered articles, poems, letters, comments (usually of a political nature) in Manx, cf.
Mona's Herald for 27.12.1833 (See Appendix B), 21.02.1834, 06.06.1834, 08.08.1834,
06.02.1835, 23.07. 1835, etc; *Manx Sun* for 20.12.1845, etc.

him (as he did at St. Matthew's) or employs a 'pious young man' in the capacity of a curate for this purpose.

2.3.1.1.10. *MANX SUN* 06.06.1842: A long letter questioning the assumption that English is understood and spoken by the rural population at large. Emphasises the need for Manx in church services. Regarding the practicalities of having Manx for business purposes the writer adds:

> It is well known, that in the principal shops in Douglas it is found absolutely necessary to employ a person conversant with the Manx language to transact business with country customers, and I have lately heard a Douglas tradesman declare that one half of the people resorting on Saturdays to the shop, in which he serves, were unable to ask for what they wanted in English (*Manx Sun* 06.08.1842).

-10a. *WILLIAM KENNISH* (1840)

Nevertheless, the falling into disuse of Manx had become sufficiently marked by 1840 as to prompt the Manx engineer and inventor William Kennish (1799-1862) to compose a 21-quatrain ballad in Manx lamenting the demise of the Manx language: *Dobberan Chengey ny Mayrey Ellan Vannin* 'lament for the mother tongue of the Isle of Man' (Moore 1896: 142-47), part of which runs thus:

> Son mish, bee fys ayd er, ta scaan y chenn ghlare
> ec cloan Vannin er my hregeil;
> Agh s'beg fys ta ocsyn de beagh eh ny share
> daue mish dy ve harroo dy reill
>
> Son mish ta er reayll yn fer joarree ersooyl
> son keeadyn dy vleintyn dy hraa;
> As va mee er reill veih yn traie gys Barool
> da Manninee dooie son dy braa
>
> Agh nish ta yn voyrn oc er chur lesh yn Vaarle
> eer seose yn glione mooar Tolt-y-Will
> as mastey ny reeastyn er lhiattee Wooar Cardle
> as creggyn yn Creg-Willy-Sill

('for it is I, you will know, who am the ghost of the old tongue, abandoned by the children of Man. But little do they know that it would be better for them for me to rule over them.

'For it is I who has kept the stranger away for hundreds of years of time. And I had ruled from the shore to Barrule for ever for true Manxmen.

'But now their pride has brought the English tongue even up the great glen of Tholt y Will, and among the wastelands on the side of Cardle Vooar and the rocks at Creg Willy Syl').

-10b. *TOM KERMODE* (1883)

In addition, when John Strachan was collecting a version of the Manx folksong *Ec ny Fiddleryn* 'at the fiddlers' in 1883 (which he later printed in the first issue of ZCP (1897)), his informant Tom Kermode of Bradda told him that he had not heard a Manx song sung "for the last forty years" (Strachan 1897: 54-58). This would suggest a similar date for the falling into disuse also of the Manx secular song tradition. For comment on songs sung in Manx, see also §2.3.1.1.1. above.

2.3.1.1.11. *MANX SUN* 21.06.1845: A long letter advocating the appointment to the vacancy at Lezayre of a person competent in Manx:

> [...] as it is a fact that two thirds of the parishioners cannot benefit from the reliogious services performed in any other language than Manx (*Manx Sun* 21. 06.1845).

In fact matters here went further than a mere letter to the newspapers. Among papers from the Farrant family of Ballamoar, Jurby, recently accessioned at the Manx Museum Library (MM.MS.9257) a memorial from landowners and inhabitants of Lezayre dated June 9th 1845 was sent to the then British Home Secretary Sir James R. G. Graham imploring the appointment of a vicar competent in Manx, advising:

> [...] That the Vicarage of the above named Parish [Kirk Christ Lezayre] is now vacant by the decease of the Revd. J. H. Lamothe the late Vicar thereof.
> That the gift of the said Vicarage lays in the hands of the Crown, dependant upon your nomination as Secretary of State for the Home department.
> That at least a Majority of the adult population of this parish are unable to benefit by the Ministration of our Holy and Venerable Church in public or in private in any other Way than through the Medium of their Vernacular tongue (that is) the Manks Language.
> That during the Incumbency of the late Revd. J. H. Lamothe, very considerable Spiritual loss has occurred to a large number of the Parishioners from the ignorance of the Manks Language on the part of their departed Vicar.
> Your Memorialists, therefore, humbly Implore you, in your appointment to the Vacant Vicarage to place over them a Man fully Competent to Converse with, and to Minister to the Inhabitants of Lezayre in their Mother tongue [...] (Farrant Family Papers MM.MS. 9257).

According to Kermode (Kermode 1954: 84-85), William Bell Christian (1815-1886) of Milntown, Lezayre, (and almost certainly a native Manx speaker) was appointed vicar 07.07.1845 and resigned in 1861 to be appointed the last member to the self-elected House of Keys, popularly elected as from 1866.

2.3.1.1.12. *LETTERS FROM BISHOP W. A. SHIRLEY* (1847)
Interesting also are two letters from Bishop W. A. Shirley of Sodor and Man (1847 only), an Englishman, from his seat at Bishop's Court:

a) to his son 05.02.1847:

> [...] You will understand one feature of this responsibility, when I tell you that though I am patron of only four vicarages, these livings, with some chapelries recently constituted in my gift, comprise more than half the population of the island, and have not an aggregate income of one thousand pounds per annum; besides which I have the additional difficulty that the Manx language is required in most of them, which limits my choice to men who, for the most part, are behind the English in vigour, education, habits of business, and even piety and their moral standard (Hill 1849: 463).

b) to his parents 18.02.1847:

> [...] The Manx papers amuse me now and then with letters from correspondents about what Bishop Shirley ought to be made acquainted with, and how he ought to act. The great point of discussion is whether Manx-speaking clergymen are to be exclusively appointed to livings. I have appointed one to a vacant vicarage; but they are a heavy set, and will soon be exhausted, for their children do not understand Manx. I am glad to hear that the children in the streets play in English. The Manx is a language without a literature, except the Bible and Prayer-book lately translated, and as far as I can make out, has neither dictionary nor grammar deserving of

the name. It is an unmitigated portion of the curse of Babel. I will send you a Manx paper - it is sad stuff (Hill 1849: 476).

Shirley had obviously not seen, or thought much of, Cregeen's *Dictionary* (1835) or Kelly's *Grammar* (1804).

2.3.1.1.13. *THE CHRISTIAN ADVOCATE AND JOURNAL* 21.08.1862. Correspondence, dated 24 June [1862], from a reader, Mrs. Phoebe Palmer. In: *Excerpts* 1: 55 §4:

> The Manks language is still spoken in the rural villages; but though in frequent use, there are probably but few who do not understand English (*The Christian Advocate and Journal* 21.08.1862, quoted after Speers 1997: 264).

2.3.1.1.14. *CHAMBERS JOURNAL* 11.06.1881. In: *Excerpts* I: 86. Comment about the people of Cregneash and their attitude towards their native tongue:

> Perched high up on Spanish Head lies the village of Craigneesh, a primitive and conservative folk who pride themselves on being the original aborigines of the island. They neither marry, nor give in marriage outside their own circle, and hold themselves as much aloof from the rest of the world as is possible in these days. Inability to speak English is with them considered an accomplishment, though, happily, the progress of education is daily more and more restricting this accomplishment to the elders of the community (*Chambers Journal* 11.06.1881 quoted after Speers 1997: 271).

-14a. *Mrs. SAGE KINVIG* (1953)

Similar comment was also recorded in Manx from Mrs. Sage Kinvig (1870-1962), Garey Hollin, Ronague, Arbory, in 1953 (YCG Tape 34; cf. HLSM/I: 338-39), referring to a period around 1880:

> Ren mee clashtyn y jishig ginsh mygeayrt eh as v'eh goll dys yn skaddan mârish as v'eh gra... va fer elley goll dys yn skaddan, v'eh woish Cregneash as cha row monney Baarle echey, as v'eh jannoo gamman jeh eshyn. Cha row Gaelg echey as v'eh gra rish yn jishig aym, 'T'eh *futile* loayrt rishyn. Cha nel eh toiggal Baarle, as cha nel ad toiggal Baarle erbee heose ayns Cregneash', dooyrt eh [..].
> ('I heard my father telling about him and he used to go to the herring with him and he was saying...there was another one going to the herring, he was from Cregneash and he hadn't any English, and he would make sport of him. He (the first man) had no Manx and he would say to my father, 'It's futile speaking to him. He can't understand English, and they do not understand any English up in Cregneash') (Mrs. Sage Kinvig 1953, HLSM/I: 338-39).

It is possibly the above sentiment that gave rise to the belief that Cregneash was the last community in Man where Manx was last spoken. Perhaps. But see Stanley Karran's comments in Section 3, fn. 19. That there was little English in Cregneash around 1840 is testified next.

-14b. *CHARLES ROEDER* Introduction to Edward Faragher's *Skeealyn Æsop* [Æsop's Fables] (1901): 9, in a section giving a brief details of Faragher's *vita* (which he would have got from Faragher himself):

> [...] There was little English taught and known in Cregneish [ca.1840], his mother being the only person who could converse with strangers. His father was a fair scholar, and wrote all the letters [in English] for the Cregneish people, and that was a great thing then [...] (Roeder 1901: 9).

2.3.1.1.15. *CASSELL'S FAMILY MAGAZINE* April 1884 "Manxland People". In: *Excerpts* II: 95:

> [The Manx language] is still spoken in the country districts, and in the remoter highlands there are still individuals unable to speak any other, but the Manx, though they love it as the old language of their country, and pride themselves upon having something of its phraseology, are too practical a race not to see that its common use would be a hindrance to the prosperity of their country, and it is now fast dying out as a spoken language. The English language alone is the common speech of the country, and as The Manx is not taught in schools, in another generation it will have become extinct (*Cassell's Family Magazine* April 1984, quoted after Speers 1997: 271).

Concerning the dialects of Manx the writer adds:

> [...] There are also marked differences in the native languages [Manx] of the two districts [North and South], differences so great as to affect their pronunciation of the English language, and amounting to dialectal peculiarities. [...] (*Cassell's Family Magazine* April 1884, quoted after Speers 1997: 272).

2.3.2. Contemporary opinion during the 20th century

In the twenties and thirties of the 20th century the position of Manx was still able to elicit comment, whereby all the ingredients pertinent to the decline of Manx were assembled together:

2.3.2.1. *DAILY MAIL* 12.07.1930 "Island's Dying Tongue. Only 2,000 Manx Speakers. Holiday "Invasion" Blamed":

> The idiom of the Lancashire visitors; burr of the Scot on holiday; general use of English for all commercial, political and social purposes, and apathy of Manx youth are among the reasons given for the decline of the native tongue which has existed for more than 1,000 years (*Daily Mail* 12.07.1930 quoted after Peter 1984: 36).

This can be reinforced by the following, whereby scapegoats are sought for the decline of Manx:

2.3.2.2. *THE OBSERVER*: 01.02.1924. Letter to the Editor from Mona Douglas:

> [...] The painful fact is that the bulk of immigrants to Mann the number of whom grows every year are of the type that disfigures our countryside with red-roofed jerry-built bungalows, laughs our traditions to scorn, and, so far from attempting to help in the preservation of our ancient tongue [rest lost] (*The Observer* 01.02.1924 quoted after Peter 1984: 36).

For further comment in this respect, cf. Section 5, Note 7.

2.3.2.3. *MANX FOLKLIFE SURVEY.* In the 1940s-1970s the Manx Folk-Life Survey of the Manx Museum collected a number of aspects of Manx folklore, folklife, and tradition (including comment on the Manx language) from informants in the field. The following will give some idea of attitudes towards it. The period referred to would be ca.1900-10. Comment from other sources are also included where relevant.

2.3.2.3.1. *Manx still spoken in some parts ca.1890s-1900s.*

Ned Maddrell (1877-1974) remembers the time when he first went to the fishing in his teens (ca. 1890s) that all the fishermen were speaking Manx, and that there was no English to be heard:

> Ta cooinaghtyn aym's er y traa va mish guilley veg goll magh mâroo as cha jinnagh shiu clashtyn un fockle dy Baarle, ooilley Gaelg
> ('I remember the time I was a wee lad when I went out with them (the fishermen) and you wouldn't hear one word of English, (it was) all Manx') (Ned Maddrell YCG Tape 32).

Edward Christian, Northop, Greeba, German, remembers when Manx was spoken on the farms in his time (ca.1900):

> There was Manx spoken on the farms in my day [...]. The old men at Glen Meay [i.e. Maye] could talk some Manx, not all of them, but a good many. They would be giving orders in Manx to the young fellows. It was always *gow shen* ['take that'] and *jean shoh* ['do this'], and the younger men must have been able to understand the order at least. I knew two men who worked for us and they could talk Manx, and they used it a lot in conversation, but when the old men died and the next generation came on they didn't bother to use the language at all. The English would be of more general use to them, and so it got to be all English that they were talking (MFLS/C-27 (1960)).

Later he adds:

> It was strange that people of varying ages differed so much in their ability or otherwise to speak Manx. It wasn't necessarily the oldest people who spoke it. Of two of my grandfathers, grandfather Wattleworth had no Manx. Grandfather Christian of Ballakilmerton [Onchan] had a great deal. My parents did not speak Manx, but people living in Dalby and Glen Meay who would be younger than them could speak it [...].
> [...] There was a man who was working for my father, old Quayle from the North and he used to be singing *Mylecharaine* [my ital. - GB] in Manx. He would always sing when he had a drop, but there was one occasion when he refused to do it for a visitor. Johnny Hall [Peel] used to sing *Ny Kirree fo Niaghtey* [my ital. - GB] in Manx (MFLS/C27E (1962)).

Comment on Manx is also attested in places the native Manx speaking fishermen would go to to fish. In his *Seanchas Chléire* 'reminiscences of Cléire (Cape Clear)' Conchobhar Ó Síothcháin, a native of Cléire, tells the story of how he met a Manx fisherman one Saturday in a local bar in West Cork ca.1890-95 and was able to hold a reasonable conversation with him in Gaelic:[26]

> Tá isteach agus amach le daichead bliain ann, lá Sathairn bhíos i dtír in nDún na Séad. Chuas is-teach i dtigh tábhairne ag ól dí mar is gnáthach go mbíonn iascairí tíortha go deo tar éis na seachtaine. Tharla go raibh stróinséarach ina shuí ar an suíochán céanna in aice liom. Is orm a bhí an ionadh nuair a labhair sé Gaeilg liom gur shamhlaíos difir inti seachas an Ghaeilg a bhí agam féin. Is cuimhin liom aon ní amháin gur *cabhall* a thugadh sé ar chapall agus gur *sligeach* a thugadh sé ar choirce. Ach chainteoimis le chéile sa deireadh díreach mar ba mhaith linn é. D'fhiafraíos de cad as é agus dúirt sé liom gurbh ó Oileán Mhanainn é, agus gurbh iascaire é i gceann de na báid sin amuigh sa chuan. D'fhiafraíos de an raibh an Ghaeilg á choinneáil suas sa bhall san, nó an raibh sí ag nach éinne ann mar a bhí sí aige féin. 'Níl mhuise', ar seisean, 'ach

---

26 I am grateful to Prof. Dr. Máirtín Ó Murchú, DIAS, for this reference. Prof. Ó Murchú points out that though *Seanchas Chléire* was (first) published in 1940, its editor Donnchadh Ó Floinn had finished putting it together by November 1936, and it would seem that Ó Síothcháin's narra-tive was taken down during the winter of 1935-36. If this is the case this would put the incident round about 1895.

amháin fáltas atá á labhairt sa tuaith di, ach níl aon fhocal á labhairt anois di i sráid ná i mbaile mór'

('One Saturday around about forty years ago I was ashore in Dún na Séad [Baltimore, Co. Cork]. I went into a bar for a drink of beer, as fishermen are usually quite parched at the end of the week. It happened that a stranger was sitting on the same seat beside me. I was surprised when he spoke to me in a Gaelic which I thought quite different from the Gaelic which I had myself. One thing I remember is that he called a horse *cabhall* and oats *sligeach* [27]. But in the end we chatted to each other just as we pleased. I asked him where he came from and he told me that he was from the Isle of Man, and that he was a fisherman in one of the boats out there in the harbour. I asked him whether the Gaelic was being kept up in that place (Man), or whether everyone else had it just as he had. 'Alas, no', he said, 'apart from a measure of it which is spoken in country areas, but there's not a word of it spoken now in village or town'') (Ó Síothcháin 1970: 167).

2.3.2.3.2. *Use of Manx as a secret code or language to keep the conversation private.*
Here Ned Maddrell, the last native speaker, Glenchass, Rushen, tells a story of how Manx speaking boys in Cregneash would have fun at the expense of those who could not speak Manx:

Va shin loayrt eh tra nagh row shin laccal naboo elley dy clashtyn eh. Un laa, ta cooinaghtyn aym nish, va vraar (*sic*) aeg Jem, as ren shin goll dy yannoo red ennagh nagh row shin laccal dy ve fys echey, as dooyrt mish rish y naboo elley, 'Ah, ta shin braew noi dhyt's, as dooyrt eh, ren eh roie thie dys y vumming as brie eh jeh'n vummig, 'C'red mama,' dooyrt eh, 'c'red ta 'braew noi dhyt'?' 'Quoi ren gra shen?' dooyrt yn vummig. 'Oh, Ned', dooyrt eh. "Oh, t'ad goll dy yannoo red ennagh nish', dooyrt ee, dooyrt y vummig [...].
('we used to speak it (Manx) when we were not wanting another neighbour to hear (what we were saying). One day, I remember now, Jem's younger brother, and we went to do something that we didn't want him to know about, and I said to the other one, 'Ah, we are *braew noi dhyt's* (dead against you)', and he said, he ran home to his mother and asked her, 'What, mama', he said, 'what is *braew noi dhyt's* ?' 'Who said that?' said the mother. 'Oh, Ned', he said. 'Oh, they're going to do something now', she said, the mother said...') (HLSM/I: 364-65).

Mr. Logan, Gordon, Patrick, born and brought up in Maughold:

(reported) Manx Spoken - On a farm in Maughold where he worked - he would not give the names of the people, the man and his wife talked Manx all the time when the men came in for meals, so that they would not be able to repeat the conversation outside. He had plenty of opportunity to learn it, but never took it up. People thought it wasn't much good unless you could already speak it, and then it was used when they wished to keep the conversation private (MFLS/ L/20-A(1965)).

And from Mrs.Ethel Flanagan, Douglas:

The grand parents spoke Manx and the children answered them in English. They always spoke in Manx when they didn't want the children to know what they were talking about (MFLS/FCE/A (1957)).

In addition, the use of Manx as a means of keeping a conversation private could turn the victim against the language because a) he could not understand it and b) it was used as a means to exclude him (J. R. Corlett, Sulby Glen, Lezayre, ca.60):

---

[27] i.e. 'shelly'. According to a Mr. Moore, Baldromma Beg, Kirk Maughold, "Shliggeragh [...] is the Manx word for 'Shilly soil'" (MFLS/M/1-A (1949)). *Sligeach* would probably refer to the husky nature of the oats and may well be a taboo word.

I know very little Manx and am not sorry. The Manx language is dead and it deserved to die because the last use it was put to in our house was to enable our parents and grandmother to carry on a conversation between themselves which my sister and I did not understand (MFLS/C/40-A (1951)).

2.3.2.3.3. *Use of English as a status symbol*
Henry Quayle, Ramsey, 86:

My father and mother could all talk Manx, though they weren't encouraging the children to speak it. There weren't all Manx teachers in the schools, and I suppose the parents would be wanting the children to speak English and not Manx. They would not be wanting them to appear backward compared with others [...] (MFLS/Q/36c (1959)).

2.3.2.3.4. *Manx held in low social esteem*
Mrs. Annie Kneale, Ballagarrett, Bride:

In my young days girls were only scoffing at Manx (MFLS/E (1949)).

Edward Christian, Northop, Greeba, comments:

[...] Among younger people of my own generation, if the old folk would say anything in Manx there would be a lot of giggling and laughing. That was the attitude of young people in my experience - they thought it was something to laugh at - a funny sound (MFLS/C/27E (1962)).

2.3.2.3.5. *Made to feel inferior at school for using Manx*
Fletcher Kinvig, Spring Valley, Braddan (orig. Ronague, Arbory, 81; son to Mr. & Mrs. John Dan Kinvig, two of the last native speakers, cf. §3.5.3. below):

(reported) He [Mr. Kinvig] has a painful recollection of his schooldays. He was the only child from the tops at Ronague who went to Arbory school. Most of the children went to Ballamodha or to Rushen, and the children at Arbory in his time were more from the lowlands where there was not much Manx to be heard. He however had Manx-speaking parents and lived with his grandparents who had Manx as well. He vowed when he was only seven years old that he would not talk Manx, because the children used to get him in the play ground and ask him the Manx word for various things and then laugh at him when he told them, and in class he was also mocked and laughed at if he used a Manx word. He said that this was the worst thing that ever happened to him and one he has never got over - this sense of inferiority that he was made to feel, because he came from the uplands of Ronague and from a home where Manx was spoken - he was regarded as stupid and backward [...]. One day Archdeacon Kewley came into the school when he was being taunted for something he said, and the other children as usual were making fun of him, and he [Kewley] gave the schoolmaster - Teare - a fearful lecture about allowing the class to do this. He of course was himself very interested in the language, and was doing all he could to keep it alive. It was not long after that that Teare (who was Liverpool-Manx) was trying to teach it himself. The Archdeacon had made him see how mistaken he was in allowing the children to think of the Manx language as thing to ridicule (MFLS/K/127 (1975)).

The intervention of Archdeacon Kewley here may just have been a one-off visit, and the taunting continued afterwards. This experience was not uncommon, as the following makes clear.
- Henry Clague, Ballahaven, Ballamodha, Malew, but of the Niarbyl, Patrick:

I went to Dalby school till I was thirteen and then I got no more education, but went to work on a farm. There were 60 or 70 scholars. When I was a boy I could speak Manx better than I could English, and I was the only child there who could. I was hearing a lot of it at home. The other children got interested and used to come to me and ask about Manx, and the master didn't like

I went to Dalby school till I was thirteen and then I got no more education, but went to work on a farm. There were 60 or 70 scholars. When I was a boy I could speak Manx better than I could English, and I was the only child there who could. I was hearing a lot of it at home. The other children got interested and used to come to me and ask about Manx, and the master didn't like it. He said I had to stop talking Manx and spoke to my mother about it too. Well, one day an inspector came to [the] school and asked the master (his name was Popplewell) if any of the children could speak Manx, and Popplewell said there was only one boy who could speak it, and so the inspector asked me to talk in Manx. I said, "The master stopped me from talking Manx before, so I'm not going to talk Manx today". Manx was a native language with me, though, and I can understand a good deal yet [...], but I have forgotten a lot of it now (MFLS C/88 (1965)).

2.3.2.3.6. *Retention of Manx in everyday phrases, prayers or in an ability to read Manx*
Mrs. Ethel Flanagan, Douglas:

As well as everyday phrases such as *Moghrey mie* [my ital. - GB]['good morn-ing'], Mother could read the first Chapter of St. John and say the Lord's Prayer in Manx (MFLS/FCE/A (1957)).

For details of the residuum of Manx in Manx English, cf. §4.7. below.

2.4. Statistical aspects of language shift in Man

Though Ravenstein (1879: 591-92) dates the decline of Manx from the beginning of the 19th century, the first survey giving a reliable general assessment of the position of Manx was made by Henry Jenner in November 1874, published in 1875 (Jenner 1875). The survey consists of a series of questions directed at the Anglican clergy in all 17 parishes (exclusive of Douglas) as to the numbers of people who spoke Manx and/or English and the necessity or otherwise of Manx for church services. The questions were as follows (Jenner 1875):

1. Is English or Manx the prevailing language in your parish?
2. If English, about how many persons speak Manx as their mother-tongue?
3. How many speak no English, and of what ages and class are they?
4. Do you ever preach or perform divine service or any part of it in Manx? If so, how often and what part? And is a knowledge of Manx necessary in your parish work?
5. Which language do children of the present generation learn? Do they grow up with a knowledge of both?
6. Is the Manx of the present day substantially the same as that of Kelly's Grammar [1804], &c., and of the Manx Bible [1748-75] and Prayer Book [1765], and are those easily intelligible to the present Manx speakers?

The answers to these questions Jenner tabulated as follows (Jenner 1875, also Kneen 1931: 18-19; the abbreviations are mine):

Table 1: *Competence in Manx and English in the Isle of Man 1874-75* (Jenner 1875)

Parish	Pop.	Speaking Manx habit. about	Speaking no Eng. about	Lang. spoken by children	Lang. in church	Mx. necessary in parish work
Bride	880	44	12	Eng. & little Mx.	Eng. Until 3-4 yrs. ago Mx. used 4 times a yr.	(Living vacant)
Andreas	1757	600	50	Eng. & little Mx.	English	Not necessary
Lezayre	2500	2000	0	Eng. only	English	Not necessary
Michael	1267	300	0	Eng. & Mx.	English	Useful, but not absol. nec.
Ballaugh	1077	250	10	English only	English	Useful
Jurby	788	600	0	Eng. & little Mx	Eng. (Mx. used 14-15 yrs. ago)	Useful
Lonan	3741	1850	10	English only	English	Necessary
Maughold (incl. Ramsey)	4567	2000	1	Eng. & Mx.	English	Desirable but not absol- utely nec.
German (incl. Peel)	4700	50	10	English only	Eng. No Mx. for 30 yrs.	Hardly necessary
Patrick	2888	700	50	English only	English	Not absolutely necessary
Marown	1121	100	1	English only	English	Hardly nec.
Rushen	3200	600	12	English only	English	Useful
Arbory	1350	1200	12	Eng. & Mx.	Eng. Mx. on 4th Sunday morning of the month	Indispensible
Malew (incl. Castletown)	5000	60	0	English only	Eng. (priv. com- munion with old people occ. Mx.)	Not absol. necessary
Santan	628	0	0	English only	English	Not nec.
Braddan	4000	1000	12	English only	Eng. Mx. occ. introduced	Useful
Onchan	1620	600	10	English only	English	
Total	*41084*	*12350*	*190*			

These statistics are exclusive of the town of Douglas

Though in some cases the clergy could not give accurate details for their parish (either be- cause the living was vacant, or that they were not in a position to answer some of the ques- tions), nevertheless Jenner was able to show that the 'strongest' areas where, according to his figures, Manx was habitually spoken were (in the North) the parishes of Bride, Lezayre and Jurby, and (in the South) in Arbory. According to him, out of a total population of 41,084 for all the parishes 12,350 spoke Manx habitually and 190 spoke no English at all. With the exception of Kirk Arbory, where the language (for church work) was 'indispensible', Manx for the others was considered at the most 'useful'. With regard to the children, as can be seen above, Jenner comes to the following conclusions:

English and Manx (Michael, Maughold, Arbory).
English and a little Manx (Bride, Jurby, Andreas).

English only (the remaining 11 parishes) (Jenner 1875: 23). [28]
However, as is known from the last native speakers and their birthplaces, scattered families continued to speak Manx.

In addition Jenner printed the following comments (Jenner 1875: 24):

From the Rector of Kirk Andreas:
Children pick up a little Manx when they leave school. Old people, so to speak, 'dream in Manx'. Servants like to keep it up as a class language not understood by their masters.

From the Vicar of Kirk Arbory:
Dissenters [?Methodists] make considerable way owing to the neglect of Manx by the [Anglican] Church.

From the Vicar of Kirk Lonan:
Manx is preferred by the country people (in parochial ministrations), as they can understand *every* [Jenner's italics] word, which they cannot in English.

From the Vicar of St. George's, Douglas:
In country parishes one finds three generations in one cottage. The old speaking Manx only, the middle Manx and English, and the children English only (Jen-ner 1875: 24).

However, as Kneen (Kneen 1931: 17) commented:

Of course these statistics can hardly be taken to represent a perfect language census of the Island, and it would be very difficult to obtain such a thing by answers from different people, as each man (as regards Mr. Jenner's second question at any rate) would have his own standard to judge by, and without doubt these standards vary considerably. Compared with the Census of 1901 many discrepancies will be noted which can only be accounted for in one way, that the vicars of certain parishes must have had a very uncertain knowledge of those who spoke Manx or English in their respective parishes. Still Mr. Jenner's tabulation may be said to give a fair approximate of the philological state of the Isle of Man in the year 1875 (Kneen 1931: 17).

It might be added that any non-Manx speaking vicars would not be in any position to answer question 6.

In April 1875 Jenner, according to his own account (Jenner 1875: 25), visited Man himself and attended a Manx service at Kirk Arbory held on the fourth Sunday after Easter. Although the congregation joined in the service 'very heartily', he noticed after the service that:

such of the congregation as remained talking together in the churchyard and near it, almost always spoke in English. Indeed I heard but little Manx talked during my stay in the Island, excepting when done for my edification, though the English of many of the old people showed plainly that they must be more at home in Manx (Jenner 1875: 25).

The Rev. Wm. Drury of Kirk Braddan told Jenner (Jenner 1875: 25) that he sometimes used Manx in his sermons "to clinch the matter" (as Drury put it) for the benefit of the older people. Jenner adds:

---

[28] There appears to be some inconsistency here. "English and Manx" (?50-50) is given for the children of Michael with a proportion of 1267 (pop.): 300 (adult habitual speakers), but "English and a little Manx" for Jurby (788 : 600), a parish equally, if not more, remote.

During the whole of my tour I only met with one person who could not speak English, though I went into a good many Manx cottages on various pretexts of resting, asking the way, etc, so as to find some such person [who had Manx] if possible (Jenner 1875: 26).[29]

In conclusion Jenner writes:

From the shape and situation of the Island, the phenomenon of a gradual receding of the boundary line between the two languages, so clearly to be seen in the case of Cornish, Welsh, or Scotch, is totally absent in Manx. One cannot speak of any district as the *Manx speaking* [Jenner's italics] part of the Island, though it prevails in some districts more than others, and those furthest from the four towns of Douglas, Ramsey, Peel and Castletown have preserved more of it than the rest. Still there is but little difference on that account, since no place in the Island is more than ten or twelve miles at the most from one or other of these towns. On the whole the 'Manxest' parts of the Isle are Dalby, a hamlet in the parish of Kirk Patrick, Cregneash and the neighbourhood of Spanish Head in Kirk [Christ] Rushen, the parish of Kirk Bride and the north part of Kirk Andreas, and the hill country at about the junction of the three parishes of Lezayre, Maughold and Lonan.[30] If there ever comes to be such a thing as a single Manx district, it will probably be the west coast from Peel to Spanish Head. [...] but there is a decided feeling on the part of the people, especially the Manx speakers themselves, that the language is only an obstruction, and that the sooner it is removed the better (Jenner 1875: 26-27).

Rhys, during his visits to Man (1886-1893), painted a similar picture, but added that he had only come into contact with one all-Manx speaking family in Cregneash, where the woman

was an octogenarian who had two sons living with her, together with a granddaughter in her teens. That girl was the only Manx speaking child that I recollect meeting with in the whole Island (Rhys 1894: ix).

He was also of the opnion that

in ten or fifteen years the speakers of Manx Gaelic may come to be counted on the fingers of one hand (Rhys *ibid.*).[31]

In a letter to the *Observer* of 08.04.1928, extracts of which are printed in *Chronique* 356-57/VIII, J. Cubbon noted:

---

[29] It is perhaps not surprising that Jenner heard little Manx during his visit, simply because he was a stranger, and he would have been spoken to in English, albeit in broken English. Rhŷs experienced something similar ten years later and commented:
When I met people in the roads and lanes in places where I was known, I used to ask them questions in Manx. They would invariably answer in English; for Manxmen, when addressed by a stranger in Manx, regard him as taking liberties with them, and feel altogether different from my own countrymen, who usually dote on any stranger who learns a few words of Welsh (Rhys 1894: viii).

[30] This comment is rather curious, as the junction mentioned is uninhabited mountainous area save for a few sheep. What is probably meant is the hill area south of Glen Tramman in Lezayre and in and at the head of Sulby Glen, which apparently was heavily populated till the latter quarter of the 19th century, when the application of the Disafforestation Act of 1861 resulted in the removal of many sqatter-farmers (see above).

[31] Marstrander made a similar comment some thirty five years later:
The material I have collected [from the native Manx speakers] will without doubt have significant value when Celtic speech has completely disappeared from the island in 5-10 years time [..] (Marstrander 1929-33b: 63; see Appendix A).

There is no one living, nor any one existed for thirty-six years, speaking only Manx and no English. The last such person died in 1892. Ten years before that the monolinguists had dwindled to under half a dozen. See *Notes and Queries* October 1, 1887, where Rev. E. B. Savage, M.A., F.S.A., Vicar of St. Thomas, Douglas, wrote: "Four or five years ago I made minute inquiries as to how many Manxmen survived who could not speak English. I found about six, but that small number is sadly thinned by this time" (*Chronique* 356-57/VIII, MM. MS.H140/lx/ 151).

In a letter he wrote to *Révue Celtique* the Manx *Heimatforscher* J. J. Kneen (1872-1938) noted (*Révue Celtique* XLIV (1927): 467):

When I was a boy between 40 and 50 years ago, I was acquainted with several old people, who were 'not at home' - as one might say - in English and spoke Manx much better. And quite a few spoke a broken English dialect interspersed with Manx words and idioms. In the house [in Douglas] where I was reared, about 6 spoke Manx fluently, and at least 2 of them spoke English very haltingly.

30 years ago [ca. 1900] I have passed the Quarter Bridge, outside of Douglas, and have seen about a dozen men sitting on the the bridge-wall and conversing in Manx only. I have gone into a country inn, - and on Saturday, market day, into a Douglas inn, - and heard nothing but Manx [...]

But then added:

[...] But now it is all gone, and one has to search a great deal to find a Manx speaker (*Révue Celtique* XLIV (1927): 467).

2.5. Census enumerations

The first census enumeration in Man taking into account the Manx language was that of 1871. Subsequent enumerations including this category were made in 1901, 1911, 1921, 1931, 1951, 1961, 1971. The 1981 census ignored the matter, as by that time no native speakers of Manx were living. However, the 1991 census included information on Manx which is given below in Section 5.

Table 2: *1871-1971 official census figures for Manx Gaelic and English speakers*

Year	Total pop.	Manx only	Manx/Eng.	Total speakers	% of total population
1871/74	54042	190	12340	13530	25.04
1901	54752	59	4598	4657	8.51
1911	52016	31	2351	2382	4.58
1921	60284*	19	896	915	1.52
1931	49308		529	529	1.07
1941	(no census made because of the Second World War)				
1951	55253		355	355	0.64
1961	48133		165	165	0.34
1971	54581		284	284	0.52

Source:
1. For 1871-1971 official census figures. For 1911 figures for Manx speakers unofficially published in *Mannin* 2 (Nov. 1913): 80.
2. For 1874 Jenner (1875: 23). * Census taken in June; figures also include visitors.

Table 3: *1871-1971 census figures of Manx speakers according to age:*

Age group	1901 Mx.	ME	1911 Mx.	ME	1921 Mx.	ME	1931 Mx.	ME	1951 Mx.	ME	1961 Mx.	ME	1971 Mx.	ME
All ages	59	4598	31	2351	19:	896		529		355		165		284
3-4:			1	5						1		5		
5-9:		27	2	6		7		4		5		5		6
10-14:			6	11		11				15		10		8
15-24:	7	105	9	51	3	35		24		42		9		31
25-44:	28	631	4	179	5	67		58		72		37		76
45-64:	21	2167	7	868	5	232		140		124		57		109
65+	3	1668	1	1230	6	544		303		96		42		54
Not stated			1	1										

Source:
Official census figures Manx Museum Archive. Mx. = Manx; ME = Manx & English.

Figure 3: *Diagram showing the decrease in Manx speakers 1871-1971*

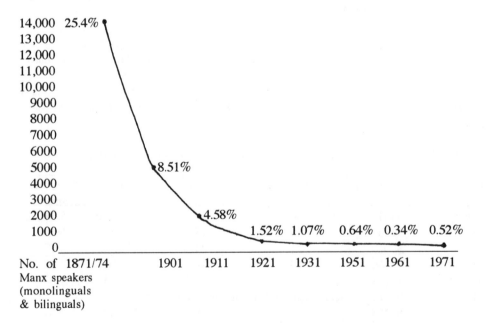

Comments

1. The number of 59 for the monoglot Manx speakers in the 1901 census, being made up of 57 males and 2 females, may represent some inconsistency on the part of the enumerator, as the census enumerator for 1921 remarks (Census 1921: xv), though the total figure in itself would not be out of proportion with the 190 recorded by Jenner only 27 years before. That Jenner and Rhys met with very few monoglots does not mean that they did not exist (cf. note 24). However, from the figures of 28 and 21 for monoglots in the age-group 25-44 and 45-64 respectively, particularly for the former, one would have expected greater figures for this age range well into the 1920s & 1930s, if not later. The fact that such figures do not appear would indicate an exaggeration in the relevant 1901 figures, and perhaps we should read something between 7 and 3 for the two groups respectively.

2. The figure of 27 in 1901 for bilingual speakers for the age-groups 3-4, 5-9, 10-14 is suspect, given the fact that the ages of the last native speakers (cf. below) indicate a date of birth between 1860 and 1880, and should either be discounted or drastically reduced. The appearance of such doubtful figures in the 1901 census (and in 1911 for monoglots in the same age range) may be due to revived interest Manx promoted by *Yn Cheshaght Ghailckagh* 'the Manx Language Society', founded in 1899 on the model of *Conradh na Gaeilge* 'the Gaelic League', set up in Ireland in 1893.[32]

3. The sharp decrease in the number of bilinguals between 1901 and 1921/31 would suggest that the language was not being passed on to the children, because the people were not speaking it any more.[33] As Jenner's comments show (cf. above) Manx lingered on in some areas more than in others, but seems to have passed on as a community language around the turn of the century. According to local knowledge Cregneash, probably because of its isolation, seems to have been the last bastion of Manx as a community language, passing from there around 1910.

4. In 1929 Marstrander could only find some 40 people with any Manx at all, though in an Island the size of Man, it would not be too difficult to miss potential informants.[34] His comment in 1934 that

---

[32] The 'Revival' began ca.1890, if not before, and embraced also the collecting of folk songs and folk music, principally by general practitioner Dr. John Clague of Castletown (1893-98) and A. W. Moore (1895-96), though letters regarding the use of Manx (cf. Appendix B) may suggest some superficial efforts in the 1820s. For details of and comment on the Revival, see Section 5.

[33] Comments even today (1997) by older people in their 80s/90s that their parents or grandparents spoke Manx when they didn't want the children or grandchildren to understand are common. The use of Manx as a 'secret language' in this way is a facet of language death (cf. Section 1, p. 12 & Figure 2, and §2.3.2. above). Questions asked of older people in the northern parishes of Jurby, Andreas, and Bride in August 1989 as part of work for the Manx Place-Name Survey as to whether Manx had been heard or spoken within their lifetime largely produced a negative response. In other words Manx, according to their memories, had not been spoken as a community language in that area since ca.1900, if not earlier.

[34] This is evidently the case. According to his diary (Diary: 57) Marstrander was given the name of a 'Mr. Kneen' (then) of the Lhen whom he apparently never visited. This same 'Mr Kneen' turned out to be one John Kneen (the Gaaue) (later) of Ballaugh Curragh, one of the most profuse of the last native Manx speakers (cf. HLSM/I: 230ff.).

as far as I know, there is at present only one person left who could probably be described as a native speaker [Harry Kelly, Cregneash (1853-1935)] (Marstrander 1934: 292),

though some 3-4 others had good Manx and about 30 others smatterings (Marstrander *ibid*; cf. also Marstrander 1929-33b: 74-75) was not quite accurate, as shown by Charles W. Loch in 1946 (Loch 1946: 2-3). In April of that year Loch visited Man and interviewed some twenty Manx language enthusiasts from whom he was able to produce a list of twenty persons who were regarded as native speakers, i.e. people whose first language was Manx, or who had acquired Manx in early childhood.[35] This list was published by A. S. B. Davies in 1948 (Davies 1948: 89-91).

By 1950 this number had decreased to 10 and by 1955 to 7 (Jackson 1955: 2-3). By the time of the 1961 census only two known native speakers were still alive: Mrs. Sage Kinvig, Ronague, Arbory (b.1870) and Ned Maddrell, Glenchass, Rushen (b.1877). Mrs Kinvig died on 13 April 1962.[36]

5. Loch (1946: 4) noted that in 1946 there were four classes held in various parts of Man for learners of Manx, which probably accounts for the figures of 355 (including the known native speakers) in the 1951 census. The same would apply to the figures for 1961 and 1971, i.e. that the adults had acquired it in classes (or from native speakers) in their adult life, and the children, either from them or at school where, depending on the availability of a competent teacher, they could learn Manx in some form or other. In any event English would be their first language. For an assessment of the situation today and comment on the 1991 census figures, see Section 5.

The passing of Manx as a community language took place ca.1870/80-1900/10, with the last native speakers living through the 1920s to the 1950s, decreasing in number gradually towards the end, and resulting in the death of the last reputed native speaker Ned Maddrell on 27 December 1974.[37]

---

[35] The late Mr. Chalse Craine of Ballaugh (d.1979), one of the enthusiasts of that time (also mentioned by Loch) and an employee of the Ramsey branch of the Isle of Man Bank, told me when I visited him on 7 July 1974 that a search began for the last native speakers during the mid-thirties as a result of Marstrander's visits. He told me he was personally instrumental in 'discovering' three of the four or five surviving native speakers from the north ca.1936 when they would be making their weekly visit to the bank (Craine 1974).

[36] General Registry, Douglas.

[37] For the semi-speaker Ewan Christian of Peel, cf. Section 3.6.9.-10. below.

3. Studies on Language and Language Use in Man

3.1. Early observations of language use

Observations on Manx Gaelic by laymen and antiquarians, mostly English, date back to the 16th century. The first known notice of a Gaelic language spoken in Man similar to that of either Ireland or Scotland, or both, is found in Camden's *Britannia* of 1586:

> Incolae tamen, & lingua & moribus ad Hibernicos proxime accedunt, ita autem ut *Norwagicum* [Camden's italics] quiddam admisceatur 'the inhabitants, however, both in language and in customs lean towards the Irish, with a certain Norwegian admixture' (Camden 1586: v.s. "Yle of Man"),

and in giving the various names which Man was/is known by Camden has:

> [...] Menaw Britannis, incolis Maning [...] '(the island is called) Menaw by the Welsh, and Maning (G. *Manainn*) by the local inhabitants' (Camden 1586 *ibid.*).

This was confirmed in statements made in 1611 by John Speed whereby

> ...the common sort of people both in their language and manners, come nighest unto the *Irish* [Speed's italics]...(Speed 1611 quoted after Price 1984: 73),

as in contradistinction to the

> wealthier sort...do imitate the people of Lancashire, both in their honest carriage and good housekeeping... (Speed 1611 quoted after Price 1984: 73).

Some 45 years later James Chaloner, Governor of Man 1658-60 during the Cromwell 'Protectorate' (as the period is called), observed that the language of the Manx people

> ...is the very same with that of the Scottish-Irish...(Chaloner 1656 quoted after Moore 1889-92: 130).

However, the first known specific reference to the Gaelic language of Man comes from Bishop John Phillips in a letter to Robert Earl of Salisbury, Lord Treasurer of England (responsible for the Isle of Man during the brief period of English suzerainty 1607-10) regarding a number of matters, including his translation into Manx of the Anglican Book of Common Prayer (cf. also §§2.2.1.-2. above):

> [...] That whereas I, with my clergy did this year purpose to have perused the Mannish Book of Common Prayer by me translated [...] (Letter 01.02.1610/11 quoted after Moore & Rhys 1893-94: xi).

This was followed the same month by a letter from John Ireland, the then Governor of Man, to Phillips:

> [...]the Book of Common Prayer said to have been translated into the Mansche speech; [...] the Book translated by the new Bishop of Sodor [Phillips] into Mannish (Letter of John Ireland to John Phillips quoted after Moore & Rhys 1893-94: xii; see also footnote 10 in Section 2).

Edmund Gibson in his 1695 edition of Camden's *Britannia* notes that

[...] the people [of Man] are styled Manksmen and their language is Manx [...] (Gibson 1695 quoted after Moore 1889-92: 130).

Following on from that William Sacheverell, Governor of Man 1693-96, made the comment in 1702:

The Manks language, according to the best information I can get, differs no more from Irish than Scotch [i.e. Scots] from English and that both are different idioms of the Erse, or Highland (Sacheverell 1702 quoted after Feltham 1798: 61).

In addition Sacheverell in 1702 made the comment that:

in the Northern part of the Island they speak a deeper Manx, as they call it, than in the South (Sacheverell 1702 quoted after Price 1984: 73).

This could be taken to mean either that the Manx in the North was less affected by English speech, the South being nearer the centre of government at Castletown, or more probably this should be taken as an acknowledgement of their being two identifiable dialects in the Man.

The first known scholarly attempt to record anything of Manx speech was made 1703/4 by Edward Lhuyd, Keeper of the Ashmolean Museum at Oxford, when he collected a considerable number of Manx Gaelic lexical items as part of his greater survey of Gaelic and British languages, etc, ninety-five words of which were published in 1707 in his *Archaeologia Britannica* (Lhuyd 1707, Thomson 1969b). In or about 1977 a further thousand or so of such items were discovered by Dafydd Ifans of the Llyfrgell Genedlaethol Cymru (National Library of Wales) in Aberystwyth in the Mysevin collection of manuscripts formed from the papers of the Welsh grammarian and lexicographer William Owen [-Pughe] (1759-1835). They were transcribed by Ifans and edited with full commentary by Robert L. Thomson (Ifans and Thomson 1979-80). Lhuyd's Manx word list is arranged under various sections according to topic, e.g. trees, fish, domestic animals, etc, John Ray's *Dictionariolum* being used as the questionnaire. The "General Alphabet" as used by Lhuyd, based on Welsh, was intended as a phonetic rendering in those conventions as modified by Lhuyd. It was also intended to be as accurately representative as possible of the sounds of Manx. Unfortunately for us Lhuyd's actual work-books do not survive, only copies of them, in which it can be shown that errors have crept in during copying. Nevertheless, Lhuyd's collection is an event of the first importance in Manx Gaelic studies.

The first notice of Manx containing sentences illustrating its idiom is found in a short description of Man, particularly its inhabitants and its language made by the Vicar-General James Wilks in 1777 (Wilks 1777), but first published in 1887 (cf. Moore 1887: 178-80). A more detailed notice of Manx is found in Feltham (Feltham 1798/5) where a separate chapter is devoted to the language. Here texts of translations of morning and evening hymns are printed, as well as some sentences, and a list of works in Manx. Following on from this Rev. J. G. Cumming (Cumming 1848) produced a sketch of the Manx language as an appendix to his work. In 1861 Christoll Terrien (Terrien 1861) presented parts of St. Luke's Gospel in Manx along with parallel texts in Irish and Scottish Gaelic, and Breton, for comparison.

A brief examination of Manx was made by W. S. Kerruish in 1881 (Kerruish 1881) in a paper entitled 'Manx Gaelic' read at the 13th Annual Session of the American Philological Association, Cleveland, Ohio, in July of that year. Six years later A. W. Moore (Moore

1887) presented the first known historical sketch of the Manx language printed in the *Transactions of the Celtic Society of Montreal* and in *Yn Lioar Manninagh* /I (Moore 1889-92).

A more detailed account of Manx Gaelic and its literature, particularly the Bible, religious writings, ballads, and folklore appeared in Germany in 1909 (Stern 1909), followed by G. W. Wood in 1911 (Wood 1911) which contains an excursus on Manx literature to the middle of the 19th century. A more thorough account of Manx literature, based to a large extent on Wood, was made in 1924 by Manx Museum librarian William Cubbon (Cubbon 1924). This deals primarily with the literature translated into Manx, as well as with original material in Manx, and appends a bibliography of literature relating to that language.

More recently a brief general overview of Manx Gaelic and its literature was compiled in 1988 by Thomson and Pilgrim (Thomson & Pilgrim 1988) and on the history of Manx by Brian Stowell and Diarmuid Ó Breasláin (Stowell & Ó Breasláin 1996).

3.2. Descriptions of Manx

3.2.1. Grammars

The first known comment on the grammar of Manx was made by Dr. Vallancy in his Irish grammar of 1782. According to Cubbon (Cubbon 1939: 815), Vallancy corresponded with Rev. Philip Moore, editor of the Manx Bible, from whom he obtained his sample. The first grammar as such was prepared and completed by Rev. John Kelly in 1780, but not printed till 1804. Kelly's *Grammar* was reprinted in 1859 by the Manx Society, with an introduction by Rev. Wm. Gill. For a detailed assessment of Kelly's *Grammar* see Thomson (1969a: 185-202).

In 1847 Heinrich Leo produced a grammar of Manx from Manx versions of the New Testament (Leo 1847). However, its imperfections secured its obscurity. A more scientific, if scant, overview of Manx and its grammar was made in 1875 by Henry Jenner (Jenner 1875) and published by the Philological Society of London (see also below).

In 1931 John Joseph Kneen produced *A Grammar of the Manx Language* (Kneen 1931), though completed in 1910 (cf. Cubbon 1939: 823). However, it is marred by antiquarianism, as it is merely a transcript of the Christian Brothers' Irish Grammar. In passing comment on Kneen's *Grammar* Thomson (1969a: 189 footnote 1) adds:

> Kneen's description of the language should not be relied upon except where it is independent of its source or other evidence onfirms it. By way of extenuation it can be properly urged that the writing of a grammar without a model is a difficult task, that the model is that of a cognate language, and that the work was done early in Kneen's career, left in manuscript for a long period, and then published in haste without revision. [...]. The foregoing will explain why, with real regret, I have not been able to include in this survey of the native Manx grammarians any mention of one whose reputation stands so high amongst his fellow Manxmen (Thomson 1969a: 189 footnote 1).

Since then the only known grammar to have been produced is that by George Broderick (Broderick 1984a/I) of the later stages of Manx Gaelic from the last native speakers.

3.2.2. Dictionaries

The first known dictionary relating to Manx was produced in 1808 by Rev. John Kelly (see also above). It was in fact a triglot dictionary of Manx, Irish, and Scottish Gaelic equivalents of an amplified version of Shaw's English-Gaelic half of his dictionary of 1780 (cf. Shaw 1780). However, due to a catalogue of disasters the book never appeared and partially exists in manuscript form in the Manx Museum Archive (MM.MSS.1477 & 1045-47; cf. Cubbon 1939: 815-16, Thomson 1977). However, though the story is somewhat complex (cf. Thomson 1984c), his dictionary of Manx (1805-08), like his grammar, was prepared for Bishop Hildesley and the Bible translators (Thomson 1977), and was to follow his grammar to the press, but never appeared until printed by the Manx Society (Vol. VIII) in 1866, along with an English-Manx version edited by Rev. J. T. Clarke and John Ivon Mosley. The printed version of 1866 contains also material from Cregeen (see next). However, his dictionary must be regarded as unsatisfactory in comparison with that of Cregeen, since, although it was not entirely faithfully reproduced from the original mss. and whilst it contains more vocabulary, some of it unashamedly culled directly from Shaw's Scottish Gaelic dictionary (Shaw 1780), it is prone to much dubious etymology and fatuous deduction. The Manx-English part was reprinted by *Yn Cheshaght Ghailckagh* in 1977 (Thomson 1977).

Meanwhile Archibald Cregeen produced a Manx-English dictionary ca.1834-35, though, according to the 'Memoir' to Cregeen produced as a preface by J. M. Jeffcott, High-Bailiff of Castletown, the work first appeared in 1838. It draws its material from printed religious material available at the time, as well as oral material from his neighbourhood of Kirk Arbory. Even with its imperfections (cf. Thomson 1969a), it is much more reliable than that of Kelly.

The next lexical work after Cregeen and Kelly is the English-Manx pronouncing dictionary of J. J. Kneen (Kneen 1938). Here Kneen used an English-based phonetic script which, within these limitations, provides a reliable guide to Manx pronunciation, if properly interpreted (cf. also Jackson 1955: 5). The next is a substantial English-Manx dictionary compiled by Douglas C. Fargher (Fargher 1979), produced as part of the then surge of interest in the revival of Manx. The dictionary takes its material, not only from Cregeen and Kelly, and Robert L. Thomson's *Glossary of Early Manx* (Thomson 1954-57; see also §3.3. below), but also from de Bhaldraithe's English-Irish Dictionary for neologisms and idioms felt to be lost in Manx. The aim here is prescriptive, not descriptive, since its production was to serve the interests of the revival (see Section 5), and there is a certain attempt at antiquarian restoration of the case system, particularly the genitive case, whose loss can be shown to be an internal development (cf. Thomson 1969a, Broderick 1991). Nevertheless, Fargher's dictionary is essentially a reservoir of genuine material, complementing the works of Cregeen and Kelly. A Manx-English version of Fargher's dictionary was produced in 1991 by Manx teacher Phil Kelly (Kelly 1991) to facilitate reference to the former. As a complement to the latter Kelly (Kelly 1993) produced a two-volumed work of some 26,000 examples of Manx usage, taken mainly from Fargher 1979 to make more easily available Manx idiom and expression buried in Fargher under the various headwords in English.

In 1984 George Broderick produced a Manx-English dictionary of Late Spoken Manx as part of his work on the Manx of the last native speakers (Broderick 1984/II). It contains some 3000 items of Manx Gaelic, with items in phonetic script from the respective informants, and gives an idea of the extent of vocabulary current during the last phase of the language (see also below).

3.2.3. Phonologies

A small amount has been published on the phonology of Manx. The pioneer in this regard was John Rhys, with 'The Outlines of the Phonology of Manx Gaelic' (Rhys 1894), printed as an appendix to Bishop John Phillips' Manx translation of the Anglican 'Book of Common Prayer', edited by himself and A. W. Moore (Moore/Rhys 1893-94). This provides quite an amount of information, but, as Jackson also observed (Jackson 1955: 4), it is not always easy to understand, and in some cases his accuracy is suspect. After Rhys there is John Strachan's semi-phonetic transcription in ZCP I: 54-58 (Strachan 1897) of the Manx folksong *Ec ny Fiddleryn* 'at the fiddlers', taken down from Tom Kermode, Bradda, in 1883. In 1928 F. G. Ackerley made comment on Rhys 1893-94 in his 'Manx Marginalia' published in *Y Cymmrodor* 39: 20-38 (Ackerley 1928).

Then followed J. J. Kneen with his 'Place-Names' (Kneen 1925-28, see §3.2.4. below), his 'grammar' (Kneen 1931), and a Manx-English 'pronouncing dictionary' (Kneen 1938; see §3.2.2. above). In the first two works Kneen makes use of an IPA-type of phonetic script, but as Jackson also noted (Jackson 1955: 4-5), it is not certain whether he fully understood it. His 'pronouncing dictionary' is more reliable (see above).

Much more reliable, however, is Carl Marstrander (Marstrander 1932), a professional Celtic scholar who had access to good Manx speakers, whose description, though brief (pp. 52-75), is comprehensive, though limited in scope. As Jackson also noted (Jackson 1955: 5), the article is in Norwegian and the comparisons are mainly with Modern Norwegian phonemes, which restricts its usefulness. His critique of Kneen (1925-28) (Marstrander 1934), though a review, is nevertheless valuable, so far as it goes.

Less satisfactory, however, is Francis J. Carmody's 'Manx Gaelic sentence structure' (Carmody 1947) where he uses only one informant, a woman living in California who learned her Manx in language classes; her pronunciations in some cases are highly suspect. In addition there are a number of mistranslations of examples and even errors in the choice of examples, and the mutilation of them to make them apply where they do not apply (cf. Thomson 1950-51: 264). Better is his later article 'Spoken Manx' (Carmody 1953) for which he interviewed genuine native Manx speakers during a visit to Man in July 1949 (see also §3.6.6. below).

Much more comprehensive is the phonology produced by Kenneth Jackson (Jackson 1955), based on a two-week visit made over Christmas 1950-51. The phonology, largely made up of individual lexical items, links Manx to the developments that took place in Irish and Scottish Gaelic since the 'Common Gaelic' period (ca. 13th century; cf. Jackson 1951) and as such is a diachronic study. Of the seven informants he used, Jackson was only able to go completely through his questionnaire with one, Mrs. Eleanor Karran, an elderly lady from Cregneash in the very south of Man. His phonology is, therefore, essentially a description of her Manx, with added details from others. Nevertheless, it is a pioneering work in diachronic phonology intended as a pilot study for later planned similar works on Irish and Scottish Gaelic phonology, which (with the exception of a brief diachronic overview of Irish as an appendix to his edition of *Aislinge Meic Con Ghlinne* (Jackson 1990)), sadly never materialised. From this point of view it is extremely useful (see also §3.6.8. below).

At about the same time Heinrich Wagner, who visited Man for three weeks during the summer of 1950 (which occasioned Jackson's visit six months later), discusses Manx sentence structure in his comprehensive analysis of the development of the verb in the Insular Celtic languages of the British Isles (Wagner 1959a) and later produces a word-list in his 'Atlas' (Wagner 1958-69) and an extensive collection of sentences, all from native Manx speech, in Vol. 4 of his 'Atlas', point 88. Additional works by Wagner which comment on spoken Manx appear in Wagner 1959a and O'Driscoll 1982 (see also §3.6.7. below).

Following on from that the latest and perhaps most comprehensive phonology of Manx to date is that of George Broderick (Broderick 1986) which forms Vol. 3 of his 'Handbook' (Broderick 1984-86). It contains both a synchronic and diachronic study. The synchronic part essentially describes Late Spoken Manx, i.e. the last phase of Manx as a living language, while the diachronic part follows that of Jackson, but is more comprehensive in that Broderick had access to additional material. It omits parallel comments on similar developments in Irish and Scottish Gaelic supplied in Jackson (1955), as matters here have been dealt with more comprehensively by others in the respective fields of dialect research (see Section 1.3.).

3.2.4. Place-Names

The subject of place-names could for our purposes here be regarded as a sub-section of Phonology, since their development is pertinent to that discipline. Apart from the products of mapmakers (cf. PNIM: Intro.), the first known scientific work on Manx place-names is that of A. W. Moore (Moore 1891), which looks at a list of place-name elements and comments on their meaning and distribution. From 1853 to 1925 a number of smaller articles of various sorts on Manx toponomy appeared (cf. Cubbon 1939: 832-34).

The first known comprehensive survey of Manx place-names (extracted from known sources, assembled in chronological order and discussed) is that of J. J. Kneen (Kneen 1925-28) in 6 vols. For a critique see Marstrander 1934.

This was followed shortly afterwards by Carl Marstrander in a comprehensive study of essentially the Old Norse elements in Manx place-names (Marstrander 1932), with some discussion of the problems involved, taking into consideration ON and Mx. phonology in arriving at his conclusions (which Kneen had been unable to do). Marstrander followed this in 1934 (Marstrander 1934) with additional comment. In 1929 and 1963 Walter Gill (Gill 1929 & 1963) published a considerable number of place-names mostly derived from oral tradition.

In 1970-71, as part of the then ongoing debate concerning the proportion of Old Norse and Gaelic speakers in Man during the Scandinavian period (9th-13th-cent.), Margaret Gelling (Gelling 1970, 1971) contributed two important articles on Manx place-names, examining their early forms and elements as found in pre-16th-century sources, arguing for an ON hegemony and a reintroduction of Gaelic into Man after the Scandinavian period. These were followed in 1976, as part of the same debate, by Basil Megaw (Megaw 1976 & 1978). He set Manx place-names in the context of a re-assessment of the evidence relating to the Scandinavian period, dating a vital source about 100 years earlier than previously thought. He argued for a continued Gaelic presence in Man throughout the same period. This was followed in

1983 by Robert L Thomson (Thomson 1983) who was able to demonstrate the continuity of Gaelic in Man from the Old Irish period right through to the present day.

Additional contributions on aspects of Manx place-names have to date been made by Eleanor Megaw (Megaw 1978), Robert'L Thomson (Thomson 1978, 1991), Per Sveas Andersen (Andersen 1983), Gillian Fellows-Jensen (Fellows-Jensen 1980, 1983, 1985, 1987, 1993), Margaret Gelling (Gelling 1991), and George Broderick (Broderick 1978, 1979a, 1980-81a, 1981c, 1981-82, 1987, 1993c).

In 1978 Manx local historians William & Constance Radcliffe produced a comprehensive book on the place-names of the parish of Kirk Maughold and the town of Ramsey (Radcliffe 1978). This was followed in 1983 by their joint work on the parish of Kirk Bride (Radcliffe 1983). It was as a result of these two books that it was realised that a fresh and more comprehensive survey needed to be made of Manx place-names, particularly as those elder members of the native-born Manx community, who would have a knowledge of the older names, would be extremely small.

This point was recognised by Prof. Dr. Máirtín Ó Murchú, Director of the School of Celtic Studies at the Dublin Institute for Advanced Studies, and Robert L. Thomson who made available initial funding to enable field-work to be carried out in Man on behalf of the Manx Place-Name Survey, set up at the University of Mannheim as a research project in 1988 by George Broderick. During the years following further funding was also forthcoming from the Leverhulme Trust, London, the Manx Museum and National Trust and the Manx Heritage Foundation, Isle of Man (the latter two co-ordinated through the Manx Place-Name Survey Trust, set up in December 1994). To date three volumes (of an anticipated eight) have been published (Broderick 1994, 1995, 1997).

3.3. Other works relating to Manx Gaelic linguistics

Foremost in this area in this regard over the past forty years or so has been Robert L Thomson, former Reader in Celtic at the University of Leeds. Prompted by Carmody's inadequate handling of Manx syntax (cf. Carmody 1947) Thomson began with his analysis of the verb and its construction in Manx (Thomson 1950-51). He then moved on to compile his *Glossary of Early Manx*, namely a dictionary of lexical items and their various forms found in Bishop John Phillips' Manx translation of the Anglican Book of Common Prayer (made ca.1610, though the only known surviving ms. dates from ca.1630) (Moore/Rhys 1893-94) listed where possible under their standard orthographical forms (Thomson 1954-57). Following this Thomson's works on Manx include:

- a look at the function of svarabhakti in certain consonant clusters in Manx and its effects (Thomson 1960),
- an analytical edition of the 'Manannan or Traditionary Ballad', from internal evidence composed ca. 1500 and containing a number of lexical items obsolete by the 18th century (Thomson 1960-63),
- an overview of Manx Gaelic and its literature, with comment on the decline of the case system and a critique of the earlier scholarship, including the dictionaries of Cregeen (1835), Kelly (1866), and the grammars of Kelly (1804) and Kneen (1931) (Thomson 1969a),
- comment on the composition of non-native elements in Manx (Thomson 1965, 1991),

- a phonemic analysis of a Manx idiolect, being the speech of Thomas Christian, Ramsey, one of Marstrander's informants (v. §3.5.2. below) (Thomson 1976),
- comment on the composition of Manx place-names (Thomson 1978, 1991a),
- a linguistic analysis of the Manx translations of St. John's Gospel (Thomson 1981),
- comment on the continuity of Gaelic speech in Man from ca.500AD through to the present day (Thomson 1983),
- a consideration of Manx personal names and general vocabulary as a continuation of the thesis propounded in the foregoing (Thomson 1984c),
- a detailed look at Rev. Dr. John Kelly as a lexicographer (Thomson 1987),
- an edition of Thomas Christian's *Pargys Caillt*, a Manx version of Milton's 'Paradise Lost', and Parnell's 'Hermit', with linguistic commentary (Thomson 1995), and
- an edition of the Homilies in Manx (Thomson 1997).

Contributions from others include: some notes on Manx phonology, morphology, and lexis by T. F. O'Rahilly (O'Rahilly 1932), an edition of the Manx stories and reminiscences of Ned Beg Hom Ruy (Edward Faragher of Cregneash 1831-1908), who wrote in a conversational 19th century style. The edition is accompanied by an introduction and English translation, with linguistic notes (Broderick 1982-83), an excursus into language decline and death, i.e. into the latter stages of Late Spoken Manx (Broderick 1991; see also below). A re-assessment of the system of stress in Manx is made by Diarmuid Ó Sé (Ó Sé 1991).

A number of traditional Manx Gaelic song-texts edited by George Broderick and containing linguistic notes or other comments have also been published (cf. Broderick 1980-81b, 1982b/c, 1984b-d, 1990).

3.4. Didactic works on Manx

The first known didactic works on Manx are those of Rev. Hugh Stowell, Rector of Ballaugh, in his 'Lessons and Stories for Good Children' (Stowell 1808), though this in strict terms is not didactic as such in content, but rather a collection of several prayers in Manx and English, which could be used for didactic purposes. The first known lesson book as such was also prepared by the same author (Stowell 1818), and was taken as a model for later teachers of Manx Gaelic, such as Robert E. Christian of Baldromma, Kirk Maughold, who produced a book of lessons ca.1880 (Christian 1880). This was followed by a series of simple lessons in Manx by J. J. Kneen (Kneen 1890), printed in the *Isle of Man Examiner* 1890ff, and another by him in *Celtia* for June 1901. In 1898 Joseph Cain and William Kneen produced a book of lessons (Cain & Kneen 1898), which in reality is a regurgitated version of Stowell 1818.

The first systematic lesson book covering most, if not all aspects of Manx grammar, presented in a simple way is that of Edmund Goodwin in his *First Lessons in Manx* (originally entitled *Lessoonyn ayns Chengey ny Mayrey Ellan Vannin* ('lessons in the mother tongue of the Isle of Man')) (Goodwin 1901). First developed from blackboard use at Manx language classes held at Peel, Goodwin, encouraged by the Manx folksong collector Dr. John Clague of Castltown, prepared them in book form and they were then published by the Celtic Association and the Manx Society (Goodwin 1901: [5]; Cubbon 1939: 822). The main aim of the book was to "[...] enable people to acquire a reading acquaintance with the Manx Bible and

Prayer Book" (Goodwin [4]1974): [5]), but not to speak the language, as the preface to the 1901 edition makes clear:

> The pleasure to be had from reading the wonderfully beautiful and idiomatic Manx version of the Scriptures would amply compensate for a year's labour in the study of the language [..] (Goodwin 1901: [5], König 1996: 38).

Goodwin's *First Lessons* were reprinted in 1947, 1966 and 1974 by *Yn Cheshaght Ghailckagh* ('The Manx Language Society'), with revisions by Robert L Thomson in the last two editions.

In the early years of the 20th century teaching by the 'direct method', i.e. through conversation and every-day life situations, was becoming fashionable, and in the Isle of Man this was promoted by J. J. Kneen in his *Saase Jeeragh* (the Direct Method of Teaching Manx) (Kneen 1911). In 1914 Deemster Henry Percy Kelly produced a book of Manx reading lessons, with texts translated from the Irish of Norma Borthwick (Kelly 1914). The simplicity of the lessons (with illustrations) suggests that they were perhaps geared more for children than adults (cf. Peter 1984: Appendix VIII, König 1996: 38). In 1926-27 J. J. Kneen was responsible also for another series of Manx lessons, his *Lessoonyn Gailckagh Aashagh* ('easy Manx lessons') published in *Ellan Vannin* Magazine for 05.01.1926, 06.08.1926, 07.01.1927, 08.06.1927 (Kneen 1926-27). Nevertheless, the situation seemed somewhat *ad hoc*.

In an interview with Edward Christian (1907-1996) of Ramsey during the summer of 1983 (and on later occasions), he told me that he and others set up a Manx class in Ramsey in the early 1930s and arranged for Mona Douglas to come and teach them. He added that though there had been Manx lessons published from time to time in the Manx press (cf. foregoing) there was nothing available in any ready form (Goodwin's *First Lessons* had apparently long been out of print), which presented problems for those wishing to hold or attend classes (Christian 1983; cf. also Peter 1984: 48-49). To attempt to rectify this situation Mona Douglas produced a series of weekly lessons for teachers and learners of Manx, which were printed weekly in the *Mona's Herald* and based almost entirely on Goodwin's *First Lessons*. Douglas's lessons were gathered together and made available in a more permanent form by the Manx Language Society and published in 1935 under the title *Beginning Manx Gaelic. A Manx Primer* (Douglas 1935).

So far as is known, no further book of Manx lessons was published until after the Second World War when a number of works began to appear in connection with the third phase of the Revival (see Section 5). Such works include Brian Stowell's *Gaelg Trooid Jallooghyn* 'Manx through pictures' (Stowell 1968) and *Bunnydys* 'beginning' (Stowell 1970), the latter based on the Irish series *Buntús Cainte*. This was followed in 1966 and 1974 by revised editions of Goodwin's *First Lessons in Manx* (Goodwin 1966, 1974) published by YCG (see also above), and in 1977 by Juan Gell's *Conversational Manx* (Gell 1977). This is based upon genuine native Manx speech which he had heard from the old native speakers, with the sentences given also in a very helpful English spelling-based phonetic script. In 1981 Robert L. Thomson produced his *Lessoonyn sodjey sy Ghailck Vanninagh* (Thomson 1981) intended to assist learners in their reading of St. John's Gospel (cf. also §3.3. above) and to progress beyond *First Lessons* and as an introduction to the language for speakers of Irish and Scottish Gaelic. In 1986 *Abbyr Shen* 'say that' by Brian Stowell (in co-operation with Douglas C. Fargher) (Stowell 1986) appeared, produced with three accompanying cassette tapes by Manx Radio, and more recently, as part of the Government programme of teaching Manx in schools, the course *Bun Noa* 'new beginning' by Brian Stowell (Stowell 1992ff.), using the 'direct method', has been produced by *Yn Unnid Gailckagh* 'the Manx Gaelic Unit' at Santan and published by the Isle of Man Government Dept. of Education.

3.5. Sound-recordings of native Manx Gaelic speech

3.5.1. Vienna Recordings

The first known sound-recordings of spoken Manx were made by Dr. Rudolf Trebitsch for the Österreichische Akademie der Wissenschaften in Vienna 5 - 8 August 1909. Trebitsch's visit to Man formed part of a survey of his at that time to record the extant Insular Celtic languages. The Manx sound-recordings are extant on ten phonograph cylinders (nos. 1087, 1088-96) and are housed in the above academy. They were made of the following speakers:
1. William Joseph Cain,(1825/26-1911) Glendhoo, Onchan,
2. William Cowley (b. 1842/43- Lezayre) of Douglas,
3. Thomas Moore (b. 1835/36 Ballaglionney Lhag, Bradda) of Brookfield, Port Erin,
4. John Nelson (b. 1839/40 Andreas) of Ramsey.
For further details of recordings, cf. Broderick 1984e.
The material recorded ranges from readings from the Manx Bible to recitations of some Manx folksongs, etc. The recordings are accompanied by texts provided by the informants themselves (though written out in Trebitsch's own hand) of their own material. There is no connected speech on them, only read or recited material, and consequently their usefulness is restricted.

3.5.2. Marstrander Recordings

The first known extensive sound recordings of native Manx speech were made on phonograph cylinders by Carl J. S. Marstrander, Profssor of Celtic Languages at the University of Oslo, in late January/early February 1933. According to his own account (Marstrander 1929-33a: 597ff.), he made 48 cylinder recordings of the following speakers:
1. Harry Kelly (1853-1935) of Cregneash, Rushen (28 cyl; nos. 2-29)
2. William Quane 83 (b. 1850) of Peel (5 cyl.)
3. Caesar Cashen (b. ca.1850 Dalby) of Peel (2 cyl.)
4. Mr. Fayle (b. ca.1860) of Staward, Sulby, Lezayre (2 cyl.)
5. John Cain (b. ca.1860) of Ballamoar, Jurby (2 cyl.)
6. Thomas Quayle 'the Gardener' (b. Ronague, Arbory) of Castletown (1 cyl.).
For further details cf. HLSM/III: xii-xviii.
In addition three other cylinder recordings were made of Harry Kelly, one of J. J. Kneen (not a native speaker) and three of William Cubbon, then librarian at the Manx Museum (also not a native speaker). Of the 48 cylinder recordings made only 23 have so far come to light (Oftedal 1982: 18); one is of J. J. Kneen, the rest are of Harry Kelly (nos. 2-24, excl. no. 7 which is missing, as is also part of no. 14). The contents include much folklore and folklife

which is missing, as is also part of no. 14). The contents include much folklore and folklife material delivered in separate sentence form[1], particularly about farming and fishing, some recited song and hymn fragments, and a number of individual word items. The sound quality, though scratchy, is an improvement on the Vienna Recordings, and with the accompanying texts much can be gleaned from them. Nevertheless, they are in poor condition. In a letter to me dated April 1978 Dr. Magne Oftedal, Professor of Celtic at the University of Oslo and one of Marstrander's pupils, relates the following regarding the cylinders:

> The cylinders were retrieved, after Marstrander's death, in a cardboard box in his attic, directly under the roof, where they had apparently been stored for several years and exposed to very great variations in temperature. The cylinders are now in my custody [at the University of Oslo] and I have had them copied. The copy was made mechanically, with a microphone, and contains much noise from the scraping of the needle. We hope in time to be able to copy the cylinders electronically, whereby the noise of scraping may perhaps be reduced (Magne Oftedal, pers. comm. April 1978; cf. also Oftedal 1982: 18).

Copy-tapes from this copy were sent to various interested parties, including myself, in May 1978. To date, so far as I am aware, no such electronically produced copies have been made.

In addition to the phonographic cylinders Marstrander made substantial recordings of native Manx speech in phonetic script contained in four manuscript volumes (Marstrander 1929-33a) bound in red with gilt tooling and presented to the Manx Museum on behalf of the Norwegian Government on 2 July 1951 as part of the 'Festival of Britain' in which Man took part. A fifth volume in the form of a box contains sundry items, including letters concerning the recordings, photographs of some of the informants (some photographs also appear at the start of vol. I), and a diary (see below). In addition to the phonetic transcriptions of the material on the cylinder recordings (except those of Kneen and Cubbon) written out in vol. I (almost all of which is written out again in vol. III, but seems to be a separate rendering, and is probably the first taking of Kelly's *vita* taken down on 31.08.1930 (Diary: 73)), the four volumes extend to some 2630 pages of material in phonetic script and much linguistic comment. The volumes include material from:

1. Thomas Christian (1849-1930 Slieau Lewaigue, Maughold) of Ramsey.
2. Joseph Woodworth (1854-1931 The Smelt, Gansey, Rushen) of Port Erin.
3. Thomas Taggart (b. 1846 Ballagilbert, Malew) of Grenaby, Malew.
4. Edward Kennah (b. 1859 Ballaclery, Arbory) of Ronague, Arbory.
5. Thomas Crebbin (b. ca.1854) of Bradda Village, Port Erin.

The contents include passages read from the Manx Bible, a good number of texts almost exclusively from Thomas Christian, with proverbs, lore, songs and rhymes (mostly fragmentary) from the other speakers.

In addition, during the course of his tour of 1929 Marstrander noted material of a minor nature (e.g. numerals, individual lexical items, recitations of the Lord's Prayer, one or two rhymes, etc.) in his diary (cf. Marstrander 1929-33b in Appendix A) from the following informants:

1. John Joseph Corrin (b. 1857-58, Ballacroshey, Ballaugh) of Ballachurry, Jurby.
2. Wilfred Wade, Sandygate, Jurby (latterly of Orrisdale, Michael).
3. John Christian (b. 1844-45), Sulby Glen, Lezayre.

---

[1]   Most of the sentences are repeated three or four times, as Marstrander wanted to make sure he obtained the material satisfactorily, since the recording machine he was using was apparently faulty (Diary: 81-82).

4. Mr. Cowley (b. 1843-44), Creggan, Tholt-y-Will, Lezayre.

5. Mr. Farakyl (*sic*) [?Faragher] (b. 1864-65), Sulby Glen, Lezayre.

6. Mr. Fayle, Stauard, Sulby, Lezayre; see also above.

7. Mr. Mylechreest (b. 1854-55), ?Ballaskeig Beg, Maughold.

8. James Kewley (b. 1850-51 Lezayre), Maughold.

9. Mr. T. Watterson (b. ca.1864), Glenchass, Rushen.

10. Mr. Gawne (b. ca. 1860), West Nappin, Jurby.

11. John Cain, Ballamoar, Jurby; see above.

12. William Quane, Peel; see above.

In all Marstrander made three visits to Man (in 1929, 1930, and 1933 when the sound-recordings were made. Information in this respect is almost exclusively to be found in a contemporary diary forming part of the contents of vol. 5 (see also above; cf. Marstrander 1929-33a) of his Manx material now in the Manx Museum. The diary is in Norwegian and was translated in 1983 by Knut Janson of Dublin at my request (cf. Marstrander 1929-33b & Appendix A).

According to the diary (Diary: 1-66), Marstrander's first (and most extensive) visit took place from mid-June to the second week in September 1929. Having arrived in Man via Newcastle, London, and Liverpool (stopping off in London to see his old friend the Celtic scholar Robin Flower), he began making a tour of the Island by bicycle in a clockwise direction starting from Douglas (see Map 3 in Appendix D). He would stop at various places on the way and would enquire of the local people about Manx and who, if anyone, still spoke it or could remember some of it. He would either be advised of the best person or persons to go to for material, or be informed that no one in the district spoke Manx at all. Sometimes those asked might say that their parents or grandparents spoke it, but that they did not. In this way Marstrander was able to build up a fairly accurate picture of the distribution of Manx speakers, or of those that had some Manx, in the Island at that time. What he came across was in reality a *Trümmerlandschaft* (see Map 3) where all that remained were the 'ruins' of a language.

> My first victim was a 60 year old man from the farm Kewaigue, 1-2km from Douglas. The old people in those parts didn't speak Manx any longer, he said. His old parents spoke a little Manx, but they preferred English, and refused to have their children speak Manx. His grandparents, however, spoke mainly Manx and spoke English with an accent (Diary: 9).

Although it was mostly older people who would have Manx, if at all, Marstrander did come across younger people with a smattering of it:

> [...]Later on that evening [15.06.29] I had a pleasant conversation [in the Union Hotel, Castletown] with the older and younger people from Castletown and the surrounding area. However, none of them spoke Manx. There was one exception, however, in a relatively young man whom I estimated to be in his forties; he had learned a little Manx, typically enough, from his grandfather. When I took a random sample and asked him what was "it is a cold day" in Manx, his reply was quite correct. (Diary: 10).

One of the persons recommended to him was Thomas Taggart of Grenaby, Malew, whom he first visited on 16 June 1929. Of him he says:

> Thomas Taggart turned out to be a jolly old man with a great apostolic beard, and quite a talkative man with a brilliant sense of humour. His pronunciation appears to me to be inarticulate, not only in Manx but also in English (which, however, doesn't say much, because my

knowledge of Manx is practically nil).[2] He lisps a little bit, certainly he doesn't have all his teeth, and some of the words appear to stick in his beard. But as far as I can see his Manx is impeccable. He told me that he also knew several Manx songs of the sort you couldn't tell in public.[3] I'm quite sure I can use the man; I have to keep him in mind, but at the moment I have to carry on on my round[4] (Diary: 16).

It was also during this initial *cuairt* that he came into contact with Harry Kelly, Joseph Woodworth, and Thomas Crebbin, all of whom he later visited and obtained material from (cf. HLSM/I Texts). Of Harry Kelly he writes:

Harry Kelly, 77 yrs. old, who lives at the bottom of the village on the right hand (south) side of the road. A nice old man with a clear pronunciation. The few sentences I gave him to translate -they were quite simple - he managed without any difficulty. His father spoke practically only Manx [...] Kelly knows the names of all the small islands and skerries outside here. A skerry is known as [krɛg ə lˊɛmən [*Creg y Lhieman*] ([lˊɛm] 'a jump'; Ir. *léim*), the exact form I couldn't be quite sure of. 'How many horses have you?' is [kwɔd kævəl tæd] [*c'woad cabbyl t'ayd?*] or something like it (Correct! Aug. 1930). Kelly can be used without doubt (Diary: 18-19).

When Marstrander returned to Man in August 1930, he visited Kelly again and noted, this time making linguistic comments on his Manx pronunciation:

[...] I took a trip to Cregneish and met old Kelly. He makes a very good impression. He grew up in a house where the parents spoke Manx to each other. He has always understood Manx himself - even as a small boy he was able to speak a little. He only achieved complete mastery of the language when, as with Woodw[orth], he went fishing with the older men when he was around 15 yrs. old. It was most interesting to observe that K. did not have a broad fronted *l*, as in *laa* 'day'. There is a question here whether we are up against a change in the old Manx dialect in the Port Erin district, or the loss of this feature could be that W[oodworth] and K[elly] grew up with English as their main language. The problem will have to be solved. It is of considerable general interest (Diary: 71).

That Kelly and Woodworth grew up with English as their main language is possible, given that their birth dates (1853 and 1854 respectively) are relatively late. But, as we shall see (Section 4, §4.2.3.), even by the Classical Manx period the resonants had been reduced to a single neutral and palatal in opposition, viz. (in the case of *l*) a neutral dental /l/ and a palatalised dental /lˊ/, the neutral forms having lost their velar quality. It would therefore not be surprising if Kelly failed to produce "a broad fronted *l* ", as Marstrander put it (*ibid.*).

With some informants, however, it was clear that though they had heard Manx first hand from native speakers (probably their parents or grandparents) their knowledge of it was shaky, i.e. of that of a semi-speaker:

Watterson [of Glenchass, Rushen] gave me the impression that he was able to hold a conversation in Manx, although his knowledge of the language probably wasn't perfect judging from several examples [...] Watterson was, however, not quite certain when he exceeded 40. He mentioned 60 as [tri: ˈki:d [*tree keead*] which has to be 300, but he corrected himself later [...] [su:lˊ] [*sooill*] 'eye' (which he, however, couldn't remember immediately, and it was only after I mentioned the Irish word for it [*súil*] that he did remember it) (Diary: 20-22).

---

2   Until he had (later on) learned Manx Marstrander judged the accuracy of the answers his informants gave him to his test questions from his knowledge of Irish.

3   cf. Abraham Juan in HLSM/I: 390-91.

4   In fact he went back to Taggart during his second visit in 1930.

In a similar instance in the North where his 70+ yrs. old informant John Kissack of Ballachrink, near Kirk Michael, had 'semi-speaker' competence in Manx, Marstrander noted:

> [...]He knows amongst other things the Our Father [Lord's Prayer] in Manx - but appears strangely enough not to be able to count to 10 (Diary: 35).

Again with a Mr. Cowley, Creggan, at the far (southern) end of Sulby Glen:

> He is now 85 yrs. old, almost blind and rather rheumatic, but his pronunciation is quite clear. His memory seems somewhat weakened. Even when he speaks English he hesitates and seems to be rooting for the words. It was impossible for him to remember what 'head' was in Manx. It wasn't until I mentioned the southern Manx [k´ɔ: n] [kione] that he gave me his pronunciation of it as [k´ɔun]. He also had problems differentiating between 'with him' and 'with her', but things like that will hopefully diminish fairly naturally in more connected speech (Diary: 42).

In another instance his informant was literate in Manx (i.e. he could read the Manx Bible) which was appparently noticeable in his Manx. It seems that in this case neither Marstrander nor his informant took to each other very well:

> [...] I called on carpenter Wilfred Waid [Wade], Sandygate, Jurby, who is hardly much of a number. His pronunciation seems quite clear. He can read quite a lot of the Bible [...], which one notices in all his conversation. [...] Wade was extremely dissatisfied with my pronunciation (Diary: 39).

As we have seen on his own admission, Marstrander had little or no Manx when he first came to the Island, and on his circuit he was looking for someone with whom he could work regularly to learn from and question. He found his ideal person on 21 June in Thomas Christian of College Street, Ramsey, whom he describes as:

> an excellent old man, a Nordic type through and through. Here I seem finally to have found the man to work with. His pronunciation is clear, the man is intelligent, patient, and understands that he can be of great service to scholarship by making himself available. He answers small test samples quickly and idiomatically[5] (Diary: 47-48).

Marstrander arranged to visit Christian on a regular basis to learn Manx from him, and he began his lessons with him the following Tuesday (25 June). He tells us (Diary: 54) that he would work with him from ca. 10-12 in the morning and from 2-4pm in the afternoon and adds:

> Christian without doubt knows a lot of Manx. But it is quite clear that even he is a long time without practice at speaking the language. He often neglects the ordinary rules of mutation [i.e. lenition], eclipsis, but maybe that is part of the development of the dialect he is speaking[6] (Diary: 54).

Marstrander evidently worked regularly with Christian till just prior to his departure in September. On 8 September 1929, the day before his departure, Marstrander was satisfied that he had "really got the hang of Manx [...]" (Diary: 64). However, just prior to his departure Marstrander wrote to *Chronique* on 03.09.1929 from Ramsey and made the following comment:

---

5   Potential informants would first be asked to translate simple sentences into Manx. Then, if they were able, more difficult ones. One of Marstrander's favourite test questions to elicit the use of the conditional/past subjunctive in unreal conditional clauses was 'I would not have beaten him, had he not been a bad man'.

6   For details cf. HLSM/I §§7-27.

I have spent about three months in this beautiful island; I started by crossing it in all directions to gain an impression on the positions of the Manx. I am sorry to say I have come at least five years too late. There is no fluent Manx speaker left, three or four pretty good speakers and about thirty who have got smatterings of it. The language is practically dead without hardly any phonetical transcriptions having been taken (*Chronique* 248/V MM.MS.H140/lx/151).

Marstrander returned to Man the following summer, arriving (via Newcastle, London, and Liverpool - the route he took on all three visits) at the beginning of August 1930. The purpose of his visit on this occasion was to investigate the southern dialect which he regarded (correctly) as differing "to a significantly greater degree than is generally thought from that in the northern part of the island" (Diary: 64).[7] During that second visit he worked mainly with Thomas Taggart, Grenaby; Edward Kennah, Ballaclery; Joseph Woodworth, Port Erin; Thomas Crebbin, Bradda; Harry Kelly, Cregneash, and from Peel with William Quane (Marstrander's main informant for the northern dialect, Thomas Christian, had died on 21 February 1930). He found Taggart a disappointment:

Now working with Taggart in Grenaby. He is is a bit of a disappointment; he is over-rated. He has forgotten most of his Manx; he does not remember the most ordinary of words like 'shoulder', 'knee', etc, and this is probably not because of his great age. I will probably give him up shortly (Diary 67-68),

and a difficult subject to deal with:

Taggart is a very difficult subject to put it mildly. First of all he is deaf and a continuous conversation with him is almost impossible. His memory is also weakened to a considerable degree. All his information will have to be checked and used with the greatest care. False associations with synonyms or similar sounding English or Manx words would often lead him to produce completely mad forms, such as [æ:-kəl] 'limekiln' (under the influence of Eng. 'kiln' for [i:l] = [G.] *aoil*!! ['lime']. I'll have to arrange some phonetic system of what he has explained. Yesterday we were shouting for a full four and a half hours which I'm sure could be heard all over the parish - and we were both completely knackered when we were finished (Diary: 70-71).

He regarded Kennah as a trustworthy man, but noted that he did not speak Manx with ease. Better he found was Joseph Wordworth whom he noted (Diary: 68):

was clear and certain, and his Manx seems to be with him something more than just memories (Diary: 68).

Nevertheless, his best informant from the south was Harry Kelly who:

appears to have an extraordinarily good knowledge of Manx. I've still not been able to get to know him very well, but it would not surprise me that of all the speakers I have met he is the one who speaks best and most idiomatically.[8] Made him tell me his "Life" in English; I'll take it down in Manx tomorrow morning [31.08.30] at 9 o'clock. Kelly is supposed to be very unapproachable - a fishmonger who passed by was surprised that I ever got Kelly to speak Manx (Diary: 72).

---

7   As well as investigating the southern dialect it was also Marstrander's intention (Diary: 64) to excavate an old 'keeill' (church) site "in a very Norse district, and perhaps find a few runic crosses". Marstrander was an acknowledged expert on runes and runic monuments (Borgstrøm 1967, Oftedal 1982). Bearing in mind that Man once formed (a major) part of the 'Norse' kingdom of Sodor (Man and the Hebrides) till 1266, Marstrander's interest in Manx and Celtic studies, particularly the cultural and linguistic relations between the British Isles and Scandinavia during the 'Viking Age', has to be seen in the context of a surge in interest in matters Germanic at that time (cf. also Borgstrøm 1967).

8   An observation he confirmed when he met him the following day (Diary: 73).

In fact, Marstrander did experience some initial difficulty in getting Kelly to honour his agreement, for he noted:

> [...] he is a difficult man to handle. When I called in this morning at 9 o'clock as we had agreed he had no time to spare. I'll have to come to a permanent arrangement with him (Diary: 73).

He managed to get Kelly's *vita* from him nevertheless, plus other information relating to fishing and farming customs and practices (cf. HLSM/I: 324ff.).

Marstrander returned a little over 16 months later (in mid-January 1933) to Man, this time with a phonograph cylinder recorder and a graph to "determine the sonority, nasality, consonant and vowel sounds" (Diary: 82). However, neither machine was evidently working satisfactorily. There was apparently something faulty with the stylus on the phonograph recorder which meant that at least one fifth of the wax cylinder could not be used (Diary: 81). In addition the machine could not be used when the temperature was less than 20 degrees centigrade, which in the Isle of Man in January was (and still is) difficult to attain, even indoors.[9] With regard to the graph it was seemingly difficult to get the oscillations to show on the paper, and Marstrander thought he could improve things if he changed the nibs. At any rate, he admitted (Diary: 82) that the machine could not be compared with the French variety he had used previously in Brittany.[10]

Nevertheless, in spite of the difficulties, Harry Kelly was evidently to be his star performer. He made contact with him on 24 January 1933, and began recording him at the Station Hotel, Port Erin, (to where he brought him) on 25th. He made 29 cylinder recordings of Kelly (Diary: 83) and finished work with him on 30 January 1933. He regarded the recordings, however, as being rather uneven:

> Kelly's voice is somewhat hoarse, is a bit squeaky and not very sonorous, but the result improves when he speaks relatively softly and has his mouth very close to the horn (Diary: 81-82).

He had some success also with the graph, the main result being:

> faintly voiced media in *dorcha* are voiced; *p, t, k* considerably weaker aspiration than in Norwegian; [ɑun´] 'river', [dɑun´] 'deep' have a non-nasal vowel (Diary: 83).

Before returning to Norway on 5 February 1933 he made five cylinder recordings in Peel of Quane and two of Cashen, two of Fayle (Sulby), and the last two of John Cain of Jurby. Of Fayle Marstrander commented:

> [...] an impossible subject, hoarse and had a squeaky voice; and barked the words into the horn (Diary: 84).

He noted also that:

> Quane's voice didn't turn out to be very good either for the recordings, and his knowledge of Manx is probably rather limited. He is not like Kelly and Cashen born with Manx, but has learned it, as he says himself, by listening to the old people when he was a boy. His pronunciation often varies for the same words, it seems to me (Diary: 83).

On the other hand, Marstrander had a good impression of John Cain:

---

[9] Apart from anything else Manx people generally prefer to live in cool conditions - GB.

[10] According to Oftedal (Oftedal 1982: 14), Marstrander collected material in Brittany during the 1920s which apparently has never been published. Some 120 notebooks containing his Breton material are at present housed in the Dept. of Celtic at the University of Oslo (*ibid.*: 14).

John Cain confirmed completely the good impression I got of him in 1929. [...] It is a pity I
hadn't met him before. He would have been one of my main informants together with Christian, Woodworth, and Kelly (Diary: 85).

From his diary we also learn that Marstrander had a fetish for acquiring old Manx Bibles and
prayer books, whether he bought them or had his informants part with them, and would be
put out if an informant did not want to sell it! The regularity with which he mentions his acquisition of such books suggests that they were as important to him as the Manx he was
eliciting from his informants. One example will suffice to show this:

[Harry] Kelly has a Manx Bible which Karran [also from Cregneash] has (he's the oldest of
them), but none of them wanted to part with it. Taggart in Grenaby also has a Bible from 1819
[...] (Diary: 28).

Marstrander, it seems, also like to indulge in some mild boyish mischief. While at Kirk
Michael on his cycle tour in 1929 he found the flat surface of a gatepost quite irresistible and
carved on it in runes: "I Carl erected this stone". He hoped that no one would find it and take
it seriously! (Diary: 35).

So far as is known, Marstrander did not return to Man again till 1965 (and then on a private visit), shortly before his death later that same year. For his publications of 1932 and
1934 (cf. Marstrander 1932, 1934) he used only his linguistic commentaries and place-name
material in the volumes cited. The publications cited in fact consist mainly of place-name
material, which he must have noted elsewhere, as little or none of this material appears in
the above volumes. The textual material in phonetic script, whether from the Bible or original pieces (mostly of a folkloristic nature), Marstrander never published, and it had to wait
till 1984 before the original material, at any rate, saw the light of day (cf. HLSM/I: 168-229;
312-319; 324-341; 388-401). It was not until 1948 that the next systematic sound-recording
of native Manx speech was made (see §3.5.3.1. below).

3.5.3. Recordings of the last native speakers

Although in 1932 Marstrander believed (incorrectly) that at that time there was only one person who could properly be described as a native speaker (Marstrander 1932: 292), it was as a
result of his visits and the publicity they received in Man that Manx Gaelic enthusiasts began combing the countryside in search of surviving native speakers (Craine 1974). In consequence a Welsh visitor, Arthur S. B. Davies, of Mochdre, Colwyn Bay, using their discover-
ies (cf. also Loch 1946) was able to publish the names and addresses of twenty people who
were believed to have spoken Manx from infancy (Davies 1948). For reference they were:
   1. Wilfred Wade, Sanygate, Jurby (also visited by Marstrander).
   2. Charles Kneale, Ballagarrett, Bride.
   3. Mrs. [Annie] Kneale [his wife], Ballagarrett, Bride.
   4. John Tom Kaighin, Ballagarrett, Bride.
   5. John Kneen [the Gaaue], Lhen Mooar, Andreas.
   6. Robert Fayle, Ramsey.
   7. Capt. James Kinley, Peel (orig. Ballafesson, Rushen). [Not a native speaker].
   8. Mrs. Clague, Dalby, Patrick.
   9. Miss. Kaye, Onchan (of Glen Maye, Patrick).

10. Harry Boyde, Ballaugh.
11. Edward (Ned) Maddrell, Glenchass, Rushen (of Corvalley, Rushen).
12. John Maddrell (his brother), Port St. Mary.
13. Mrs. [Eleanor] Karran, Cregneash.
14. Mr. [Thomas] Crebbin, Cregneash.
15. James Karran, Cregneash.
16. Mrs. [Emily] Lowey, Kirkill, Rushen.
17. Thomas Leece, Moaney Mooar, Malew.
18. John Kinvig, Ronague, Arbory.
19. Mrs. [Sage] Kinvig [his wife], Ronague, Arbory.
20. Mrs. [Catherine] Watterson, Colby, Arbory (of Glenchass, Rushen).
See also Broderick 1984a, 1984e, 1986.

3.5.3.1. Irish Folklore Commission Recordings

On 23 July 1947 Éamonn de Valéra, then Taoiseach of Ireland, came to Man on a one-day visit whose main purpose was apparently cultural (when later in opposition he made similar visits to Wales and Scotland), during which he was escorted to various places in the Island by the then Director of the Manx Museum, Mr. Basil Megaw, and Mr. Ramsey B.Moore, then Attorney-General.[11] One of the places visited by de Valéra and his party was the recently re-opened (in 1946) open-air folk museum at Cregneash (in the very south of the Island), whose curator was Ned Maddrell, a native Manx Gaelic speaker.[12] According to the Museum's Annual Report for 31.03.1948 (Annual Report 1948: 2), de Valéra was much impressed by the Cregneash folk museum, and when he was told[13] that no really adequate sound-recordings had been made of the few surviving native speakers of Manx Gaelic,[14] he said that, if it would be helpful, he would be glad to ensure that the best technical facilities and 'know-how' were made available for the purpose. After consultation with of *Yn Cheshaght Ghailckagh* (YCG) 'the Manx Language Society' this offer was warmly accepted by the Manx Museum Trustees (Annual Report 1948: 2). In consequence de Valéra approached Prof. Dr. Séamas Ó Duilearga, Director of the Irish Folklore Commission (IFC) to arrange for the Commission to visit Man to make sound-recordings of the native Manx speakers that were then living. In an interview with Dr. Caoimhín Ó Danchair on this subject on 27 May 1981 I learned from him that de Valéra was told that the Commission had no sound-recording unit at all. De

---

[11] Basil Megaw pc. 10.12.1976. See also Annual Report (1948: 2).

[12] As it later turned out he was the last native Manx speaker (†27.12.1974). De Valéra and Ned Maddrell evidently got on well together, and each began talking to the other in his own Gaelic language. Maddrell told me on the only occasion that I visited him (see below) on 17.08.1972 that he began reciting the Lord's Prayer in Manx and de Valéra joined him in Irish about half-way through. He said also that Mr. de Valéra's visit to him was the one he cherished most.

[13] Some believe that it was Ned Maddrell himself who urged de Valéra to do something about the precarious situation of Manx in which it then was. Maddrell was away at sea at the time of the Marstrander visits.

[14] Marstrander's phonographic recordings had evidently been forgotten, or were not known about. In fact some 23 of the original cylinders were retrieved after Marstander's death and their contents were transferred on to playing tape in 1978 (Magne Oftedal: pers. comm. April 1978; cf. also §3.5.2. above).

Valéra ordered that one be obtained, and on 21 April 1948 Dr Ó Danchair was sent on his own with the van containing the recording unit to Man on board the B & I cattleboat SS *Longford*. Ó Danchair added that his visit to Man was the first sound-recording undertaken by the IFC (Ó Danchair 1981).

The boat arrived at the Battery Pier, Douglas, at about 06.00hrs on the morning of 22 April 1948 and was met by Basil Megaw. The van had been placed in the ship's hold, and when it was winched out it was found that the roof of it was completely covered in cowdung. Once on the quayside they drove via the back streets of Douglas to the Manx Museum where it was hosed down and cleaned (Ó Danchair 1981).

> That was the start of a wonderful fortnight. A fine team of young Manxmen, including Mark and Tom Braide, Charles Craine, John Gell, Leslie Quirk, and Bill Radcliffe, happily gave up their time to accompany Kevin Danaher [Caoimhín Ó Danchair] to the ends of the Island, and to introduce him to all the notable speakers then living. Kevin [Caoimhín] and the Manx folk took to each other instantly, and not many hours were left for sleeping [...] (Basil Megaw: pc. 29.04.1976).

The machinery his van contained included two recording decks set on a table immediately behind the front seats and powered by batteries recharged each night at the Museum. When out on field-work, said Ó Danchair, care was taken to park the van on level ground. The microphone was then positioned according to the requirements, depending on whether the interview was to be conducted indoors or not. The sound-levels would then be checked, and when all was correct the recording would begin. The sounds would be monitored through headphones. The second deck would be put into operation as the disc on the first deck was coming to an end, hence there would be certain amount of overlap. The recording arm would work from the centre outwards as it cut the disc. In this way between 22 April and 5 May 1948 the Irish Folklore Commission was able to collect on twenty six 12- and 16-inch double-sided discs just over four hours of recorded material. The original disc recordings are housed in the archives of the old Irish Folklore Commission, now the Department of Irish Folklore, at University College Dublin. I was shown the discs by Dr. Ó Danchair when I interviewed him on 27.05.1981. Copy-tapes as well as the 35mm negatives of the photos of the informants were later forwarded to the Manx Museum (Tape Archive Nos. MM36-41). The IFC recordings were done with the active help of the Manx Museum Director and staff, as well as members of *Yn Cheshaght Ghailckagh*. Dr. Ó Danchair returned to Dublin via Liverpool (Ó Danchair 1981).

The material recorded contains over sixty different items including much folklife material, stories, conversations between speakers, recitation of some song-fragments, one or two hymns, and version's of the Lord's Prayer (cf. HLSM/I Texts). The speakers recorded were:

1. Mrs. Annie Kneale (ca.1865-1949), Ballagarrett, Bride.
2. John Tom Kaighin (1862-1954), Ballagarrett, Bride.
3. Harry Boyde (ca.1870-1953 Bishop's Court, Ballaugh), Ballaugh.
4. John Kneen (the Gaaue) (1852-1958 St. Jude's, Andreas), Ballaugh Curragh.
5. Ned Maddrell (1877-1974 Corvalley, Rushen), Glenchass, Rushen.
6. Thomas Leece (1859-1956 Ronague, Arbory), Kerrookiel, Malew.
7. Mrs. Sage Kinvig (1870-1962), Garey Hollin, Ronague, Arbory.
8. Mrs. Eleanor Karran (1870-1953), Cregneash, Rushen.

See also HLSM/I & III Intro.

64

3.5.3.2. Manx Museum Recordings

As a direct result of the Irish Folklore Commission's visit to Man, the staff of the Manx Museum's Folklife Survey (MM)[15] set about making their own collections of native Manx speech on paper tapes (provided by Prof. Francis J. Carmody, University of California at Berkeley, in July 1949) between early 1950 and autumn 1952. According to Basil Megaw (Megaw pers. comm. 29.04.1976) the first set of tapes were made by YCG volunteers for the Folklife Survey on a machine borrowed from Prof. Carmody. The Museum was then later equipped with a tape recorder provided by one of the Friends of the Manx Museum to make recordings for preservation in the Folklife Survey archives (Megaw *ibid.*). The native speakers recorded were:

1. John Kneen (the Gaaue), Ballaugh Curragh.
2. John Tom Kaighin, Ballagarrett, Bride.
3. Harry Boyde, Ballaugh.
4. Mrs. Eleanor Karran, Cregneash, Rushen.
5. Tom Karran (1877-1959), Cregneash, Rushen (Mrs. Karran's brother).

The Manx Museum Recordings are catalogued MM. 22, 25, 26, 28, 32, 35 in the archive index, and along with the IFC copy-tapes were re-processed on to polyethylene tapes by the School of Scottish Studies, University of Edinburgh, in 1973. The material on the MM recordings is similar to those on IFC.

3.5.3.3. Carmody Recordings

In July 1949 Professor Francis J. Carmody, University of California at Berkeley, visited Man made some recordings of his own which he used for the basis of his article in Carmody 1953. These recordings were not available for consultation for Broderick 1984/86. In addition, Carmody provided a tape recorder for the Manx Museum to make some of its recordings (see foregoing). The material he collected was obtained from the following:

1. John Kneen (the Gaaue), Ballaugh Curragh.
2. John Tom Kaighin, Ballagarrett, Bride.
3. Harry Boyde, Ballaugh.
4. Ned Maddrell, Glenchass, Rushen.
5. Mrs. Catherine Watterson (1858/59-1951), Colby, Rushen (of Glenchass).

3.5.3.4. Yn Cheshaght Ghailckagh Recordings

Following on from the example of the IFC and MM *Yn Cheshaght Ghailckagh* began making their own series of sound-recordings on paper tapes from late 1951 to ?mid-1953. The recording machine used, a "Sound-Mirror", was bought and provided by Manx enthusiast and

---

[15] The Manx Folklife Survey was set up in May 1948 and put into operation some six months later on the appointment (on 01.10.1948) of Eric Cregeen (Annual Report 1949).

YCG member John Gell,[16] and the recording sessions would take place usually on a Sunday afternoon. The speakers recorded were:

1. John Kneen (the Gaaue), Ballaugh Curragh.
2. Ned Maddrell, Glenchass, Rushen.
3. Harry Boyde, Ballaugh.
4. John Tom Kaighin, Ballagarrett, Bride.
5. Danny Caine (1860/61-1952), Little London, Michael.
6. Tom Karran, Cregneash, Rushen.
7. Mrs. Sage Kinvig, Ronague, Arbory.
8. Tommy Leece, Kerrookeil, Malew.

The recordings of John Kneen (the Gaaue) were usually undertaken in Bill Radcliffe's house in Ramsey, as Kneen had no electricity in his own house out at Ballaugh Curragh. The recordings of Harry Boyde were made at the Mannin Infirmary, Braddan, where he spent the last few years of his life (d. 02.02.1953). In most cases speakers were interviewed in their own homes, usually by two or more interviewers. On one occasion (09.10.1952) three speakers, viz. Tommy Leece, Ned Maddrell, Mrs. Sage Kinvig, gathered in the house of Tommy Leece at Kerrookeil, Malew, with five interviewers (Walter Clarke, Douglas C. Fargher, Tom Braide, John Gell, and Robert L. Thomson), and the rapport and excitement engendered by all present produced some interesting material.

Twenty-nine tapes were made in all (YCG nos. 1-24, 29, 30, 32-34), including a copy of part of the recordings made on wax cylinders by a Mr. Gelling of Liverpool in 1947 of the following speakers:

1. Mrs. Emily Lowey (1869-1947), Kirkill, Rushen (YCG.29 & pt. 30).
2. Wilfred Wade (ca.1860-1948), Orrisdale, Michael (YCG.29).

See also Private Recordings below.

The contents include material similar to that of the IFC and MM, but more of it. In only one case (YCG.32-33) is there conversation between native speakers. Mostly the recordings are of speakers on their own with the interviewer(s). The recordings were transferred on to polyetheline tapes by the School of Scottish Studies in 1961. See also Broderick 1984a, 1984e, 1986.

3.5.3.5. Private Recordings

The Private Recordings (PR), are they as classified here, were made by individuals between 1947 and 1962. They are PR.1 made by Mr. Gelling, as mentioned above, on wax discs, PR.2 made by Walter Clarke, Ramsey, of Ned Maddrell ca.1960, and PR.3 by Brian Stowell and Bernard Caine, Douglas, of Ned Maddrell on 13 June 1962. PR.2. has Maddrell talking about his younger days and at the fishing, while PR.3 contains some anecdotes and a number of lexical items sought through conversation. The original tapes in the last two cases are with their owners. It is not known what became of the original Gelling cylinder recordings.

---

[16] The Manx Museum apparently for insurance reasons refused permission sought by YCG volunteers to use its machine.

3.5.3.6. BBC and RTÉ Recordings

In May 1949 Eric Jolly recorded a number of native speakers for a BBC programme. On 14 November 1969 Proinsias Ó Conluain of Raidió Teilifís Éireann (RTÉ) interviewed Ned Maddrell in the presence of two members of *Yn Cheshaght Ghailckagh* Douglas C Fargher and Leslie Quirk. The subjects discussed touched on seasonal customs, fishing, etc. By this time Maddrell was the only known surviving native speaker, Mrs. Kinvig having died in 1962.

3.5.3.7. Linguistic Survey of Scotland Recordings

In August 1972 Professor Kenneth Jackson of the Dept. of Celtic, University of Edinburgh, sent David Clement of the Gaelic section of the Linguistic Survey of Scotland to Man to see what he could glean from Ned Maddrell, then the only surviving native speaker. The material he obtained from Maddrell, as well as from Ewan Christian (1907-1985), a semi-native speaker from Peel (see Section 2, note 34, and below), include a number of lexical items sought in the form of a questionnaire, stories, and some small anecdotes. The tapes are numbered LSS.902, 903, 908, 909 in the archive. The same archive contains copies of some of the recordings made by Gelling in 1947 (LSS.901). The LSS archive also houses 'cleaned up' copies of the IFC recordings on LSS.951 and 952. LSS.951 contains material not on other copies. Clement came again in August 1973, but found that Maddrell's hearing had deteriorated so considerably that he was not able to elicit any information at all, even though Maddrell himself was willing enough to give it.

In addition to the sound recordings of native Manx Gaelic speech, as outlined above, recordings in phonetic script were made by John Rhys (1886-1893; cf. Rhys 1894), Marstrander (1929-1933; cf. Marstrander 1929-33a), and later by Francis J. Carmody (1949; cf. Carmody (1947 & 1953), Heinrich Wagner (1950; cf. Wagner 1969), and Kenneth Jackson (1950-51; cf. Jackson 1955). See also below.

3.5.3.8. Broderick Recordings

Two tape recordings were made of the semi-speaker Ewan Christian of Peel in May and August of 1978 by George Broderick. Thereafter, occasional visits were made and material (single lexical items) collected in phonetic script until 1983 (see also §3.6.10. below).

3.6. Assessment of the material collected

3.6.1. Vienna Sound Recordings

These recordings are very scratchy, and were they not accompanied by texts provided by the informants themselves (though written in Trebitsch's own hand) of their own material they would be very difficult to make out. In addition there is no connected speech on them, only read prose pieces or recited songs[17] (cf. HLSM/I Texts), which restricts their usefulness.

3.6.2. Marstrander Sound and Phonetic Recordings

3.6.2.1. Marstrander Sound Recordings

The 23 surviving wax cylinders from an original total of 48 (cf. Marstrander 1929-33a: 579ff.) are also scratchy, but are much more intelligible than the Vienna Recordings. However, even here some parts are quite difficult or well nigh impossible to make out, and Marstrander's own phonetic versions of these have been most helpful. Because of the faulty equipment he was evidently using (see above) the material sought is elicited in separate sentence form, each sentence being repeated on average three or four times. Consequently the overall presentation is somewhat jerky with little flow, and therefore not a good sample of natural connected speech. Nevertheless, from the point of view of pronunciation the material is useful.

3.6.2.2. Marstrander Phonetic Recordings

By far the greater part of Marstrander's recordings exist in phonetic script contained in four ms. volumes spanning some 2635 pages (cf. Marstrander 1929-33a). The contents are as follows:
- *Vol. 1* (MM.MS.5354) contains 732 ([15] + iii + 714) pages of material mostly from Thomas Christian. The first 15 pages are taken up with photographs of various persons and scenes, including the following speakers: Thomas Christian (Ramsey), Joseph Woodworth (Port Erin), Harry Kelly (Cregneash), Thomas Taggart (Grenaby), William Quane (Peel). Then follow three pages of contents. Then comes the following mat-erial from Christian:
    1. One or two rhymes;
    2. Readings from the Biblical books of Jonah, Proverbs, Lamentations, Jeremiah, Song of Solomon, Joel;
    3. Readings from two manuscript sermons;
    4. Readings from folklore material in Moore 1891a and carvals from Moore 1891b, and the tract *Carrey yn Pheccagh* 'the sinner's friend', plus some additional Bible readings;
    5. Details of contents of the phonographic cylinders made of J. J. Kneen (not a native Manx speaker), Harry Kelly, William Quane, Caesar Cashen. Material from latter three given in phonetic script.
- *Vol. 2* (MM.MS.5355) contains 767 pages (numbered 715-1481) comprising the following:
    1. Linguistic material relating to irregular and regular verbs, some adverbs, and material from Cashen's *Manx Folklore* (Cashen 1912);

---

[17] viz. Moore's reading of his own Manx Gaelic version of the Manx National Anthem and two small pieces about Port Erin, Nelson's reading of two songs from Moore 1896, and a poem translated from English.

2. Original material from Thomas Christian (cf. HLSM/I Texts) intermingled with material from Cashen 1912;

3. More readings from the Manx Bible.

- *Vol. 3* (MM.MS.5356) contains 713 pages (1482-2195) comprising the following:

1. Original material from Joseph Woodworth, notes on Woodworth's phonology (incl. recitation of 8 stanzas of Manx trad. song *Mylecharaine*), plus some readings from Genesis.

2. Original material from Harry Kelly (cf. HLSM/I Texts), plus place- and field names in and around Cregneash;

3. Phonological notes on Kelly's and Christian's Manx.

- *Vol. 4* (MM.MS.5357) contains 429 pages (2208-2637) and comprises the following:

Original and other material from Thomas Taggart (Grenaby), Edward Kennah (Port Erin), Thomas Crebbin (Bradda), William Quane (Peel), Caesar Cashen (Peel), Mr. Fayle (Sulby), Thomas Quayle (Ballaugh), and John Cain (Jurby) (cf. HLSM/I Texts), plus some phonetic notes.

- *Vol. 5* (MM.MS.5358B) is made up as a box containing the following items:

1. Marstrander's diary (in Norwegian) of his visits to Man (cf. §3.5.2. above and Appendix A);

2. notebook containing some notes on Mx. phonology (but mostly blank);

3. folder containing photos and negatives of the speakers;

4. notebook containing some of Rhys's notes on Mx. phonology (cf. Rhys 1894);

5. Copy of A. Trampe Bødtker, 1929. Engelsk Lydlære. Oslo, annotated by M;

6. Copy of *Cummey Shirveish Ashoonagh* (Douglas 1930);

7. four orig. mss. of sermons in Manx;

8. sundry papers.

The first four volumes are made up of a series of exercise books containing the material in phonetic script, usually written in ink or pencil on the right hand page, the left hand page usually given over to notes on the speaker's pronunciation, lexical items used, etc. However, when gathering the books for binding (for presentation to the Manx Museum; see above) Marstrander (or whoever) grouped them more according to the speaker, rather than having regard to the chronological order. Thus, for example, his taking down of Harry Kelly's *vita* (which from his Diary (p. 73) took place on 31.08.1930) appears in Vol. 3, while the transcriptions of the phonograph cylinder recordings of the various speakers (made in late Jan./early Feb. 1933; see above) appear in Vol. 1.

The phonetic transcription of Christian's original and more informal contributions in Vol. 2 appear to be less settled thatn that of his Bible readings in Vol. 1, particularly for the vowels (though this may reflect the variance of pronunciation on the part of the speaker which Marstrander had noted elsewhere; cf. for Quane above), e.g. he writes [æ], sometimes [ẹ] or [ɛ] to represent [ɛ] (cf. Thomson 1976: 255-63).[18]

---

[18] It is clear from Marstrander's Diary (Marstrander 1929-33b) that the purpose of his visits was to collect as much data as possible to gain a fairly accurate idea of the pronunciation and sound system of Late Spoken Manx (LSM). However, it is also clear from looking at the material that from the point of view of phonology the system he used (i.e. having his informants read or recite large tracts of the Manx Bible, etc, or supply original material (stories, etc)), was somewhat haphazard. There seems to have been no questionnaire used to obtain examples of the var-

It is clear from Marstrander's material that his informants, such as Thomas Christian and Harry Kelly, had a firmer command of Manx, with a wider knowledge of idiom, than had later speakers recorded by IFC, MM, YCG, though even with Marstrander's informants the abandonment of lenition, for example, was not uncommon (as Mars-trander himself had noted; see above). It is clear also from the material that his informants were much more in contact with the old traditions and folklore of the Isle of Man (as witnessed in the texts) than later speakers. This suggests that in the forty years or so between the earliest informant recorded, i.e. William Joseph Cain (b. 1825/26) and the latest, i.e. Ned Maddrell (b. 1877) the old traditions and lore, as well as the language, were becoming lost and forgotten (cf. also Broderick 1986: xxiv-xxvi).

3.6.3. Irish Folklore Commission Sound Recordings

As we have seen, the IFC recorded material comprises some sixty different items ranging from long conversations to stories, recitations (from memory) of some song fragments, one or two hymns, to versions of the Lord's Prayer. The speakers involved in the conversations were (from the North) John Kneen and Harry Boyde, John Kneen and John Tom Kaighin, and (from the South) Ned Maddrell and Tommy Leece (also Ned Maddrell and Emily Lowey on PR. 1; see above. The speakers would be brought together for the purpose of the recording, and some interesting material from this interaction was collected. However, the distance between the various speakers' homes was in most cases sufficiently far enough away to prevent ordinary day-to-day contact which would have produced a different sort of relationship between them (i.e. one of more familiarity), rather than one of formality on the occasion(s) of the recordings.[19] That is to say, that had the speakers been on more familiar terms with each other, more idiom and *Umgangssprache* might possibly have been elicited than at times the somewhat stilted and more reserved speech actually recorded. In the case of the Kneen-Kaighin conversations there is an almost total domination of the scene by Kaighin. However, given the scarcity of speakers living at the time nothing else could have been done. One result of such encounters was that Ned Maddrell and Tommy Leece apparently met each other

---

ious sounds of LSM. Although, as we have seen above, he made extensive notes on the sounds of Christian's and Kelly's Manx (in Vol. 3), his thoughts here seem only to have been tentative; and when he had committed them to print (cf. Marstrander 1932) it is noticeable that his transcription is broad, at times too broad, the analysis is limited in scope, and the comparisons are made with Norwegian phonemes which, as Jackson had already experienced (cf. Jackson 1955: 5), restricted its usefulness.

[19] Though this is no guarantee that they would have spoken Manx with one another. Mrs. Annie Kneale, Ballagarrett, Bride, lived next door on the same quarterland as her native Manx speaking neighbour John Tom Kaighin. To judge from Mrs. Kneale's Manx on the recordings it is apparent that she had been without practice for quite some time, and probably would have spoken to Kaighin in English whenever she met him.

In a Manx Place-Name Survey interview on 23.01.1991 with Stanley Karran (b. 1910), Cregneash, whose mother Eleanor Karran was a Cregneash native Manx speaker who had been interviewed by Wagner and Jackson (see below), Mr. Karran told me that his mother only spoke Manx once a year to a particular neighbour who lived a short distance away at Corvalley. He also told me that with the other native Manx speakers in Cregneash, e.g. Harry Kelly, she spoke only English. He added that in his time Harry Kelly and the others who could speak Manx generally spoke to one another in English.

fairly frequently afterwards. At the only get-together of speakers recorded (by YCG 09.10.1952; YCG.32-33) the atmosphere was one of informality.

3.6.4. Manx Museum Sound Recordings

The Manx Museum recordings are similar to those of IFC with the exception that they lack pieces of conversation between speakers.

By the very nature of the work of the Irish Folklore Commission and the Manx Museum their recordings of native Manx speech are of necessity geared to the collection of folkloristic and folklife material. Consequently any linguistic approach designed to obtain a phonology of the language simply did not apply. That was undertaken by others.

The policy with the IFC and MM was to let the native speakers themselves talk, and the interviewers only to come in either to prompt the speaker whenever he/she would get stuck or to lead the speaker(s) on to another topic.

3.6.5. Yn Cheshaght Ghailckagh Sound Recordings

The material recorded by YCG is similar to that of IFC and MM, but there is much more of it - in fact roughly twice as much as the IFC and MM collections put together. The interviewers for IFC, MM, and YCG were essentially the same people who had the advantage of knowing the speakers quite well, and some speakers, such as John Kneen and Ned Maddrell, became their friends and would be visited a lot more often by them without a tape recorder. This contact enabled the interviewers to get to know the reservoir of material the speakers had, e.g. anecdotes, stories, folklife information, etc (though there is none of the traditional folktales or songs as collected in Scotland or Ireland), and so when the recording sessions would take place the interviewers knew what to elicit. In this way they were quite successful, so that in the case of John Kneen, for example, they were able to obtain extensive information about such things as working at the smithy, turf-cutting, building sod-houses, etc, as well as his fund of stories and anecdotes.

The IFC, MM, and YCG recordings, in spite of some short-comings, provide by far the major part of the sound-record collection of native Manx Gaelic speech that we possess.

3.6.6. Carmody Phonetic and Sound Recordings

3.6.6.1. Carmody Phonetic Recordings ˙

In 1947 Prof. Francis J. Carmody published an article entitled 'Manx Gaelic Sentence Structure' (Carmody 1947) at the University of California. This contains some introductory remarks on phonetics and some short textual material obtained from a woman living in California who had obtained her Manx from Manx classes. In some cases the pronunciation is impossible, as Jackson (Jackson 1955: 5, 6) has already noted, e.g. [nəhi], [nhi] for *nhee* 'thing' (in fact [nji:]), [lhiəm] for *lhiam* 'with me' (in fact [lʼæm]), and [ðə tʃöLʼjə] for *dy chooilley* 'every' (in fact [ðə xǫljə], [də xǫljʋ]. For the above reasons the article cannot be used in any serious study of Manx.

3.6.6.2. Carmody Sound Recordings

Much better is the following. In July 1949 Prof. Francis J. Carmody visited Man and recorded on tape material from five native speakers (see above), on the basis of which he published an article 'Spoken Manx' in ZCP XXIV (1954): 58-80 (cf. Carmody 1953). The article takes the form mainly of a brief overview of the morphology of LSM, and the examples he cites are given in his own form of phonetic script and accompanied by a version in standard Manx orthography. In addition to five native speakers he interviews a non-native speaker and makes use of his material. Leaving this aside, and so far as it goes, Carmody's contribution gives a fairly accurate account of LSM as it then was. As Carmody's informants are also those of Wagner and Jackson (and mostly of the IFC, MM, YCG), there is nothing new in his material that is not in these collections.

3.6.7. Wagner Phonetic Recordings

From the information provided in Davies 1946 (1948) Dr. (afterwards Prof.) Heinrich Wagner, then of the Dublin Institute for Advanced Studies, spent three weeks in Man (two of them with the Celtic scholar Miles Dillon) during the summer of 1950. In section IX of the introduction to vol. 1 of his *Atlas* Wagner comments on his visit:

> [...] I collected a fair amount of material from the remaining native speakers of Manx Gaelic, which is practically dead now (Wagner 1958/I: xxi-xxii).

He views Manx as:

> [...] a Gaelic language which has been influenced in its structure by Britannic Celtic and later by English, in its phonetics and vocabulary also by Norse. It is a very mixed Celtic dialect (Wagner 1958/I: xxii).

Like Marstrander, Wagner noticed distinct differences between the northern and southern dialects and he classified his material accordingly in his *Linguistic Atlas and Survey of Irish Dialects* (cf. Vol. 1 (Wagner 1958) and Vol. 4 (Wagner 1969)). His informants were:

From the North:
1. John Kneen (the Gaaue), Ballaugh Curragh.
2. Harry Boyde, Ballaugh (c/o Mannin Infirmary, Braddan).
3. John Tom Kaighin, Ballagarrett, Bride.
From the South:
1. Mrs. Catherine Watterson, Colby, Rushen.
2. Mrs. Eleanor Karran (1870-1953), Cregneash, Rushen.
3. Ned Maddrell, Glenchass, Rushen.

He adds:

> [...]. All these informants belong to the rural population of the island (Wagner 1958/I: xxii).

Contrary to the general layout of the *Atlas*, in which the material gathered from various points is arranged according to a 1175-item questionnaire (with or without additional vocabulary and texts), the Manx material (point 88) appears in alphabetical order under English headwords. Wagner told me (1982) that this arrangement was decided upon, as he had difficulty applying the questionnaire owing to the imperfect memory of his informants. The material is presented in sentence form, thus giving the realisation of each word as it naturally appears in connected speech. But the individual lexical items would need to be marshalled into some sort of order before any phonological study could be made of them.

There are one or two curious phrases in the collection that deviate from the norm, e.g. [tɒ lɑːm lʹeʃ ɛrə 'vaːnjəlN 'there is a lot of froth on the milk', with [lɑːm] probably for [rɑːm] *ram* 'a lot' and [lʹeʃ] for [keʃ] *kesh* 'froth', with [lʹ] likely influenced from [l] in [lɑːm]. But as Wagner put it (Wagner 1958/I: xxii):

> [...] The pronunciation of our informants was mostly unclear and therefore an accurate acoustic reception was seldom forthcoming. Our phonetic notations must be used with great care. In how far our material is "corrupted" is hard to say (cf. also Jackson op. cit. [Jackson 1955] 3 s.)[...] (Wagner 1958/I: xxii).

Nevertheless, in spite of some odd forms, Wagner's material contains vocabulary and idiom not encountered on the sound-recordings, or even in other collections, and is therefore of substantial value (cf. also Wagner 1956 & 1959a).

3.6.8. Jackson Phonetic Recordings

Prompted by Wagner's visit to Man some months earlier Prof. Kenneth Jackson of the Dept. of Celtic Studies, University of Edinburgh, spent a period of a fortnight during the Christmas and New Year of 1950-51 in Man and collected material from the following speakers (the comments in smaller print are those of Jackson (cf. Jackson 1955: 2, 3)):

From the South-West
1. Mrs. Eleanor Karran, Cregneash, Rushen
About 80. She was my chief source, with whom I worked right through the questionnaire (Jackson 1955: 2).
2. Ned Maddrell, Glenchass, Rushen. Aged 72.
3. Mrs [Catherine] Watterson, Colby, Rushen. Aged 91.
4. Tommy Leece, Kerroomooar, Kerrookeil, Arbory.
Aged 91. A very good speaker, from whom I got some valuable material. He remembered an old woman living next door about 80 years ago who spoke no English.
From the North
1. Harry Boyde, Ballaugh.
[...] now in the [Mannin] Infirmary, Douglas [i.e. Braddan]. Aged 82. Blind. Another very good speaker, who was most useful.
2. John Kneen [the Gaaue], Ballaugh. Aged 97.
3. John Tom Kaighin, Ballagarrett, Bride. Aged 89. Blind.

Jackson was apparently unable to visit Thomas Karran (brother to Mrs. Eleanor Karran), and John Dan & Mrs. Sage Kinvig. He noted that Mrs. Kinvig could read Manx (Jackson 1955: 2, 3).

Jackson's visit to Man, as he himself says (Jackson 1955: v), was made under the auspices of the Linguistic Survey of Scotland (LSS; see also §3.5.3.7.above & §3.6.9. below) and was able to justify it as follows:

> Though Man is not part of Scotland, the Manx language is so closely linked to Scottish Gaelic that it may be regarded as an early offshoot of it; or more properly, the two are really comparatively recently formed dialects of a common Eastern Gaelic ancestor [cf. here Jackson 1951]. Hence the great importance of Manx for any historical study of Scottish Gaelic, and the interest of the Linguistic Survey in it (Jackson: 1955: v).

With regard to the above speakers Jackson made the following comments:

> Some of the above are a good deal more fluent than others, but all have long ceased to use Manx as their daily medium of intercourse, mostly for many years, though the efforts of the new generation of Manx students have caused them to rub some of the rust off more recently. Hence they frequently forget, especially since in addition they are almost all very old, and it was often impossible therefore for me to get anything like all the words and phrases I asked for. Thus some would often know a singular but not its plural, and so on, and would be unable to give the Manx for the commonest things. In addition it is probable that their Manx pronunciations have been considerably influenced by English, as is only to be expected now that Manx is no longer used in daily conversation, and is only more or less dimly remembered by a handful of people who have regularly spoken nothing but English for years. This appears to account for one aspect of the treatment of *r*-sounds (see p. 18), and may also explain a number of other features in the speech of these people which appear un-Gaelic. The uncorrupted fluent Manx which was still available to Marstrander exists no longer in its purity[20] (Jackson 1955: 3, 4).

On his return to Edinburgh Jackson was able to make the following notes of his visit:

> I took with me a questionnaire already prepared to cover the phonology of Manx from a historical point of view, but circumstances prevented my collecting information quite as complete as I could have wished (hence the qualified title of this book). Some of the words and forms in the questionnaire were not known to my informants (cf. p. 3); for instance, where a genitive was included to illustrate attenuation, they could very rarely give anything but the nominative.[21] Only two speakers had any real fund of continuous narrative material, in the form of little anecdotes or verses; and the inaccessibility of their homes, the number of distracting casual visitors present, and the fact that of the two one is blind and the other very old, made in their case an insuperable barrier to the accurate recording of phonetic texts other than single words and brief phrases. Unluckily the youngest and much the most fluent and alert of the surviving speakers, Mr. Maddrell, was in hospital until the last day of my stay, when I got some very valuable material from him.
>
> In spite of these difficulties, I was able to make use of seven of the ten remaining native speakers of Manx, and to get quite enough matter recorded in phonetic script to constitute a pretty complete picture of the outlines of the phonology of present-day spoken Manx (Jackson 1955: v, vi).

Jackson's material, printed in his *Contributions to the Study of Manx Phonology* (Jackson 1955), largely consists of individual lexical items drawn up under various phonological headings, thus giving the development of a particular sound in 'Common Gaelic' (cf. Jackson 1951) into its Manx reflex. But the lack of prose pieces makes it difficult to assess the reali-

---

[20] It is not certain what Jackson meant here by "uncorrupted" and "purity". Presumably he felt that Marstrander's informants had a firmer command of Manx than his. However, a perusal of Section 4 will reveal that the Manx of Marstrander's informants also had its imperfections.

[21] This is because the genitive (and other cases) had even by the Classical Manx period of the late 18th century ceased to exist as a separate constituent case form, except in nominal and fossilised phrases (cf. Thomson 1969a: 194-201; Broderick 1991: 66-79).

74

sation of each lexical item as it occurs in connected speech. His organisation of the material is in fact the opposite to that of Wagner. In view of the abundance of native Manx speech material now available, Jackson's view (Jackson 1955: 4) that claims for North/South dialectal differences do not stand up to examination cannot be endorsed.

The timing of his visit to Man over the Christmas and New Year period when people visit each other and when bad weather may prevent accessibility to remoter areas, and the fact that probably his best informant Ned Maddrell was indisposed (in hospital) till the last day of his visit (cf. above) was perhaps not conducive to obtaining as complete a picture as one may have desired. It is unfortunate that Jackson was not able to return to Man shortly after, even if only to work through the questionnaire with Ned Maddrell, a task that was to be left to LSS to attempt more than 20 years later in 1972 (see below).

Jackson's main informant, as he himself says (Jackson 1955: 2), was Mrs. Eleanor Karran of Cregneash, with whom he worked right through the questionnaire. For one reason or another (cf. above) he was not able to do the same with his other informants.[22] Consequently they only play a supporting role with the relatively small amount of information they provide. His phonology therefore is essentially descriptive of the southern (Cregneash) dialect of Manx with additional information from other parts. Nevertheless, Jackson's phonology of Manx provides a valuable insight into the sound system of Late Manx and as such is a pioneering work in Gaelic diachronic phonology (see also §3.2.3. above).

3.6.9. Linguistic Survey of Scotland Sound Recordings

In August 1972 Jackson sent David Clement of the Linguistic Survey of Scotland (LSS) to interview Ned Maddrell, by then the last of the native Manx speakers. The material collected by Clement exists on four polyethylene tapes (cf. above) recorded on an Uher Report 4000 machine. The first recording session took place on Thursday 17 August 1972 in Ned Maddrell's house in Glenchass near Port St. Mary. Present at the recording session were Clement, Walter Clarke of the Manx Museum, and myself. Our visit took place three days before Maddrell's 95th birthday, and on this the only occasion I met him he had white hair and a short white beard, and had some difficulty seeing. His diction was perfectly clear and he was more than willing to help us. However, he had quite some difficulty hearing, and once or twice the interview had to be interrupted by contributions from Walter Clarke (who knew Maddrell well) to enable Maddrell to tell one or two short stories and to regain his composure. Nevertheless, the information elicited included a number of lexical items sought through a questionnaire similar to that used by Jackson with Mrs. Eleanor Karran more than 20 years before. Some short stories and anecdotes were also collected. It is clear from the material elicited that Maddrell knew a lot more Manx than the IFC, MM, and YCG recordings

---

[22] Manx enthusiast and former Manx Museum employee Walter Clarke, who was assigned to accompany Jackson this day, told me some years ago that when they went to visit the Gaaue (John Kneen) in Ballaugh Curragh Jackson began his interview by speaking to Kneen in Manx, which Kneen apparently had difficulty in understanding owing to Jackson's middle class English accent. Clarke added that Jackson in turn had considerable difficulty in understanding Kneen, who by that time was 98 years old and had few teeth, and after about twenty minutes or so broke off the interview as a fruitless exercise. Nevertheless, Jackson was able to get some useful material from Kneen.

imply (even though there Maddrell is alert and fluent). Had he been systematically worked on much earlier it is very probable that much more material from him would have been available to us for analysis. Clement returned to Maddrell the following day on his own and obtained additional material, some of it in English. Clement came again to Man the following year (in August 1973) to seek to obtain more material from Maddrell. However, by that time Maddrell's hearing had deteriorated to such an extent that an interview was hopeless. Nothing was obtained from him.[23]

The other informant recorded by the LSS in 1972 was Ewan Christian of Peel, an energetic 65-year old. The first recording session took place in his house at 58 Patrick Street, Peel, on Thursday 24 August 1972, with David Clement of LSS, Christian's close friend Lewis Crellin of Peel, and myself. Ewan Christian was chosen as a subject, as (Ned Maddrell apart) he was the only other person in the Isle of Man, so far as we knew, who had learned Manx at an early date. He told us he first learned Manx from two old ladies in the same street when he was about five years old, and later from farmers and fishermen in and around Peel. He admitted to us that he had also gone to Caesar Cashen's Manx classes that were held in Peel before the Second World War. In the recording sessions Jackson's questionnaire was not used because it became clear that Clement was beginning to experience the same problems Jackson had had earlier with fuller speakers. (cf. above). Instead Christian would reel off *stante pede* the Manx names of various birds and fish, sometimes giving the Peel variant. The information was elicited mainly by Lewis Crellin who knew what Christian could offer. Without being asked Christian would relate a couple of stories in Manx about incidents in and around Peel. He was also literate in Manx and could recite long passages from the Manx Bible. One suspects that some of his vocabulary was derived from literary sources, and at times his grammar was somewhat shaky, due either to lack of practice or to imperfect learning. Nevertheless, it was quite clear from his pronunciation that he had learned his Manx from native speakers at an early date in his life, and in that respect his contribution is valuable. Christian was apparently great friends with Ned Maddrell, and he told us that they would visit each other fairly regularly.

3.6.10. Broderick Sound and Phonetic Recordings

I myself made two tape recordings of Ewan Christian in May and August 1978, and visited him on occasions after that to make some notes in phonetic script till 1983. The material collected was similar to that of LSS, with additional vocabulary plus some traditional songs and chants in English. In the context of the foregoing my recordings here can only be regarded as complementary.

On 27 December 1974 Ned Maddrell died and now lies buried in Rushen parish churchyard. As with others I attended his funeral at which not a word of Manx was uttered or sung. This I

---

[23] Ned Maddrell was by far the 'youngest' of the native speakers recorded, and he was exceptional in that most of his contemporaries of his generation were brought up without Manx. Maddrell told us when we visited him 17.08.1972 that he was born at the Corvalley, about a mile NE of Cregneash, and because of the size of his family was farmed out to relatives when he was about two and a half years' old to be brought up by an old aunt, Paaie Humman (Margaret Taubman) in Cregneash who had little or no English.

understand was the wish of his immediate family, though I suspect not his. With Ned Maddrell's death native Manx Gaelic speech passed into history.

The semi-speaker Ewan Christian died in the White Hoe Hospital, Douglas, in mid-January 1985, aged 78.[24]

---

[24] One small problem encountered by interviewers was the attitude of the informant's relations to Manx and the collecting of it. The story is told of a visit one Sunday to record John Kneen who was then living with two daughters. When the interviewers arrived one of the daughters put on a record of 1920s music, which apparently elicited a giggle from one of the interviewers. This was seemingly taken as a comment by the daughter on her favourite music, whereupon the interviewers were asked to leave immediately without recording a word from Kneen. Apparently it took an amount of diplomatic skill on the part of one of their company to persuade the daughters to allow them to return on a subsequent occasion.

Towards the end Ned Maddrell, after a good Manx speaking session with enthusiasts or a successful interview with academics, would allegedly become moody after the excitement of the visit and 'take it out' on his daughter then living with him. In the end, to avoid further unpleasantness, the daughter apparently discouraged any further Manx visits.

It is said that similar experiences were encountered from Ewan Christian's lady friend in Peel (who apparently had learned Manx and taught it in local classes) with whom he was then living (late 70s till his death), as she apparently had to suffer moodiness from Christian after a Manx visit. I personally did not encounter this problem at all.

4. The Formal Linguistic Development of Manx

4.1. Introduction

Manx is a VSO and an Insular-Celtic language. Insular Celtic is divided into two branches: Goidelic (comprising Irish, Scottish Gaelic, and Manx), and Brittonic (Welsh, Cornish, and Breton).[1] Manx is a descendant of Old Irish and ran parallel with Irish until the thirteenth century and with Scottish Gaelic until the fifteenth century (cf. Jackson 1951). Thereafter the evolution of Manx became more progressive in its development from a synthetic to an analytic type, while at the same time preserving archaisms from the Old Irish period, lost in other branches of Gaelic (cf. Thomson 1983).[2] The social and political factors which cut off Manx from its sister dialects (cf. Section 2) helped this more progressive evolution which made available a variety of alternative constructions and innovations, e.g. in the verbal system (cf. Thomson 1950-51, Broderick 1993: 248-60) and nominal and case system (cf. Thomson 1969a: 194-202; Broderick 1991: 66-74) which had taken place by the late 18th century, but which do not entirely displace the old. For the purpose of our study here three periods of Manx are distinguished:

1. EM: Early Manx - 17th century; essentially that of the Manannan or Traditional Ballad (MB ca.1500; cf. Thomson 1961-62) and Bishop John Phillips' Manx Gaelic translation of the Anglican Book of Common Prayer (PB ca.1610; cf. Moore & Rhys 1893-94, Thomson 1954-57).[3]
2. CM: Classical Manx - 18th century; essentially that of the Manx Bible translation (1744-75) and various tracts, sermons, and traditional song texts (cf. Thomson 1969a).
3. LM: Late Manx - 19th/20th centuries; essentially that of the stories of Ned Beg Hom Ruy (1831-1908; cf. Broderick 1981-82) and the native speakers (ca. 1840-1974; cf. Broderick 1984-86). The period of language death falls within the latter phase of the native speakers.

One of the first to discuss in some detail aspects of phonology in a decaying Celtic language (Breton) is Wolfgang Dressler in his article *On the Phonology of Language Death* (Dressler 1972b). Here he prefixes his study with the comment:

---

[1] For an overview of the various branches of Celtic and their linguistic components, cf. Russell 1995.

[2] Such archaisms would include: Mx. *lhisagh* 'ought', OIr. *dless-*, subjunctive stem of *dligid* 'is entitled to, deserves', in MIr. 'ought, is bound to' (DIL: D 160-62), cf. Thomson (1983: 171, HLSM/II: 275 s.v. *lhisagh*; Mx. *cha b'loys* 'would not dare', viz. *cha* 'not' + *b* (past tense of copula) + *lámhas* (pret. paasive of OIr. *ro-laumur* 'I dare', or + fut. rel. *lamas* (cf. HLSM/II: 63 s.v. *cha b'loys*).

[3] Though this work serves as a good example of 17th century Manx, it must be borne in mind that Bishop John Phillips was not a native Manx, but a native Welsh speaker (from North Wales). However, he would almost certainly have been assisted in the task of translation by his assistant, probably Hugh Cannell (a native Manx speaker), vicar of Kirk Michael and his nearest neighbour at Bishop's Court (seat of the bishopric of Sodor and Man) (cf. Thomson 1969a: 180-81).

From time immemorial language death has been viewed as an extreme case of language contact. The victorious language slowly replaces the dying language, and in this process the phonology of one language adjusts to the phonology of the other one: these are the classical cases of substratum and superstratum influence. So language death would boil down to the borrowing of items (e.g. Petrovici 1967, Keller 1968) and of rules (Hamp 1968, 1970), and to the loss of those rules and items in the dying language which have no counterparts in the victorious language (cf. [...] Silverstein 1971) (Dressler 1972b: 448).

But then poses the question:

[...] If the dying language has, e.g. 5 phonological rules which have no counterparts in the victorious language, are all 5 rules lost at the same time? If not, how could we predict which one is lost first, and which is the last one to be lost? Is there any rule governed hierarchy in the degradation of linguistic competence? This is distinct from borrowing phenomena (Dressler 1972b: 448).

In his study of the dialect of Buhulien near Lannion (Trégorrois area) in the north-eastern Breton-speaking part of Lower Britanny Dressler discusses the Breton initial mutations of lenition (voices unvoiced initial stops and spirants and spirantised voiced non-continuants), provection (unvoices voiced stops and spirants), and spirantisation (spirantises voiceless stops) and the frequency of their use by older and younger generations alike. With the younger generation he noted that "some or all of the mutations are lost" (Dressler 1972b: 449), to explain which he introduces the term "lexical fading", whereby:

A rule is slowly dropped by successively withdrawing words from its imput [...]. This principle [...] applies to Breton mutations in two ways: There are specific words whose initial consonants are mutated, in contrast to other words, e.g. ['paːrus] 'parish' is a resistant word, whose initial consonant is often spirantized by youngsters who otherwise have replaced spirantization with lenition. They may say [ma 'vaːrus] 'my parish' with spirantization, but [ma 'bɛnː] 'my head' with lenition from /maS pɛnː/ (Dressler 1972b: 452).

And if a rule is optional with the older generation, so argues Dressler (*ibid*: 452), it is lost with the younger generation[4]:

So we may formulate the following hypothetical principle of language death: If a rule is optional with the older generation which has a full and varied command of a still vigorous language system, it is lost in the disintegrating language of a younger generation (Dressler 1972b: 452).

From his experience with the Breton mutations in Buhulien Dressler (*ibid*: 453) argues that "lexical fading" may progress very slowly at the beginning, then an initial minor loss may expand very rapidly to a major loss:

i.e. the major rule remains a major rule for a long time with a slowly increasing number of exceptions, and then suddenly it shrinks rather rapidly into a minor rule (Dressler 1972b: 453).

---

4   However, Hennessey (1990: 212) has argued that such changes may not necessarily have anything to do with language death at all, since evidence can be produced to show lenition after numerals attested in Breton as early as 1710, and that change of mutation in numerals can be dated from at least the 1870s, if not earlier. Nevertheless, given that Dressler's sample shows generation-, and not solely dialect-based divergencies, in this case these seem to be symptomatic of language death, rather than a result of earlier internal development.

Finally, Dressler remarks that in a disintegrating language, "characterised by fluctuations and uncertainties of its speakers" (Dressler 1972b: 454), free variation in its phonology increases, which often renders perception difficult. This, says Dressler,

> is due to the restriction of the use of the decaying language to ever fewer speech situations and to generalization of the styles used in these situations (Dressler 1972b: 455).

The situation of Manx is slightly different in that it is not possible to make a contrast between older and younger generations of native speakers, since all native speakers of Manx, whether full or semi, have now passed on. It may have been possible at one time. However, the methods of linguistic research now in use were then not in place. In addition, the system of initial mutation in Manx is different from that of Breton. Nevertheless, it is possible to make some comparisons (see below).

In her assessment of language death in East Sutherland Gaelic (ESG) Nancy Dorian (Dorian 1981b) examines the application or otherwise of initial mutation (of labial or velar stops) in determining gender and case in the nominal system. For gender she found a gradual-to-marked reduction in application of mutation: (for nasalisation[5] in masculine nouns after the definite article) with Older Fluent Speakers (OFS) 100%, Younger Fluent Speakers (YFS) 87.5%, and with Semi-Speakers (SS) 61%; (for lenition in feminine nouns) with OFSs 100%, YFSs 92%, and SSs 38% (Dorian 1981b: 126). A similar falling-off in the application of initial mutations was also found in attributive adjectives (*ibid*: 127-28), though here SSs lenited adjectives for both genders (i.e. an "abuse" or hypercorrect use of lenition occurred in the masculine of adjectives (cf. §4.2.4.3.)). In addition the following morphological developments were also noted:

1. generalisation of the masculine pronoun for all nouns (Dorian 1981b: 124-25),
2. loss of the inflected genitive in ESG; possession expressed instead by a prepositional phrase (Dorian 1981b: 130),
3. reduction of the appropriate initial mutation in the dative, or prepositional case, except in some fossilised phrases (Dorian 1981b: 131-33),
4. loss of initial lenition and final mutation (i.e. palatalisation of final -s) in the vocative (Dorian 1981b: 134-35),
5. marked movement in simplification in the nominal system, i.e. 67% of SSs use the simple plural suffix /ən/ (Dorian 1981b: 136),
6. confusion in the application or otherwise of lenition in the tenses of the verb: application of lenition in the (inflected) future tense, and failure of lenition in the conditional (Dorian 1981b: 139), or other tenses given for conditional, or outright loss of the conditional (Dorian 1981b: 140),
7. loss of number in the verbal system (Dorian 1981b: 141-42), imperative sg. and pl. fall together (homonomy) when no suffix is applied (Dorian 1981b: 142),
8. confusion in application of various forms of the periphrastic passive (Dorian 1981b: 143-44),
9. ESG lexical items linger on longer after language dies out (Dorian 1981b: 146).

As with Dressler (cf. above), Dorian was able to work with speakers of varying competence and age, and thus able to show the varying degrees of language change or decay from one set

---

[5]   For a definition of the terms Nasalisation and Lenition in Goidelic, cf. §4.3.

of speakers to the next, or even within the group as a whole (e.g. the loss of the genitive right across the board; cf. Dorian 1981b: 147). Nevertheless, when one compares the situation with Late Manx (where it will be seen that the onset of decay is much more advanced), attrition in ESG is much less marked, and Dorian's assertion "that none of the major grammatical changes under way in ESG has a conditioned phonetic basis" (Dorian 1981b: 152) may well apply to ESG (where "the noun plural is [...] the grammatical category which shows *least* change between fluent speakers and SSs" (*ibid*: 152, note 39)). But in LM, as will be seen (cf. §4.3.), the opposite is the case simply because the amount of decline and decay is greater. Manx Gaelic was in full flow and vibrancy up until the Classical Manx period at least, and we shall take this as our starting point on our excursion into language death in Man.

4.2. Phonology

4.2.1. The vowel phonemes of Classical Manx

The vowel system of CM includes long and short vowels and diphthongs which can be sketched as follows:

Figure 4: *The vowel phonemes of Classical Manx* (cf. also Thomson 1984b: 316).

```
/i(:)                                                          u(:)
        e:                        ə(:)                o:
                ɛ(:)                      ɔ(:)
                        a(:)/
```

Long vowels and diphthongs are confined to stressed syllables and original long vowels in unstressed syllables have become short or indeterminate (Thomson 1984b: 315, HLSM/III: 122ff.). All vowels can be long or short, with the exception of /e/ and /o/ which (apart from occasional shortening) are long.

The vowels /a/, /ɛ/, /ə/ can form both *i*- and *u*-diphthongs, /ɔ/, /u/ only *i*-diphthongs, while /i/ and /u/ can form ə-diphthongs. These last are later developments resulting from the weakening or vocalisation of /r/, e.g. /mi:r/ 'morsel' -> /mi:ə/, /mu:r/ 'big' -> /mu:ə/. Except in monosyllables before /l/, /r/, the *i*- and *u*-diphthongs result from the vocalisation of palatal and labial (occasionally dental) spirants, viz./gra:i/, /grɛi/ cf. Gaelic (Ir./ScG.) *gráidh* 'love', /lau/ G. *lámh* 'hand'. The diphthongs /iə/ and /uə/ can be subject to monophthongisation, e.g. /biəl/ -> /bi:l/ 'mouth' G. *béal*, /ku:əg/ -> /ko:g/ 'cuckoo' G. *cuthag*. Quite often in Mx. the first element of a diphthong can be long, cf. /gra:i/ above.

4.2.2. Destabilisation of the vowel phonemes in Late Manx

However, in LM the more the language fell into disuse the greater the uncertainty and consequent destabilisation in the realisation of the phonemes. This resulted in a wider range of allophones for each phoneme than was formerly the case, and to an extent an overlapping of allophonic variants between the phonemes. In addition the separate phonemes in CM of /e:/
and /ɛ:/, /o:/ and /ɔ:/ fall together and appear in LM as /e:/ and /o:/ respectively (cf.
HLSM/III: 50-52, 54-56).

4.2.2.1. Free variation of allophones (=wild allophonic variation)

The wild allomorphy in LM may be partially due to the various transcription systems used
in the collection and analysis of Late Manx material, i.e. those of Marstrander, Wagner,
Jackson, and myself (cf. HLSM/III: xxxiii), though every effort has been made to regularise
them to conform to the system used in HLSM/III and here. Nevertheless, free variation
(including the introduction of new variants), as Dressler also noted (Dressler 1972b: 454-55),
is a symptom of language death.

4.2.2.1.1. The short vowels

The range of possibilities for each of the short vowels is as follows (the first ex. in the list
would repr. the usual pron.) (cf. HLSM/III: 35ff., Broderick 1993: 231ff.):

1. /i/ = [ɪ], [i] varying freely with /i:/, /e(:)/, /a/, particularly in stressed monosyllables or
initially stressed syllables of polysyllables:
cleaysh /kl[i]s´/, /kl[ø:]s´/, /kl[e:]s´/ 'ear' G. *cluas, cluais.*
cheet /t´[ɪ]t/, /t´[ɛ]t/, /t´[e]t/, /t´[ø]t/ 'coming' G. *tidheacht.*
greimey /gr[ɪ]mə/, /gr[i:]mə/, /gr[a]mə/ 'gripping' G. *greimeadh.*

2. /e/ = [e], [ȩ], [ɛ], varying freely with /u/, /ə/, /ɛ:/, /i/, /a/ in stressed monosyllables or
in initial position:
ben /b[e]n/, b[ȩ]n, /b[ɛ]n/ 'woman' G. *bean.*
Gailck /g[e]lk/, /g[i]lk/ 'Manx Gaelic' MIr. *Gaidilg.*
bentyn /b[ɛ]ntən/, /b[ȩ]ntən/, /b[a]ntən/ 'touching' G. *beantainn.*

3. /a/ = [a], [æ], [ɑ]. In stressed or unstressed initial syllables there may be free variation
with /o/, /e/, /i/, /ə/ especially in the environment of laterals and nasals, or before /x/, and
/a(:)/ and /u/:
chiass /t´[a]s/, [t´[æ]s/ 'heat' G. *teas.*
chiollagh /t´[ɔ]lax/, /t´[a]lax/ 'hearth' G. *teallach.* Here w. /o/ infl. from /l/.
anmagh /[a]mənax/, /[ɪ]mnax/, [ɛ]mnax/, /[ɔ]nmax/ 'late' G. *anmoch.*
fammynagh /f[æ]mərax/, f[ø]mərax/ 'seaweed' G. *feamnach.*
clashtyn /kl[a]s´t´ən/, /kl[a:]ʃt´ən/ 'hearing' G. *claisteann.*

4. /o/ = [o], [ǫ], [ɔ], [ɒ], [ɑ]. In initial position or in stressed monosyllables there may be free variation with /e/:

goll /g[o]l/, /g[ǫ]l/, /g[ɔ]l/, /g[ɑ]l/ 'going' cf. G. *dol.*

fod /f[ǫ]d/, /f[ɛ]d/ 'can' G. *faod.*

5. /u/ is normally advanced and poorly rounded. Sometimes there is [ǫ] or [y], varying with /o/:

punt /p[u]nt/, /p[ǫ]nt/ 'pound' G. *púnt.*

sliught /ʃ´[ǫ]x(t)/, /ʃl[y]x/ 'progeny' G. *sliocht.*

shassoo /ʃɑːs[u]/, /ʃaːs[o]/ 'standing' G. *seasamh.*

6. /ə/: [ə] usually in unstressed position. Sometimes [ɪ] after palatal. /l/, /n/. May vary freely with /i/, /e/, /a/, /o/.

carrane /k[ə]'rɛːn/ 'sandal' G. *cuarán.*

balley /baːl'[ə]/, /baːl´[ɪ]/ 'town' G. *baile.*

dooinney /dun´[ə]/, /dun´[ɪ]/ 'man' G. *duine.*

argid /aːrg[ə]d´/, /aːrg[i]d/ 'money' G. *airgead, airgid.*

faasaag /f[ə]'seːɡ/, /f[ɛ]'seːɡ/ 'beard' G. *féasóg.*

faagail /f[ə]'geːl´/, /f[a]'geːl´/ 'leaving' G. *fágáil.*

buggane /b[ə]'geːn/, /b[o]'geːn/ 'sprite' G. *bócán.*

4.2.2.1.2. The long vowels

As for the short vowel phonemes we have a wide range of allophonic variance:

1. /iː/ = [iː], [ɪː]. Also in free variation with /i/, /eː/, /uː/, /ei/, /ai/, /iə/:

freayl /fr[iː]l´/, /fr[uː]l´/ 'keeping' G. *friotháil.*

geayl /g[iː]l/, /g[i]l/, g[u]l/, /g[y]l/, /g[øː]l/, /g[u]l/ 'coal' G. *gual.*

cloie /kl[iː]/, /kl[ɛi]/, /kl[ai]/ 'play' G. *cluich.*

beeal /b[iː]l/, /b[iə]l/ 'mouth' G. *béal.*

2. /aː/ = [aː], [ɑː], in free variation with /a/, /e(ː)/, /ai/:

niart /nj[aː]t/, /nj[ɑː]t/ 'strength' G. *neart.*

argid /[aː]gəd/, /[ęː)gəd/ 'money' G. *airgead.*

aile /[aː]l´/, /[ai]l´/ 'fire' G. *aingeal.*

3. /uː/ as with /u/ is normally advanced and poorly rounded in its articulation. It may be realised as [yː], [øu], and vary freely in stressed monosyllables or initial stressed syllables with /u/, /o(ː)/, /i(ː)/, /eu/, /au/:

doo /d[uː]/, /d[yː]/, /d[øu]/ 'black' G. *dubh.*

oor /[uː]r/, /[oː]r/ 'fresh' G. *úr.*

liurid /lj[uː]rid/, /lj[u]rid/ 'length' G. OIr. *libra* w. *-id.*

liorish /lj[uː]riʃ´/, /lj[ɔː]riʃ´/, /lj[ɔ]riʃ´ 'by' G. *láimh ris.*

jiu /d´[uː]/, /d´[øu]/, /d´[ɡu]/ 'today' G. *an diugh.*

4.2.2.1.3. Merging of the earlier phonemes /e:/ and /ɛ:/, /o:/ and /ɔ:/

4.2.2.1.3.1. /e:/ and /ɛ:/

Some lexical items demonstrate more close realisations, others more open. The former suggest an original distinction between /e:/ and /ɛ:/, now merged or fallen together in LM as one phoneme. Under more constrained conditions the following minimal pair may have applied:

1. *eash* */e:s´/ 'age' G. *aois* : *aash* */ɛ:s´/ 'rest' G. *áis*,
now realised in LM as:
eash /[ẹ:]s´/, /[i:]s´/ (HLSM/II: 140 s.v. *eash*)
aash /[ẹ:]s´/, /[ɛ:]s´/ (HLSM/II: 2 s.v. *aash*).

2. *breag* */bre:g/ 'lie' G. *bréag, breug* : *braag* */brɛ:g/ 'shoe' G. *bróg*
now hopelessly mixed in LM as:
breagyn 'lies' /br[ẹ:]gən/, /br[ɛ:]gən/ G. *breugan* (HLSM/II: 44 s.v. *breag*)
braagyn 'shoes' /br[ɛ:]gən/, /br[e:]gən/ G. *brògan* (HLSM/II: 41 s.v. *braagyn*).
For G. /o:/ in Mx. as /ɛ:/, cf. Jackson (1955:41), HLSM/III: 134).

In stressed monosyllables and initial stressed syllables there may be free variation as follows:
with [e:] and [ɛ:]: *eayst* /[ẹ:]s/, /[e:]s/, /[ẹ:]s/, /[ɛ:]s/ 'moon' OIr. *ésca*.
with /e:/ and /o:/: *laa* /l[ɛ:]/, /l[e:]/, l[ø:]/, /l[ọ:ə]/ 'day' G. *lá*.
aalin /[ɛ:]lin´/, /[ø:]lin´/, /[ɑ:]lin´/ 'fine, beautiful' G. *áluinn* (cf. HLSM/III: 50-52).
with /e(:)/ and /i/: *eaddagh* /[e:]dax/, /[e]dax/, /[i]dax/ 'clothing' G. *éadach*.

4.2.2.1.3.2. /o:/ and /ɔ:/

As with original /e:/ and /ɛ:/ more close realisations are restricted to some and more open to other items, suggesting two former contrasting phonemes /o:/ and /ɔ:/ that could have given the following near minimal pair:
boayl */bo:l/ 'place, spot' G. *ball* : *Boaldyn* */bɔ: ldən/ 'May' G. *Bealltuinn*.
now realised as:
boayl /b[o:]l/, /b[ɔ:]l/, b[ọ:]l/, b[ɔ:]l/
Boaldyn /b[ɔ:]ldən/, /b[ɑ:]ldən/, though both orig. /a/ + /l/.
In stressed monosyllables and initial stressed syllables there may be free variation with /o/, /u:/, and /e:/ before original /r/:
loayrt /[ɔ:](r)t/, /l[ɛ:]t/, /l[ọ:]t/, /l[ʌ:]t/ 'talking' G. *labhairt*.
boayrd /b[ø:]rd/, /v[ŏ:]rd/ (len. form), /b[y:]rd/ 'table' G. *bord*.
purt /p[ọ:]t/, /f[u:]rt/ (len. form) 'harbour' G. *port*.

As can bee seen from the above, the phonemic instability as occasioned by the wild allomorphy would have had rendered any accurate perception difficult (cf. also Dressler 1972b: 455).

4.2.3. The consonant phonemes of Classical Manx

It will be noted from the table below that the palatalised variants of the consonants in CM (with perhaps the exception of the labials), so far as we are able to establish, are intact. In LM, as we shall see, there is a general trend towards loss of palatalisation as a general charactistic of language change in Man, which took place long before the onset of any instability in the consonants of LM. The consonant phonemes of Classical Manx may be illustrated as follows:

Figure 5: *The consonant phonemes of Classical Manx* (cf. Thomson 1984b: 314; Broderick 1993: 234):

	Labial	Dental	Velar	Glottal
Voiceless stops	p [p´]	t t´	k k´	
Voiced stops	b [b´]	d d´	g g´	
Voiceless fricatives	f [f´]	s s´	x x´	h h´
Voiced fricatives v [v´]			ɣ ɣ´	
Voiced laterals		l l´		
Vibrants		r r´		
Voiced nasals	m [m´]	n n´	ŋ ŋ´	
Semivowels	w	j		

As can be seen the consonant system demonstrates an opposition between neutral and palatal articulation in the stops, fricatives, and voiced nasals, though the contrast (with perhaps the occasional exception; hence given here in square brackets as allophones of their non-palatalised counterparts) is lost in the labials.[6] Also most consonants exhibit a contrast between voiceless and voiced, and stop and fricative articulation.

The four-way system in the Old Irish resonants /L, N, R/ involved a double phonemic contrast as follows:

(a) neutral-palatalised: /L : L´, l : l´, N : N´, n : n´, R : R´, r : r´/
                    [L : L´, l : l´, N : N´, n : n´, R : R´, r : r´]

(b) fortis-lenis: /L : l, L´ : l´, N : n, N´ : n´, R : r, R´ : r´/
           [L : l, L´ : l´, N : n, N´ : n´, R : r, R´ : r´]

This developed into a two-way system in CM for /L, N, R/, viz./l: l´, n: n´, r: r´/ (cf. Thomson 1984b: 314), i.e. their uvular and velar manner of articulation changed to a dental and alveolar articulation, giving rise to a simplified two-way resonant system in CM, in which the old /L, N, R/ were lost.

---

[6] For palatalisation of labials in Scottish Gaelic, cf. Oftedal 1963 and MacAulay 1966; for the same in Gaelic in general, cf. Jackson 1967.

Original /θ/ and /ð/ fell in or merged with /h/ and /ɣ/ (both neutral and palatal) respectively. However, since the latter part of the 18th century there has been a tendency to make lenis single intervocalic voiced stops and fricatives, or to voice single intervocalic voiceless stops. So /b, d, g/ becomes /v, ð, ɣ/ (the latter becoming lost altogether), and /p, t, k/ becomes /b, d, g/. In addition, a new [ð] has developed from modified articulation of single /t, d, s/ in intervocalic position, and a voiced variant of /s/, viz. [z] and [z´] from /s´/ or /d´/, and /ɣ/ from /x/.

Palatalised /t´/ and /d´/ are realised as the affricates [tʃ] and [dʒ] respectively.

The distribution of some of the above is restricted as follows:

- /f, v, ð, ɣ, x´/ do not occur in word-final position;

- [ð, z, z´] do not occur initially;

- /ɣ, ŋ, w, v, h/ only appear under conditions of initial mutation (lenition or eclipsis) or in loanwords (see below);

- /h/ sometimes occurs in permanent lenition with no radical alternative, e.g. the negative particle *cha* /ha/ 'not' (cf. Thomson 1984b: 314-15, Broderick 1986, 1993: 234-35).

The earlier initial clusters /kn, gn, tn, dl, tl/ had by the end of the 18th century fallen in with /kr, gr, tr, gl, kl/: G. *cnoc* /knuk/ 'hill' -> Mx. *cronk* /kroŋk/, and /mn/ became /mr/: G.*mnathan* 'women' -> Mx. *mraane* /mreːn/; /kd/ resulting from syncope became /kr/ (cf. Thomson 1984b: 314-15; Broderick 1993: 234-35).

By the beginning of the 18th century original /sr/ had largely fallen in with /str/, viz. G. *sráid* 'street' -> Mx. *straid* /stred/, and medial and final /sk, s´k´/, with one or two exceptions, had fallen in with /st, s´t´/, viz. G. *iascadh* 'fishing' -> Mx. *eeastagh* /jistax/, G. *uisce* 'water' -> Mx. *ushtey* /usət´ə/. Final /t/ after /s/ and /x/ tends to be lost, the former in the 18th the latter as early as the 17th century, though usually preserved in the standard spelling, viz. G. *sliocht* 'progeny' -> Mx. *sliught* /sləux/.

In monosyllables the original length in unlenited /L, N, R. m/ is transferred to the preceding vowel either increasing its length or forming a *u*-diphthong:

- G. *ceann* 'head' /kəaɳ/ -> Mx. *kione* /kəaun/.

Other modifications of the late 18th century include preocclusion, the development of a weak variety of the corresponding voiced stop before final /m/, /n/, and /ŋ/ in stressed monosyllables, generally causing shortening in original long vowels:

- *trome* 'heavy' /troːm/ -> /tro[bm]/, *kione* 'head' /k´oːn, k´aun/ -> /k´o[dn]/, *lhong* 'ship' /loŋ/ -> /lo[gŋ]/.

In addition there is a tendency to replace /g/ with /d/ in proclitics: Mx. *gy* 'that' /gə/ -> *dy* /də/; *gys* 'to' /gəs/ -> *dys* /dəs/; *gyn* 'without' /gən/ -> *dyn* /dən/ (cf. Thomson 1984b: 315, HLSM/III, Broderick 1993: 235-36).

4.2.4. Simplification of consonant phonemes in Late Manx

In contrast to CM we see here partial loss of palatalised variants as part of the process of simplification taking place in LM. The consonant phonemes of Late Manx can be sketched as follows:

Figure 6: *The consonant phonemes of Late Manx* (cf. also HLSM/III: 2).

	Labial	Dental	Velar	Glottal
Voicess stops	p	t t´	k k´	
Voiced stops	b	d d´	g g´	
Voiceless fricatives	f	s s´	x [x´]	h [h´]
Voiced fricatives v			[ɣ], [ɣ´]	
Voiced laterals		l l´		
Vibrant		r [r´]		
Voiced nasals	m	n n´	ŋ [ŋ´]	
Semivowels	w	j		

As can be seen, from the transition from CM to LM, i.e. during the course of the late 18th century and into the 19th century, Mx. had (with one or two scattered examples; cf. HLSM/II: 34 s.v. *blein*) lost its palatal labials. In addition other segments such as the palatalised voiceless velar fricative [x´], the palatalised glottal fricative [h´], both the voiced velar fricatives [ɣ, ɣ´], the palatalised vibrant [r´], and the palatalised voiced velar nasal [ŋ´] (see below) are marked as phonetic variants, since they occur no longer as phonemes in their own right, but as allophones of their respective non-palatalised variants (hence their appearance above in square brackets); in the case of [ɣ(´)] these occur as allophones of /d(´)/ or /g(´)/ (see below). Palatalisation in LM in association with high front vowels is weak, but with back and low front vowels it is quite pronounced as if C + [j]: *king* 'heads' /k´iŋ/ [k´ıŋ] G. *cinn*, but *kione* 'head' /k´o:n/, [kjo:n] G. *ceann* [k´aN]. Manx has developed a tendency towards a glide between the consonant and the back vowel and thereby the consonant has lost its palatal quality.

4.2.4.1. Loss of morphophonemic variation in the consonants of Late Manx

Also there is a loss of morphophonemic variation in that the initial velar stops /k/ and /g/ gradually cease to be lenited to fricatives,[7] but which does not alter the sense or impede understanding, i.e. lenition here has become superfluous.

---

[7]   This may have been in evidence even as early as the late 18th century, as possibly attested in the title of the Manx Bible itself - *Yn Vible Casherick*. Here *Bible* is marked as a fem. noun with len. after the def. art. This would require spirantising of the initial voiceless velar stop in the following adjective, viz. /k/ -> /x/, recognised in the orthography as *Ch-*, viz. *Yn Vible Chasherick* 'the Holy Bible'. In the first edition of the Old Testament (1771) the title runs: *Yn Vible Casherick; ny Yn Chenn Chonaant...* 'the Holy Bible; or the Old Testament...'. We see here that the initial spirant /x/ in *Conaant* (< E. 'covenant') is recognised in the orthography as *Ch-*, but not in *Casherick* (*Conaant* follows the leniting preposed adj. *shenn* 'old'), itself len. after the def. art. (to /t´/), thus marking *Conaant* as a fem. noun). It does not necessarily follow, of course, that omission of *h* in *ch-* indicates loss of the spirant in everyday speech. However, its omission here in the title of a book of this nature is either a misprint, or suggests (as I believe it does) that even by that date (1771) the contrast /x/ : /k/ (and possibly /ɣ/ : /g/, /d/) in initial position was in a state of flux, i.e. its application was optional.

4.2.4.1.1. In initial ch- (/x/, /x´/)

1. Initial /x/ may vary with /h/, /k/, k´/ or is not realised at all, i.e. there is glottalisation of fricatives or loss of friction in a wild distribution in LM (cf. HLSM/III: 21). Compare the following examples:

cha 'not' /[x]a/, /[h]a/, /a/, ScG. *cha*.

cheayll 'heard' /[x]i:l/, /[kʰ]il/, G. *chuala*.

chaie 'went, past' /[x]ai/, /[kh]ai/, /[k´ˤ]ai/, G. *chaith*.

chraa 'shook' /[x]re:/, /[kʰ]re:/, G. *chraith* (though the 'correct' form is *chrie*).

However, still in 1883 Strachan (Strachan 1897: 54-58) recorded (in his own brand of phonetic script) initial /x/ as a lenited form of /k/ in *yn chied* [an x´ed] 'the first' G. *an chéad* (i.e. [x´]), *my chree* [mə 'xri:] 'my heart' G. *mo chroidh*, *cheayl* [xλ1] 'heard' G. *chuala* (i.e. [x]).

In medial position /x/ is sometimes retained as [x] or realised as [ɣ], but also stopped as [g] (cf. HLSM/III: 94).

In final position it is retained as [x] or stopped to /k/ ([k]) (cf. PNIM/I: 143, s.v. *mullagh mooar, mullagh vane*).

2. Initial /x´/ as a lenited form of /k´/ is largely lost in LM, but survives in the following (cf. HLSM/III: 21-22):

my huyr 'my sister' /mə '[x´]u:r/; len. form of /s´/.

my chione 'my head' /mə '[x´]o:n/, len. form of /k´/; also /mə '[k´ˤ]o:n/.

my-mychione 'about me' /məmə'x´odn/ (cf. HLSM/II: 314).

O Hiarn! 'O Lord!' /o '[x´]a:n/; len. of /t´/

da cheilley 'to each other' /de '[x´]elə/, *ry cheilley* 'together' /re ke:l´ə/

(here with failure of both palatalisation and lenition).

In medial and final positions /x´/ is lost early in Manx; cf. HLSM/III: 93-94.

4.2.4.1.2. In initial gh- (G. dh-, gh-) (ɣ, ɣ´)

In initial position neutral *gh-* in LM represents lenition of /d/ and /g/ respectively and is sometimes realised as [ɣ], viz. LM *dy chooilley ghooinney* 'everyone' /də xul´ə '[ɣ]un´ə/, ScG. *a h-uile dhuine* /ə hul´ə 'ɣun´ə/, but is mostly stopped to /g/, viz. /ɣ(´)/ -> /g/, /d/, i.e. loss of the fricative:

1. *ghaa ny tree* : ScG. *dhà na trí* [ɣɑ: nə 'tʰri:]
/[ɣ]anə 'tri:/, /[g]anə}tri:/ HLSM/III: 91-92
'two or three'

2. *cred traa t'eh, dooinney?* : *ghooinney* (G. *a dhuine*)
/krəd 'tre: ti dun´ə/ N/HLSM/I: 250-51
'what time is it, man?'

Initial [ɣ] in *ghooinney* (voc. of *dooinney*) 'man!' can be lost in Mx. and is replaced by prothetic /w/, viz. /wun´ə/.

Initial palatal *gh-* may appear as [ɣ´] before /l´/, viz. *yn ghlion* 'the glen' /ən '[ɣ´]l´odn/, but in LM is also stopped to [g], viz. /ɣ´/ -> /g/ or /j/:

3. *y glion* /ə '[g]oun/'the glen'

4. *my ghuilley* /mə '[j]il´ə/ 'my lad',

more often non-lenited as [g] /mə 'g)il´ə/; cf. HLSM/III: 93, i.e. loss of the fricative. The loss of /ɣ/ and /x/ in initial position is most likely to be attributed in late speakers to the absence of these two phonemes in English. In Mx. internal and final neutral and palatal *gh* are lost early; cf. HLSM/III: 92.

4.2.4.1.3. In initial palatalised /h´/

In Mx. original /h´/ appeared as a lenited form of initial /s´/, /t´/; it is realised everywhere as [h] in LM, viz. /h´/ -> /h/, i.e. loss of palatalisation:
  1. *ta yn braar aym ny hassoo* 'my brother is standing' (lit. 'is my brother in his stand-ing') /te ən 'brɛːr em nə'[h]aːsu/ G. *tha an bràthar agam ina sheasamh*; */te ən 'brɛːr em nə '[h´]aːsu/ (cf. HLSM/II: 392 s.v. *shassoo*).
  2. *cum dty hengey* 'hold your tongue!' /kum də '[h]en´ə/; cf. ScG. *cum do theanga!* */kum də '[h´]en´ə/ (cf. HLSM/II: 74 s.v. *chengey*).

4.2.4.1.4. Loss of the palato-velarised nasal /ŋ´/

After front vowels the velarised nasal /ŋ/ in LM may be realised in a fronted (i.e. palatalised) velar form, viz. [ŋ̟], but this is rare, and in the few attested exx. non-fronted variants are also found (cf. also HLSM/III: 110), but generally /ŋ´/ -> /ŋ/, /ŋg/, i.e. loss of palatalisation:
  ching 'sick' /t´i[ŋ´]/ (also /t´i[ŋ]/ and in combination w. /g/, viz. /t´i[ŋ]g/ G. *tinn*.

4.2.4.2. Simplification of the system of resonants in Late Manx

The double phonemic contrast in OIr. /L, N, R/ as outlined in §4.2.3. above is largely sim-plified in CM and LM to a single opposition of neutral : palatal in initial position in each of the three. In some cases in LM there is even further simplification to /l, n, r/, i.e. that the neutral : palatal opposition is completely given up. As can be seen, there is loss of uvular quality in /N/ and /R/ and of velar quality in /L/. In addition (except for the odd example) there is loss of palatalisation in original palatalised variants:

  1. /L/ -> /l/ [l]:
  laa 'day' /[l]eː/ G. *lá* /Lɑː/
  Nollick 'Christmas' /no[l]ik´/ G. *Nollaig* / NoLək´/
  moal 'slow' /moː[l]/ G. *mall* /maːL/ (/a/ + /l/, w. lengthening from unlenited /l/ in a monosyllable).

  2. /L´/ -> /l´/ [lj]:
  lioar 'book' /[lj]oːr/ G. *leabhar* /L´oːr/
  shilley 'sight' /s´i[lj]ə/ G. *silleadh* /s´iL´ə/
  keyll 'wood, copse' /ke[lj]/ G. *coill* /kaiL´/

3. /l/ -> /l/ [l]:
my laue 'my hand' /mə'[l]e:u/ G. *mo lámh* /mə'la:u/
lhie 'lay' (pret.) /[l]ei/, G. *laigh* /ləi/

4. /l´/ -> /l´/ [l´], [lj], /l/ [l]:
le 'with' /[l´]e/, /[l]e/ G. *le* /l´e/
balley 'town' /ba:[lj]ə/, /ba:[l]ə/ G. *baile* /bal´ə/
schoill 'school' /sko[lj]/, /sko[l]/ G. *scoil* /skol´/

5. /N/ -> /n/ [n]:
nuy 'nine' /[n]i:/ G. *naoi* /Ni:/
creeney 'wise' /kri:[n]ə/ G. *críonna* /k´r´i:Nə/
ayn 'in it' /o:[n], u:[n]/ G. *ann* /a:N/

6. /N´/ -> /n´/ [nj], /n/ [n]:
nhee 'thing' /[nj]i:/ G. *ní* /N´i:/
bainney 'milk' /ba:[nj]ə/ G. *bainne* /baN´ə/
awin 'river' /au[nj], au[n]/ G. *abhainn* /auN´, awəN´/

7. /n/ -> /n/ [n]:
my naboonyn 'my neighbours' /mə '[n]a:bunən/, cf. ScG. *mo nàbuidh* /mə 'na:pi/
annym 'soul' /a[n]əm/ G.*anam* /anəm/

8. /n´/ -> /n´/ [n´], [nj], /n/ [n]:
nee 'will do' /[n´]i:, [n]i:/, ScG. *nì* /n´i:/ cf. Ir. *do-ghní*)
bannish 'wedding' /ba[n]is´/ G. *bainis* /ban´əs´/
blein 'year' /ble:[nj]/, /bli[n]/ G. *bliadhain* /b´l´iən´/

9. /R/ -> /r/ [r]:
reayrt 'view' /[r]e:t/ G. *radharc* /Rairk/
arragh 'spring' /a[r]ax/ G. *earrach* /aRəx/
baare 'top' /be:[r], be:/ G. *barr* /ba:r/

10. /R´/ -> /r/ [r´], [r]:
roih 'forearm' /[r]i:/ G. *righe* /ri:/
rio 'frost' /[r´]o:/, /[r]o:/ G. *reodh* /ro:/
cur 'put' /ko[r]/, /ku[r]/ G. *cur* /kur´/

11. /r/ -> /r/ [r]:
roie 'ran' /[r]ei/ G. *ruith* /rʰi/
arryltagh 'willing' /a[r]altax/ G. *earaltach* /erəLtəx/
mooar 'big' /mu:[r]/, /mu:ə/ G. *mór* /mo:r/

12. /r´/ -> /r/:
breck 'speckled' /b[r]ek/ G. *breac* /b´r´ak/
arrey 'notice' /a[r]ə/ G. *aire* /ar´ə/

cair 'proper' /keː[r]/, /keːə/ G. *cóir* /koːr´/

As can be seen from the foregoing, neutral consonants having uvular or velar articulation in Irish and Scottish Gaelic have largely lost these qualities in Manx.

4.2.4.3. 'Abuse' of palatalisation in Late Manx through hypercorrection

Due to the loss of vitality of the language in LM 'abuses' of various sorts through hypercorrection began creeping into the phonology, one of which was the application of palatalisation in places where it is not expected or is unhistorical. Velars seem to have been particularly susceptible to this 'abuse':

1. *gaaue* 'smith' /g´aːu/ N/HLSM/II: 182-83 : /gaːu/, cf. G. *gobha.*
2. *gaccrys* 'hungering, hungry' /g´aːgərəs/ S/HLSM/II: 183 : /gaːgərəs/, cf. G. *(ag) acras.*
3. *mraane* /mreːn´/ S/HLSM/II: 308 : /mreːn/, cf. ScG. *mnathan.*
4. *hie mee dys ny margey*
/hai mi dosnə 'mər´g´ə/ (N/Diary: 38) : /...mərgə/.
'I went to the market', w. abuse of palat. in the cluster /rg/ (cf. G. *margadh*), as if
*mairgeadh. For *dys ny margey* see §4.6.3. below.
(cf. HE /kjɑːr/ 'car', /gjɑːrdən/ 'garden' < 18th cent. Eng. affection - RLT).

For "abuse" of lenition in LM, cf. §4.3.2.3. below.

4.2.5. Summary

The following developments can be seen as taking place in the transition from CM to LM:

1. Fixed value of vowel phonemes in CM becomes destabilised in LM with the onset of wild allophonic variation (§4.2.2.) probably due to imperfect perception (cf. also Dressler 1972b: 455), leading to the collapse of once distinct phonemes.

2. Simplification of the consonant phonemes from CM to LM leading to loss of palatalised variants (§4.2.4.1.). In addition, simplification of the resonant system (§4.2.4.2.) already underway in CM, but accelerated in LM, in the loss of neutral : palatal contrast, leading on to 'abuse' or hypercorrect use of palatalisation.

4.3. Morphophonology

The main morphophonological pattern of Manx, as with other Insular Celtic languages, is the system of consonant replacement in initial position in nouns, verbs, and adjectives. In certain environments the distinctive features which make up certain of the initial consonants or consonant clusters are wholly or partially replaced, and the result shares an articulatory position with the radical consonant. Such replacements are systematic and can be predicted for certain environments, e.g. def. art, prep. + art, some poss. particles, some adverbs, one or two numerals, etc (cf. HLSM/III, Broderick 1993).

In common with the other branches of Goidelic (Irish and Scottish Gaelic) two forms of initial replacement are discernible in Manx. Lenition and nasalisation (or eclipsis). Lenition essentially spirantises bilabials, labio-dentals, dentals, and velars. Nasalisation - also called Eclipsis - voices /p, t, k/ to /b, d, g/ and converts /b, d, g/ into their corresponding homorganic nasals, viz. /m, n, ŋ/. The system (including palatalised variants) for initial single consonants can be sketched for CM as follows:

Figure 7: *System of lenition and nasalisation in Early and Classical Manx* (cf. Thomson 1984b: 314; Broderick 1993: 237):

Radical	/p	t	t´	k	k´	b	d	d´	g	g´	m	f	s	s´	/
Lenited	[f	h/x	h´/x´	x/h	x´	v	ɣ/-	ɣ´/j	ɣ	ɣ´/j	v	-	h	h´/x´	]
Nasalised	[b	d	d´	g	g´	m	n	n´	ŋ	ŋ´			v		]

In his discussion of the criteria under which initial mutation can take place in Manx Robert L. Thomson (Thomson 1969a: 189-90) comments:

> [...]It will be obvious to any Gaelic reader that Manx has much less in the way of mutation [lenition and nasalisation] than its sister languages, and that according to the text examined what there is may seem to be in some disorder. There is, of course, nothing at all abnormal in the reduction or simplification of the mutational system. Even the most extensive type is a simplification of what would have occurred if the results of phonetic change had been left without analogical rearrangement. For example, the tying of mutation in the adjective to the gender (and case) of the noun rather than to its stem-formation is already a simplification. At the same time, the inhibition of mutation for phonetic reasons introduces irregularities into the system. Then again the reduction or loss of the case-system introduces a further simplification so that in Manx the incidence of mutation becomes more like that in Welsh than in Gaelic. Finally there is the distinction between such mutations as bear some functional load of meaning and such as may be regarded as redundant in this respect and therefore expendable. Furthermore, mutation and gender are mutually supporting systems and the reduction of one will necessarily involve the other (Thomson 1969a: 189-90).

To set the loss of initial mutation in LM in context an overview of the situation in EM and CM is sketched briefly below. Here only nouns and adjectives are dealt with. Loss of initial mutation in the verb-phrase is confined to LM, so far as our evidence goes.

4.3.1. Initial mutation affecting nouns and adjectives in Early and Classical Manx

Without wishing to enter the realms of a historical grammar, the situation regarding initial mutation in nouns and adjectives in Early and Classical Manx is briefly presented as an example to set in context the loss of initial mutation in Late Manx. The examples are given in standard Manx orthography.

4.3.1.1. In Early Manx

4.3.1.1.1. Lenition

In the context of nouns and adjectives lenition in EM is generally found in the following circumstances (cf. Thomson 1969a: 201):

4.3.1.1.1.1. *Nouns*:

a) in the nominative singular feminine after the definite article (*ben* 'woman' -> *y ven* 'the woman'),

b) in the vocative both singular and plural (*carrey* 'friend' -> *y charrey* 'friend!', *y chaarjyn* 'friends!'),

c) in masculine nouns in the genitive singular after the definite article (*baatey* 'boat' -> *kione y vaatey* 'end of the boat'), in the dependant genitives (*Juan* 'John' -> *thie Yuan* 'John's house', and in feminine nouns where the nominative is used as a genitive (*ben* 'woman' -> *kione y ven* 'the head of the woman, the woman's head').[8]

d) in the prepositional or 'dative' case, i.e. after a prep. + def. art. + noun, in both masculine and feminine nouns (*baatey* 'boat' -> *er y vaatey* 'on the boat'; *ben* 'woman' -> *er y ven* 'on the woman').

e) /h/ is prefixed to nouns with initial vowel in the fem. gen. sg. (*oie* 'night' -> *dooid ny h-oie* 'blackness of the night') and nom/acc. pl. after the def. article (*uinnagyn* 'windows' -> *ny h-uinnagyn* 'the windows') and after the poss. part. *e* 'her' (*ayr* 'father' -> *e h-ayr* 'her father').

4.3.1.1.1.2. *Adjectives*:

a) after the nominative feminine singular noun (*mooar* 'big', *ben vooar* 'big woman'),

b) the vocative singular of both genders (*Juan* 'John' -> *y Yuan* ; *Joney* 'Judith' -> *y Yoney*),

c) usually not lenited after the genitive singular masculine (*mooar* 'big' -> *kione y vaatey mooar (vooar)* 'end of the big boat'),

d) equally divided between lenition and non-lenition after dative singular masculines, but normal after feminines, with gender coming to be the dominant factor (*mooar* 'big' -> *er y vaatey vooar/mooar* 'on the big boat', *er y ven vooar* 'on the big woman').

e) after attenuated plurals (*mooar* 'big' -> *mac mooar* 'big son', *mec vooarey* 'big sons' (also w. suffix).

For further details and exceptions, cf. Thomson (1969a: 201-02).

4.3.1.1.2. Eclipsis / Nasalisation

The genitive plural of the noun is frequently eclipsed after the definite article (*baatey* 'boat' -> *kione nyn maatey* 'end of the boats'), while *n*- is prefixed to nouns with initial vowel (*eean* 'bird, fowl' -> *magher ny n-eean* 'field of the birds, fowl') (cf. Thomson 1969a: 201).

---

[8] In PB the older inflected genitive forms *ny myny, ny mynii* 'of the woman' (cf. G. *na mná*; though the Mx. forms suggest dative sg. *mnaoi*) are also attested.

4.3.1.2. In Classical Manx

4.3.1.2.1. Lenition

In the same context lenition in CM is generally found under the following circumstances (cf. Thomson 1969a: 195-201):

4.3.1.2.1.1. *Nouns*:
a) in the nominative singular feminine after the definite article (as above),

b) in the vocative both singular and plural (as above),

c) in the masculine genitive singular after the definite article (as above), in dependent genitives (as above), and in feminine nouns where the nominative is used as a genitive (as (above).[9]

d) in the prepositional case in feminine nouns (*ben* 'woman' -> *er y ven* 'on the woman'), occasionally, though not regularly, in masc. nouns (*baatey* 'boat' -> *er y vaatey, er y baatey* 'on the boat') .

e) /h/ is prefixed to nouns with initial vowel in the fem. g. sg. and nom/acc. pl. after the def. article and after the poss. part. *e* 'her' (as above).

4.3.1.2.1.2. *Adjectives*:
a) after the nom./acc. feminine singular noun (as above),

b) in the vocative after nouns of both genders (though the examples are rare) (as above),

c) in the prepositional case after a feminine noun (as above),

d) after attenuated plurals in adjectives (*mooar* 'big' -> *mic vooar(ey)* 'big sons') and dependent genitives (*Juan* 'John' -> *thie Yuan* 'John's house').

• Lenition is *not* usually found in:

a) the adjective following a masculine genitive singular after the def. art,. (as (c) above)

b) in the prepositional case after masculine nouns (as (d) above).

For further details and exceptions see Thomson (*ibid.*).

4.3.1.2.2. Eclipsis / Nasalisation
Eclipsis does not occur in the genitive plural of nouns after the def. article, and vestiges of this feature are now almost exclusively restricted to place-names:

(N Art. Ngpl.(nas.)):

1. *glion ny mreck* 'glen of the trout', nom.sg. *breck*, G. *gleann na mbreac*, nom.sg. *breac*.

2. *creg ny voillan* 'rock of the seagulls' nom.sg. *foillan*, G. *creag na bhfaoileann*, nom.sg.

faoileann (cf. PNIM/I: xxxiv).

For *n-* prefixed to vowels see §4.3.3.1.3.9. below.

For fuller details see §4.3.3.1. below.

---

[9] The older inflected genitive form of *ben*, viz, *ny myny, ny mynii* of PB, is lost in CM.

4.3.1.3. Summary

In short, the development affecting nouns and adjectives from EM to CM can be listed as follows:

1. Full application of lenition in masculine nouns in the prepositional case in EM to occasional application in CM.

2. Occasional application of lenition in the adjective after the genitive singular masculine in EM to non-application in CM.

3. Application of eclipsis in the genitive plural of the noun after the definite article in EM to non-application in CM (now confined to place-names).

4.3.2. Loss of initial mutation (lenition and nasalisation) in Late Manx

However, associated with the simplification of phonemes and loss of allophonic variation (cf. Section 4.2.4. above), there also occurred loss of initial mutation which in LM ceased to have any grammatical or other function, and as meaning could be conveyed without it, its failure to appear became more marked in the transition from CM to LM.

4.3.2.1. Loss of lenition in Late Manx

Lenition and loss of lenition in LM are found side by side without altering the intended meaning, and they can be regarded as being in a state of flux bearing no functional load. Such free variation can be found in the following environments (all exx. are taken from HLSM/I: 9ff, except where specifically stated). From being phonemic rules (used in the expression of case, number, tense, etc) they have become phonetic rules of allomorphic variation. The arrow denotes the loss of lenition:

4.3.2.1.1. After the def. art. governing an original feminine in nom./acc. (except in dental consonants)

1. *ben* 'woman' /ben/ : /ən 'ven/ 'the woman' -> /ən 'ben/
2. *geay* 'wind' /giː/ : /ən '[ɣ]iː/ 'the wind' -> /ən '[g]iː/

4.3.2.1.2. After prep. + def. art. in nouns

1. <u>len</u>: *ayns y vaatey* 'in the boat' /unsə 'veːdə/ (S/HLSM/II: 20 s.v. *baatey*) (rad. *baatey*, G. *bàta*).
<u>non-len</u>: *ayns y baatey* 'in the boat' /unsə 'beːdə/ S/HLSM/II: 20 s.v. *baatey*.
2. <u>len</u>: *ayns y yeurey* 'in the winter' /usə 'jeurə/ N/HLSM/II: 194 s.v. *geurey* (rad. *geurey* 'winter'; G. *geimhreadh*).
<u>non-len</u>: *ayns y geurey* 'in the winter' /usə gʹeurə/ N/HLSM/II: 194 s.v. *geurey*

3. len: *er y voghree* 'in the morning' (lit. 'on the morning') /erə 'voːri/ S/HLSM/I: 366-
67 (rad. *moghrey*, G. *mochthradh*)
non-len: *er yn moghree* /ərən 'moːri/ 'in the morning' N/HLSM/II: 302 s.v. moghrey.

4.3.2.1.3. In nouns after the poss. particles *my* 'my', *dty* 'your'(sg.), *e* 'his'

1. len: *my yishig* 'my father' /mə 'jisˊigˊ/ (rad. *jishig* 'father').
non-len: *my jishig* /mə 'dˊisˊigˊ/.
2. len: *dty voir* 'your mother' /də 'vaːr/ (rad. *moir* 'mother', G. *máthair*).
non-len: *dty moir* /də 'maːr/.
Dressler (1972b: 453) also noted loss of len. after *da* 'thy' in Breton.

4.3.2.1.4. In nouns after numerals

1. len: *ane phunt* 'one pound' /eːn ·funt/ (rad. *punt* 'pound', G. *púnt*).
non-len: *ane punt* /eːn ·punt/.
2. len: *daa veeilley* 'two miles' /de: 'viːlˊə/ (rad. *meeilley* 'mile', G. *míle*).
non-len: *daa meeilley* /de: 'miːlˊə/.
3. len: *queig vlein* 'five years' /keg vleːn/ (rad. *blein* 'year', G. *bliadhain*, usu. *queig
blein, bleeaney* (pl. form used with numerals); cf. HLSM/I: 11-12.
3. len: *shey phingyn* 'six pence' /sˊe: 'fiŋən/ (rad. *pingyn* 'pennies', G. *pinginn*).
non-len: *shey pingyn* /sˊe: 'piŋgən/.
4. len: *jeih vlein* 'ten years' /dˊai vliːn/.
non-len: *jeih blein* /dˊei bliːn/ (cf. HLSM/I: *ibid*).
5. len: *feed vinnid* 'twenty minutes' /fid vinəd/ (rad. *minnid* 'minute', G. *mionaid*).
non-len: *feed blein* 'twenty years' /fid bliːn/.
6. len: *keead vlein* 'a hundred years' /kid vliːn/.
non-len: *keead punt* '100 pounds' /kid punt/.
In CM len. is found after *unnane, nane, ane* 'one' and *daa* 'two' only, occasionally after *feed*
'twenty' and *keead* 'hundred'. Its appearance after *queig* and *shey* could be regarded as an
'abuse' of lenition (cf. §4.3.2.3. below).

4.3.2.1.5. In adjectives after an original feminine noun

1. len: *earish vie* 'good weather' /irisˊ 'vaːi/ (rad. *mie* 'good', G. *maith*).
non-len: *earish mie* /irisˊ 'maːi/.
2. len: *queeyl vooar* 'big wheel' /kwiːlˊ 'vuːə/ (rad. *mooar* 'big', G. *mór*).
non-len: *queeyl mooar* /kwiːlˊmuːə/.

4.3.2.1.6. In adjectives after a qualifying adverb

1. len: *feer vie* 'very good' /fi: 'vaːi/ (rad. *mie* 'good').

non-len: *feer mie* /fiː 'maːi/.
2. len: *lieh chrooin* 'half crown' /lʹeː 'xrun/ (rad. *crooin* 'crown', G. *crúinn*).
non-len: *lieh crooin* /lʹeː 'kruːnʹ/
3. len: *ro vie* 'too good' /roː 'vaːi/ (rad. *mie* 'good').
non-len: *ro mie* /roː 'maːi/.
4. len: *shenn ven* 'old woman' /sʹaːn 'ven/ (rad. *ben* 'woman', G. *bean*).
non-len: *shenn ven* /sʹaːn 'ben/.

4.3.2.1.7. In nouns after the preposition *dy* 'of'

1. len: *boayl dy vaynrys* 'a place of happiness' /boːl də 'veːndrəs/ (rad. *maynrys* 'happines', cf. G. *méanra*)
non-len: *boayl dy maynrys* /boːl də 'meːndrəs/.
2. len: *bit dy vee* 'bit, portion of food' /bit də 'viː/ (rad. *bee* 'food', G. *biadh*).
non-len: *paart dy bee* 'some food' /peːt də 'biː/.

4.3.2.1.8. In place-names after the preposition *dy* (orig. *gy*) 'to, towards'

len: *goll dy Phurt ny Hinshey* 'going to Peel' /gol də fonə 'hindʹsʹə/.
non-len: /gol də ponə 'hindʹsʹə/ (rad. *Purt ny Hinshey* 'Peel').

4.3.2.1.9. In the infinitive after *dy* 'to'

1. len: *dy heet* 'to come' /də 'hit/ (rad *cheet* 'come', G. *tidheacht*).
non-len: *dy cheet* /də 'tʹit/.
2. len: *dy yannoo* 'to do' /də 'jenu/ (rad. *jannoo* 'do', G. *déanamh*).
non-len: *dy jannoo* /də 'dʹenu/.

4.3.2.1.10. After *er* 'after' in the perfect tense of verbs

len: *ta mee er yarrood eh* : (rad. *jarrood* 'forget', G. *dearmad*).
(SbV Pn. Prep. VbN(len.) Pn.)
/ta mi a ja'rud a/
'I have forgotten it' (lit. 'am I after forgetting it').
non-len: *t'ee er jarrood ny vraagyn* (*sic*)
(SbV Pn. Prep. VbN Art. Npl.)
/tei er dʹə 'rud nə vreːgən/ [N]/HLSM/I; 15
'she has forgotten the shoes'
For the form *ny vraagyn* see §4.3.2.3. below.

4.3.2.1.11. In definite nouns in dependent genitival position or proper names

1. len: *Kione Vradda* /k´o:n ˈvradə/ 'Bradda Head'
non-len: *Kione Bradda* /k´o:n ˈbradə/
2. len: *Kione Vaghal* /k´o:n ˈvaːxəl/ 'Maughold head'
non-len: *Kione Maghal* /k´o:n ˈmaːl/

4.3.2.1.12. In the vocative case, both singular and plural: lenition (usually restricted to exclamations or interjections)

1. *Graih Yee!*
((Prep.) Nvoc. Ngen.)
/graːi ˈjiː/ N/HLSM/II: 209 s.v. *graih*, w. loss of initial *er* 'on, for'
'for God's sake'
(lit. '(for) God's love').

2. *O vuddee voght, cre ta jannoo ort?*
(Voc.exclam. Nvoc.(len.) Adj.voc.(len.) Interrog.pn. SbV VbN Prep.pn.)
/oː vodi voh kreː te d´enu ort/ (rad. not attested; cf. ScG. *pùtach* 'young fowl, cf. Eng. 'bird') N/HLSM/II: 474 s.v. *vuddee*
'O poor creature, what's the matter with you'
(lit. 'O creature poor, what is a-doing on you?')

3. *t'eh kiare er y clag ayns y faster, wooinney*
(SbV Pn. Num. Prep. Art. N Prep. Art. N Nvoc.(len.))
/ti ˈk´eːr erə ˈklag usəˈfaːstə wun´ə/ N/HLSM/II: 476 s.v. *wooinney*
'it's four o'clock in the evening, man!'
(lit. 'is it four on the clock in the evening, man')
4. *wooinney veen!*
(Nvoc.(len.) Adj.voc.(len.))
/wun´ə ˈviːn/ (rad. *dooinney* 'man', *meen* 'dear') N/HLSM/II: 476 s.v. *wooinney*
'dear man!'

5. *woy, woy!*
(Nvoc.(len.))
/woi, woi/ (rad. *boy* 'boy' Eng.) N/HLSM/II: 477 s.v. *woy*
'boy, boy!'.

6. *my ghuillyn!*
(Poss.part. Npl.(len.))
/mə ˈjil´ən/ (also /məˈgil´ən/) S/HLSM/I: 27
'my lads!'

Otherwise non-lenition is the norm:

7. *cha row bee oc jiu, bwa*
(Neg. SbV N Prep.pn. Nvoc.(non-len.))
/a rou 'biː ok 'dˊiuː bwa/ S/HLSM/II: 51 s.v. *bwa*
'they had no food today, boy!'

8. *nish, Juan, t'eh fo raad*
(Exclam. Nvoc.(non-len.) SbV Pn. Adv.phrase)
/nisˊ dˊun ti fə 'ræːd/ (w. len. *Yuan*) N/MTT/T40: 5
'now, Juan, it [the recording machine] is going, underway'
(lit. 'now, Juan, is it underway').

9. <u>*fire*</u> yn <u>*gun*</u>, *Tom*
(Vimp. Art. N Nvoc.(non-len.))
/faiər ən 'gun tom/ (w. len. *Hom*) S/HLSM/I: 368-69
'fire the gun, Tom'.

10. *c'red* [rectius *cre'n*]*traa t'eh, dooinney*
(Interrog.pn. Art. N SbV(rel.) Pn. Nvoc.(non-len.))
/krəd (*sic*) 'treː ti dunˊə/ N/HLSM/I: 250-51
'what time is it, man?'
(lit. 'what the time (which) is it, man?').

4.3.2.1.13. /t/ before /s/ as a lenition of /s/

Lenition of /s/ after the def. art. is /t/, viz. [t] when neutral and [tʃ] when palatalised.[10] This does not occur in the clusters *sk-, sm-, sn*. It is found in the nom./acc. of original feminine nouns, in the genitive of original masculine nouns (or nouns treated as masculine), or in the prepositional case in nouns in *s-, sl-, str-* after the def. art. In LM occurrence and non-occurrence of lenition here is found:

with lenition (/s/ -> /t/), /sˊ/ -> /tˊ/):

1. *jerrey yn touree, tourey* (rad. *sourey* 'summer' G. *samhradh, deireadh an t-samhraidh*)
(N Art. Ngen.(len.))
/dˊerə ən 'tauri/ S, /dˊerə ən 'taurə/ N/HLSM/II: 235 s.v. *sourey*
'the end of the summer'
(lit. 'end of the summer').
Note in the first ex. umlaut and palatalisation in *sourey*.

2. *ayns yn theihll ainyn* (rad. *seihll* 'world' G. **anns an t-saol againne*)
(Prep. Art. N(len.) Prep.pn.)
/ənsən 'teːlˊ iŋən/ S/HLSM/II: 388 s.v. *seihll*

---

[10] The /t/ in this position originally belonged to the def. art. (cf. OIr. *int* (before *ṡ*)) (cf. Thurneysen 1946: 294).

'in our world'
(lit. 'in the world at us').

3. *yn chiaghtin shoh* (rad. *shiaghtin* 'week' G. *an t-seachtain*)
(Art. N(len.) Dem.adj.)
/ən t´aːxtən ˈsˊo̧ː/ S/HLSM/II: 400 s.v. *shiaghtin*
'this week' (lit. 'the week this').

4. *yn chenn ven* (rad. *shenn*L 'old', G. *an t-seann bhean*)
(Art. Adj.(len.) N(len.))
/ən tˊen ˈven/ S/HLSM/I: 358-59
'the old woman'.

5. *er y tlieau* (rad. *slieau*, G. *ar an t-sliabh*)
(Prep. Art. N(len.))
/erə ˈtlˊuː/ N/HLSM/II: 415 s.v. *slieau* [11]
'on the mountain'.

6. *ayn y traid* (rad. *straid*, G. *anns an t-sràid*)
(Prep. Art. N(len.))
/usən ˈtredˊ/ N/HLSM/II: 436 s.v. *straid*
'in the street'.

With non-lenition (/s/ remains /s/):

1. *ayns y seihll aym*
(Prep. Art. N(non-len.) Prep.pn.)
/usə ˈseːilˊ em/ N/HLSM/II: 388 '
in my world' (lit. 'in the world at me').

2. *er y shiaghtin*
(Prep. Art. N(non-len.))
/erə ˈsˊaːxtin/ [N]/HLSM/I: 130
'on, during the week'.

3. *jeant ec yn shenn dooinney*
(Vppp. Prep. Art. Adj.(non-len.) N)
/dˊint egən sˊaːn dunˊə/ N/HLSM/I: 280-81
'made at/by the old man'.

4. *er y slyst*
(Prep. Art. N(non-len.))

---

[11] However, init. /tl(ˊ)/ in Mx. becomes /kl(ˊ)/: *woish yn clieau* /wusˊən ˈklˊuː/ 'from the mountain', or w. len. of /k/, viz. /x/ (hypercorrection): *er y clieau* /erə ˈxˊlˊuː/ 'on the mountain' N/HLSM/II: 415 s.v. *slieau*.

/erə 'slist/ S/HLSM/II: 417 s.v. *slyst* (G. *slios*)
'on the coast'.

5. *ayns y straid*
(Prep. Art. N(non-len.))
/osə stred/ N/HLSM/II: 436
'in the street'.

4.3.2.1.14. Prefixing of /h/ to vowels

as in §4.3.1.2. above.

4.3.2.1.15. Loss of lenition in the preterite of verbs

with lenition:

1. *vrie eh jeem naillt goll ny dyn*
(Vpret.(len.) Pn. Prep.pn. Q/Cop.phrase/Pn(2sg.) VbN Prep. Neg.part.)
/vrai a 'd´ibm naːl´t´ 'gol nə 'dən/ S/HLSM/II: 473-74 s.v. *vrie*.
'he asked me if you want(ed) to go or not'
(lit. 'asked he of me if want(ed) you going or not').
2. *vrie peiagh ennagh, quoi eh shen*
(Vpret.(len.) N Adj. Interrog.pn. Pn. Dem.adj.)
/vrai paiax e·n´ax kwei e 's´en/ S/HLSM/II: 473-74 s.v. *vrie*.
'someone asked, who is that?'
(lit. 'asked someone, who is that?').

3. *chraa mee eh dy mie*   : G. *chraith*
(Vpret.(len.) Pn. Adv.)
/xreː mi a də 'maːi/ S/HLSM/II: 70 s.v. *chraa*
'I shook it well'
(lit. 'shook I it well').

With non-lenition.

A. With loss of /v-/; viz. /b-/ for /v-/:
1. *as brie yn dooinney mooar jeh*   : *vrie*...(see foregoing).
(Conj. Vpret.(non-len.) Art. N Adj. Prep.)   (Vpret.(len.)...)
/as brai ən dun´ə muːə d´eː/ N/HLSM/I: 196-97
'and the big man asked him'
(lit. 'and asked the man big of him').

2. *bwoail eh lesh y cass*   : *woaill* (G. *bhuail*)
(Vpret.(non-len.) Pn. Prep. Art. N)   (Vpret.(len.)...)

/buľ e ľesʹ ə ˈkaːs/ N/HLSM/II: 52 s.v. *bwoaill eh*
'he struck him with his foot'
(lit. 'struck he (him) with his foot').

B. With loss of /x-/; viz. /k-/ for /x-/:

1. *caill eh ooilley yn snaie echey*   : *chaill* (G. *chaill*)
(Vpret.(non-len.) Pn. Indef.pn. Art. N Prep.pn.)   (Vpret.(len.)...)
/kaľ a olʹu ən ˈsnei ega/ S/HLSM/II: 68-69 s.v. *chaill*
'he lost all his net'
(lit. 'lost he all the net at him').

2. *kiannee eh*   : *chiannee* (G. *cheannaigh*)
(Vpret.(non-len.) Pn.)   (Vpret.(len.)...)
/kʹani a/ N/HLSM/I: 86
'he bought' (lit. 'bought he').

C. With loss of /ɣ-/, /ɣʹ-/; viz. /g-/ for /ɣ/; /gʹ/ for /ɣʹ, j/:

1. *greim eh yn waagh*   : *ghreim* (G. *ghreim*)
(Vpret.(non-len.) Pn. Art. N(len.))   (Vpret.(len.)...)
/grem e ən weːx/ N/HLSM/II: 211 s.v. *greimey*
'he grasped the hare'
(lit. 'grasped he the hare').
But note that len. takes place in the noun after the def. art. (rad. *mwaagh*, G. *maigheach*,
f.).

2. *greim mee eh ayns y roih*   : *ghreim* (G. *ghreim*)
(Vpret.(non-len.) Pn. Pn. Prep. Art. N)   (Vpret.(len.)...)
/grim mi eː unsə ˈriː/ S/HLSM/II: 211 s.v. *greimey*
'I gripped him by the arm'
(lit. 'gripped I him in the arm').

3. *giall ee dy beagh jinnair mie aarloo daue*   : *ghiall* (G. *gheall*)
(Vpret.(non-len.) Pn. Conj. SbV N Adj. Adv. Prep.pn.)   (Vpret.(len.)...)
/gʹal i də biəx dʹiˈneːr maːi eːrlu deu/ N/HLSM/II: 195 s.v. *gialdyn*
'she promised there would be a good dinner ready for them'
(lit. 'promised she that would be a dinner good ready for them').

D. With loss of /h-/; viz. /sn-/ for /hn-/, /s-/ for /h-/:

1. *as snaue mee seose ny greeishyn*   : *hnaue* (G. *shnámh*)
(Conj. Vpret.(non-len.) Pn. Prep. Art. N)   (Vpret.(len.)...)
/as ˈsnau mi ˈseis nə ˈgriːsən/ S/HLSM/I: 358-59
'and I crawled upstairs'

(lit. 'and crawled I up the stairs').

2. *soie eh sheese er creg*   : *hoie* (G. *shuidh*)
(Vpret.(non-len.) Pn. Adv. Prep. N)   (Vpret.(len.)...)
/sai e sˊiːsˊer kreg/ N/HLSM/I: 172-73
'he sat down on a rock'
(lit. 'sat he down on a rock').

E. With loss of /h/, viz. /tr/ for /hr/; /t/ for /h/:

1. *treig mee eh*   : *hreig* (Don. Ir. *thréig*, vn. *tréigbheáil*)
(Vpret.(non-len.) Pn. Pn.)   (Vpret.(len.)...)
/treg mi a/ S/HLSM/II: 460 s.v. *treigeil*
'I forsook him' (lit. 'foresook me him').

2. *tuitt mee sheese ny greeishyn*   : *huitt* (G. *thuit*)
(Vpret.(non-len.) Pn. Prep. Art. Npl.)   (Vpret.(len.)...)
/tut mi siːs nə ˈgriːsən/ S/HLSM/II: 466 s.v. *tuittym*
'I fell down the stairs'
(lit. 'fell I down the stairs').

The occurrence of the inflected forms of the verb in LM is not common, it being replaced by periphrasitic forms with *jannoo* 'do' (cf. HLSM/I: 86), and when at all then most often the preterite, but even here the exx. are scarce. However, in most of the extant exx. of the preterite where lenition is possible lenition does not occur. This is in contrast to Dorian's SSs in ESG (where 90% used len.; cf. Dorian 1981b: 138), but note that in ESG there is no developed parallel periphrastic tense form with *jannoo*, as in Mx.

4.3.2.2. With non-failure of lenition

In spite of the above, failure of lenition does not occur in secondary forms without base forms. In this respect Manx consistently makes the distinction between significant and non-significant mutation (cf. also Thomson 1969a: 190). For examples cf. also HLSM/ III: 66:

4.3.2.2.1. (verbs): *va* 'was' /va/ ScG. *bha*.
4.3.2.2.2. (negative particles): *cha* 'not' /ha/, /a/ ScG. *cha*.
4.3.2.2.3. (prepositions): *harrish* 'over' /harisˊ/ G. *thairis*.
4.3.2.2.4. (pronoun): *oo* 'you' (sg.) /u(ː)/ ScG. *thu*.
4.3.2.2.5. (reflexive pron.): *hene* 'self' /hiːn/ ScG. *fhìn*.
4.3.2.2.6. (prep. pron.): *my yeih* 'after me' /mə ˈjei/ G. *imo dhéidh*, *ny yeih* 'after him' /nə ˈjei/ G. *ina dhéidh* (but *ny jeih* 'after her' G. *ina déidh*).
4.3.2.2.7. (adverb): *heese* 'down' /hiːs/ G. *shíos*, *heose* 'up' /hus/ G. *shuas*.
But note that failure of lenition occurs in the preterite of regular verbs, cf. §4.3.2. 1.15.

4.3.2.3. 'Abuse' of lenition in Late Manx through hypercorrection

As with palatalisation (cf. §4.2.4.3.), lenition occurs in places where it is unhistorical or is not expected. The following are some examples:

1. *ny vraagyn* : *ny braagyn*, i.e. in the nom/acc. pl. after the def. art.
(Art.(pl.) Npl.(len.)) (Art.(pl.) Npl.)
/nə 'vreːgən/ [N]/HLSM/I: 15
'the shoes'.

2. *er wullagh er y cheilley* : *er mullagh y cheilley*
(Prep. N(len.) Prep.phrase) (Prep. N Art. Ngen.)
/e: 'wulax erə 'keľ ə/ N/HLSM/I: 246-47
'on top of each other'
er does not normally cause lenition, cf. *er mullagh Slieau Lewaigue* /er mulax sľ uː 'ľ eːg/
N/HLSM/II: 309 s.v. *mullagh* 'on top of Slieau Lewaigue' from the same informant; see also HLSM/I: 129ff. In addition, the genitive construction without preposition would have been expected here.

3. *oh, vreck va shin eeastagh ayns Nherin* : *breck...*
(Exclam. Npl.(len.) SbV(rel.) Pn. VbN Prep. PN)
/o: vrek vas´ ən jistax os n´ eːrən´/ S/MTT/PR2: 1
'oh, (it was) mackerel we were fishing in Ireland'
(lit. 'oh, (was it) mackeral (which) were we fishing in Ireland').[12]

4.3.2.4. False delenition

As noted above, lenited neutral /d/ fell together with lenited /g/ as /ɣ/. With the loss of this spirant in intital position (cf. §4.2.4.1.2. above) initial /ɣ/ of whatever origin can be stopped to /g/. So *daa* 'two' (G. *dó, dà*) in the phrase *ghaa ny tree* 'two or three' /ɣanə 'triː/ (HLSM/II: 194) is often found in LM as /ga nə triː/, i.e. w. /ɣ/ repr. *dh-* falsely delenited to /g/ instead of /d/. So also *ghaa yeig* (G. *dhà dheug*) appears as /geː ieg/, /gai eg/ (cf. HLSM/I: 16), though note /ɣ/ to /d/ (correctly) in failure of lenition in *dooinney* (len. *ghooinney*) in the vocative in §4.3.2.1.12.

---

[12] Note here also failure of application of the particle **ag* 'at' (reduced in Mx. to *'g-* before vowels) to the verb-noun *eeastagh* to form the present participle, probably due to resistance from the initial palatalised element /j/.

4.3.3. Nasalisation

4.3.3.1. In Classical Manx

In CM nasalisation is found in the following environments:

4.3.3.1.1. it follows the plural possessive or objective particle and elements containing it, e.g. *t'ad nyn gadley* 'they are asleep', rad. *cadley* 'sleep' G. *...nan gcodladh, t'eh dyn vakin* 'he sees them' lit. 'he is at their seeing' G. *...gan bhfaicinn* (cf. also Thomson 1984b: 314, Broderick 1993: 238, 272).

4.3.3.1.2. occasionally occurs after the genitive plural of the article:

4.3.3.1.2.1. in dependence on a foregoing noun: *ayns bwoaillee ny geyrragh* 'in the sheepfold', n.sg. *keyrrey* 'sheep', G. *...na gcaorach*, n.sg. *caora* (cf. Broderick 1991: 79),

4.3.3.1.2.2. in the same after a verbal noun: *shooyll ny dhieyn* 'walking the houses' i.e. begging.

4.3.3.1.2.3. in place-names, e.g. *kerroo ny glough* 'quarterland of the stones', n.sg. *clagh* 'stone' G. *ceathramh na gcloch*, n.sg. *cloch* (cf. also PNIM/I: xxxiv).

4.3.3.1.3. In verbs affecting only voiceless stops after the following particles:

4.3.3.1.3.1. zero sign of the interrogative: **fel* 'is' *(an) vel* 'is?'.

4.3.3.1.3.2. after *cha* 'not': *cha vel* 'is not' /ha 'vel/ (also *cha nel* w. lenition).

4.3.3.1.3.3. after *dy* 'that /də/: *dy vel* 'that is' /də 'vel/.

4.3.3.1.3.4. after *nagh* 'that not' /nax/: *nagh vel* 'that is not' /nax 'vel/.

4.3.3.1.3.5. after *mannagh* 'if not' /manax/: *mannagh vel* 'if is not' /manax 'vel/.

4.3.3.1.3.6. after *roish my* 'before' /ro:s´ mə/: *roish my jem roym* 'before I go my way' (Job X 21), and without *roish*.

4.3.3.1.3.7. after *dy* 'if' /də/ in unreal conditions: *dy voddagh shiu jannoo shen* 'if you were to do that' /də vodax s´u d´enu s´en/.

4.3.3.1.3.8. after *er* 'after' in the perfect tense of verbs: *t'ou er n'yannoo feer vie* 'you have done very well' /teu e 'n´inu fi: 'vaːi/, vn. *jannoo* 'doing' /d´inu/.

4.3.3.1.4. it prefixes *n-* to vowels: *droghad ny n-eayn* 'bridge of the lambs', n.sg. *eayn* 'lamb', G. *drochaid na n-uan*, n.sg. *uan*.

4.3.3.2. Loss of nasalisation in Late Manx

In LM nasalisation is found only in the following environments:

4.3.3.2.1. in fossilised phrases containing the plural possessive particle *nyn* /nən/ 'our, your, their' e.g. *bee shiu nyn dost* 'be ye silent' /bi: s´u nən 'dost/ or in the declined forms *ta shin ooilley ny dost, ta shiuish..., t'ad* ... (cf. HLSM/II: 455-56). In LM all three persons sg. and pl. had generally become fixed in the 3rd pers. sg. masc, viz. *...ny host* (cf. Broderick 1993: 272-73).

4.3.3.2.2. Except for fossilised phrases (cf. below) this feature is only found in place-names (cf. PNIM/I: xxxiv). It is no longer found after verb-nouns: *shooyll ny thieyn* /sˊuːlˊ nə ˈtaiən/ (cf. HLSM/II: 405 s.v. *shooyll*).

4.3.3.2.3. It is still found in all the instances of No. 4.3.3.1.3 above, with the exception of 4.3.3.1.3.7. where *my* is lost and the verb is found in its independent form, viz. *roish hooar eh baase* 'before he died', earlier *roish my dooar eh baase*. 4.3.3.1.3.8. The conjunction *dy* 'if' has generally been replaced with *my* 'if' (used in real conditions).

4.3.3.2.4. This element is lost altogether in LM and is found only in place-names.

4.3.3.3. With non-failure of nasalisation in Late Manx

As with permanent lenition (cf. §4.2.2.2. above) non-failure of nasalisation occurs in examples showing permanent nasalisation (though it is not perceived as such):

4.3.3.3.1. (verbs): *vel* 'is, exists' /vel/ (dep. pres. of *ta*) following zero particle of interrogation cf. Ir. *bhfuil* (cf. §4.3.3.1.3 above & other exx. there).

4.3.3.3.2. (adverbs): *mygeayrt* 'around' /məˈgit/, cf. Ir. *mun gcuairt*.
  myrgeddin 'also' /marˈgedən/, cf. Ir. *mar an gcéadna* 'like the first'.

4.3.4. Loss of final mutation in Late Manx

Final mutation in Manx manifested itself as palatalisation of dentals and laterals to indicate attenuated plural forms (of the *o*-stem type):
  1. *kayt* /ket/ 'cat', pl. *kiyt* /ketˊ/
  2. *bwoid* /bod/ 'penis', pl. *bwhid* /bwidˊ/
  3. *eayn* /jeːn/ 'lamb', pl. *eayin* /jeːnˊ/
  4. *shiaull* /sˊoːl/ 'sail', pl. *shiauill* /sˊoːlˊ/
  5. *cabbyl* /kaːbəl/ 'horse', pl. *cabbil* /kaːbilˊ/
However, as the palatal element became indistinct (possibly due to contact with English where final /nˊ/ and /lˊ/ are not normally found (except perhaps in loanwords)), so did the distinction between sg. and pl., thus giving rise to suffix pl. forms: /ketən/, /bodən/, /sˊoːlən/, /kaːbələn/, etc. For other exx. cf. HLSM/I: 35. See also below §4.4.2.2.

In ESG Dorian (1978b: 596-98, 1981b: 136) found that, though her OFSs and YFSs were conservative in their use of the various plural formation devices (11 in all), her SSs show considerable increase in the use of suffixes to form plurals, especially the suffix /ən/, i.e. that final mutation as an aspect of plural formation was being lost in ESG. This sudden increase is probably due to English influence, where suffix plurals are the norm, than to morphological innovation due to loss of final mutation.

4.3.5. Summary

As we have seen, there has been a tendency towards simplification and reduction in the application of initial and final mutation in LM. Dressler (1972b) noted a similar tendency in the dialect of Breton he investigated. In this regard, as noted earlier, he formulated the following hypothetical principle of language death:

> If a rule is optional with the older generation which has a full and varied command of a still vigorous language system, it is lost in the disintegrating language of a younger generation (Dressler 1972b: 452).

How far this applied to Manx is uncertain, since the informants had all died before this investigation took place. Nevertheless, it is possible to give examples of the loss of the lenition rule. From the transition from CM to LM the following are noted:

1. Simplification of the application of lenition, already begun in CM, proceeds apace in LM towards non-application (cf. §4.3.2.1.), affecting gender, case, after possessive particles, after numerals, in adjectives after original feminine nouns, in adjectives after qualifying adverbs, after various prepositions, in the infinitive, in the perfect tense of verbs, in definite nouns in dependent genitival position, in the preterite of verbs.

2. But lenition is retained in secondary forms without base forms (§4.3.2.2.).

3. The reduction in application of lenition due to "lexical decay" and perhaps imperfect perception leads, as in the case of palatalisation above (§4.2.4.3.), to the "abuse" or hypercorrect use of lenition (§4.3.2.3.) and false delenition (§4.3.2.4.).

4. Simplification in the application of nasalisation, already under way in CM but attested in a number of environments (§4.3.3.1.), accelerates in LM (§4.3.3.2.) to be retained only in fossilised phrases, place-names, and after certain pre-verbal particles.

5. Nasalisation is retained in circumstances showing permanent nasalisation (§4.3.3. 3.), as in verbs and adverbs.

6. Final mutation, i.e. the palatalisation of dentals and laterals to indicate attenuated plural forms (of the o-stem type), becomes lost due to indistinction and imperfect perception, resulting in the application of a suffix.

4.4. Morphology

4.4.1. Nouns in Classical Manx

4.4.1.1.Gender: loss of distinction

In Manx nouns may be divided into two genders: masculine and feminine; the former is unmarked. In CM nouns can essentially be regarded as masculine unless there is evidence to suggest they are not . Even when an inanimate noun has clearly been marked as feminine, the pronoun referring to it is only exceptionally the fem. *ee* (G. *i*) (cf. Thomson 1969a: 197). Any gender distinction appears in the third-person singular personal pronoun, but even here discrepancies are frequent, as the notion of 'it' is almost exclusively expressed by *eh* /e/ 'he, him' (cf. Broderick 1993: 239). In CM there is even an attempt to distinguish orthographically between the sense 'he is' (*t'eh*) and 'it is' (*te*), though, as Cregeen notes (C.196), "[...] both words are sounded alike [...]".

4.4.1.2. Number: change of number marking

The Old Irish declensions according to stem formation are reflected in CM only in the contrast of two types of plural: internal or attenuated, or suffixal (cf. Broderick 1991: 65-73). The former continue or imitate original *o*-stem plurals: *fer* 'man, one' /fer/, pl. *fir* /fir/, G. *fear*; the latter the rest, with occasional continuation of the historical consonant stem formation infixed before the common plural suffix -*yn* /ən/: *sooill* 'eye' /suːl/ (orig. *i*-stem), pl. *sooillyn* /suːlʹən/ G. *súil*; *carrey* 'friend' /karə/ (orig. stem in -*t*, pl. /karədʹ/) G. *cara*, pl. (Mx.) *caarjyn* /kəːrdʹən/, cf. ScG. *càirdean*.

4.4.1.3. Case: the simplified system of Classical Manx

4.4.1.3.1. The nominative, accusative, and dative singular

By the period of CM the original nominative, accusative and dative singular had long fallen together, generally under the old nominative: *carrey* 'friend' /karə/ (orig. a/d. /karidʹ/), but frequently under the old accusative or dative: *thie* 'house' (old dative; old nom. /tʹex/). The dative singular is found also in one or two nominal phrases: *er c(h)osh* 'on foot, up':

- *cha nel eh er-cosh foast*
(Neg. SbV Pn. Prep. N(dat.) Adv.)
/ha ˈnel i erə (*sic*) kaːsˊ foːs/ N/HLSM/II: 147 s.v. *er-cosh*
'he is not up yet'
(lit. 'not is he on foot yet').

4.4.1.3.2. Maintenance of marking in the vocative

The vocative is the common case lenited with or without prefixed particle /ə/: (sg.) *carrey* /karə/ 'friend', voc. *y charrey* /əˈxarə/, (pl.) *y chaarjyn* /ə ˈxəːdʹən/ (cf. also §§ 4.3.1.1.1. & 4.3.1.2.1. above). There is no evidence of final mutation in the expression of the vocative in CM due to absence of relevant examples.

4.4.1.3.3. The genitive singular: loss and maintenance

4.4.1.3.3.1. Feminine

The genitive singular survives in a number of examples, usually with the suffix /ə/ (*a*-, *i*-, *u*-stems) and generally feminine: *muck* 'pig' /muk/, g.sg. *ny muickey* /nə ˈmukʹə/ (w. def. art.) (cf. also Thomson 1969a: 197)).

4.4.1.3.3.2. Masculine

Occasionally attenuated masculine genitives are found (usually in nouns in *-agh* /ax/ or nouns (or verb-nouns) in *-ey* /-ə/, with genitive in *-ee* /-i/: *ollagh* 'cattle' /olax/, g.sg. *ollee* /oli/, *poosey* 'marrying' /puːsə/ , g. *poosee* /puːsi/), but almost exclusively in nominal phrases: *thie-ollee* 'cowhouse' /tai 'oːli/, *car y phoosee* 'wedding reel' /kaːrə 'fuːsi/.

Except for examples such as the foregoing the inflected form of the genitive in CM is not generally used where it would be expected:

> 1. *laa yn chaggey* (N Art. Ngen.(len.) Hosea X 14 (1773)
> 'the day of the battle'
> : not g. *-chaggee* (Ngen.(len. & pal.))
> (though *sheshaght-chaggee* (N Ngen.(len. & pal.)) 'army' (lit. 'band of war') universally).

> 2. *pooar y vaase* (N Art. Ngen.(len.) Hebrews II 14 (1767)
> 'the power of death'
> : not g. *y vaaish* (Art. Ngen.(len. & pal.)).

> 3. *baase yn fer* (N Art. Ngen. (non-len.) Hosea IX 16 (1767)
> 'the death of the man'
> : not *yn 'ir* (Art. Ngen.(len. & pal.))
> (cf. Thomson 1969a: 196).

In general the genitive singular, when it appears, occurs in set phrases: Isaiah VII 20 (1773) *folt y ching* 'the hair of his head' (nom. *kione*), *siyn cloaie* 'vessels of stone, stone vessels' (nom. *clagh*) (cf. Thomson 1969a: 195), or in *fer* /fer/ 'man' + verb-noun to express agent: *fer-ynsee* 'teacher' /fer 'insi/ (lit. 'man of teaching'; nom. *ynsagh*).

4.4.1.3.4. The genitive and dative plural

Apart from traces of genitive plurals having the same form as the nominative singular (as in *o*-stems, etc): (placename): *Bul na garvel* 'fold of the horses' (Mx. *bwoaill' na gabbyl*, nom.sg. *cabbyl*, G. *buaile na gcapall*, nom.sg. *capall*) (cf. PNIM/II: 21), and of dative plurals in *-oo* /-u/ in phrasal prepositions and adverbs: *er-beealloo* 'in front of' (lit. 'at the lips of') /er 'biːlu/ (G. *ar béalaibh*), *er-my-chooylloo* 'behind me' (G. *air mo chùlaibh*), there is only one common case in the plural (cf. Thomson 1969a: 194-201, Broderick 1991: 65-79, 1993: 239-40).

4.4.2. The noun in Late Manx

4.4.2.1. Gender: loss of marking

The tendencies that produced a simplified system of gender in CM have been carried further in LM. The methods by which gender can be distinguished, viz. the genitive case, the presence or absence of *t-* after the def. art. in the nom. and acc. sg. of nouns in *s-*, the lenition or non-lenition of the initial consonant after the def. art., or the lenition or non-lenition of a qualifying adjective or noun genitive following the noun, have in LM for the most part disappeared.

The use of the pronoun to determine gender in LM does not help us at all, as the form used is almost always the masc. form *eh* /e/, irrespective of what it represents, and the use of the fem. pronoun would seem to be arbitrary (e.g. *brashlagh* 'wild mustard' is repr. by both masc. and fem. pronouns in the same text, which clearly indicates the loss of gender distinction, cf. HLSM/I: 202-03). However, the only occasion masc. and fem. pronouns indicate the gender of nouns they replace are when they refer to persons or animals (cf. HLSM/I: 25ff.):

1. *Dan Caley, [...] v'eh soie ayns stoyll-dreeym mooar*
(Pers.N ... SbV Pn. VbN Prep. N Ngen.(unmarked) Adj.)
/daːn 'kˊeːli, ...vi 'sai us stol drim 'muːə/ N/HLSM/I: 230-31
'Dan Caley, ...he used to sit in a big armchair
(lit. 'Dan Caley, ...was he sitting in an armchair big').

2. *Ren [...] yn jouyl eh hene cheet gys Aaue tra v'ee goll mygeayrt y garey*
(V...Art. N Pn. Reflex. VbN Prep. Pers.N Conj. SbV Pn. VbN Prep. Art. N)
/rin...ən dˊeul a'hiːn tˊet gus ɑu treː vei gol mə'giːrt ə 'geːrə/ N/HLSM/I: 198-99
'the devil himself...came to Eve while she was going about the garden
(lit. 'did...the devil himself coming to Eve while was she going about the garden').

3. *Tra haink ee ayns imbagh v'ee currit ayns cart...*
(Conj. V Pn. Prep. N SbV Pn. Vppp. Prep. N)
/treː heŋk i uns embax vei kurətˊ uns 'kaːrt.../ N/HLSM/I: 216-17
'when she (the sow) came into seson she would be placed in a cart...'
(lit. 'when came she in season was she put in a cart').

Personal names of males are usually masculine:

Juan Mooar Etty
/dˊuːn muːr 'eti/ N/HLSM/II: 488
'Juan Mooar Etty'
(i.e. Big Juan, son of Hetty').

But failure of concord in the qualifier also occurs:

Caine Veg Doodlee
/keːn veg 'dudəli/ (instead of *Beg*) N/HLSM/II: 483
'Caine Beg Doodlee ' (i.e. Little Caine (son of) Doodlee').

Similarly personal names of females are usually feminine:

Bess Wooar
/bes 'wuːr/ S/HLSM/II: 483

'big Bess'

But cf. *Mary Mooar Vaarlagh/Baarlagh*

/meːɾi mur(ə)'veːrlax/beːrlax/ N/HLSM/II: 490

'Big Mary the English speaker' for older **Mary Vooar Vaarlagh*, w. len. in both quali-
fiers.

In ESG Dorian (1981b: 124-25) noticed that pronoun replacement as a gender signal shows

a good deal of decay. The masculine pronoun /a/ is being extended to use with all inanimates,
presumably on the model of English "it". Six reliable feminine nouns in the gender texts
should have produced replacements with the feminine pronoun /i/, but OFSs used only 16 in 24
opportunities (66.5 percent), and YFSs used only 7 in 24 opportunities (29 percent) [...]. SSs
[...] used none (Dorian 1981b: 125).

4.4.2.2. Number: change of marking in Late Manx

As with EM and CM, nouns in LM have two numbers: singular and plural. The singular is
used with the numerals 1 and most of the time with 2 (also with 11 and 12): *unnane thie*
'one house' /u'neːn 'taːi/, *daa vee* 'two months' /deː 'viː/. The plural is also found with 2: *daa
deiney* 'two men' /deː 'diːn´ə/ (cf. HLSM/I: 274-75).

The noun *blein* /blɛːn/ 'year' has a special plural with numerals, viz. *bleeaney: hogh
bleeaney* /hoːx bliənə/ 'eight years' (cf. HLSM/II: 34, s.v. *blein*. In LM the usual plural
form *bleeantyn* /blintən/ is also found with numerals: *tree bleeantyn jeig* /triː blintən 'd´eg/
'thirteen years' (cf. HLSM/I: 360-61).

However, whereas internal or attenuated plurals in CM can be formed by application of final mutation (cf. also §4.3.4. above), whereby a final neutral consonant (usu. in orig. *o*-
stems) in n/a. pl. is palatalised (cf. Broderick 1991: 69) , this rule is all but lost in LM.

	Singular		Plural
(older)	*cabbyl* /kaːbəl/ 'horse'	:	*cabbil* /kaːbil´/ 'horses'
			w. raising in final syll. before palat. /l/.
			-> *cabbylyn* /kaːbələn/ in LM

However, as /kaːbəl/ also occurs side by side with /kaːbil´/ to express the n/a.pl, viz. *as yn
tree cabbyl echey* /as ən triː 'k´aːbəl egə/ 'and his three horses' N/HLSM/I: 236-37 (but notice *ta ram cabbil aym* /ta 'ram 'kabəl´ em/ (w. final mutation) N/HLSM/II: 55 s.v. *cabbyl*),
and because of the loss of final mutation, the sg. and pl. forms have become homophonous.
As a result the suffix plural marker /-ən/ has been applied to /kaːbəl/ to distinguish it from
the singular, i.e. the loss of allophonic variation has thus led to morphological innovation in
LM.

Note a similar development in ESG (cf. Dorian 1981b: 136). For further information on
plural formations in LM, cf. HLSM/I: 33-35.

4.4.2.3. Case: loss of marking in Late Manx

As with CM the common case for the singular is mostly that of the old nominative (with exceptions as in CM; cf. also Broderick 1991: 77-78). There may be survival of signalling (lenition) in the vocative case in LM.

4.4.2.3.1. Loss of the vocative

Survival of initial lenition to indicate the vocative is rare and is mainly restricted to interjections or exclamations. There is no evidence of final mutation suffixation For examples see §4.3.2.1.12. above.

Gradual loss of signalling in the vocative in ESG is also attested, cf. Dorian (1981b: 134-35), dropping off sharply with SSs.

4.4.2.3.2. The genitive singular

The genitive singular, once used in possessive constructions or expressing the 'part-of-relationship', has disappeared as a distinct form in LM. Instead the dependent noun occurs with or without the definite article or possessive particle uninflected, i.e. as a lexical base form.

LM	Earlier
1. *sheshaght-chaggey*	: *sheshaght-chaggee* (G. *seiseacht* + *chogaidh*)
(N Ngen.(len.))	(N Ngen.(len. & pal.)) (always in CM in this ex.)

/sˊesˊax ˈkaːgə/ S/HLSM/II: 399 s.v. *sheshaght*.
'war-band/host, army'
(lit. 'band/host of war').

2. *mullagh y glion*	: ...*y ghlionney* (G. *gleann*, g.sg. *gleanna*)
(N Art. N)	(...Art. Ngen.(len. & suffix))
/mulax ə ˈglˊeun/ N/HLSM/I: 28	: */...ə ˈɣˊlˊonə/

'top of the glen'.

In the foregoing two examples in LM the possession or 'part-of-relationship' is expressed only by position, whereas earlier it was marked by lenition and palatalisation only if the def. art, poss. pn, etc, preceded, or the head-noun was fem. sg.

cooyl my chione	: ...*my ching* (G. *ceann*, g.sg. *cinn*)
(N Poss.part. Ngen.(len.))	(...Poss.part. Ngen. (len./Umlaut/ Pal.)
/kuːl mə ˈxˊoːn/ N/HLSM/II: 234 s.v. *kione*	: */...mə ˈxˊiŋˊ/

'the back of my head'.

In ESG Dorian (1981b: 130-31) found that the genitive singular, even by OFSs, was being replaced by a prepositional phrase. Her SSs used it almost exclusively. In LM there are some examples of prep. phrases to express the relationship 'part of':

1. *bit dy bee*　　　　　: *bit bee*　(E. 'bit', G. *biadh*, g. sg. *bidh*)
(Pn. prep. N)　　　　　: (Pn. N)
/bit də 'biː/ S/HLSM/II: 33 s.v. *bit*
'a bit of food'.
Note also:
bit eeym, bit arran
(Pn. N,　Pn. N)
/bis (*sic*) 'ibm, bis (*sic*) aran/ S/HLSM/II: 33 s.v. *bit*
bit of butter, bit of bread'.

2. *jeih as feed dy keirdeeyn*
(Num Conj. Num. Prep. Npl.)
/dʹai as fid də keːdiən/ [N]/HLSM/I: 50
'thirty smithies'
(lit. 'ten and twenty of smithies').
Earlier this would have been expressed as
jeih keirdee(yn) as feed　(lit. 'ten smithy/ies and twenty').

4.4.2.3.3. Survival of the genitive singular in fossilised phrases in Late Manx

However, in LM there are still examples of the genitive singular, both masculine and feminine, which occur in some fossilised phrases. The following syntactic structures have preserved the old genitive:

4.4.2.3.3.1. Masculine nouns occurring with def. art. or possessive adjective

1. *mullagh e king*
(N Poss.part. Nmasc.gen.(umlaut & pal.))
/mulax ə 'kiŋ/ N/HLSM/II: 254 s.v. *kione.*
'top of his head'
(nom.sg. *kione* 'head') (w. failure of len. in *ching*)

2. *jough y dorrish*
N Art.(masc.gen.) VbNgen.(pal.))
/dʹɒːx ə 'dorasʹ/ (*rectius* *dorisʹ/ S/HLSM/I: 239 s.v. *jough*
(but also
/dʹoːx ə dorəs/) S/HLSM/II: 239 *ibid.*
(N Art. Ngen.(unmarked))
'drink of/at the door' (the last drink before one departs)(n.sg. *dorrys* 'door')

4.4.2.3.3.2. Masculine nouns with genitive in compounds or in combination

1. *cleigh cagliee* (nom.sg. *cagliagh* 'boundary')
(N Nmasc.gen.(umlaut & pal.))

/kLei kagLi/ N/HLSM/II: 57 s.v. *cagliagh*
'boundary fence' (lit. 'fence of boundary').

2. *doagh feeyney* (nom.sg. *feeyn* 'wine')
(N Nmasc.gen.(suffix))
/do:x 'fi:nə/ N/HLSM/II: 122
'wine vat' (lit. 'vat of wine').

3. *stoyll drommey* (nom.sg. *dreeym* 'back')
(N Nmasc.gen.(umlaut + suffix))
/s′to:l 'drumə/ S/HLSM/II: 435 s.v. *stoyll*
'armchair' (lit. 'chair of back', i.e. with a back on it)

With genitives of verbal nouns:

4. *clagh shleeuee* (n.sg. *shleeuagh* 'whetting')
(N VbNgen.(umlaut + pal.) (pal. ending lost in Mx.)
/klɑːx 's′1′ui/ S/HLSM/II: 80-81 s.v. *clagh*
'whetting stone' (lit. 'stone of whetting').

5. *greie kiaullee* (nom.sg. *kiaulleeagh* 'making music, playing, singing')
(N VbNgen. (umlaut (in final syll.) + pal.)) (final syll. & pal. ending lost here)
/grei 'k′o:li/ N/HLSM/II: 210 s.v. *greie*
'musical instrument' (lit. 'instrument of musicking').

6. *mwyllin bwoaillee* (nom.sg. *bwoalley* 'striking')
(N VbNgen.(umlaut + pal.)) (pal. ending lost here)
/mul′in′ 'buli, bul′ə/ N&S/HLSM/II: 311
'threshing mill' (lit. 'mill of beating, thrashing').
For other exx. see HLSM/I: 28.

4.4.2.3.3.3. Feminine noun with def. art. or possessive adjective

1. *dooid ny h-oie* (nom.sg. *oie* 'night')
(N Art.(fem.gen.) Pref. h- N)
/du:əd′ nə 'hi:/ S/HLSM/II: 125 s.v. *dooid*
'the blackness of the night'.

2. *eaghtyr ny marrey* (nom.sg. *muir* (m.), g.sg. (f.) *marrey*)
(N Art.(fem.gen.) Nfem.gen.(umlaut + suffix))
/i:xtə nə 'ma:rə/ S/HLSM/II: 139 s.v. *eaghtyr*
'the surface of the sea'.

3. *cassan ny greiney* (nom.sg. *grian* 'sun')
(N Art.(fem.gen.) Nfem.gen.(umlaut + suffix))

/kasən nə 'greːnə/ N/HLSM/II: 61
'the Zodiac' (lit. 'footpath of the sun').

4.4.2.3.3.4. Feminine nouns with genitive in compounds or in combination

1. *croae snaidey* (nom.sg. *snaid* 'needle')
(N Nfem.(suffix))
/kreu 'snedˊə/ S/HLSM/II: 106
'eye of a needle'.

2. *meeyl keyrragh* (nom.sg. *keyrrey* 'sheep')
(N Nfem.gen.(change of suffix))
/midl 'kiːrax/ S/HLSM/II: 296 s.v. *meeyl*
'sheep louse' (lit. 'louse of sheep').

3. *Shamyr hoshee lhongey* (nom.sg. *toshiagh* 'beginning, forward'; *lhong* 'ship')
(N Nmasc.gen.(umlaut + pal.(lost)) Nfem.gen.(suffix))
/sˊembər hosˊi 'luŋə/ N/HLSM/II: 391 s.v. *shamyr*
'ship's forward room' (lit. 'room of forward of ship').

In the last ex. the form *hoshee* w. initial lenited /t/ shows *shamyr* as a fem. noun. Had *shamyr* been treated as a masc. then no len. would have taken place, and we would have had *toshee*, cf. *fer-toshee* 'leader' (lit. 'man of/at the beginning, front'). For other exx. see and HLSM/I: 29.

4.4.2.3.3.5. Genitive forms in personal and place-names

Thomas Pherick (nom.sg. *Perick* 'Patrick')
(Pers.N Pers.Nmasc.gen.(len.))
/toməs 'ferik/ S/HLSM/II: 493
'Thomas (son) of Patrick'.

Here the genitive is marked by lenition as well as position, as is usual with (masc.) personal names.

Port y Vwyllin (nom.sg. *mwyllin* 'mill', G. *muileann*, g. *muilinn*)
(N Art. Nmasc.gen.(len. + pal.(lost))
/poːrtə 'vulˊən/ N/HLSM/II: 508 (place-name)
'harbour of/by the mill'.
For further exx. cf. PNIM/I/II/III.

4.4.2.3.3.6. Genitive forms in bird names

lossyr ny keylley (nom.sg. *keyll* 'wood')
(N Art.(fem.gen.) Nfem.gen.(suffix))

/laːs nə 'keːilˊə/ N/HLSM/II: 283
'goldfinch' (lit. 'flame of the wood').

4.4.2.3.3.7. Genitive forms after verb-nouns

1. *va mee laccal fosley yn dorrish*
(SbV Pn. VbN VbN Art.(gen.) Nmasc.gen.(umlaut + pal.))
/va mi laːl foːslə ən doresˊ/ S/HLSM/I: 358-59
'I was wanting to open the door'
(lit. 'was I wanting an opening of the door').

2. *v'ad freayll yn faail...son giarrey*   : nom.sg. *faayl* /faːl/
(SbV Pn. VbN Art.(masc.gen.) Nmasc.gen.(umlaut + pal.)
/vad friːlˊən faːilˊ...son 'gˊaːrə/
'they were keeping the turf-spade...for cutting'
(lit. 'were they a-keeping of the turf-spade...for cutting').

3. *va ny guillyn aegey whistlal dy geddyn geayee* : nom.sg. *geay*, G. *gaoth*, *-gaoith*
(SbV Art. Npl. Adj(pl.) VbN Vinf. (Prep.+ VbN) Nfem.gen.(pal.))
/va nə gilˊən 'eːgə hwistlal də gedən 'gəːi/ S/HLSM/I: 328-29
'the young lads were whistling to get wind'
(lit. 'were the lads young whistling for a getting of wind').
As examples of this featrure are rare, they could be viewed as survivals in fixed phrases, esp.
the first and third exx.

4.4.2.3.3.8. Genitive forms in prepositional phrases

fud ny h-oie (nom.sg. *oie* 'night', G. *oidhche*)
(Nom.prep. Art.(fem.gen.) Pref. h N)
/fud nə 'hiː/ S, /fud nə 'hei/ N/HLSM/II: 178-79 s.v. *fud*
'all through the night' (lit. (on) length of the night').
Mx. *fud*, G. *ar fad* (prep. + noun) is used as a nominal preposition and therefore its governing noun occurs in the genitive case.
As the g.sg. form here is the same as the nom. the genitive is marked by the fem. g. sg.
form of the def. article.

4.4.2.3.4. The genitive plural

The genitive plural as a separate morphological feature does not exist in LM. Nouns in genitival position have the same form as the nominative/accusative plural and are genitive only
by position (Npl. Npl, N Art.pl. Npl., or VbN Art.pl. Npl.):
1. *thieyn claghyn*
(N Npl.)
/taiiən 'klaːn/ HLSM/II: 81 s.v. *clagh*
'houses of stones, stone houses'

2. *smoghan ny lossree* (nom.sg. *lossragh* 'herb', G. *lusrach, -aich*)
(N Art. Npl.)
/smɔxən nə 'loːsəri/ N/HLSM/II: 418 s.v. *smoghan*
'the scent of the herbs'.
The pl. form is usu. *lossreeyn*, i.e. w. a double pl.

3. *shooyll ny thieyn* (nom.sg. *thie* 'house')
(VbN Art. Npl.)
/sʹuːlʹ nə 'taiən/ N/HLSM/II: 405 s.v. *shooyll*
'(a) walking (of) the houses' (i.e. 'begging').

In the first two exx. the plural *claghyn* is probably quite late, since the singular would be more natural as a quasi-adjective. For further exx. see HLSM/I: 29.

4.4.2.3.5. The dative plural

The dative plural of nouns in LM is the same in form as the nominative plural:

v'ad currit lesh thie ec ny deiney dy ve bwoailt lesh suishtyn
(SbV Pn. Vppp. Prep. Adv. Prep. Art. npl. SbVinf. Vppp. Prep. Npl.)
/ved kurətʹ lʹesʹ taːi ek nə deːnʹə də ve bulʹtʹ lʹesʹ susʹtʹən/ S/HLSM/I: 326-27
'they (the bundles of corn) would be brought home by the men to be threshed with flails'
(lit. 'were they brought home at the men to be thrashed with flails').

There are, however, occasional survivals of the old dative plural in nominal phrases:

er-beealloo (rad. *beeal* 'mouth, lip')
(Prep. Ndat.pl.(inflec.))
'before' (lit. 'on lips (of)'); cf. also §4.4.1.3.3. above.

In the context of noun gender, number, and case in LM it can be seen that reduction in or simplification of the foregoing occurred as an internal development in CM (but taken further in LM) primarily as a result of loss of the final mutation distinguishing number and case particularly, which led to a reduction in case marking (cf. also Broderick 1991: 66-68) and an increased use in suffixes to distinguish plural from singular (see also above).

In ESG the dative singular becomes indistinguishable from the nom/acc. among OFSs and YFSs, i.e. use of lenition in the dative is replaced (in ESG) with nasalisation (as in the nom/acc.), except in fossilised phrases (cf. Dorian 1981b: 131-32). However, though many of her SSs used lenition in the dative (and Dorian regards this being more conservative on their part), nevertheless this could simply be a case of attempted hypercorrection (as in LM, cf. §4.3.2.3), and that the application of lenition may just be a lucky strike.

4.4.3. The adjective in Classical Manx

4.4.3.1. The attributive adjective

Adjectives in CM usually follow the noun they qualify and are usually invariable as to gender and case, though there may also be lenition in an adjective following a feminine noun: *mooar* /muːr/ 'big' *ben vooar* /ben 'vuːr/ 'big woman'. However, a handful, mainly monosyllabic adjectives, may form a plural in *-ey* /ə/ in attributive position only:

> *dooinney mooar* /dunʹə 'muːr/ 'man big', viz. 'a big man',
> pl. *deiney mooar<u>ey</u>* /deːnʹə 'muːrə/ 'men big', viz. 'big men'.

In nominal use adjectives in *-agh* /-ax/ and one or two other *o*-stem types may form a plural by a vowel change: *peccagh* /pekax/ 'sinner', pl. *peccee* /peki/ 'sinners', *baccagh* /bakax/ 'lame', pl. *ny baccee* /nə 'baki/ 'the lame'.

4.4.3.2. Comparative and superlative in the adjective

With regard to comparison, the framework is a relative clause introduced by the copula *'s* /s/ (rarely the past *by* /bə/ + adj. when attributive), and relative *ny* /nə/ + copula + adjective, usually without any modification of form: *gloyroil* /gloː'roːlʹ/ 'glorious', /nəs'gloːroːlʹ/ 'more glorious' (lit. 'that which is more glorious'). In such cases, however, the periphrastic construction with *smoo* /smuː/ 'greater, more' + positive form of the adjective is normal: *ny smoo gloyroil* /nəs'muː gloːˈroːlʹ/ 'more glorious' (lit. 'that which is more glorious').

Modification, when it does occur (in monosyllables), usually involves raising of the stem vowel + palatalisation of the following consonant + suffix in *-ey* /-ə/:

> *shenn* /sʹen/, /sʹaːn/ 'old' -> *ny shinney* /nə 'sʹinʹə/ 'older' (lit. 'that which is older');

adjectives in *-agh* /-ax/ generally substitute *-ee* /-i/:

> *berchagh* /bertʹax/ 'rich' -> *ny s'berchee* /nəs 'bertʹi/ 'richer' (lit. 'that which is richer').

Irregular comparison also occurs: *mie* /mai/ 'good' -> *ny share* /nə sʹeːr/ 'better' (lit. 'that which is better').

In CM there is no distinction between comparative and superlative. The former is indicated by *na* /na/ 'than': *t'eh ny shinney na mish* /ti nə 'sʹinʹə na 'misʹ/ 'he is older than I', the latter when the noun followed by the compared adjective is definite: *yn fer share* /ən fer 'sʹeːr/ 'the best man/one' (lit. 'the man/one who is best') (cf. Thomson 1984b: 311-12; Broderick 1993: 240-41).

4.4.4. The adjective in Late Manx

4.4.4.1. The attributive adjective: loss of number agreement

The adjective in LM, whether monosyllabic or polysyllabic, following a plural noun is usually in the singular (Npl. Adj.sg.):

118

LM	Earlier

1. *fammanyn mooar liauyr*   : *fammanyn mooarey liauyrey*
(Npl.(ən) Adj.sg. Adj.sg.)   (Npl. Adj.(pl.(ə) Adj.(pl.)(ə))
/famanən muːə 'lˊauə/ N/HLSM/II: 236-37 : */famanən muːrə 'lˊaurə/
'big long tails' (lit. 'tails big long')

2. *pohnaryn beg*   : cf. also *ny pohnaryn beggey*
(Npl.(ən) Adj.sg.)   (Art.pl. Npl.(ən` Adj.(pl.(ə))
/poː nˊarən 'beg/ S/HLSM/:326-27 : /nə poːnˊarən 'begə/ S/HLSM/II: 332
'little children' (lit. 'children little').   s.v. *pohnar*

3. *ny Guillyn Bane*
(Art.pl. Npl.(ən) Adj.sg.)
/ne gilˊen 'beːn/ S/HLSM/II: 215 s.v. *guilley* :
'the white boys' (lit. the boys white), i.e. 'the White Boys' (folklore)

4. *ny deiney aeg*
(Art.(pl.) Npl. Adj.(sg.))
/nə deːnˊə eːg/ N/HLSM/I: 174-75
'the young men' (lit. 'the men young').

Nevertheless, a plural form of the (monosyllabic) adjective is also attested:

5. *boaylyn boggey*
(Npl.(ən) Adj.(pl.)(ən))
/boːlən 'bɔgə/ N/HLSM/I: 38.
'marshy places' (lit. 'places marshy').

6. *keimyn liauyrey*
(Npl.(ən) Adj.(pl.)(ən))
/keːmən 'lˊaurə/ N/HLSM/II: 277 s.v. *liauyr*.
'long steps' (lit. 'long steps')

7. *[ny] Guillyn Baney*
((Art.pl.) Npl.(ən) Adj.(pl.)(ən))
/[nə] gilˊən 'beːnə/ S/HLSM/II: 214 s.v. *guilley*.
'the white boys' (lit. the boys white'), i.e. 'the White Boys' (folkore)

8. *deiney aegey*
(Npl. Adj.(pl.)(ə))
/deːnə 'eːgə/ N/HLSM/II: 3-4 s.v. *aeg*.
'young men' (lit. 'men young').

However, the trend is towards non-agreement is to be seen as a simplification; cf. HLSM/I: 38. In ESG (Dorian 1981b: 127-28) there seems to be a tendency to lenite attributive adjectives after masc. nouns, even by OFSs, but increasing in use by YFSs and indiscriminately used by SSs. This perhaps could be attributed either to hypercorrection or a failing in knowledge as to correct usage. There is also non-mutation in the adjective after both genders.

4.4.4.2. The comparative and superlative adjective

The situation is similar to that for CM, but there is a greater tendency to simplify and to avoid inflection, i.e. the positive form of the adjective is used, and we find older and simplified forms side by side.

1. *aeg* /eːg/ 'young', *ny s'aeg* /nə 'seːg/ N/HLSM/II: 328 s.v. *ny s'aeg* 'younger'. This is made up of the rel. part. *ny* + rel. of copula *s* + positive form of the adjective, viz. 'that which is younger'.
: also *ny saa* /nə seː/ N/S/HLSM/II: 328.
Here we find also the comparative form of the adjective *aeg*, viz. *aa*.

2. *deyr* /deːr/ 'dear', *ny s'deyr* /nə 'steːr/ N/HLSM/I: 41 'dearer'
: also comparative form *ny s'deyrey* /nə 'steːrə/ S/HLSM/II: 329.

3. *lajer* /leːd´ə/ 'strong', *ny s'lajer* /nəs'leːd´ə/ S/HLSM/II: 331 s.v. *ny s'lajer* 'stronger'
: also comparative form *ny stroshey* /nə 'stroːs´ə/ N/HLSM/II: 333.

4. *shenn* /s´en/ 'old', *ny shenn* /nə s´en/ S/HLSM/II: 330 s.v. *ny shenn* 'older'
: also comparative form *ny shinney* /nə s´in´ə/ S/HLSM/II: 330.
For further exx. see HLSM/I: 41-42.

The attributive in LM also leans towards greater simplification:

LM	Earlier
1. *yn dooinney s'berchagh*	: ... *s'berchee*
(Art. N Rel.cop. Adj.)	: *.../sɹ̩ertˊiː/
/ən dunˊə sɹ̩eːrtˊax/ N/HLSM/II: 381 s.v. *s'berchagh*)	
'the man who is richest, the richest man'.	

And sometimes the predicative form is found:

2. *yn yiarn ny share*	: *yn yiarn share*
(Art. N Rel.part. Cop. Adj.) :	* /in jaːn 'sˊeːr/
/in jaːdn nə sˊeː/ N/HLSM/I: 43	
'the iron which is better/best, the best iron'.	

For further details of influences from English see §4.6. below.

4.4.5. The definite article in Classical Manx

The article in Manx can only be definite. There is no indefinite article: /beːdə/ 'boat', or 'a boat'.

The forms of the definite article are:

<u>Singular:</u> (nom/acc/dat. case): *y* /ə/ or *yn* /ən/, /in/;

(gen. masc.): *y/yn* + len.;

(gen. fem.): *ny* /nə/ (when the fem. has a distinctive form)

<u>Plural:</u> *ny* /nə/.

4.4.5.1. Singular nom/acc/dat.

yn dooinney /ən 'dunˊə/ 'the man' (nom.)

ta mee fakin yn dooinney /ta mi faːɡən en 'dunˊə/ 'I see the man' (acc.)

ec yn dooinney /ek ən 'dunˊə/ 'at/by the man' (dat. or prepositional case).

4.4.5.2. Singular masculine genitive

ayns mean y vaatey /uns meːn ə 'veːdə/ 'in the middle of the boat'

w. lenition; rad. *baatey* /beːdə/ 'boat'.

4.4.5.3. Singular feminine genitive (in set phrases only)

leigh ny foalley (Romans IV 1 (1767)) 'the law of the flesh'; rad. *feill* 'flesh'.

dooid ny h-oie /duːədˊ nə 'hiː/ 'the darkness of the night'; rad. *oie* /iː/ 'night'.

4.4.5.4. Plural forms

ny claghyn /nə 'kɫaːxən/ 'the stones' (nom.)

v'eh ceau ny claghyn /vi 'kˊeu nə 'kɫaːxən/ 'he was throwing the stones' (acc.)

er oirr ny claghyn /er 'oːr nə 'kɫaːxən/ 'on the edge of the stones' (gen.)

er ny claghyn /er nə 'kɫaːxən/ 'on the stones' (dat./prep.case).

For further details see Broderick (1993: 245-48).

4.4.5.5. The singular article in titles

The singular article is also used in titles: *Yn Sushtal liorish yn Noo Mian* 'the Gospel according to St Matthew' (St. Matthew's Gospel 1748), though here in a prep. phrase. Exx. of this sort are rare in Mx.

4.4.5.6. The article in constructions containing a definite genitive

The article is usually omitted from its noun in constructions containing a definite genitive (the year refers to date of publication; cf. Thomson 1969a: 194, fn. 1):

freayney ny marrey 'the surge of the sea' (Isaiah V 30 (1773).

ushtey ny h-awin 'the water of the river' (Exodus IV 9 (1771).

biljyn y cheyll 'the trees of the wood' (Isaiah VII 2 (1773).

messyn y thallooin 'the fruits of the earth' (Judges VI 4 (1771).

For additional exx. see Thomson (1969: 195-97).

4.4.6. The definite article in Late Manx

The forms of the definite article in LM are the same as those for CM. However, in LM there is a tendency to reduce the number of forms of the article to one, viz. *y(n)*, irrespective of gender, number or case, as found in English.

4.4.6.1. Reduction of the number forms of the definite article in Late Manx

The form generally used with the plural of nouns is *ny.*

1. *ny kirree as ny goair*
(Art.(pl.) Npl. Conj. Art.(pl.) Npl.)
/nə kiri as nə goːr/ N/HLSM/I: 72
'the sheep and the lambs'

2. *ayns gien mie lesh ny ferrishyn*
(Prep. N Adj. Prep. Art.(pl.) Npl.)
/uns gin maːi lˊesˊ nə 'ferisˊən/ N/HLSM/I: 180-81
'in good standing with the fairies'
(lit. 'in standing good with the fairies').

3. *mârish ny eeasteyryn*
(Prep. Art.(pl.) Npl.)
/meːrisˊ nə ji'steːrən/ S/HLSM/I: 366-67
'with the fishermen'
For further exx. see HLSM/I: 72.

However, in LM, particularly among the last of the native speakers (recorded from 1948 on-wards) who had apparently not spoken Manx for some time, the singular forms *y, yn* are quite often found with plural nouns, as in English:

4. *y ferrishyn* /ə 'feːrisˊən/ 'the fairies' (also *ny ferrishyn* /nə 'feːrisˊən/).

5. *y colbeeyn* /in koːlbiən/ 'the heifers' (also *ny colbeeyn* /nə koːlbiən/).
For further exx. see HLSM/I: 72.

6. *cha row ad soit er y king*   : *...er ny king, er nyn ging* (w. eclipsis)
(Neg. SbV Pn. Vppp. Prep. Art.(sg.) Npl.) (...Prep. Art.(pl.) Npl.(ecl.))
/ha rou ad 'soitˊ erə 'kiŋ/ N/HLSM/I: 194-95
'they (stones) were not set on the(ir) ends'
(lit. 'were they set on th(ir) ends').
Here the sg. of the art. is used with a pl. noun *king* 'heads, ends'.

7. *er y cassyn echey*   : *er ny cassyn echey*
(Prep. Art.(sg.) Npl. Prep.pn.)   (Prep. Art.(pl.) Npl. Prep.pn.)

/erə kaːsən egə/ N/HLSM/I: 204-05   : /...nə kaːsən.../
'on his feet' (lit. 'on the feet at him')

8. *ayns yn boaylyn cair*   : *ayns ny buill chair*
(Prep. Art.(sg.) Npl. Adj.)   (Prep. Art.(pl.) N(infl.pl.) Adj.)
/usən bulən 'keːə/ N/HLSM/I: 232-33   :*/...nə buĺ 'xeːr.../
'in the right places' (lit. 'in the places right').

9. *sheidey yn bollaghyn*   : *...ny bollaghyn*
(VbN Art.(sg.) Npl.)   (...Art.(pl.) Npl.)
/sʹeːsʹən 'bolaːn/ N/HLSM/I: 232-33   :*/...nə bolaxən/
'blowing the bellows'

10. *nane jeh'n deiney*   : *nane jeh ny deiney*
(Num. Prep. Art.(sg.) Npl.)   (Num. Prep. Art.(pl.) Npl.)
/neːn dʹen 'diːnʹə/ N/HLSM/I: 270-71   : /...dʹe nə diːnʹə/
'one of the men'

11. *dys y thieyn-ollee*   : *dys ny thieyn-ollee*
(Prep. Art.(sg.) Npl. Ngen.)   (Prep. Art.(pl.) Npl. Ngen.)
/dosə taidʹnʹ 'oli/ S/HLSM/I: 332-33 :*/...nə taidʹnʹ 'oli/
'to the cowhouses' (lir. 'to the houses of cattle').

12. *v'ad thoo yn thieyn*   : *...ny thieyn*
(SbV Pn. VbN Art.(sg.) Npl.)   (...Art.(pl.) Npl.)
/vad 'tuː ən 'taːiən/ N/HLSM/I: 294-95   :*/...nə 'taːiən/
'they were thatching the houses' (lit. 'were they thatching the houses').

13. *v'eh faagail ooilley yn obbyr da'n deiney elley*   :...*da ny deiney elley*
(SbV Pn. VbN Indef.pn. Art. N Prep. Art.(sg.) Npl. Adj.)   (...Prep. Art.(pl.) Npl. Adj.)
/vi fəgeːlʹ ulʹu ən 'oːvər dən deːnʹə 'elʹa/ S/HLSM/I: 386-87 */...deː nə 'deːnʹə 'elʹa/
'he would leave all the work to the other men'
(lit. 'was he leaving all the work to the men other').

4.4.6.2. Omission of the article in titles in Late Manx

In contradistinction to CM the article is usually omitted in a title preceding a surname or personal name, perhaps influenced from English (though the examples are very few):

            LM   Earlier
1. *Saggyrt Drury ve* [rect. *v'eh*] *dooyrt eh*: EF141   **Yn Saggyrt Drury...*
((Zero cop.) N Pers.N SbV(rel.) Pn. V Pn.)   ((Zero cop.) Art. N Pers.N...)
'he said he was Parson Drury'
(lit. '(it was) Parson Drury was he said he')

2. *honnick Ayr Kellhee eh* EF161
(Vpret. N Pers.N Pn.)
'Father Kelly saw him'
(lit. 'saw Father Kelly him')

*honnick yn Ayr Kelly eh
(Vpret. Art. N Pers.N Pn.)

3. *Saggyrt Qualteragh*
(N Pers.N)
/saːgət 'kwaltərax/ N/HLSM/I: 290-91
'Parson Qualtrough'.

:

*Yn Saggyrt Qualteragh
(Art. N Pers.N)
* /ən saːgət 'kwaltərax/

But is retained with designations following the personal name:

4. *Caine y Lord*
(Pers. N Art.(nom.sg.) N(nom.sg.))
/kʹeːnə 'laːd/ N/HLSM/II: 484
'Caine the Lord' (nickname on a local Methodist preacher).

5. *Caine ny Perrickyn*
(Pers.N Art.(g.pl.) N(g.pl.))
/kʹeːn nə 'perikʹən/ N/HLSM/II: 483
'Caine of the Petticoats'
("He always dressed as a woman but worked in the fields like a man").

6. *Jem y Snieggan*
(Pers.N Art.(nom.sg.) N(nom.sg.)
/dʹibm ə 'snʹeːgən/ N/HLSM/I: 258-59
'Jim the Ant' (in rhyme).

4.4.6.3. The article in constructions containing a definite genitive

In contrast to CM the article occurs with its noun in genitive constructions, almost certainly due to influence from English:

LM		Earlier
1. *ayns y keird yn gaaue*	:	*ayns keird yn ghaaue*
(Prep. Art. N Art.(g.sg.) N(g.sg.))		(Prep. N Art.(g.sg.) N(g.sg.))
/osə kʹed ən 'gau/ N/HLSM/I: 74, 232-33 :		* /os kʹeːrd ən ɣaːu/
'in the trade of the smith'.		

2. *ec y bun ny greeishyn*
(Prep. Art. N Art.(g.pl.) N(g.pl.))
/egə bun nə 'griːsən/ S/HLSM/I: 74, 358-59 :
'at the foot of the stairs'.

:

ec bun ny greeishyn
(Prep. N Art.(g.pl.) N(gpl.))
*/ek bun nə 'griːsən/

3. *yn thie Juan*   :   *thie Yuan*
(Art. N Ngen.)   (N Ngen.)
/ən tai dˊun/ N/HLSM/I: 74, 248-49   :   */tai ˈjuan/
'the house of Juan, Juan's house'.

4. *ny schoillaryn Purt Chiarn*   :   *schoillaryn Phurt Chiarn*
(Art. Npl. PN)   (Npl. PN(len.))
/nə skolarən poːrtˊaːrn/ S/HLSM/I: 326-27:   */skolarən foːrtˊaːrn/
'the pupils of/at Port Erin'.

In the last 2 examples note also the failure of lenition in the dependent genitive (cf. also §4.3.2.1.11.).

4.4.7. Summary

In the transition from CM to LM we note the following developments:

1. In CM the system of noun gender had been reduced to one form (masc.), with some exceptions in the old feminine (§4.4.1.1.). This system pertains also in LM (§.4.4.2.1.)

2. In CM the distinction of singular and plural is maintained in LM. However, the occurrence of internal or attenuated plural forms in CM practically disappears in LM (§4.4.1.2. & §4.4.2.2.).

3. The already simplified case system of CM (§4.4.1.3.), e.g. the nom/acc/dat, the vocative, genitive singular (fem. rare; masc. in fossilisaed phrases, both in place-names), genitive plural, and dative plural (fossils only), is further simplified in LM to one case only (nominative (whether derived from oblique cases or not), with some fossils in the genitive singular and plural and dative plural. Otherwise case is marked by position or prepositional phrase only.

4. The marking of attributive adjectives after feminine singular nouns or with suffix after plural nouns in CM (§4.4.3.1.) becomes optional in application.

5. The use of inflection in the compared adjective in CM falls away in LM (§4.4.3.2. & §4.4.4.2.), so that the compared form becomes indistinguishable from the positive form.

6. In the definite article in LM we see the number and case forms (of CM §4.4.5.) reduced to one form in LM (§4.4.6.1.), its application in titles (rare) in CM (§4.4.4.5.) lost altogether in LM (§4.4.6.2.), its non-appearance in constructions containing a definitive genitive in CM (§4.4.5.6.) moving towards its appearance on the model of English (§4.4.6.3.).

4.5. Morphosyntax and Syntax: Disturbance and reduction in Late Manx

Syntax in LM is essentially similar to that of CM (cf. Thomson 1984b: 307-13, Broderick 1993: 268-81). However, disturbances do occur in LM which for the most part seem to be influenced by English idiom. The following have been noted:

4.5.1. Loss of number distinction in the imperative of the verb

In Manx the imperative is used in commands and exhortations and exists in the second-person singular and plural only, the singular with zero inflection (V + ø), the plural with suffix (V + -*jee* /-dˊiː/ or + *shiu* /sˊu/):

> *gow* /gou/ 'take' (2 sg.)
> *gow jee* /gou dˊiː/, *gow shiu* /gou sˊu/ 'take ye' (2 pl.).

For the imperative in other persons, cf. Broderick (1993: 270).

However, in LM the singular form of the imperative is sometimes used to refer to a plural noun which is in the vocative:

> 1. *giu seose, my guillyn, as gow unnane elley*
> (Vimp. Adv. Poss.part. Npl.(voc.) Conj. Vimp. Pn. Adj.)
> /gˊu 'susˊ (sic) məgilən as gou əˈnen elə/ N/HLSM/I: 87-88
> 'drink up, my boys, and take another one'
> (lit. 'drink up, my boys, and take one other')
> : *iu-jee/shiu...gow-jee/shiu* */ju dˊiː, sˊu...gou dˊiː, sˊu.../

> 2. *tar, my guillyn, dy pluckey freoagh*
> (Vimp.(2sg.) Poss.part. Npl.(voc.) Vinf. N)
> /taːr mə gilˊən də plugə freːx/ N/HLSM/II: 178 s.v. *freoagh*
> 'come, my boys, to pluck heather'.
> : *tar-jee/shiu...*/taːr díː, sˊu.../

Here the singular has probably been used on the pattern of the English invariable imperative. The form *giu* in the first example contains the particle **ag* 'at' preposed before a verbal-noun to form the participle, i.e. has coalesced with the verb stem used also to form the 2 sg. imperative.

Or there is use of both sg. and pl. (or formal) forms for the same person in the same sentence:

> 3. *cre t'ou laccal aynshoh [...]? Reue-shiu ass shoh!*
> (Interrog.pn. SbV Pn.(2sg.) VbN Adv. ... Vimp.(2pl.) Adv.phrase)
> /kreː teu laːl unsó: [...]? reusˊu as 'sˊo:/ N/HLSM/I: 186-87
> 'what do you (sg.) want here...? Get ye out of here!'
> (lit. 'what (is it that) are you wanting here? (Go) before you (2pl.) out of here').
> : *...fow royd ass shoh!* (...Vimp.(2sg.) Adv.) */feu 'roːd as 'sˊo:/ 'get you (sg.) out of here'.

This feature is not uncommon:

> 4. *fuirree ort, verrym braghtan diu; ta shiu dty guilley speeint*
> (Vimp.(2sg.) Prep.pn. V(infl.) N Prep.pn. SbV Pn.(2pl.) Prep.part.(2sg.) N Vppp.)
> /furi ort, verəm 'braːxtan deu teːsˊu də gilə spiːnˊtˊ/ N/HLSM/I: 212-13

'wait (sg.), I'll give you (pl.) a sandwich to you (pl.); you (pl.) are a smart lad'
(lit. 'wait on you (sg.), I'll give a sandwich to you (pl.); you (pl.) are in your (sg.) lad smart').
Here both sg. and pl. forms are intermingled to refer to the same person. The impv. *fuirree ort* (sg.) 'wait', (pl.) *fuirree-jee erriu* has likely been fossilised in the sg. form, the pl. being too cumbersome.
: *fuirree ort, verrym braghtan dhyt; t'ou dty ghuilley speeint*
(Vimp.(2sg.) V(infl.) N Prep.pn. SbV Pn.(2sg.) Prep.part.(2sg.) N Vppp.).

5. *trooid-shiu gys shoh mairagh as cur-lesh-mayrt hoght straueyn-oarn*
(Vimp.(2pl.) Prep. Dem.pn. Adv. Conj. Vimp.(2sg.) Num. Npl. Ngen.)
/trud´ s´u gəs 's´oː 'meːrax as kər 'l´es´ 'meːrt hoːx 'straːuən 'oːrn/
N/HLSM/I:218-19
'come here tomorrow and bring with you eight straws of barley'
(lit. 'come you (pl.) to here tomorrow and bring with you (sg.) eight straws of barley')
: *trooid gys shoh mairagh as cur lhiat hoght.../ cur-lesh-mayrt hoght straueyn-oarn*
(Vimp.(2sg.) Prep. Dem.pn. Adv. Conj. Vimp.(2sg.) Num.../Vimp.(2sg.) Num. Npl. Ngen.).
Here we have also the idiom *cur lesh* 'bring with' (taking decl. forms of *lesh* 'with', viz. *ta mee cur lhiam...* 'I bring with me...') fossilised in *cur lesh* as 'bring', w. decl. forms of *mârish* 'with'. CM has both preps. regularly when the sense is 'bring <u>with</u>'.

For loss of the 2 plural imperative in ESG, cf. Dorian (1981b: 142), where her YFSs used the impv. pl. suffix only 43% of the time. She has no exx. of mixed 2 sg./pl. forms.

4.5.2. Use of the verbal noun as an imperative form in Late Manx

In LM the verbal noun can be used as an imperative, implying that the traditional imperative form had been forgotten.

1. *na cheet shiu [cheu]sthie jeh shoh!*
(Neg.part. VbN Pn. Adv. Prep. Dem.pn.)
/nə t´ət s´ə stai d´e 's´oː/ N/HLSM/I: 176-77
'don't you (pl.) come in(side) of this (circle)'
(lit. 'not coming you (pl.) inside of this').
Here the verb-noun *cheet* 'coming' has been used instead of the traditional imperative form *tar-jee / tar-shiu* 'come ye!'
: *na tar-shiu cheusthie jeh shoh*
(Neg.part. Vimp.(2pl.) Adv. Prep. Dem.pn.)

2. *loayrt Gailck*
(VbN N)
/loːt gilk´/ N/MTT/IFC/T37:4
'speak Manx!' (lit. 'speaking Manx').
The verb-noun *loayrt* 'speaking' is used as the impv. instead of *loayr*.

: *loayr Gailck!* (Vimp. N).

Unless we take this as omission or suppression of the auxiliary *jannoo* 'do', viz. *jean*, in the impv: *ny jean cheet...*' lit. 'not do a coming', *jean loayrt Gailck!* lit. 'do a speaking (of) Manx!'.

4.5.3. Confusion of forms in close relationships and forms of address

(father complaining to his son that the son is walking quicker than he):
Mannagh jinnagh shiu fuirraghtyn son sheshaght jeem's cha bee shiu mac jeem's (N/HLSM/I: 270-71)
(Conj.neg. Vcond. Pn. VbN Prep. N Prep.pn. Neg. SbV Pn. N Prep.pn.)
/manax dʹinax sʹu 'furaxtən son sʹeiax dʹiməs haː biː sʹu 'mak dʹiməs/
'if you won't wait for my company, you'll not be a son of mine'
(lit. 'if not would do you (pl.) waiting for company of me (emph.), not will be you a son of me (emph.)').
Here the sg. form *oo* should have been expected in a father-son relationship. For *jean* in the protasis, see §4.5.4.3. below.
: *mannagh jean oo...cha bee oo...*
Here the choice of pronouns of address has been disturbed due to influence from English, where one simple form of address is used: 'you'.

4.5.4. Confusion in the tenses and tense forms

In LM the expected form of the verb does not always turn up after various conjunctions, here in temporal and conditional clauses, suggesting uncertainty as to the form required.

1. *tra bee'm scrieu reesht* EF117   : *tra nee'm screeu reesht*
(Conj. SbV(inflect.) VbN Adv.)
'when I (will) write again'
(lit. when will be I writing again').
Here the future indic. of the substantive verb, viz *bee*, has been used after *tra* 'when' where the relative form of the future, *vees*, would be expected, though the auxiliary here with a following verb-noun would be *jannoo* 'do', not *ve* 'be, viz. *tra nee'm....*

2. *my bee ee bio bee ee bio*   : *my vees ee bio bee ee bio*
(Conj. SbV Pn. Adj. SbV Pn. Adj.)
/mə biː i 'bjoː biː i bjoː/ N/HLSM/I: 180-81   : */mə viːs i bjoː.../
'if she'll live, she'll live'
(lit. 'if will be she alive, will be she alive')
As with *tra* the ordinary future indic. form *bee* has been used in the subordinate clause after *my* 'if', instead of the expected relative fut. form *vees*.

3. *mannagh jinnagh shiu fuirraghtyn son sheshaght jeem's cha bee shiu mac jeem's* (N/HLSM/I: 270-71). See foregoing.

(Conj.neg. Vcond. Pn. VbN Prep. N Prep.pn. Neg. SbV Pn. N Prep.pn.)

'if you won't wait for my company, you'll not be a son of mine'

(lit. 'if not would do you (pl.) a waiting for company of me (emph.), not will bee you (pl.) a son of me (emph.)').

Here we have the conditional form of *jannoo* 'do', viz. *jinnagh*, where we would expect the future, viz. *jean*, as in the main clause with *bee* (fut. of *ta* 'is')

: *mannagh jean oo...cha bee oo...*

4. *cha row mee er bwoailley eh [man]nagh bee eh drogh dooinney*

(Neg. SbV Pn. Prep. VbN Pn. Conj. SbV Pn. Adj. N)

/ha rou əmi ha buḷe eː na bi e drox dunˊə/ (Diary 37)

'I would not have struck him had he not been a bad man'

(lit. 'not was I after striking him, (if) not will bee he bad man')

Here we have the future in the protasis, instead of the imperfect. The indicative in the apodosis is quite normal, though the exx. are not frequent. The use of the imperfect for the pluperfect of *ve* is also not unusual.

: *cha row mee er (b)woailley eh mannagh row eh ny ghrogh ghooinney.*

(Neg. SbV Pn. Prep. VbN Pn. Conj. SbV Pn. Prep.part. Adj.(len.) N(len.))

This was translated by Joseph Woodworth (one of Marstrander's more proficient informants, cf. §3.5.2.) as:

mannagh beagh eh er ve drogh ghooinney.../manax bexe əˈveː drox ˈgunˊə.../ (Diary 23) where the pluperfect subjunctive has been used - lit. 'if he were not to have been a bad man...'.

For the form *ny ghrogh ghooinney* above, cf. §4.5.8.1. below.

In ESG Dorian (1981b: 138-41) noticed confusion in the use and form of the various tenses, e.g. non-lenition in the preterite, lenition in the future, non-lenition or unrecognisable forms in the conditional, or outright loss of the latter.

4.5.5. In the passive

The passive in CM can be expressed in three ways, all of which are periphrastic (cf. Thomson 1950-51: 278)[13]:

Type 1: by the substantive verb *ve* + noun/pronoun + past participle passive ending in *-t*, *-it*:

va mee bwoailt

(SbV N/pn. Vppp.)

'I was struck' (lit. 'was I struck').

---

[13] Of the original inflected passive or impersonal Mx. preserves only *ruggyr* 'is/was born' (cf. G. *rugadh*; the *-r* in Mx. would be from the G. pres. impers. ending *-r*) (cf. Thomson 1950-51: 278).

Type 2: by the substantive verb *ve* + noun/pronoun + *er* 'after' + possessive particle + verbal noun passive in *er n-* plus possessive particle (varying according to person) + verbal noun. Depending on the poss. part. is whther any initial mutation occurs in the following verbal noun:

va mee er my woalley (w. len. of *b-* to *v/w-* after *my* 'my')
(SbV N/Pn. Prep. *er* Poss.part.(len./nas./ø) VbN)
(lit. 'was I after my striking').

Type 3: by the substantive verb *ve* + noun/pronoun + *goll er* 'going on/after' + verbal noun:

va mee goll er bwoalley
(SbV N/pn V*goll* Prep.*er* VbN)
(lit. 'was I going after striking').
or verb *goll* (inflected tense form) + noun/pronoun + verbal noun:
hie mee er boaley
(V *goll* N/pn Prep.VbN)
(lit. 'went I after striking').

In LM Type 2 is reduced to the 3 sg. (masc.) analogical for all persons (with or without len.; cf. HLSM/I: 101-02):

1. *Va feailley mooar er ny cummal ayns Balley Cashtal*
(SbV N Adj. Prep. Prep.part. VbN Prep. PN)
/va feːlˊə ˈmuːr eː nə ˈkomal uns baːlˊə ˈkaːsˊtˊal/ S/HLSM/I: 402-03
'there was a big fair held in Castletown'
(lit. 'was a fair big after its holding in Castletown').

2. *ta mee er ny doalley lesh coau oarn*
(SbV Pn. Prep. Prep/part. VbN Prep. N Ngen.)
/te mi ernə doːlə lˊesˊ kou oːrn/ N/HLSM/II: 122 s.v. *doalley*
'I am/have been blinded by barley chaff'
(lit. 'am I after my blinding with chaff barley').

3. *ta yn thie er ny hroggal* (w. len.; rad. *troggal*)
(SbV Art. N Prep. Prep.part. VbN(len.))
/teː ən taːi ernə ˈxrogal/ S/HLSM/II: 463 s.v. *troggal*
' the house has been built'
(lit. 'is the house after its building').

4. *ta ooilley ny boallaghyn er ny huittym* (w. len.; rad. *tuittym*)
(SbV Indef.pn. Art. Npl. Prep. Prep.part. VbN(en.))
/te ˈolˊu nə ˈbaːlaən ernə ˈhodˊəm/ [S]/HLSM/I: 102
'all the walls have been fallen/felled'
(lit. 'are all the walls after their falling').
In this last exx. we would have expected in CM the 3 pl. poss. part. *nyn* + nas, viz. *er nyn duittym*.

Dorian also noticed a reduction in this form of the passive in ESG, with inappropriate use (or lack of use) of intitial mutation (cf. Dorian 1981b: 143-44).

In CM Type 2 is the more common form of the passive, in LM Type 1. Type 3 is rare in Mx. altogether (for exx. cf. Thomson 1950-51: 278, HLSM/I: 102).

4.5.6. Changes in answers to 'yes-no' questions in Late Manx:

In LM in answers to 'yes-no' questions, as in other branches of Gaelic, the verb in the question (in its dependent form) is repeated in the answer without express subject maintaining concord of mood and tense (in its dependent form if negative, in its independent form if affirmative):

1. *vel yn arroo ooilley cuirit echey? - Ta*
(Q/zero part. SbV(pres.) Art. N Adv. Vppp. Prep.pn. - SbV(pres.affirm.))
/vel ən 'aːru ul´u kwirət´ egə - teː/ S/MTT/YCG33: 2
'has he sown all the corn? Yes'
(lit. 'is the corn all sown at him - Is').

2. *nagh row ad baghey ayns Colby? - Va.*
(Q/neg.part. SbV(pret.) Pn. VbN Prep. PN - SbV(pret.affirm.))
/na 'rau ad beːxə əs kolbi - veː/ S/MTT/YCG33: 6
'weren't they living in Colby? Yes'
(lit. 'not were they living in Colby? Were').

3. *nee woish chibbyrt ta shiu geddyn yn ushtey? - She*
(Q/cop.pn. Prep. N SbV(indep.) Pn. VbN Art. N - Cop(affirm.).pn.)
/niː wus´ 't´s´uvət ta s´u gidən ən 'us´t´ə - s´eː/ S/MTT/YCG32: 4
'is it from a well you're getting the water? It is (Yes)'
(lit. 'is it from a well are you getting the water. - Is it').
This last example asks the question with the copula in a cleft sentence.

However, in LM sometimes the present tense of the substantive verb can answer a question asked with a different verb in a different tense, i.e. using *ta* and *cha nel* ('is, not is') to mean 'yes' and 'no' respctively, thus copying English syntax:

4. *Oh, va mee smooinaghtyn dy row ad ooilley marroo?. - Cha nel*
(Exclam. SbV(pret.) Pn. VbN Conj. SbV(pret.) Pn. Indef.adj. Adj. - Neg. SbV (pres.))
/oː va mi smun´an də 'rau ad ol´u maru, ha 'nel/ S/MTT/YCG33: 6
'Oh, I was thinking that they were all dead. - No'
(lit. 'oh, was I thinking that were they all dead. Not is')
: *...Cha row.

This feature is rare in the LM corpus, which suggests that in this respect at least the language was fairly intact. Had Manx lived on longer than it did, this aspect might have become more widespread.

4.5.7. Change in the placement of object pronoun and prepositional phrase in Late Manx

In Mx, even as late as LM, the object pronoun can be found *after* a prepositional phrase, in accordance with normal Gaelic practice:

   1. *yiow jeeragh eh* MH1833
   (Vfut. 2pn.sg. Adv. Pn.)
   'you'll get it right away'
   (lit. 'you'll get right away it').

   2. *ceau dys y derrey cheu eh*
   (Vimp. Prep. Art. Adj. N Pn.)
   /kʹeu dəs derə tʹeu a/ S/HLSM/II: 120 s.v. *derrey* 'other'
   'throw it to the other side'
   (lit. 'throw to the other side it').

   3. *v'ad cur magh er y geinnagh ad*
   (SbVPn. VbN Adv. Prep. Art. N Pn.) *V'ad* is an elision of *Va ad*
   /vad kər ˈmaːx erə ˈganax ed/ N/HLSM/II: 191 s.v. *geinnagh*
   'they were putting them out on the sand'
   (lit. 'were they putting out on the sand them').

However, placing the object pronoun *before* the prepositional phrase (as in English) becomes the norm:

   3. *troggal eh seose erskyn e kione*   : *erskyn e kione eh*
   (VbN Pn. Adv. Prep. Poss.part. N)
   /trogəl e ˈsuːs erˈskin ə kʹeun/ N/HLSM/I: 176-77
   'lifting it up above his head'.

   4. *v'ou jannoo eh son daa skillin as kiare pingyn*
   (SbV Pn. VbN Pn. Prep. Num. Npl. Conj. Num. Npl.)
   /vou dʹenu a son deː skilʹən as kʹeː a ˈpiŋin/ N/HLSM/I: 234-35
   'you were doing it for two shillings and four pence'
   (lit. 'were you doing it for two shillings and four pence').
   : ...*son da skillin as kiare pingyn eh*

   5. *veagh ad cur eh er y clagh mooar shoh*
   (SbVcond. Pn. VbN Pn. Prep. Art. N Adh. Dem.adj.)
   /vix ad hure erə kɬaːx ˈmuːə sʹoː/ S/HLSM/I: 344-45
   'they would be putting it on this big stone'
   (lit. 'would be they putting it on the stone big this').
   : ...*cur er y clagh mooar shoh eh*

Dorian (1981b: 155, note 42) noted that this was normal practice only with her semi-speakers. Her fluent speakers adopted normal Gaelic practice.

4.5.8. In the predicate

4.5.8.1. Loss of the prepositional particle in the indefinite predicate:

In indicating a state of affairs or function (job) the indefinite predicate noun appears in Manx usually with the substantive verb in the following formula: *ta* + Subject + 'in' + possessive particle coalesced with the preposition + predicate:

> 1. *t'eh ny^{L}wooinney litcheragh*
> (SbV Pn Prep/Poss.Part. N Adj.)
> /te nə wun´ə 'lit´ərax/ S/HLSM/II: 125 s.v. *dooinney*
> 'he is a lazy man'
> (lit. 'is he in his man lazy').

Here the prepositional particle *ny* 'in his' (viz. a contraction of *i^N* + *e* 'his') lenites the following predicate, as is the case with *my* 'my' and *dty* 'thy, your':

> 2. *cha row mee rieau my^L veshtey*
> (Neg.part. SbV Pn Adv. Poss.part. Adj.)
> /ha rau mi ru: mə 'ves´t´ə/ N/HLSM/I: 44.
> 'I was never drunk' (lit. 'I was never in my drunkenness') [14]

> 3. *bee dty^L host*
> (SbVimpv. Prep.part. N.)
> /bi də 'host/ N/S/HLSM/II: 455 s.v. *tost*
> 'be quiet!' (lit. 'be in your silence').

> 4. *t'ad nyn^N dost*
> (SbV Pn Prep.part. N)
> /tad nə 'dos/ S/HLSM/II: 455 s.v. *tost*.
> 'they are silent'
> (lit. 'are they in their silence').

Here the particle *nyn* 'in our, your, their' nasalises (voices) the following predicate (from *t* to *d*). For the complete paradigm of *tost* see HLSM/II: 455.

Usually there is concord in the prep. + possessive particle, but already in CM this was becoming generalised in the 3 person singular masculine irrespective of the person or number of the anticedent:

---

[14] Unless this is a false memory of *er meshtey* 'drunk' or *my veshtalagh* 'drunkard'.

1. *ta mee my chadley* /ta mi mə 'xadlə/ -> *ta mee ny chadley*, with or without lenition after the particle *ny* 'in his'. For exx. of this see under *cadley* 'sleeping' (HLSM/II: 56) and *shassoo* 'standing' (HLSM/II: 392).

2. *tra va shinyn pohnaryn beg*   : ...*nyn bohnaryn beggey*
(Conj. SbV Pn(emph.) N+ən Adj.)
/trɛː va sʹiŋən poːnʹərən ˈbeg/ S/HLSM/I: 326-27 :*/...nən boːnʹərən ˈbegə/
'when we were little boys/children'
(lit. 'when were we children little').

Note here also non-declension in the adj. following a plural noun (cf. also §4.4.4.1. above). However, the same speaker earlier on has: *va shinyn nyn pohnaryn* /ve sʹiŋən nə ˈpaːnʹərən/ (S/HLSM/I: 324-25) without nas. after *nyn*.

However, confusion in this construction is also found in LM:

3. *vel oo nyn dost*   : *vel oo dty host*
(Zero Q part. SbV Pn Prep.part. N)
'are you silent?'
(lit. are you (sg.) in your (pl.) silence?')

The 2 pl. of the predicate has been used with the 2nd singular of the verb. See also §4.5.1. above for combination of 2sg. + 2pl.

4. *ta yn shuyr aym nyn dost*   : ...*ny tost* (without len. after *ny* 'in her')
(SbV Art. N Prep.pn.Prep.part. N)
/te ən sʹuːr ebm nə 'dos/ S/HLSM/II: 455 s.v. tost
'my sister is silent'
(lit. 'is the sister at me in their silence')

Here there is confusion between 3 sg. and pl.

5. *ta mee dty ayr jeh tree paitchyn*
(SbV Pn. Poss.part. N Prep. Num. Npl.)
/tɛː mi də eːr dʹe triː petʹən/ N/HLSM/I: 45
'I am a father of three children'
(lit. 'am I in your father of three children').

Here the inappropriate poss. part. has been used, i.e. *dty* 'your' for *my* 'my', unless we take *dty* to be the Eng. def. art. 'the'.

: *ta mee my ayr jeh tree paitchyn*
(lit. 'am I in my father of three children').

In LM, probably due to English influence, the prepositional particle is left out altogether and we can have:

6. *va mee cadley mâree*
(SbV Pn. V Prep.pn.)
/va mi ˈkadlə meːri/ S/HLSM/II: 56 s.v. *cadley*,
'I was sleeping with her'.
with *cadley* treated as an active, not as a stative verb.

4.5.8.2. Loss of ayn as predicate:

When the substantive verb is used absolutely without predicate, the position of the predicate is filled by the 3 sg. masc. prep. pn. *ayn* /o(ː)n/, /u(ː)n/ 'in it'. In LM *ayn* may be lost, thus rendering the sentence like its English counterpart:

1. *va dooiney ayn*
(SbV N Prep.pn.)
/ve ˈdunˊə ˈun/ HLSM/I: 168-69
'there was a man'
(lit. 'was a man in it')

2. *va shenn dooiney boght*   : *...ayn*
(SbV Adj. N Adj.)
/ve sˊan dunˊəˈbox/ HLSM/I: 170-71
'there was a poor old man'
(lit. 'was an old man poor').

4.5.9. Loss of the fusion between prepositions and pronouns in prepositional pronouns

In LM the system of inflection can remain, but there is a tendency to detach pronouns from their prepositions. Thus many prepositional pronouns have 'decomposed' forms (i.e. prep. + pn.) alongside their inflected forms. The tendency towards decomposition likely derives from English usage:

1. *va soar mooar...cheet veih-eh*   : *...cheet veih*
(SbV N Adj. VbN Prep. Pn.)
/ve ˈsoːr muːr...tˊet ve a/ N/HLSM/I: 174-75   : /...tˊet vei/
'there was a great smell...coming from it'
  (lit. 'was a smell big...coming from it')

Here the prep. pn. *veih* 'from it' (3 sg. masc. which also functions as the simple prep. form 'from') is found with the pn. *eh* 'he, him, it', viz. *veih eh*.

2. *jannoo red gollrish bonnag jeh-ad*   : *...jeu*
(VbN N Prep. N Prep. Pn.)
/dˊenu rid gorisˊ bonag dˊe əd/ [N]/HLSM/I: 240-41
'making something like bonnag (soda cake) (out) of them'

(lit. 'making a thing like bonnag of them').

Here *jeu* 'of them' has been decomposed to *jeh* 'of' + pn. *ad* 'them'.

    3. *t'ad jannoo gamman jeh'd*   : ..*jeu*
    (SbV Pn. VbN N Prep. Pn.)
    /tad d´inu 'gaman d´ed/ S/MTT/YCG32: 4
    'they are making sport of them'
    (lit. 'are they making sport of them'). See foregoing.

    4. *ta ram cleighyn jeant ec mish*   : ...*aym's*
    (SbV Pn. N Vppp Prep. Pn(emph.))
    /ta 'raːm kleiːjən d´int ek 'misʹ/ N/HLSM/I: 276-77
    'I have built a lot of hedges'
    (lit. 'there are a lot of hedges built at me')

Here the inflected emphatic form *aym's* (1st pers. sg. of *ec*) has been decomposed to *ec* 'at' and *mish* 'me' the emph. form of pn. *mee*.
    5. jeeagh *er-shiu*   : ...*erriu*
    (Vimp. Prep. Pn.)
    /d´ix eː 'sʹu/ S/HLSM/I: 356-57
    'look at you'
    (lit. 'look on you').

Here the inflected prep. pn. *erriu* 'on you (pl.)' has been decomposed to the prep. *er* 'on' and pers. pn. *shiu* 'you (pl.)'.

    6. *geddyn markiaght son mee*   : ...*er-my-hon, son-aym*
    (VbN N Prep. Pn.)
    /gen maːkax son mi/ N/HLSM/I: 234-35 .
    'getting a ride for me'.
    (later he has) *geddyn markiaght son-aym*
    /gen 'maːk´ax sonəm/ *ibid.*/I: 238-39
    (lit. 'getting a ride for at-me')

In the first example the nominal preposition *er-my-hon* 'for my part, for me' has been decomposed to prep. *son* 'for' and pn. *mee* 'me'. In the second example the form with *ec* 'at' is used, w. *ec* inflected, attached to the nominal part *son* 'sake', cf. HLSM/I: 60ff.

4.5.10. In conjunctions and subordinate clauses

4.5.10.1. In co-ordinating conjunctions: transfer of Eng. 'but' for Mx. *agh*

In LM the co-ordinative conjunction *agh* 'but' comes to be replaced by Eng. 'but':

1. *cha row eh feer vonney edyr* <u>*but*</u> *shen va shin geddyn*
(Neg. SbV Pn. Adv. Adj. Adv. Conj. (zero cop.) Dem.adj. SbV(rel.) Pn. VbN)
/ha 'rau a fiː 'vonə but 'sˊen vasˊin 'gˊedinˊ/ N/HLSM/I: 140
'it wasn't very often at all, but that was what we were getting (as wages)'
(lit.'not was it very often at all, but that (it was) that (which) were we
    getting').

2. *ta'n eirinagh geddin argid son dy chooilley red t'eh jannoo,* <u>*but*</u> *ta'n gaaue, t'eh foast*
gobbyragh
(SbV Art. N VbN N Prep. Adj. N SbV(rel.) Pn. VbN Conj. SbV Art.N
SbV Pn. Adv. VbN)
/tan irinˊax genˊ 'egid son də hulə rid ti dˊunu but tan gˊaːu ti foːs ə gobərax/ N/HLSM/I:
140
'the farmer gets money (from the Government) for everything he does, but the smith, he's
still working (for his)'
(lit. 'is the farmer getting money for everything (which) he does, but is the smith, is he
still working').

4.5.10.2. Subordinating conjunctions and subordinate clauses: generalisation of subordinators

In the use of subordinating conjunctions there is a tendency towards simplification, using
one subordinator where previously there had been two (as in *if*-clauses), and in subordinate
clauses to avoid more complicated constructions in favour of parataxis, as in English.

4.5.10.2.1. with *dy* or *my dy* 'if' in unreal conditional clauses:

1. *dy beagh yn earish fihn mairagh harrin dys yn eeastagh*
(Conj. SbVcond. Art. N Adj. Adv. Vcond(infl.). Prep. Art. N)
/də beːx ən 'irisˊ faːin 'meːrax harənˊ dəs ən 'jiːstax/ S/HLSM/: 144
'if the weather were fine tomorrow I would go to the fishing'
(lit. 'if would be the weather fine tomorrow would-go I to the fishing').

2. *my dy beagh yn earish er ve fihn jea veagh shin er goll dys yn Cholloo*
(Conjj. SbVcond. Art. N Prep. SbVpart. Adj. Adv. SbVcond. Pn. VbN Prep. Art. N)
/ma də beːx ən 'irisˊ er ve fain dˊeː 'vex sˊin er gol dəsən kolu/ S/HLSM/I: 145
'if the weather had been fine yesterday we would have gone to the Calf (of Man)'
(lit. 'if would be the weather after being fine yesterday, would be we after going to the
Calf').

4.5.10.2.2. with *my* 'if' for *dy* 'if' in unreal conditional clauses:

In LM *my* 'if' in real conditions comes to take the place of *dy* or *my dy*:

1. *My yeanagh dooinney ôna erbee treishteil boa ny cabbyl, er fer jeu, fegooish yn argid laue...veaagh eh bunnys shikyr jeh surranse coayl* MH1854
(Conj. Vcond. N Adj. Adj. VbN N Conj. N Adv. Pn. Prep.pn. Prep. Art. N Ngen. SbVcond. Pn. Adv. Adj. Prep. VbN N)
'if any innocent man trusts a cow or horse, even one of them, without money in the hand, he would be almost certain of making a loss (lit. suffering loss)'
(lit. 'if would do a man innocent any trusting a cow or horse, even one of them, without the money hand...would be he almost certain of suffering loss').
Here the conj. *my* 'if', used normally with the indic. in real conditions has supplanted *dy* 'if' (G. *dá*) + conditional + dep. form of verb.
: *dy jinnagh...*

2. *mor yannagh ad chebbal bee dow dy jeanyn ghoaill eh* EF140
(Conj. Vcond. Pn. VbN N Prep.pn. Conj. V(infl.) VbN Pn.)
'if they were to offer me food I would eat it'
(lit. 'if would do they offering food to me that would do-I taking it').
: *dy jinnagh ad...*

3. *My yinnagh fer taggyrt dy enmey ennym jeh nane oc shoh veagh eh foarst greimey piece dy yiarn ayns e feeackleyn*
(Conj. Vcond. Pn. VbN Vinf. N Prep. Pn. Prep.pn. Dem.pn. SbVcond. Pn. Vppp VbN N Prep. N Prep. Poss.psrt. Npl.)
/ma ˈjenax feːr taːxərt də ˈemnə ˈenəm dˊe neːnok ˈsˊoː viːx a ˈfoːs gramə́ˈpiːstəˈjaːrn əsə ˈfiːklən/ S/HLSM/I: 328-29
'if anyone happened to mention a name of one of these he would have to grip a piece of iron in his teeth'
(lit. 'if would do anyone happening to name a name of one at these, would be he forced gripping a piece of iron in his teeth').
: *dy jinnagh....*

4. *My yinnin quirr ny lieenyn ayns Poyll Veeill yinnin geddyn skaddan*
(Conj. Vcond. VbN Art. Npl. Prep. PN Vcond(infl.) VbN N)
/maː ˈjininˊ kwir nə ˈliːnˊən uns pulˈviːl jinin gˊidən ˈskadan/ S/HLSM/I: 348-49
'if I were to cast the nets into Pooillveeill I would get herring'
(lit. 'if would do-I casting the nets in Pooillveeill would do-I getting herring').
: *dy jinnin...*

4.5.10.2.3. Loss of the preposition *da* 'to' after *lurg* 'after' in temporal clauses:

After *lurg* 'after, on the track of' there comes the inflected prep. pn.*da* 'to' (uninflected w. noun) + substantive verb participle *ve* 'being' + past participle passive of the verb (if passive), or the verb-noun; sometimes *ve* may be omitted. In both cases the subject (or agent) is expressed by the preposition *da* 'to, by':[15]

1. *lurg da yn arroo ve giarrit va yn Meilliaman goit ec ny mraane aegey*
(Conj. Prep. Art. N SbVpart. Vppp SbV Art. N Vppp Prep. Art.pl. Npl. Adj.pl.)
/lərg deːən aːru vi gˊaːrətˊ ve ən 'melˊəman gotˊ ek nə ma'reːn 'eːɡə/ S/HLSM/ I: 142
'after the corn had been cut, the Meilliaman was taken by the young women'
(lit. 'after to the corn being cut was the Meilliaman taken at the women young').

2. *lurg dooin cheet woish y cheayn*
(Conj. Prep.pn. VbN Prep. Art. N)
/lərg 'dunˊ tˊət wisˊə 'xˊin/ S/HLSM/I: 142
'after we had come from the sea'
(lit. 'after to us coming from the sea, after a coming from the sea by us', with the prepositional pronoun following the conjunction in Mx, instead of the verbal noun, cf. OIr. example in footnote 11 below).

However, from some of the last native speakers the elements *da* and *ve* are omitted, thus rendering it similar to the English:

3. *lurg mee faagail Creneash...ha row mi clashtyn monney Gaelg*
(Conj. Pn. VbN PN...Neg. SbV Pn. VbN Pn. N)
/log mi fe'ɡeːl kre'neːsˊ...ha rau mi klaːsˊtˊən monə ɡilɡ/ S/HLSM/I: 142
'after I left Cregneash...I wasn't hearing any Manx'
(lit. 'after me leaving Cregneash...not was I hearing any Manx').

4.5.10.2.4. Loss of *my* in *roish my* 'before' in temporal clauses:

After *roish my* the (nasalised) dep. form of the verb is expected. In LM the *my* element can fall away and the independent form of the verb is used:

1. *roish my neemayd scarrey veih-my-cheilley*
(Conj. V(infl.) VbN Prep.phrase)
/roːsˊ mə 'niː mad skaːrə vei mə 'kelˊə/ S/HLSM/I: 142
'before we part from one another'
(lit. 'before will do-we parting from one another').
Here we have the indep. form of the future of *jannoo* 'do', viz. *nee*, instead of the dep. form *jean*, as in the next example.
: *roish my jeanmayd...*

---

[15] cf. W. *ar ôl iddo fynd* 'after he had gone' (lit. 'after to him going'), OIr. *iarna grísad dond araid* 'after being urged on by the charioteer' (lit. 'after his urging on by the charioteer'), cf. DIL D: 176 s.v. *do*.

2. *bee eh mean-oie roish nee shiu goaill toshiaght*
(SbV Pn. Npred. Conj. V Pn. VbN N)
/biː e menˈiː roːsˊ ni sˊu goilˊ ˈtoːiax/ S/HLSM/: 143
'it will be midnight before you get started'
(lit. 'will be it midnight before will do you taking beginning').
: ...*roish my jean shiu goaill toshiaght*

4.5.10.2.5. Loss of the (future) relative verb-form after *tra* 'when' in temporal clauses:

For exx. here see under §4.5.4. above.

4.5.10.2.6. Loss of the particle *dy* 'that' after *er-yn-oyr, er-y-fa* 'because', *shen-yn-oyr, shen-y-fa* 'that's why' in causal clauses:

After *er-yn-oyr, er-y-fa* 'because (lit. 'on the reason that'), *shen-yn-oyr, shen-y-fa* 'that is why' (lit. 'that (is) the reason') the dep. form of the verb introduced by *dy* 'that' is expected. In LM the element *dy* can be omitted and the following subordinate clause introduced by the indep. form of the verb in direct parataxis, as in English:

With *dy*:

1. *hug mee dhyt eh er-yn-oyr dy vel taitnys aym ort*
(Vpret. Pn. Prep.pn. Pn. Conj. Part. SbV N Prep.pn. Prep.pn.)
/hog mi dətˊ eː erə ˈnoːr də vel ˈtatˊnˊəs em ort/ S/HLSM/I: 140-41
'I gave it to you because I like you'
(lit. 'gave I to you it because that is pleasure at me on you').

2. *shen yn oyr dy vel shin gyllagh Ooyl Adam da cront ny scoarnagh*
(Conj. Part. SbV. Pn> VbN N N Prep. N Art. Ngen.)
/sˊedn əˈnoːr də vel sˊinˊ gilax uːl ˈadam de kront nə ˈskornax/ N/HLSM/II: 344 s.v. *oyr*.
'that's the reason that we call the knot in the throat the Adam's Apple'
(lit. 'that (is) the reason that are we calling Apple Adam to knot of the throat').

Without *dy*:

3. shen y fa *cha vel eh*... MH1833
(Conj. Neg. SbV Pn. ...)
'that is why it is not...'
(lit. '(is) that the reason not is it...').
English does not require 'that' in this construction, where parataxis is the norm. In Mx. *dy* 'that', *nagh* 'that not' would be required after *shen y fa*, viz.*shen y fa nagh vel*...

4. shen y fa *ren* mee... EF118
(Conj. V Pn. ...)
'that's the reason I did...'
(lit. 'that (is) the reason did I...')
: *shen y fa dy ren mee...*

5. shen yn oyr *v'ad* jannoo shen
(Conj. SbV Pn. VbN Dem.pn.)
/s´eːən oːr veːd d´enu s´en/ N/HLSM/I: 168-69
'that is why they were doing that'
(lit. 'that (is) the reason were they doing that')
: *shen yn oyr dy row ad jannoo shen.*

4.5.10.2.7. with *ga* 'although' in concessive clauses:

The CM usage is *ga* + indep. form of the verb; *ga dy* + dep. form is probably imitative of *ga nagh* 'although not'. In LM both forms are found:

1. *cha jeanym ginsh dhyt ga dy vel fys aym er dy mie*
(Neg. V(infl.) VbN Prep.pn. Conj. Part. N Prep.pn. Prep. Adv.)
/ha d´enəm ˈgiːns´ dətˊ ˈgeː də vel ˈfis ebm er də ˈmaːi/ S/HLSM/I: 141
'I'll not tell you although I know it well'
(lit. 'not will do-I a-telling to you although that is knowledge at me on it well').

2. *ga v'eh mitchooragh t'eh mie dy gobbyragh*
(Conj. SbV Pn. Adj. SbV Pn. Adj. Vinf.)
/geː vi miˈt´uːrax ti ˈmaːi də gobərax/ N/HLSM/I: 141
'although he is mischievous he's good to work'
(lit. 'although was he lazy is he good to work').

4.5.10.2.8. Loss of the relative particle *nagh* 'that not' in negative relative clauses:

In negative relative clauses, direct or indirect, the conjunction is *nagh* + dep. form of the verb. In LM *cha* is also found, but w. indep. form of the verb, thus making the expression as formally paratactic as the corresponding affirmative (as in English):

With *nagh*:

1. *as fer nagh row jannoo cairagh*
(Conj. N/Pn. Neg.conj. SbV VbN Adv.)
/as ˈfaː na ˈrau d´enu keːrax/ N/HLSM/I: 147
'and a man/anyone who was not doing it right/properly'
(lit. 'and a man/anyone who not was doing (it) right/properly').

Without *nagh*:

2. *va mee beaghey ayns boayl cha row monney sleih mygeayrt ec y traa*
(SbV Pn. VbN Prep. N Neg. SbV Pn. N Prep. Adv.phrase)
/va mi biax əs boːl ha 'rau monəslai ma'git egətreː/ N/HLSM/: 147
'I was living in a place (where) there were not many people about at the time'
(lit. 'was I living in a place not was many people about at the time')
: *va mee beaghey ayns boayl nagh row monney sleih mygeayrt ec y traa*.

4.5.10.2.9. Loss of the particle *dy* 'that' in sentences expressing possibility:

Possibility is usually expressed with *foddee* 'perhaps, it may be' + *dy* 'that' + dep. form of
the verb. In LM the element *dy* can be lost, whereupon the indep. form of the verb follows,
thus rendering the whole as in English:

With *dy*:

1. *foddee dy vel ad ersooyl dy geddyn poosit*
(V Part. SbV Pn. Adv. Vinf. Vppp.)
/fodi di 'vel ad e'suːl di gedin´ 'puːsit´/ S/HLSM/I: 153
'perhaps (it may be that) they are away to get married'
(lit. 'perhaps that are they away to get married').

Without *dy*:

2. *foddee bee eh chyndaa*
(V SbV Pn. VbN)
/fodi bi e t´in'deː/ N/HLSM/I: 153
'perhaps it will change'
(lit. 'perhaps will be it changing')

4.5.10.2.10. Loss of the preposition *da* 'to' after *lhiggey* 'let, allow' in sentences expressing permission or exhortation:

This is mostly expressed by forms of *lhiggey* 'let' + prep. *da* 'to'. In LM this preposition
can be omitted, thus presenting the sentence as in English:

permission:
with *da*:

1. *lhig daue goll*
(Vimp. Prep.pn. VbN)
/l´ig dau 'goːl/ S/HLSM/I: 153
'let them go'

(lit. 'let to them going').

without *da*:

2. *lhig ad goll*
(Vimp. Pn. VbN)
/l´ig ad 'goːl/ N/HLSM/I: 153
'let them go'
(lit. 'let them going').

exhortation (in 1 pl.):
with *da*:

3. *lhig dooin goll dys Doolish*
(Vimpv. Prep.pn. VbN Prep. PN)
/l´ig´ doːn´ gol dəs gulis´(*sic*)/ S/HLSM/II: 274 s.v. *lhiggey*.
'let us go to Douglas'
(lit. 'let to us going to Douglas').

without *da*:

4. *lhig shin geam stiagh yn fifer*
(Vimp. Pn. VbN Prep. Art. N)
/l´ig´ s´in gebm 's´t´aːx ən 'faifə/ N/HLSM/I: 254-55
'let us call in the fifer' (lit. 'let us calling in the fifer').

4.5.11. Summary

The syntax of LM is essentially that of CM. However, in the Manx of the last native speakers matters begin to go seriously astray, showing confusion of idiom and/or influence from English:

1. Use of both singular and plural forms in the imperative of the verb for the same person (§4.5.1.).

2. The verb-noun used as an imperative (§4.5.2.).

3. Use of formal forms of the verb in close relationships (§4.5.3.), thus indicating uncertainty in the form required for a particular circumstance.

4. In the tenses and tense forms the disappearance of the future relative in temporal and real conditional clauses, confusion of tense forms in unreal conditions whereby the conditional form is gradually replaced by the future (§4.5.4).

5. The 3 sg. masc. of the possessive particle becomes generalised (with or without initial mutation in the following verb-noun) in Type 2 of the passive (§4.5.5.) - in so far as this type is used.

6. The introduction of standard answer forms in answers to yes-no questions, equating English 'yes' and 'no' irrespective of mood, tense or person, replacing the traditional replies (as found in CM) using a reduced form of the verb, but in the same mood and tense (§4.5.6.).

7. The placing of the object pronoun before the prepositional phrase (as in English), instead of after (as in more traditional Manx) (§4.5.7.).

8. Reduction, then loss, of possessive particles in the indefinite predicate (§4.5.8.1.), and the loss of *ayn* 'in it' in the predicate, thus rendering the sentence as in English (§4.5.8.2.).

9. Decomposition of prepositional pronouns, whereby forms inflected with a pronoun become separated from the pronoun, as in English (§4.5.9.).

10. Replacement of Eng. 'but' for Mx. *agh* 'but' as a co-ordinating conjunction (§4.5.10.1.).

11. Reduction in the number of subordinating conjunctions to one for a given clause, where previously there may have been more than one (as in conditional and temporal clauses) (§4.5.10.2.).

12. Replacement of the use of the dependent form of the verb with the independent form in direct parataxis after certain subordinating conjunctions, and in sentences expressing possibility, thus rendering the syntax as in English (§4.5.10.2.).

13. Similarly in negative relative clauses we find replacement of the conjunction *nagh* 'that not' with the simple negative particle *cha* 'not' in direct parataxis, as in English (§4.5.10.2.).

14. Omission of the preposition *da* 'to' after *lhiggey* 'let' in the expression of permission or exhortation, thus rendering the sentence as in English.

All in all we see a deep penetration of anglicisation of Manx syntax in the latter stages of LM.

4.6. Other English influences

As we have seen in §4.5, by far the greatest disturbance in LM is the influence from English. Right through the 300 years or so of the existence of Manx, from Phillips onwards, adaptation of English lexical items and syntax has taken place, especially in translated material, where it was perhaps felt that the Manx ought to reflect the English original. In commenting on Phillips' Manx translation of the Anglican Book of Common Prayer (made ca. 1610; cf. Moore and Rhys 1893-94) Robert L. Thomson (Thomson & Pilgrim 1988: 14) notes:

> The quality of the translation is uneven, much of it exhibiting good Gaelic idiom, but with occasional lapses into the most literal renderings of the English original[...]. There is a clear distinction on linguistic grounds between the Prayer Book proper and the Psalter attached to it. This work gives a valuable insight into the state of the [Manx] language at a time when the influence of bilingualism had scarcely begun and its effects were still confined to the vocabulary (Thomson & Pilgrim 1988: 14).

With regard to the Manx Bible translation Thomson (*ibid.*: 15) comments:

> The translators' drafts were revised by a small editorial group who normalised the spelling and terminology, and sometimes removed renderings which seemed insufficiently close to the original, but generally seemed not to have scrutinised the translation very closely [...]. Many of the freer renderings of obscure passages derive from the translators' own understanding or from the commentators available at the time. Though the standard of the Manx varies from book to book, and the editors seem rarely to have corrected their colleagues' grammar, the work as a whole is of a high standard [...] (Thomson & Pilgrim 1988: 15).

For comment on the earlier English (and other) vocabulary in Manx (cf. Thomson 1991).

Translated material may or may not reflect what is actually spoken on the ground, since there will always be a certain amount of editorial interference for one particular reason or another. Nevertheless, during the course of the Late Manx period the contact with English rapidly accelerated. The initial effects were not insignificant borrowings of English vocabulary followed by adaptation of LM to English syntax and idiom, which finds it climax in the Manx of some of the later terminal speakers.

4.6.1. Transfer of English for native words

4.6.1.1. 'Manxified' items with various Gaelic suffixes, etc

During the process of assimilation of English lexical items into LM various Mx. suffixes, such as verb-noun, plural suffixes, etc, were attached. Such items may have become completely absorbed into Manx phonology had Manx survived.

1. - Shimmey oor *plesal* te cur orrin ceau MH1833
(Cop. (Sh') + Adj(immey) N VbN SbV Pn. VbN Prep.pn. VbN)
'it (reading the paper) provides us with many an hour's pleasure'
(lit. 'is many an hour pleasing/pleasure is it puttting on us spending').
E. 'please' + Mx. vn. suffix *-al*.   : Mx. *taitnys* 'pleasure'
: *shimmey oor taitnys te cur orrin ceau.*

2. - Rebrezentashyn, t'ad *gusal* mennick eh MH1833
(N SbV Pn. VbN Adv. Pn.)
'Representation, they're often using it (this word)'
(lit. 'representation, are they a-using often it').
E. 'use' w. Mx. vn. suffix *-al* and the whole w. prep. *ag* or *'g* 'at' prefixed to form the present participle.
Mx. *goaill ymmyd jeh* 'using' (lit. 'taking use of');
: *Rebrezentashyn, t'ad goaill ymmyd jeh (dy) mennick.*

3. - ren mee *passal* ny claghyn sceilt MH1834c
(V Pn. VbN Art. Npl. Vppp)
'I passed the Cloven Stones (place-name)'
(lit. 'did I a passing of the Stones Cloven')
E. 'pass' + Mx. vn. suffix *-al*; : Mx. *goll shaghey* 'going past', G. *dol seachad*.
: ren mee *goll shaghey* ny Claghyn Skeilt.

4. - veagh eh *ny sesal* yannoo MH1834a
'it would be easier to do it'
(lit. 'would be it that which is easier its doing').
Here E. 'easy' + Mx. adjectival ending *-al* after removal of *-y*, then adapted to the construction of comparison, viz. rel. pn. *ny* 'that which' + copula *'s* 'is' + positive form of adj. (without inflection; cf. §4.4.4.2. above). Older is *sassey*, G. *is asa, 's asa*.

: *by-assey eh y* yannoo.

5. - *Readal* yn pabyr eu MH1834c
(VbN Art. N Prep.pn.)
'reading your paper'
(lit. 'reading the paper at you (pl.)').
E. 'read' + Mx. vn/pres. part.. suf. *-al*   : Mx. *lhaih* 'reading', G. *leughadh*.
Here a present participle has been used to replace a subordinate clause (here a conditional
clause) on the model of English syntax.
: *dy jinnin lhaih* yn phabyr eu
(lit. 'if I would do a reading (of) the paper at you...').

6. - as *clappal* bassan MH1834c
(Conj. VbN Npl.)
'and clapping hands'
(lit. 'and clapping palms (of the hand)')
E. 'clap' + Mx. vn. suffix *-al*
The Mx. idiom is *bwoalley bassyn* (lit. 'striking palms');
: as *bwoalley* bassyn.

7. - tessyn ny *ridge*yn
(Prep. Art. Npl.)
/tesən nə ˈridˊən/ N/HLSM/I: 190-91
'across the ridges'
E. 'ridge' + G. pl. suf. *-yn*   : Mx. *immyr* 'ridge', G. *iomair(e)*.
: tessyn ny *immyryn*.

8. - daa *vlister* vooar
(Num. N(len.) Adj.(len.))
/de: vlistər ˈvuːə/ N/HLSM/I: 248-49 Mx. *bolgan* 'blister'
'two big blisters'
E. 'blister' + len. & sg. after *daa* 'two'   : Mx. *bolgan*.
Here the number rules have been applied, w. len. also in the adj..
: daa *volgan* vooar.

9. - as hooar eh *wedge*yn mooar as *mallet*yn
(Conj. V Pn. Npl. Adj. Conj. Npl.)
/as ˈhuːre wedˊən muːr as ˈmalətən/ N/HLSM/I: 170-71
'and he got big wedges and mallets'
(lit. 'and got he wedges and mallets')
E. 'wedge' & 'mallet' + Mx. pl. suffix *-yn*
Mx. *jeenys* 'wedge' (C.102), *thornane* 'wooden hammer, mallet' (C.198)
: as hooar eh *jeenyssyn* as *thornaneyn*.

4.6.1.2. 'Non-manxified' items

Here items have been transferred from English, either to replace native words having a slightly different meaning from the borrowed item, or because there is no native word for the concept introduced, or simply because the native word has been forgotten or fallen out of use.

1. - Ta moghree *fihn* ayn MH1833
(SbV N Adj. Pred.)
'it is a fine morning'
(lit. 'is a morning fine in it', w. *ayn* 'in it' as predicate).
E. 'fine', Mx. *aalin*
: *ta moghree aalin ayn.*

2. - Rebrezentashyn, t'ad *gusal* mennick eh MH1833
(N SbV Pn. VbN Adv. Pn.)
'Representation, they often use it (this word)'
Here E. 'representation' has been borrowed into Manx and partly 'manxified' in its phonology, viz. *[rɛbrəzən'teːʃən]. Though *chaghterys* (< *chaghter*, G. *teachtaire* 'messenger') is used now to mean 'representation', in 1833 Mx. probably had no word for this concept in a political sense, since such would not have existed then.

3. - Jeeagh sy *Dicksinerry*, ghooinney, as yiow jeeragh eh MH1833
(Vimp. Prep. + Art.(coalesced) N Nvoc. Conj. V Adv. Pn.)
'look in the dictionarry, man, and you'll find it (the word) straightaway'
(lit. 'look in the Dictionary, man, and will find you straightaway it').
Though Cregeen has *fockleyr* and *focklioar* (C.75) 'word-book, dictionary' (cf. Ir. *foclóir*, ScG. *faclair*), these forms do not seem to appear in the literature, and may not have been current in everyday speech.
Note that E. /ksˊ/ is repr. here in the Mx. form as /ks/ (<-ks->).

4. - cur lesh *luck* mie   E; Mx. *aigh* /eːx/, *sonnys* /sonəs/
(VbN Prep. N Adj.)
/kur lˊesˊ luk 'mai/ S/HLSM/I: 328-29
'bringing good luck'
(lit. 'putting with it (bringing) luck good').
Mx. *aigh*, originally treated as fem, is found in the farewell greeting, viz. *aigh vie dy row lhiat* /eːx 'vai də rou 'lˊat/ (HLSM/II: 6 s.v. *aigh*) 'good luck' (lit. 'may there be good luck with you'), and because of this association the Eng. loan was likely introduced to express 'luck' in other contexts. *Sonnys* 'luck' also has the meaning of 'abundance, saiety' (C.185), which would not be the sense required here. I am reminded by RLT that Wilson in *Coyrle Sodjey* (Wilson 1707: 78) already has *laghyn luckee as neu-luckee* 'lucky and unlucky days', though w. the Mx. neg. prefix *neu-* (G. *neamh-*) 'un-' in the second example.

5. - v'eh jannoo skeabyn as *scrubbing*   E. 'scrubbing'.
(SbV Pn. VbN Npl. Conj. VbN)

/vi d´enu skiːbən as 'skrubən/ N/HLSM/I: 170-71
'he was making brushes and scrubbing (?pulling heather)'
(lit. 'was he doing/making brushes and scrubbing').

6. - t'ad coodit lesh *tar*   E. 'tar', Mx. *terr* (< E. 'tar').
(SbV Pn. Vppp Prep. N)
/təd 'kuːdət lesˊ tar/ N/HLSM/I: 192-93
'they are covered with tar'.

7. - v'eh agglit ass *mercy*   E. 'mercy', Mx. *myghin*, G. *meachainn*.
(SbV Pn. Vppp Adv.phrase)
/viː agələtˊ as 'maːsi/ N/HLSM/I: 202-03
'he was extremely frightened'
(lit. 'was he frightened out of/beyond mercy').

8. - ny kirree va rey rish y *tup*   E. 'tup', Mx. *rea*, G. *reithe*
(Art. Npl. (zero rel.part.) SbV Adj. Prep. Art. N)
/nə kiri ve reː risˊ ə top/ N/HLSM/I: 204-05
'the sheep that were rid of, had been with the tup'.

9. - va shin geddyn *plank* liauyr dy fuygh   E. 'plank', Mx. *deal*
(SbV Pn. VbN N Adj. Prep. N)
/veː sˊin gedinˊ plăŋk lˊeuər də fei/ N/HLSM/I: 212-13
'we were getting a long plank of wood'
(lit. 'were we getting a plank long of wood').

10. - v'eh goaill yn *sod* vooar   E. 'sod', Mx. *foaid*, G. *fód*
(SbV Pn. VbN Art. N Adj.)
/vi 'goːilˊ ən sod 'vuːə/ N/HLSM/I: 240-41
'he was taking/would take the big sod'.

11. - as va dooinney lesh yn *flail* goll mygeayrt yn slane vlein
(Conj. SbV N Prep. Art. N VbN Prep. Art. Adj. N)
/van dunˊe lˊesˊən fleːl gol məˈgit ən slen vˊlˊin/ N/HLSM/I: 244-45
'and a man with the flail would go about (from place to place) the whole year'
(lit. 'and was a man with the flail going around the whole year').
E. 'flail', Mx. *sooist*, OIr. *súst*.

12. - va my chassyn eisht geddyn *sore*   E. 'sore', Mx. *gonnagh*, MIr. *gonach*.
(SbV Poss.part. Npl. Adv. VbN Adj.)
/va mə 'kˊaːsən esˊ gedn soː/ N/HLSM/I: 248-49
'my feet were then getting, becoming sore'

13. - va'n *grease* ec y vullagh   E. 'grease', Mx. *smarrey*, G. *smearadh*.
(SbV Art. N Prep. Art. N)
/van griːs egə vulax/ N/HLSM/I: 254-55

'the grease was at the top'.

14. - v'eh *porridge* ayns y voghree   E. 'porridge', Mx. *broghan*, G. *brochan*.
(SbV Pn. N Prep. Art. N)
/vi porad´ unsə voːri/ N/HLSM/I: 266-67
'it was porridge in the morning'.

15. - shey *feet* ayns *height*   E. 'feet' Mx. *trie* 'foot' G. *troigh*.
(Num. N Prep. N)   E. 'height', Mx. *er yrjid*, G. *i n-áirde*
/s´eː fit us heit/ N/MTT/IFC/T37:1
'six feet in height'
: *shey trieyn er yrjid* (lit. 'six feet on height').

16. - va'n *priest* goll mygeayrt   E. 'priest', Mx. *saggyrt*, G. *sagart*.
(SbV Art. N VbN Prep.)
/veːn priːs gol mə'git/ S/HLSM/I: 372-73
'the priest was going about'.

17. - as ren mee skeouw yn *umbrella*
(Conj. V Pn. VbN Art. N)
/as ren´ mi skjau ən umbə'relə/ S/HLSM/I: 376-77.
'and I cut the air with the umbrella'
(lit. 'and did I cutting air with the umbrella')
E. 'umbrella', Mx. *fasscadagh* (C.71), / *scaaliaghee* (C.161) (lit. 'rain shade').

18. - t'eh *foreigner*   E. 'foreigner', Mx. *joaree*, G. *deoraidh*.
(SbV Pn. N)
/ti 'forona/ S/HLSM/I: 376-77
'he's a foreigner'.

19. - v'ee feer feer *smart* as *busy*
(SbV Pn. Adv. Adv. Adj. Conj. Adj.)
/vei fiː fiː smaːt əs bisi/ S/HLSM/I: 386-87
'she was very, very smart and busy'.
E. 'smart' Mx. *skybbylt*, G. *sgiobalt*,   E. 'busy', Mx. *tarroogh*, G. *tarbhach*.
: *v'ee feer feer skybbylt as tarroogh*.

4.6.2. Copying of English idiom and calques

Towards the end as LM lost its vitality English syntax and idiom was copied in substantial quantities, varying from speaker to speaker.

4.6.2.1. Copying of indefinite pronominal phrases: all the N:

Ooilley as a qualifying adjective would normally be expected to follow its noun whether definite or indefinite (as in Phillips), and indeed we find exx. of this in LM:

1. *eeasteyryn ooilley*
(Npl. Indef.pn.)
/jis'teɹən 'ul´i/ HLSM/II: 341 s.v. *ooilley*
'all fishermen'
(lit. 'fishermen all').

2. *t'eh goll trooid ny creearyn ooilley*
(SbV Pn. VbN Prep. Art. Npl. Indef.pn.)
/ti 'gol 'truːd´nə 'kriːrən ol´u/ N/HLSM/I: 202-03
'it (wild mustard) goes through all the sieves'
(lit. 'is it going through the sieves all').

However, even in the Manx Bible *ooilley* is found used on the English analogy: *ooilley ny
jagheenyn* 'all the tithes' (Hosea III: 10), and so in LM, but also replacing older Mx. idiom:

1. *ooilley yn laa*   E. 'all the...'
(Indef.pn. Art. N)
/ul´u ən 'laː/ HLSM/II: 341 s.v. *ooilley* :
'all day long, all the day'
: *feiy y laa* /fei 'leː/ HLSM/II: 164 s.v. *feiy y laa* 'all day long, all through the day'.

2. - *ooilley ny deiney aeg*   E. 'all the...'
(Pn. Art. Npl. Adj.)
/ol´u nə deːn´ə eːg/ N/HLSM/I: 174-75
'all the young men'.

4.6.2.2. Loss of the order 1 pers. pn, 2 pers. pn, 3 pers. pn. (& self) in emphatic reflexives

The syntax in Gaelic is that the 1st, 2nd, and 3rd persons follow in that order, and not as in
English with the speaker last, though evidence for this in Mx. is very scanty.

1. - Ta Juan Bowyr as *mee hene* MH1833
(SbV Pers.N (3 Pers.) Conj. Pn.1 Refl.)
'there is Juan Bouyr/Deaf Juan and myself'.
: *ta mee hene as Juan Bowyr* (SbV Pn.1 Refl. Conj. Pers.N (3 pers.)

2. - *'neen as mee hene*   E. 'a daughter and myself'
(N(3 Pers.) Conj. Pn.1 Refl.)
/n´iːn´ əs mə 'hiːn´/ N/HLSM/I: 236-37

'daughter and myself'
: *mee hene as 'neen* (Pn.1 Refl. Conj. N(3 Pers.)) 'myself and a daughter'.

4.6.2.3. Disturbances in the syntax of the numerical system

The numerical system in LM is remarkably unaffected from copying from English. In Mx. the noun is placed after the first element in a sequence of elements; the noun is usually found in the singular after numerals, except for *blein* 'year', pl. *bleeantyn*, which has a special plural after numerals, viz. *bleeaney*.

1. *daa punt jeig*
/deː punt dˊeg/ HLSM/I: 49
'twelve pounds'
(lit. 'two punds ten').

2. *hogh blein as feed*
/hoːx bliən əs fid/ HLSM/I: 49
'twenty-eight years'
(lit. 'eight years and twenty')

3. *shiaght keead punt as tree feed*
/sˊaːx kid punt as triː fid/ HLSM/I: 50
'seven hundred and sixty pounds'
(lit. 'seven hundred pound and three score').

4. *oor dy lieh*
/uːr də leː/ HLSM/I: 51
'an hour and a half'
(lit. 'an hour to a half').

However, disturbances do occur and seem modelled on English syntax:

5. *queig jeig bleeaney*
/kweg dˊeg blinə/ HLSM/I: 49
'fifteen years'
(lit. 'fifteen years')
: *queig bleeaney jeig* (lit. 'five years and ten').

6. *feed as jeih aker*
/fid əs dˊai 'eːka/ HLSM/I: 49
'thirty acres'
(lit. 'twenty and ten acres')
: *jeih aker as feed* (lit. 'ten acre and twenty').

7. *keead as feed punt*
/kid as fid punt/ HLSM/I: 50
'one hundred and twenty pounds'
(lit. 'one hundred and twenty pounds')
: *keead punt as feed* (lit.'a hundred pound and twenty'), or
: *shey feed punt* (lit.' six score pound').

8. *daeed punt as lieh*
/daid punt aːs ĺeː/ HLSM/I: 51
'forty and a half pounds'
(lit. 'forty pound and a half').
Here the preposition *dy* has been omitted.
: *daeed punt dy lieh* (lit. 'forty pound to a half').

4.6.2.4. Assorted idioms and calques copied from English

1. - myr boallagh *eh* MH1833   Older Mx. *myr boallagh da*
(Conj. Cop.(past/cond).+Adj. Pn.)   (Conj. Cop.(past/cond.)+Adj. Prep.pn.)
'as it would be accustomed'   (lit. 'as would be it customary/usual
(lit. 'as would be customary it').   to/for it').

2. - *shen-y-fa, shen-yn-oyr, er-y-fa, er-yn-oyr*; see §4.5.10.2.5. above.

3. - *dy gheddyn* yn baathey *aarloo*
(Vinf. Art. N Adv.)
lit. 'to get the boat ready'
Mx. *geddyn* 'getting' + *aarloo* 'ready' < E. 'get ready'.
: *dy aarlaghey yn baatey*
(Vinf. Art. N)
'to prepare, make ready the boat', or
: *dy yannoo aarloo yn baatey*
(Vinf. Adv. Art. N)
'to make ready the boat'.

4. - ta cooinaghtyn aym's er dty vummig as dty jishig *geddyn poost*
(SbV Npl. Prep.pn. Prep. Poss.part. Nlen. Conj. Poss.part. Nlen. VbN Vppp)
/ta ˈkuːnaxtən ems eːtə ˈvumig´ as də ˈd´isˊigˊ gidən ˈpuːs/ S/HLSM/I: 382-83
'I remember your mother and your father getting married'
(lit. is memories at me on your mother and your father getting married')
Here the Eng. idiom. 'get' + past part. has been taken over in Mx.
: ...*poosey* 'marrying'.

5. - cha voddyn *gheddyn* doinney erbee *doosht* EF120
(Neg. Vcond. VbN N Indef.adj. Vppp)
'I couldn't get anyone awake'

(lit. 'not could I getting man any woken').
Mx. *doostey* 'awakening', G. *dúsgadh*
: *cha voddin doostey dooinney erbee*
(Neg. Vcond. VbN N Indef.adj.)
'I couldn't wake anyone'(lit. 'not could I waking man any').

6. - v'eh feer *fond* jeh lhune   E. 'fond of'
(SbV Pn. Adv. Adj. Prep. N)
/ve fiːə 'fond dˊe 'lun/ S/HLSM/I: 360-61
'he was very fond of ale'
Here E. idiom 'fond of' has partly been adapted from the E. and partly trans. into Mx, w.
the Mx. prep. *jeh* 'of' replacing E. 'of'. However, the Mx. idiom is either *graiagh er* 'fond
of' (lit. 'loving on'), viz.
: *t'eh graihagh er lhune*
(SbV Pn. Adj. Prep. N)
(lit. 'is he loving on ale'), or *currit da* 'given to' (*currit* verbal-adj. of *cur* 'put, give'), viz.
: *t'eh currit da lhune* (SbV Pn. Vppp. Prep. N) 'he is given to ale'.

7. - v'ad *coamrit ayns jiarg as paart oc ayns gorrym as paart oc ayns gial*
(SbV Pn. Vppp. Prep. N Conj. Indef.pn. Prep. N Conj. Indef.pn. Prep. N)
/ved komritˊ uns dˊərg as 'pert ok uns gurəm as pert ok uns gˊal/ N/HLSM/I: 168-69.
'they were dressed in red and some of them (were dressed) in blue and some of them in
white'
(lit. 'were they dressed in red and some at them in blue and some at them in white').
In Mx. 'wear' is idiomatically expressed by a prep. phrase with *er* 'on', viz.
: *va eaddagh jiarg orroo*
(SbV N Adj. Prep.pn.)
'there was red clothing on them' (lit. 'was clothing red on them').
coamrit 'clothed' usually describes the manner in which one is dressed, e.g. *v'eh coamrit
gollrish bwoid gonnagh* 'he was dressed like a sore prick/penis', i.e. overdressed.

8. - *foddey veih roie ersooyl*   : E. 'far from running away'
(Adv. Prep. VbN Adv.)
/foːdə vei rei er'suːl/ N/HLSM/I: 172-73
'far from running away'
: *ayns ynnyd roie ersooyl*
(Prep. N VbN Adv.)
'instead/in place of running away'.

9. - *hooar ny deiney ersooyl lesh ny vioys*   : E 'get away with their lives'
(V Art. Npl. Adv. Prep. Poss.part. N)
/huːr nə dəːnˊə er'suːl lesˊ nə vjoːs/ N/HLSM/I: 174-75
'the men got away with their lives'
: *ren ad scapail bio*
(V Pn. VbN Adv.)
'they escaped alive' (lit. 'did they escaping alive').

10. - ec y *chied*   : E. 'first'
(Prep. Art. N)
/egə 'k´ed/ S/HLSM/I:: 70 s.v. *chied*
'at the start, at first'
Here the Mx. ordinal number *kied, chied* 'first' has been used to mean 'start, beginning' influenced from E. 'at first'.
: ec y *toshiaght* (Prep. Art. N) 'at the start, beginning'.

11. - ren eh yn cooid share *dy geddyn yn obbyr jeant* E. 'to get the work done'
(V PN. Art. N Adj.(comp.) Vinf. Art. N Vppp.)
/rin e ən kud´ s´eːr də gedin´ ən 'obər 'd´en´t´/ N/HLSM/I: 176-77
'he did his best to get the work done'
: ..*dy chur jerrey/mullagh er yn obbyr*
(Vinf. N Prep. Art. N)
'to put an end/a top on the work'.

12. - ren my ayr *tuittym ching*   : E. 'fall ill'.
(V Poss.part. N VbN Adv.)
/rin mə 'eːr tod´əm t´iŋ/ N/HLSM/I: 184-85
'my father fell ill' (lit. 'did my father a falling ill, sick')
: ren my ayr *gaase ching*
(V Poss.part. VbN Adv.)
'my father became ill' (lit. 'did my father becoming/growing ill').

13. - booa va *er-y-hon*   : E. 'for it' (i.e. wanting the bull)
(N SbV(rel.) Prep.phrase)
/buːa ve erə 'hon/ N/HLSM/I: 192-93. Mx. *er-dheyr*, G. *ar dáir*.
The expected idiom is then given:
booa va er-dheyr
(N SbV(rel.) Prep.phrase)
/buːə ve a'deːr/ *ibid*: 192-93
'bull that was on heat'.

14. - *veeit eh Tom er y raad*   : E. 'meet'
(V Pn. N Prep. Art. N)
/vit´ e tom erə reːd/ N/HLSM/I: 202-03
'he met Tom on the road'.
In Mx. 'meet' can be expressed by *cheet ny whaiyl* lit.'coming(in)to his/one's meeting' or adapting E. 'meet' + Mx. vn. suffix *-eil* + prep. *rish* 'to', viz.
: *veeit eh rish Tom er y raad*.
(V Pn. Prep. N Prep. Art. N)
However, in the ex. above the prep. *rish* is omitted thus rendering the sentence as in English.

15. - as va'n margey *ooilley harrish*   : E. 'all over'
(SbV Art. N Adv.phrase)

/van meːgə ulˊu herisˊ/ N/HLSM/I: 252-53
'the fair was all over'.
: vaˈn margey *ec kione*
(SbV Art. N Adv.phrase)
'...at an end' or
va kione currit er y m/vargey
(SbV N Vppp. Prep. Art. N(+/- len.)
(lit. 'was an end put on the fair').

16. - ta shin laccal *laa jeh*   : E. 'day off'
(SbV Pn. VbN N Prep.)
/ta sˊin laːl laː dˊeː/ N/HLSM/I: 230-31
'we are wanting a day off'
: ta shin laccal *laa seyr*
(SbV Pn. VbN N Adj/Adv.)
'...a free day' or '...a day free'.

17. - vˈad geam *each* elley   : E. 'each other'
(SbV Pn. VbN Indef. Pn.)
/vad gebm itˊsˊ 'elə/ N/HLSM/I: 254-55
'they were calling to each other'
Here E. 'each' is introduced, w. Mx. adj. *elley* 'other' attached, to repr. E. 'each other',
thus replacing older *y cheilley*, here *er y cheilley* 'to each other' (lit. 'on each other').
: vˈad geam *er y cheilley* (SbV Pn. VbN Prep.phrase).

18. - ren ad *cur y fuygh dys un cheu*   : E. 'put to one side'
(V Pn. VbN Art. N Prep. Adj. N)
/rinəd kuːrəfai dəs eːn tˊau/ N/HLSM/I: 232-33
'they put the wood to one side'
(lit. 'did they putting the wood to one side').
: ren ad *geddyn rey rish* y fuygh 'they got rid of the wood', though this is hardly less English.

19. - *daa deiney*   : E. "two' + pl. of noun
(Num. Npl.)
/deː 'diːnˊə/ N/HLSM/I: 274-75
'two men'.
Mx. *daa* 'two' takes the sg. of the noun and occasions len. in the initial consonant (cf.
§4.3.2.1.4. above).
: *daa ghooinney* (Num. Nsg.len.).

20. - kynnys ta shiu *freayll* ?   : E. 'keeping'
(Interog. SbV Pn. VbN)
/kən'asˊtou friːl/ N/Diary: 37
'how are you keeping?'
Here the Eng. idiom 'how are you keeping' has been trans. literally into Mx.

: kynys *t'ou* /kenəs tau/ S/HLSM/II: 257 s.v. *kynys* 'how are you?' (sg.)
: kynys *ta shiu* /kenəs 'ta s´u/ S/HLSM/II: 257 s.v. *kynys* 'how are you?' (pl.).
(Interrog. SbV Pn.)

21. - nee shen coon' *oo*   : E. 'help you'
(V Dem.pn. VbN Pn.)
/ni 's´an kŭnu:/ N/HLSM/II: 93 s.v. *cooney*
'that will help you'
Mx. *cooney* 'help' requires the use of the prep. pn. *lesh* 'with',viz.
: *nee shen cooney lhiat*
(V Dem.pn. VbN Prep.pn.), as in:
son dy cooney lhee
(Prep. Vinf. Prep.pn.)
/son də 'kunə l´ei/ S/HLSM/II: 93 s.v. *cooney*
'for to help her'.
or with *cur* and followed by the prep. pn. *da* 'to', viz *cur cooney da* 'give help to', as in:
cur cooney j'ee
(VbN N Prep.pn.)
/ku 'kunə d´i/ S?HLSM/I:: 93 s.v. *cooney*
'giving help to her, helping her'.
The none-use of a prep. pn. in the first ex. and the occurrence of *cooney* with a direct object would model English usage.

The examples are not exhaustive.

4.6.3. Inadequacy of expression, uncertainty of idiom in Late Manx

A feature of the Manx of the last native speakers is that their grasp of Mx. idiom was no longer complete. They might remember part of an idiom and complete it with something else or mix idioms or forms together, etc. As a result their Manx no longer functioned as a coherent and vibrant language. It had become bitty and tail-end, and with many had become faded. The following examples may give an insight into the extent of the 'damage'.

1. - dys boayl va goll noi ayns yn vayr
(Prep. N SbV(rel.) VbN Adv. Prep. Art. N(len.))
/dus bol va gol nai usən ve:/ N/HLSM/I: 238-39
'to a steep place on the road' (lit. 'to a place that was going against (them) on the road').
Here the Mx. for 'a steep slope' has been forgotten, and paraphrased as best as possible.
: dys ughtagh yeeragh ayns y vayr
(Prep. N Adj.(len.) Prep. Art. N(len.))
'to a steep slope on the road'.

2. - ta shen ooilley ta mee toiggal *mygeayrt-y-mysh*   E. 'about it'
(SbV Dem.pn. Indef.adj. SbV(rel.) Pn. VbN Prep.pn.)
/te s´en 'ol´u tɛ mi tegal mə'ge:rt ə 'məs´/ N/HLSM/I: 204-05

156

'that is all I know about it'.
: ...*my-e-chione*. The prep. pn. *mygeayrt-y-mysh* means 'round about it' and has replaced the inflected nominal prep. pn. *mychione* 'about, concerning', i.e. the inappropriate expression for 'about' has been used.

3. - shey *cassyn* er *height*
(Num. Npl. Prep.phrase)
/s´eː ˈkaːsən eː heit/ N/MTT/IFC/T37:1   E. 'height'
'six feet in height' (lit. 'six feet on height')
Here *cassyn* 'feet' (part of body) has been used instead of *trieyn* 'feet' (measurement) together w. E. 'height' instead of *yrjid* 'height', though the prep. *er* is used correctly.
: *shey trieyn er yrjid*.

4. - *mygeayrt my wannal aym*
(Prep. Poss.part. N Prep.pn.)
/məˈgut mə ˈwanəl em/ S/HLSM/II: 310 s.v. *mwannal*.
'around my neck'.
Here the form with the poss. adj. *my* 'my' and the periphrastic form with *ec* 'at' have been mixed.
either *my geayrt my wannal* or *mygeayrt y wannal aym*.
also - *ayns my laa aym* /us mə leː em/ N/HLSM/II: 258 s.v. *laa* 'in my day'.
either *ayms my laa* or *ayns y laa aym*.

5. - cha row monney *va jannoo* ayns yn keirdee
(Neg. SbV Pn. SbV(rel.) VbN Prep. Art. N)
/ha rau monə ve d´enu osən keːdi/ N/HLSM/I: 238-39
'there wasn't much to be done in the smithy' (lit. '...which was doing...')
: cha row monney *ry yannoo* ayns yn keirdee '...to be done...'.

6. - v'ee feer *cross er* ny paitchyn   E. 'cross with'
(SbV Pn. Adv. Adj. Prep. Art. Npl.)
/vei fiːə ˈkroːs er nə pet´ən/ N/HLSM/I: 184-85
'she was very cross with (on) the children'
Here the Mx. idiom *corree rish* 'angry with' has been confused with *trome er* 'angry with' (lit. 'heavy on').
: v'ee feer *hrome/trome er* ny paitchyn

7. - v'eh feer *fond jeh* bine dy yough   E. 'fond of'
(SbV Pn. Adv. Adj. Prep. N Prep. N)
/ve fiːə ˈfond d´e bain di ˈjaːx/S/HLSM/I: 348-49
'he was very fond of a drop of ale'.
Here the Eng. idiom 'fond of' and the Mx. idiom *graihagh er* 'fond of' (lit. 'loving, fond on') have been mixed.
: v'eh feer *ghraiagh er*...

8. - hie mee dys *ny margey* lesh ram *nollagh*

(Vpret. Pn. Prep. Art.(pl.) N(sg.) Prep. Pn. N)

/hai mi dɔsnə 'mər´g´ə les´ ra:m 'n´olax/ N/Diary: 38

'I went to the market with a lot of cattle'.

Here:

a) the pl. art. *ny* has been used with the sg. noun *margey*,

b) palatal. /n/ has been prefixed to *ollagh*, G. *eallach*, as if for *jeh'n* 'of the', w. *n* permanently attached (a misdivision), and

c) the cluster /rg/ in *margey* are unhistorically palatalised (cf. G. *margadh*), for which see §4.2.4.3. above.

: hie mee dys *y v/margey* lesh ram *ollagh.*

9. - *as v'ou smooinaghtyn nee eh cur ooilley yn vargey ayns aile*

(Conj. SbV Pn. VbN Vfut. Pn. VbN Indef.pn. Art. N Prep. N)

/as vou u smun´axən ni a kər ul´u in ve:gə us 'ail´/ N/HLSM/I: 252-53

'and you were thinking he would set fire to the whole fair'

(lit. 'and were you thinking will he do a putting (of) all the fair in fire').

Here we have:

a) parataxis of subordinate clause without conj. *dy* 'that' + dep. form of verb;

b) future form of *nee* instead of conditional in secondary tense sequence;

c) uncertainty of expression for setting fire to something

d) false lenition of *margey* after def. art. in nom/acc.

: *v'ou smooinaghtyn dy jinnagh eh cur aile da'n clane vargey*

(lit. 'were you thinking that would he do a putting/setting of fire to the whole (+ len.) fair').

10. - *as cur ad er wullagh er y cheilley*

(Conj. VbN Pn. Prep. N(len.) Prep.phrase)

/as korad e: 'wulax erə 'kel´ə/ N/HLSM/I: 246-47

'on top of each other' (lit. '...on top on each other').

Here two expressions are mixed together: *er muin y cheilley* 'on top of each other' and *er y cheilley* 'on each other'. For *er wullagh* see §4.3.2.3.1.

11. - *barouche v'ad gra son-eh*

(N SbV(rel.) Pn. VbN Prep. Pn.)

/ba´ru:s´ vad gre: son a/ N/HLSM/I: 234-35   E. 'for it'

'a barouche they were calling it' (lit. '...saying for it').

The Mx. idiom is *gra rish* 'say to', i.e. 'call'

: *barouche v'ad gra rish.*

12. - *ren eh geddyn dy loayrt da dooiney v'ad gra Casement da*

(Vpret. Pn. VbN Vinf. Prep. N SbV(rel.) Pn. VbN Pers.N Prep.)

/rin a gedn də lo:t də 'dun´ə vad gre: 'k´e:smənt de:/ N/HLSM/I: 238-39

'he got talking to a man they were calling Casement'

(lit. 'did he getting to speaking/talking to a man (which) were they saying Casement to').

Here we have:

a) direct trans. from Eng. for 'he got to talk to';

b) mixture of two idioms: *gyllagh da* 'calling to' and *loayrt rish* 'speaking to', *gra rish* 'saying to, calling';

: *ghow eh toshiaght dy loayrt rish dooinney v'ad gra Casement rish*

'he began talking to a man they called (whose name was) Casement'

(lit. 'took he beginning to speaking to a man (which) were they saying Casement to').

13. *-'neen as mee hene va goll dy goaill yn laa dy chur shilley dys yn sleityn*

(N Conj. Pn (emph.refl.) SbV(rel.) VbN Art. N Vinf. N Prep. Art.(sg.) Npl.)

/nʹiːnʹ əs mə ˈhiːnʹ vi gol də goːilʹ in ˈlaː də kə ˈsʹilʹədəs ən ˈslɛːtʹən/ N/HLSM /I: 236-37

'daughter and myself who were going to spend the day up in the mountains'.

(lit. 'a daughter and myself who were going to take the day to put a sight to the mountains').

Here we have:

a) *mee hene* misplaced; ought to come first in grammatical order of persons; see also §4.6.2.

b) inappropriate verb *goaill* 'take' instead of *ceau* 'spend'

c) inappropriate idiom with inappropriate prep, viz. *cur shilley er* not *dys*;

cur shilley er 'visit' (lit. 'put a sight on') used when visiting people or specific places.

d) use of sg. art. with pl. noun *sleityn* 'mountains', cf. §4.4.6.1.

: *mee hene as 'neen va goll dy c(h)eau yn laa heose ayns ny sleityn*

'myself and a daughter who were going to spend the day up in the mountains'.

14. *- neeym bwoalley hoo my jean shiu shen*

(Vfut.(infl.) VbN Pn.(2sg.) Conj. Vfut.(dep.) Pn.(2pl.) Dem.pn.)

/nim bulʹəxu me ˈdʹin sʹu ˈsʹen/ (N/Diary: 43)

'I'll beat you if you do that'

Here in the protasis the dep. form of the verb is used after *my* 'if' instead of the indep. form. In a future after *my* the future relative form (if a separate form exists) is used.

: *...my nee shiu shen* (...Conj. Vfut.(indep.(rel.)) Dem.pn.).

The list is not exhaustive.

4.6.4. Summary

In the transition from Manx to English speech in Man during the 19th century influences from English, in addition to those noted above, are also discernible:

1. Increase in lexical borrowing from English (§4.6.1.), though to an extent some are 'manxified', i.e. become absorbed into Manx phonology and morphology (§4.6.6.1.).

2. Adaptation to English idiom and calques (§4.6.2.) which leads to

3. Inadequacy of expression and uncertainty of idiom (§4.6.3.), and finally to

4. Replacement of Manx by the Target Language (English).

4.7. Manx Gaelic lexical and syntactical influence in the English of the Isle of Man today

4.7.1. Introduction

The English spoken today in the Isle of Man by native born and bred Manx men and women, showing varying degrees of phonological, syntactic and lexical influences from Manx Gaelic, is known as Manx English (MxE.). As we have seen (Section 1 p. 12 & Figure 2), residue of a dead language in the phonology, syntax, and lexis of the Target Language is a facet of the process of language death. This can be seen in the case of Manx English. We have seen (Section 2) that the language shift from Manx Gaelic to English essentially took place during the 19th century owing to increased migration of English speakers into the island, though English had been spoken in the towns and centres of administration since the advent of English suzerainty in Man in the early 15th century. In addition, primarily due to the ferry services, connections with Man for the better part of the 19th century to date have been with Liverpool (cf. Section 2.2.4.). Liverpool dialects show strong affinities with Hiberno-English (Barry pers. comm. 1977). For details of studies into and the phonology of Manx English, cf. Barry 1984; Broderick 1997b).

4.7.2. Lexical borrowings from Manx Gaelic

When the language shift had taken place a residue of vocabulary from the Abandoned Language, or substratum language (Manx), would have been retained in the Target Language (English) in Man. When Moore, Morrison & Goodwin made their collection of Manx English lexical items and idiom from both oral and literary sources (Moore, Morrison & Goodwin 1924), they were able to record over 750 lexical items from Mx. in MxE. Ten years later Walter Gill, essentially drawing his material from one literary source (cf. Gill 1934), recorded a further 250 or so items from Manx Gaelic. During fieldwork in Man in 1958 and again in 1966 Michael Barry was only able to record some 126 items from Mx. in MxE, mainly from a Mrs. Sage Kinvig in the south of the island (cf. Barry 1984). Looking briefly through Moore, Morrison and Goodwin (1924) and Gill (1934) I have noted a number of loan-words still in use from personal observation and while conducting fieldwork for the Manx Place-Name Survey (1989-92). They include the following semantic fields:

4.7.2.1. Farming

> *bithag* 'thick milk for churning'.
> *clash* 'furrow, ditch'.
> *cregs* (Mx. *carage*) 'beetles', w. Eng. pl.
> *cushag* 'ragwort'. Has to be cut by law, as it is poisonous to horses - OT.
> *jeush* 'sheep shears'.
> *jokal* [dʒɒkəl] 'spell of ploughing'; lit. 'yoking' < E. *yoke* w. radicalised init. conson. + Mx. vn. suffix *-al*. 'I've done my jokal for today'.

lhergy 'hillslope'.
loghtan 'tawny'; applied to native Manx sheep.

4.7.2.2. Fishing

ahley 'fishing ground', N only.
gobbag, govvag 'dogfish'; still used as a mild term of contempt for a Peel man.
mollag 'dogskin'; in the past inflated and tarred and used as a buoy to float herring nets.

4.7.2.3. Houshold

bonnag 'bannock' (a circular flat loaf).
braghtan 'griddle cake sandwiched with cheese, meat, etc'.
bravvag 'warming the legs by the fire'; 'to have a bravvag (by the fire)'.
chiollagh 'hearth'.
cooish 'talk, chat'. 'we met for a cooish'.
skuthan 'scum around inside of pan'.

4.7.2.4. Societal

drollane 'indolent, sluggish person'.
joushag 'chattering woman', cf. Mx. *jouish* 'sheep-shears'.
spiddhag 'person small in stature'.
toot 'fool, simpleton' - 'he's no toot'.
yisseh, yusseh 'you!' ?Eng. response 'yes sir'.

4.7.2.5. Folklore and tradition

augh-augh 'spell' (onomat.) - 'she put the augh-augh on Ballagawne'.
bollan bane 'white wort'; worn on Tynwald Fair Day (5 July).
buggane 'a sort of goblin'.
Hop-tu-naa, Hopthenei 'Hollantide'.

4.7.2.6. Curses and exclamations

cum-dty-hengey! 'hold your tongue!'.
shee [i.e. *Jee*] *bannee mee!* 'oh, dear!'; lit. 'God bless me'. Used in exclamations.
sloo my hudn! 'lick my arse!' (= E. 'fuck off!') Mx. *shliee my hudn* [s´lʼiː mə 'hudn]
N/HLSM/II: 405 s.v. *shliee*, cf. Ger. *leck' mich am Arsch*.

4.7.2.7. General

boghnid 'poorness'; now used in the sense of 'nonsense' - 'that's a lot o' boghtnid!'
bree 'vigour' - 'there's no bree in her'.
bun 'bottom, base' - to get to the bun of it - to get to the root, bottom of something.
fud-y-cheilley 'confused'; lit. 'through each other'.
jarrood 'forgetting' - 'I'm in a bit of a jarrood' - I'm in a forgetful state of mind.
jeeill 'damage' - 'there's plenty o' jeeill done at 'im' - he's done a lot of damage.
sluight 'some, a little, a trace' - 'a sluight of religion' (obtained by going to church).
traa dy liooar 'time enough, plenty of time'. Still in common use.

The list is not exhaustive.

4.7.3. Some syntactical influences from Manx Gaelic

4.7.3.1. Calques on Mx. idioms:

1. *it was done at him* 'he did it'
Mx. *v'eh jeant echey*
(SbV Pn. Vppp. Prep.pn.).

2. *it's forgotten at me* 'I've forgotten it'
Mx. *t'eh jarroodit aym*
(SbV Pn. Vppp. Prep.pn.)
(with use of personal forms of *ec* 'at' as agent with verbal adjective in both exx).

3. *we'll put a sight on him* 'we'll visit him'
Mx. *cur shilley er* 'visit'
(VbN N Prep.pn.)
(lit. 'putting a sight on (him)')
: *neemayd cur shilley er.*

4. *that field was put to it (the farm) last year*, i.e. 'added to'
Mx. *cur gys/hug* (VbN Prep.) 'putting to, adding to'
: *va'n magher shen currit huggey nurree.*

5. *that's the field they were calling the big field to* i.e. 'they called'
Mx. *gra rish* (VbN Prep.) 'say to, call, name', or *gyllagh da* (VbN Prep.) 'call to'.
In LM these two idioms were confused.
: *shen yn magher v'ad gra yn Magher Mooar rish.*

4.7.3.2. Use of Mx. present continuous for the present habitual or present perfect in Standard English:

I'm hearing that he's dead 'I hear/have heard that he has died/is dead'.
Mx. *ta mee clashtyn dy vel eh marroo*
(SbV Pn. VbN Conj. SbV Pn. Adj.).

4.7.3.3. Use of Mx. past continuous for the preterite in Standard English:

that field was belonging to him 'that field belonged to him'.
Mx. *s'lesh/b'lesh* (Cop.(pres./past) Prep.pn. *lesh*) 'is/was with him'
va...lesh (SbV(past)...Prep.pn. *lesh*) 'is/was (etc)...with him', i.e. belonging to him
: *s'lesh yn magher shen* (Cop.(pres.) Prep.pn. *lesh* Art. N Dem.adj.)
: *va'n magher shen lesh* (SbV Art. N Dem.adj. Prep.pn. *lesh*)
Forms in *s'lesh* are usually relative 'whose...it is, was'.Note also that the present tense of the copula functions also for the past.

4.7.3.4. Use of the copula for emphasis in cleft sentences:

It's George that's in 'yes, it's George, it is George who is there'.
Mx. *she George t'ayn*
(Cop. Pers.N SbV(rel.) Prep. *ayn* (3 sg. masc.)).[16]

4.7.3.5. Use of 'in' as predicate from Mx. ayn 'in it':

There's a fine day in 'it's a fine day'.
Mx. *ta laa mie ayn*
(SbV N Adj. Prep. *ayn* (3 sg. masc.). See also §4.5.6.2. above.
For further details here see Kewley-Draskau (fc.).

---

[16] For the use of the copula in EM/CM, cf. Thomson 1950-51: 279-85, in LM, cf. HLSM/I: 93-97. The displacement of the copula by the substantive verb was well underway in CM - in fact, in the Manx Bible translation "[...] the copula constructions, which are at variance with the corrsponding English expression, are fairly frequently altered, and in this respect the finished product may be less representative of the language of the period then were the [translators'] drafts" (Thomson 1969a: 186). Nevertheless, use of the copula constructions survives well into the Late Manx period, even down to the last native speakers themselves. The last native speaker, Ned Maddrell, made constant use of it (cf. §4.5.6.(3).). In such circumstances replacement of copula by substantive verb constructions are not regarded here as an aspect of language death, but of *Sprachwandel.*

4.7.4. Summary

In the process of language shift the Abandoned Language (Manx Gaelic) has left its mark on the Target Language (English) and includes the following:

1. Lexical borrowings from Manx Gaelic which come to be used in everyday speech in Man and become part of the English of Man (Manx English) (§4.7.2.).

2. Syntactical borrowings from Manx and calques on Manx idioms which become part of the everyday English speech of Man (§4.7.3.1.), e.g. the use of the present continuous tense for the present habitual or present perfect, and the past continuous for the preterite in Standard English (§§4.7.3.2.-3.), use of the copula for emphasis in cleft sentences (§4.7.3.4.), and the use of 'in' (< Mx. *ayn* 'in it') as predicate (§4.7.3.5.).

The list is not exhaustive.

4.8. Conclusion

The present description of the death of Manx is hopefully a contribution to a better understanding of the major phenomenon of language death, whereby both sociohistorical and formal linguistic factors have been taken into consideration. Unlike other Gaelic dialects perhaps,[17] Manx is fortunate in having a detailed documented history from the 17th century onwards. The last stages of Manx are particularly well attested, as a result of which we can witness step by step how a once vibrant and functioning language deteriorates and gives up its means of expressing thoughts. This process of destruction occurs slowly in the native Manx speakers who are exposed to various social and economic pressures from outside which lead first to bilingualism, in which English becomes more and more the dominant language, and then bilingual speakers stop speaking Manx to their children. The inability and poor quality of Manx in its latter stages results from infrequency of use by full native speakers and imperfect learning of it by semi-speakers. Examples of this latter aspect were noted and described by Marstrander in his fieldwork in Man 1929-1933 (cf. Diary in Appendix A).

4.8.1. A sociohistorical and sociolinguistic overview

In sociohistorical and sociolinguistic terms the decline and death of Manx could be summarised as follows. After the passing of Man into the English orbit in 1334, but especially after 1405, English began to establish itself as the language of administration and law, and of the towns where it existed alongside Manx without displacing it. Because of Man's isolation and owing to the necessity of the few English settlers for their sustenance to cultivate the goodwill of the Manx people, the small world in which Manx existed was thus protected.

---

[17] East Sutherland Gaelic, for instance, whose demise can be attributed more to the decline in the numbers of its speakers, rather than in having sustained a long period of attrition and attack from English. In comparison with the Manx situation ESG appears not to be at so advanced a stage of decay or deterioration.

The protected world of Manx became more and more exposed to English from ca. 1700 onwards due to a changing set of circumstances brought on essentially by the Running Trade (smuggling). Participation in the Trade led to Revestment of Man in the British Crown leading in turn to an impoverishment in Man which resulted in emigration of Manxmen (and others) in the latter part of the 18th century. Simultaneous immigration of English speakers ca. 1800-1820 and further emigration from the Manx heartland during the course of the 19th century began to tilt the balance (ca. 1840-1880) in favour of English. The advent of and increase in tourism and a more organised system of education imported from England during those years hastened this trend, so that those born to Manx households ca. 1860-1880 became the last generation to receive Manx from the cradle.

4.8.2. A formal linguistic overview

In line with the trend in Western IE languages from synthesis to analysis Manx progressed in that direction more so than her sister dialects in Ireland and Scotland, probably due to the absence, almost certainly from the beginning of the 14th century at the latest, of a literary Gaelic tradition and standard. Right through its short history Manx has gradually developed in the general direction of analysis and syncretism. Looking at the decline of Manx in formal linguistic terms we notice a definite trend towards simplification and reduction in the phonology (cf. §4.2.), morphophonology (cf. §4.3.), morphology (cf. §4.4.), and morphosyntax and syntax (cf. §4.5.), and a succumbing to English lexical influence (cf. §4.6.) in Late Manx.

4.8.2.1. Phonology

1. Here we notice wild allophonic variation in the vowel phonemes (§4.2.2.1.) leading to a collapse of the once distinct opposition between the phonemes /eː/ : /ɛː/ and /oː/ : /ɔː/ into one of each (§.4.2.2.1.3.); the simplification of the consonant phonemes, whereby, due to loss of the palatalisation rule (cf. §4.2.4.1.), the palatalised variants of /x/, /h/, /ɣ/, /r/, and /ŋ/ cease to have any phonemic status and are either lost or reduced to allophones of their neutral counterparts (§4.2.4.).

2. In addition, we notice a simplification in the resonant system (/L, N, R/) of LM (§4.2.4.2.), a process already underway in CM (§4.2.3.), leading to "abuse" of palatalisation (§4.2.4.3.), i.e. the application of palatalisation where it is not expected or unhistorical, due to uncertainty in the rules of application (see also Figure 8 below on the loss of palatalisation in the phonology of death).

4.8.2.2. Morphophonology

1. Linked to the foregoing is a simplification of the system of initial (and final) mutation in LM (§4.3.2. & §4.3.4.), whereby the the system of consonant replacement in initial position (lenition and eclipsis/nasalisation) is weakened (§4.3. 2.1.) leading to disorder and an

"abuse" or hypercorrect use of lenition (§4.3.2.3.) and false delenition (§4.3.2.4.) for similar reasons to "abuse" of palatalisation noted above.

2. In the case of eclipsis (§4.3.3.2.) and loss of final muation (§4.3.4.) the disappearance is, except for a few fossils and exceptions, complete (see also Figure 8 on the loss of lenition and eclipsis/nasalisation rules for the death of morphophonology).

4.8.2.3. Morphology

1. A simplification of the system of gender, number, and case marking was more or less complete by the Classical Manx period, if not before, resulting in only one gender (masculine), with some exceptions in the old feminine (§4.4.2.1.), and essentially only one case (nominative (whether derived from oblique cases or not)), with some fossils in the genitive singular and plural and dative plural (§4.4.2.) (cf. Broderick 1991: 65-81). This system continued into the period of Late Manx until the demise of Manx.

2. Concomitant with the foregoing and a feature of Late Manx is a process of simplification of the inflectional system of the adjective, whereby loss of the separate plural morpheme (§4.4.4.1.) as well as any inflection in the comparative (§4.4.4.2.) is found side by side with inflected forms. In the definite article we see a reduction of the number and case forms in LM to one form for all occasions (§4.4.6.1.), its omission in titles (§4.4.6.2.), but its appearance in constructions containing a definite genitive (§4.4.6.3.), all probably due to English influence.

4.8.2.4. Morphosyntax and Syntax

1. In the Late Manx period, particularly towards the end, we find uses of both sg. and pl. forms in the imperative for the same person(s) (§4.5.1.), the verb-noun used as an imperative (§4.5.2.), the use of formal forms in close relationships and forms of address (§4.5. 3.), thus revealing an uncertainty in the form required for a particular pragmatic circumstance.

2. In the tenses and tense forms we note the disappearance of the future relative in temporal and real conditional clauses, confusion of tense forms in unreal conditions whereby the conditional form is gradually replaced by the future (§4.5.4.).[18]

3. In the periphrastic form of the passive with the preposition *er* 'after' + possessive particle, varying according to person, + verbal noun (§4.5.5.), the 3 sg. masculine of the possessive particle become the standard form in LM (with or without initial mutation in the following verbal noun), in so far as this type is used.

4. In answers to 'yes-no' questions (§4.5.6.) we see the introduction of a standard answer form equating English 'yes' and 'no' irrespective of mood, tense or person, replacing the traditional replies using a reduced form of the verb, but in the same mood and tense.

5. The object pronoun (§4.5.7.), placed after a prepositional phrase (in accordance with normal Gaelic practice) even in the LM period (viz. 'put he on the table it'), comes to be

---

[18] For inflected tense forms and irregular verbs moving to inreased use of auxiliary of *jannoo* 'do' + verb-noun, cf. Thomson 1950-51: 275-76.

placed before the phrase (viz. 'put he it on the table'), as in English, by most of the last native speakers, which is evidence of bilingual competence in which English dominates.

6. In the predicate (§4.5.8.) we note a process of simplification in the indefinite predicate (e.g. *t'eh ny wooinney litcheragh* 'is he in his man lazy') whereby the use of possessive particles or particles containing them (viz. *my, dty, ny, nyn*) are first reduced in number (to 3 sg. masc.) then are lost altogether along with any initial mutation (viz. *t'eh dooiney litcheragh* 'is he (a) man lazy'). The use of *ayn* 'in it' in the predicate is also lost, thus rendering the sentence as in English, again evidence of dominating English syntax.

7. In the case of prepositional pronouns (e.g. *aym* 'at me', *erriu* 'on you (pl.)' etc.) (§4.5.9.) we witness their decomposition into preposition plus pronoun, as in English, viz. *ec mish* (emph. pn.), *er shiu*.

8. In co-ordinative conjunctions Eng. 'but' comes to replace the Mx. equivalent *agh* (§4.5.10.1.), and in the use of subordinating conjunctions there is a tendency to use one subordinator where previously there may have been two or more. The conjunction *my* 'if' used in real conditions comes to supplant *dy, my dy* (itself late) 'if' used in unreal conditions (§4.5.10.2.1.-2.).[19] After *lurg* 'after' in temporal clauses the prep. pn. *da* 'to' + the substantive verb-noun *ve* 'being' are lost and *lurg* is followed by the uninflected pers. pn. in the process of simplification (§4.5.10.2.3.).

9. After other subordinating conjunctions (§4.5.10.2.4.-7.) and in sentences expressing possibility (§4.5.10.2.9.) the indep. form of the verb comes to replace other forms as the standard, thus rendering the syntax as in English. Similarly in negative relative clauses the conjunction *nagh* 'that not' comes to be replaced by the negative particle *cha* 'not' in direct parataxis, as in English (§4.5.10.2.8.).

10. In sentences expressing permission or exhortation (§4.5.10.2.10.) the prep. *da* 'to' + noun or pronoun falls out after *lhiggey* 'letting', rendering the sentence as in English.

4.8.2.5. Other English influences

During the course of the 19th century an increase in English influence is discernible (§4.6.) in the form of massive lexical borrowings (§4.6.1.1. & 2.) and copying of English idioms and calques (§4.6.2.). As English comes to be spoken more and more, and Manx less and less, Manx begins to lose its vitality. Speakers begin to forget idiom (§4.6.3.); they may remember the singular of a noun, but not its plural (cf. Jackson's comments on this in Section 3.6.8.). Their Manx becomes more and more anglicised (and so far as our evidence goes, this is apparently the case more with speakers from the North than from the South of Man), until it becomes merely a code for English and no longer a functioning language. In such circumstances extinction and death is the unavoidable consequence.[20]

---

[19] In CM *my* may be used for *dy* if *dy* is ambiguous (i.e. can be construed in a particular context as *dy* 'that').

[20] In his treatise on Manx O'Rahilly's verdict was more brutal: "[...] it could be said without much exaggeration that some of the Manx that has been printed is merely English disguised in a Manx vocabulary. When a language surrenders itself to foreign idiom, and when all its speakers become bilingual, the penalty is death" (O'Rahilly 1932: 121).

4.8.2.6. Abwehrkampf

Nevertheless, Manx had an enormous capacity to absorb foreign elements into its phonological and morphonological systems (cf. §4.6.1.1. and Thomson 1991) and it was able to sustain an effective *Abwehrkampf* to the end, in spite of heavy pressure from English. Even the
numeric system of Manx,[21] counting as it does by twenties: (/(ta mi) kʹeːə fid as kweg dʹeg
sonən 'dunax/ '(I am) 95 on Sunday' (lit. '...four score and fifteen...') (Ned Maddrell,
18.08.1972, so far as is known the last academic interview before his death (27.12.1974)),
unlike Scottish Gaelic, for example, where numbers are often given in English: 'I am 92
years of age' /hami *ninety-two* blʹiəNə 'ɣuːsʹ/, or so I heard in the Isle of Skye in May
1972) is kept intact to the last (cf. HLSM/I: 47-52).

4.8.3. An anatomy of language death

Language death in Manx, as we have seen, affects and attacks right across the spectrum: its
phonology (both the vowel and consonant phonemes), its morphophonology (in initial and
final mutation), which inevitably leads to a simplification in its morphology. As Thomson
(1969a: 189-90) noted earlier (cf. §4.3. above) "[...] mutation and gender are mutually supporting systems and the reduction of one will necessarily involve the other". However, it is
pertinent to note that Manx consistently makes the distinction between two types of mutation (namely, the functioning morphophonemic alternation involving the initial consonant
replacement, either by lenition or eclipsis / nasalisation, cf. §4.3. above): "non-significant"
and "significant".
    1. The "non-signifcant mutation" could be dispensed with, since its abandonment would
not affect meaning or understanding, e.g. *ayns y vaatey/baatey* would still mean 'in the boat'.
    2. However, "significant mutation" cannot be dispensed with as it involves forms that
show fossilised historical lenition (§4.3.2.2.) or eclipsis (§4.3.3.3.), where failure of either
would produce unrecognisable forms, e.g. (fossilised lenition) *va* 'was' (ScG. *bha*) -> *ba*,
and thus lead to a breakdown of understanding.
    The loss of final mutation, however, which led to indistinction between singular and plu-
ral marking in the nominal system, resulted in morphological innovation in the introduction
of a suffix plural in order to maintain number distinction.
    These significant losses in the morphophonology and morphology of Late Manx were al-
ready underway during the Classical Manx period, and because the application of initial mutation became gender-based (cf. §4.4.2.), the loss of gender distinction (also at this time) would
necessarily lead to abandonment of lenition in due course. In this regard the abandonment of
non-significant initial mutation in Manx (cf. §4.3.2.) could be seen as a step in the direction
of simplification and rationalisation, but communication and understanding were still maintained. In the case of the preterite of inflected verbs (cf. §4.3.2.1.15.) communication is not
affected, since the context makes clear what tense is meant.[22] In reality, had there been no

---

[21] For use of the preposition *dy* 'of' in the Mx. numerical system, cf. §4.4.2.3.1. and HLSM/I:
50. For disturbances in the syntax of the numerical system, cf. §4.6.2.3. above.

[22] In addition, it is to be noted that inflected future and conditional forms of regular verbs (with
the exception of *goaill* 'take' and one or two scattered examples; cf. HLSM/I: 85-87) are not attested in LSM, and so any non-lenited preterite forms could not be mistaken for the same.

168

further loss or reduction, Manx could still have functioned as a viable language, albeit in a simplified form.[23]

However, in my view the real damage is done by the following: a) wild allophonic variation, particularly in the vowel phonemes, b) significant interference in the morphosyntax and syntax, as well as disturbances in idiom and expression.

The wild allophonic variation in the phonological system of Late Manx would lead to difficulty of perception resulting from so-called "stylistic shrinkage" and thereby to an inability to understand and be understood. As Dressler puts it:

> A disintegrating language is characterised by fluctuations and uncertainties of its speakers [...] (Dressler 1972b: 454).

In addition he adds:

> [...] "Stylistic shrinkage", i.e. conflation of either various social styles or of various slow speech and fast speech styles. (Stylistic shrinkage and phonetic free variation often render pre-ception rather difficult). This is due to the restriction of the use of the decaying language to ever fewer speech situations and to generalisation of the styles used in these situations. Both phonetic free variation and stylistic shrinkage point to the social and pragmatic context of language death [...] (Dressler 1972b: 454-55).

In the phonology, as we can see in Figure 8, the main result is a) wild allophonic variation, particularly in the vowels, which leads to indistinct perception (as already noted), b) loss of the palatalisation rule which leads to indistinction in number marking (though rectified by the application of a suffix), and c) the loss of fortis : lenis and neutral : palatal contrast in the resonants (/L, N, R/) which would have led to indistinction in tense marking in verbs with an initial resonant, e.g. Mx. verbal noun *roie* 'running' would earlier have been something like */Rei/ [Rei], and preterite *roie* 'ran' /rei/ [rei]. However, the loss of fortis /R/ in Mx. has rendered both forms as /rei/. The indistinction in tense marking may be one of the reasons that led to greater use of the auxiliary verbs *ve* 'be' and *jannoo* 'do', especially the latter, in the formation of tenses in Mx. to ensure clarity of meaning.

Concomitant with this shrinkage of language use is the significant introduction of confusion in the morphosyntax and syntax of Late Manx (cf. §4.5.), whereby loss of competence in expressing tense in the verbal system (cf. 4.5.1/4.) and the introduction of standard answer forms in 'yes-no' questions (cf. §4.5.6.) particularly can lead to interference in communication and understanding.[24] In addition, the copying and borrowing of idiom and lexemes from English into the syntax of LM would lead to Manx becoming merely a code for English.

However, the final death-blow was the non-use of Manx over a long period of time which would lead to inadequacy of expression and uncertainty of idiom, i.e. to significant *reduction* in the ability of Manx to function as a viable language. This, along with the negative social prejudices disadvantaging Manx at that time, would be significant and decisive for the decay

---

[23] Even in Dressler's examples for Breton (Dressler 1972b), where initial mutation is more involved than that of Manx, if everything were to be simplified down to lenition only (i.e. "if in doubt lenite" as is said for Welsh where the system of initial mutation is similar to that for Breton (cf. Russell 1995)), this in my view would not affect communication or understanding. As with Manx, there would need to be severe interference in the phonology and syntax particularly, before language death in Breton took significant hold.

[24] The adaptation to English syntax of the examples in §4.5.7/10. in Figure 8 would not impede communication or understanding, however.

and demise of Manx as a community language. In other words, the onset of the Target Language (English) at the expense of the Abandoned Language (Manx) leads ultimately to greater influence of the more on the less dominant, and finally to the demise and disappearance of Manx.

Figure 8 encapsulates the whole range of rule loss, breakdown of the phonological, morphophonological and morphological systems and the impact of English syntax on Manx. The main destructive causes of language death are to be found in the phonology, morphosyntax and syntax, lexicon and phraseology, which as if in a pincer movement combine to extirpate Manx altogether.

4.8.4. Earlier models of language death and their application to Late Manx

In Section 1 (§1.4.) Sasse's model for describing language death was discussed, based as it is on Dorian's work on East Sutherland Gaelic and that of Tsitsipis and his own on Arvanítika (cf. also Figure 2). Can his model apply to language death in Late Manx? I believe it can, but with some adjustment to meet the Manx situation.

1. Historical events: Development of education policy in Man by the Anglican Church - its overall negative attitude towards Manx from the mid-17th century onwards (cf. §2.2.),[25] Revestment of Man to the British Crown and the onset of poverty in the island; emigration of Manx speakers, immigration of English speakers (18th/19th centuries), cf. Section 2 - all this leads to political (the education system) and social pressure (English immigration) on Manx which results in a negative attitude towards it and a decision later to abandon it.

2. The aforementioned pressure leads to an uneven distribution of English in the multilingual situation of Manx and English and to a complementary distribution of linguistic domains. This in turn leads to an increase in collective bilingualism because of a restriction of domains in Manx, resulting in a negative attitude towards Manx.

3. The intrusion of English into the domains of Manx leads to lexical loss or failure of development of Manx in areas where English is favoured (commerce, tourism, industry, education, communications, etc. (cf.§2.2.4.)). This in turn leads to an increase in bilingualism, and thus to greater interference of English in the domains of Manx (contact), resulting in a further increase in competence in English and the stigmatisation of Manx (by the Anglican Church (§2.2.2.) and by the education authorities (§2.2.3.)). This leads to an increase in interference and simplification in Manx (already underway in the CM period), though Manx remains functionally intact.

4. The negative attitude towards Manx from the church and secular authorities, and the requirement of English in the sphere of economic and of social advancement leads to a total social stigmatisation of Manx amongst its speakers (*cha jean oo cosney ping lesh y Ghailck* 'you will not earn a penny with the Manx') and to a decision by them to abandon Manx. This results in an interruption of the transmission of Manx to the children and a conscious

---

[25] Except for the support for Manx from Bishops Wilson (1699-1755) and Hildesley (1755-72), as a result of whose efforts the Bible was translated into Manx, and one or two others, indifference (and at times outright hostility, cf. §2.2.2.) on the part of the Anglican Church in Man towards Manx seems to have been the norm.

avoidance of Language Transmission Skills for Manx and a prevention of an acquisition of Manx, eventually leading to its prohibition (cf. §2.4.).

5. This in turn leads to Primary Language Shift (from Manx to English) and a further loss of domains in Manx, resulting in language decay and a pathological reduction of rules and structures in the speech of semi-speakers.

6. This results in an end of regular communication in Manx. Manx is then retained by parents "who do not wish their children to understand" when discussing private matters, for example, and by others who wish to use it for elitist purposes, for purposes of group identification, or as a *Kunstsprache* (e.g. by revivalists, cf. Section 5).

7. However, during the period of bilingualism (ca. 1800 onwards) Manx leaves its mark on English in the adaptation of idioms and calques from Manx and a transfer of a substantial number of lexical items into spoken English in Man, i.e. Manx English (cf. §4.7.2.), used mainly in the traditional occupations of farming and fishing where an English equivalent may be lacking. However, even Manx English is gradually fading away and becoming enfeebled in the process of population change and increase in the arrival of other forms of English speech into Man.

The passing of Manx as a community language took place ca. 1870/80-1900/10, with the last native speakers living through the 1920s to the 1950s, decreasing in number gradually towards the end, until the death of the last native speaker on 27 December 1974.

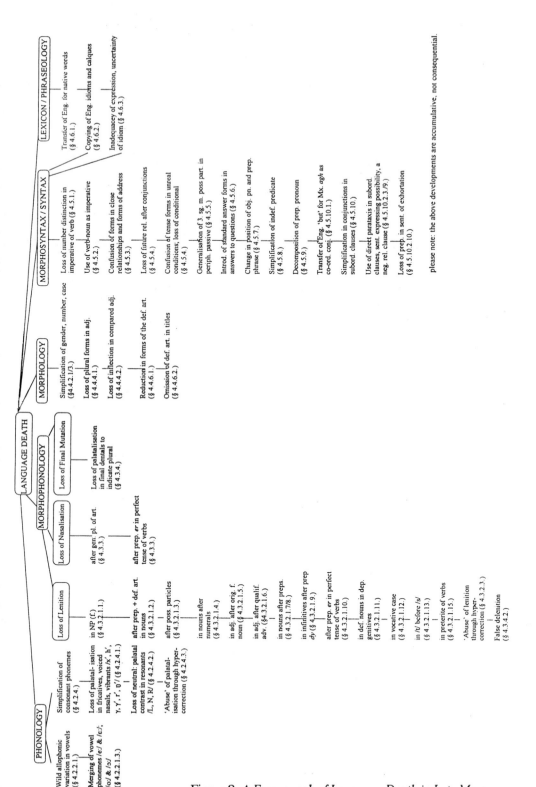

Figure 8: *A Framework of Language Death in Late Manx*

5. Excursus: Language Revival and Language Maintenance in Man[1]

5.1. Introduction

Attitudes to language use and promotion differ among those who speak a given endangered language. Some speakers regard their language as "sacred" which as a badge of the separate identity of those who speak it has to be treasured. Others take a more profane view, that the language is no longer serving the needs of the community and must give way to a language that does. They do not regard their language as "holy" and are not over-saddened when their language passes into history. There would be as many supporters who take a profane view as those who may regard their endangered language as sacred (cf. Ladefoged 1992: 809-11).

As we have seen from newspaper reports and letters (Section 2.3.1.), there was much debate about the value and use, or otherwise, of Manx and efforts to retain or abandon it, a debate that went on right through the period of decline during the 19th century. However, it was only when the decline was more or less complete that it was felt that something ought to be done about it. The inspiration for such endeavour was seemingly not home-grown, but imported from Ireland which was experiencing a similar situation (cf. Hindley 1991). Although the newspaper correspondence of the 1820s suggests some interest in 'restoring Manx' - or *cur stiagh y ghailck reesht* (cf. letter 13.12.1821 in Appendix B), as it was put, the main thrust of the Revival came in the closing years of the 19th century, and was to experience three phases.

5.2. The First Phase (ca. 1890 - ca. 1930)

The Revival of Manx could be said to have started on 22 March 1899 with the founding of *Yn Cheshaght Ghailckagh* (YCG) 'The Manx Language Society' under the presidency of Manx academic and Speaker of the House of Keys Arthur W. Moore (1836-1909).[2] The founding of a society of this nature had its roots in two main factors:

1. the general wave of interest and enthusiasm in matters Celtic emanating from Ireland which swept over all the 'Celtic Countries' (viz. Ireland, Scotland, Man, Wales, Cornwall, Brittany) during the latter part of the 19th century, and

2. more particularly relevant to the situation in Man (but mirroring a similar position in Ireland), the revelation from Henry Jenner's survey of 1874 (see Jenner 1875) of the considerable retreat Manx had sustained by the last quarter of the nineteenth century.

---

[1] As the revival of Manx is in itself a facet of language death, some details of language revival and maintenance in Man are given here.

[2] Its predecessor the 'Manx Society' had been set up in 1858 "for the publication of National Documents of the Isle of Man" and in all published 33 volumes (Cubbon 1933: 496-509). The Manx Society was wound up in 1907 (Kneen 1931: 15; König 1996: 34, fn. 36).

174

In order to engender support for the Revival, promotion of the language was linked to patriotism and national consciousness, and was seen as an indispensible part of 'Manxness', of being 'Manx'. In an article in the *Manchester Guardian* for 27.09.1913 the Manx Revival was seen to:

> [...] foster this feeling of patriotism, this earnest recognition of nationality, that the Manx Language Society was founded in 1899 [...] to promote the cultivation of the Manx language, literature and music, and the publication of modern literature in Manx [...] (*Manchester Guardian* 27.09.1913 quoted after Peter 1984: 46).

YCG is still the foremost institution in Man for the maintenance and promotion of Manx. Its
objectives and means, then as now, could be outlined from its constitution as follows:

1. The preservation of Manx as the national language of the Isle of Man.
2. The study and publication of existing Gaelic literature and the cultivation of a modern literature in Manx.

These were to be achieved through the setting up of classes, holding lectures, and encouraging those who have Manx to speak it regularly. In addition, YCG aims were to seek to have Manx taught in schools, to promote Manx music and songs, to contribute relevant material about YCG in magazines and journals, and to collect aspects of oral literature (tales, songs, etc) still thought to be extant among the people. In addition, the *Isle of Man Examiner*, then as now a leading Manx newspaper, contributed (1899-1902) to the Revival by running a column in Manx or including material on Manx folklore, especially that collected by Charles Roeder (1848-1911), a native of Gera in Thüringen, then resident in Manchester (see Roeder 1904; Cubbon 1933, 1939).

Nevertheless, the enthusiasm for the Revival of Manx was to be tempered with what was regarded as realism. At the first annual meeting of YCG (13.11.1899) the Society's first president A. W. Moore expressed his opinion that it was not desirable "to endeavour to revive the spoken Manx by teaching it to the young" (Manx Language Society 1899-1931(b): 5; König 1996: 35). Although he regarded a spoken language as valuable to the cultivation of the national spirit, he viewed a living Manx language as of little or no value to the Manx people for earning a living and concluded:

> Much as I regret to think of the day when the grand and sonorous language of Ellan Vannin will be no more heard, yet I feel that I must prefer the practical to the sentimental and acquiesce in its disappearance (*ibid*: 6).[3]

However, others at the meeting took a different view and opted for the promotion of Manx as one of the Society's main functions (*ibid*: 5; König 1996: 35).

YCG also had as one of its aims the introduction of Manx into the Island's schools. However, several problems had to be overcome. At the turn of the century the British authorities felt responsible for education in Man, where in 1872 a slightly modified version of the 1870

---

[3] As Speaker of the House of Keys Moore was an 'establishment' figure in the Isle of Man, and his comments have to be seen in that light. This was at a time when the British Empire (and English nationalist sentiment particularly) was at its zenith, and it was policy then to regard languages other than English, particularly inside the British Isles, as of little worth. Even dialects of English were considered "provincial barbarisms" (cf. Durkacz 1983: 204; Peter 1984: 35).

English Elementary Education Act was introduced,[4] and so any sanction to teach Manx in schools had to be sought from that quarter. After three years of correspondence between Whitehall and YCG it was decided to leave the matter to individual schools, with the result that evidently only one school was willing to teach Manx. The half-hour lesson per week was shortly after withdrawn, and efforts to have Manx brought into the schools on a more permanent and professional basis had to wait until 1992 (see §5.5. below).

In May 1913 YCG began publishing its journal *Mannin*, edited by YCG secretary and folklore collector Sophia Morrison. A literary publication containing much on Manx folklore, folklife, music and songs, etc, it ran twice yearly (May and November) for nine consecutive issues till May 1917, folding just after the death of its editor (in January 1917).

The demise of this publication saw a decline in enthusiasm for things Manx (not helped by the events of the First World War), which prompted YCG stalwart J. J. Kneen in 1931 to comment that "Celtic enthusiasm, always of a fugitive nature, sadly waned again during the last twenty years" (Kneen 1931: 20), and the Revival was not to see a further surge in energy and activity till about 1930.

Concomitant with, but slightly predating the surge in interest in Manx Gaelic, was the interest in Manx traditional songs, music and lore. In 1893 the Castletown general practitioner and fiddle player Dr. John Clague (1842-1908) began a systematic collection of Manx folksongs and folktunes while on his rounds, concentrating on the South of the Island (1893-96), then on the North (1896-98). His music collection contains some 270 items, plus variants, in four manuscript notebooks (though not always in his hand) (Clague 1893-98; Gilchrist 1924-26, Jerry 1987), and his fragmentary song collection (relating to the foregoing) in a further nine notebooks now in the Manx Museum (see Broderick 1982c). Clague collected a considerable amount of folklore material also (Clague 1911), in Manx Museum MS.450A. At about the same time A. W. Moore was also collecting song material, partly from oral, but predominantly from documentary sources (Moore 1896). His collection consists of 74 songs or song-fragments, of which 40 have tunes associated with them (*ibid.* 1896; see also Broderick 1982c).

As in Ireland the collection of folksong material in Man went hand in hand with the language Revival which also formed part of the general nationalist aspirations of the time. In Ireland folktunes not regarded as 'Irish' were rejected and musicians were discouraged from playing them (cf. Ó Súilleabháin 1982: v). This resulted in an apparently dramatic reduction of the repertoire available to musicians which prompted comment from some music editors (cf. also Speers 1997: 228). In Man, so far as is known, no 'political correctness' in this regard was exercised among musicians. However, it seemingly did influence the collecting process, whereby tunes known to have been played in Man during the 19th century, e.g. *the Black and the Grey* (played at weddings; cf. Speers 1997: 249) and *Flowers of Edinburgh* (played at Mellias or end of harvest gatherings; cf. Speers 1997: 258), do not appear in the available folktune collections. In other words a subconscious (or perhaps conscious) selection process was evidently underway as to what was regarded as 'Manx' and 'not Manx' during the

---

[4]   This made no provision for Manx, but had little or no effect on it, as the language shift had by then already taken place (see Section 3). But its implementation put Manx schools on a par with those in England where the language of instruction was English (for details see Bird 1995: 1-43).

collecting of the tunes. A similar 'filtration process' was apparently also underway in the collection and 'restoration' of traditional Manx dances (cf. Speers 1997: 225-47).

5.3. The Second Phase (ca. 1930 - 1940)

Personal enquiry seems to indicate that the Revival received a second major impetus in enthusiasm ca.1930 lasting till just after the outbreak of the Second World War. The catalyst here seems to have been Marstrander's visits of 1929, 1930, and 1933 which encouraged language enthusiasts to seek out those still alive who had learned Manx from the cradle (cf. Section 3, §3.5.3.ff.). In addition to the language enthusiasts, two main activists at that time figure in the 'Second Phase'. They were J. J. Kneen (1872-1938) and Mona Douglas (1898-1987).

J. J. Kneen, also active during the 'First Phase', was a producer of mint rock by profession who found time to be a prolific *Heimatforscher*. He brought out a six-volume work on Manx place-names (Kneen 1925-28), a Manx grammar (Kneen 1931), and a work on Manx personal names (Kneen 1937), not to mention a flood of smaller works, including a number of plays, connected with the Manx Revival (see Cubbon 1933, 1939). Marstrander was generous in his praise of Kneen's efforts during his visits to Man (Marstrander 1929-33b), and arranged for the Nansen Fund in Norway to grant Kneen £200.00 to assist him in his place-name work. This grant was confirmed in a letter from Marstrander to Kneen dated 16.10.1929 (MM. J. J. Kneen Papers).[5] However, in spite of Marstrander's praise Kneen was not in a position to ensure professional standards in the exercise of his academic gifts (see Thomson 1969a: 189, fn. 1 and Section 3.2.). Kneen was active in YCG, holding the posts of secretary and latterly of president.

---

5   In a letter to Kneen Marstrander sets the grant in context as follows. It is probable that the money was forthcoming primarily as a result of the arguments used by Marstrander in his last paragraph:
   I have the honour to inform you that the Trustees of the Fridtjof Nansen Fund for the Promotion of Scientific Research and the Trustees of the State Research Fund of 1919 have at their last meeting unanimously decided to offer you a grant of £200 in support of your studies on the place-names of the Isle of Man.
   Actuated by the alarming report laid before them by their delegate to the Island [i.e. Marstrander] on the state of the Gaelic language, they consider that every possible effort should be made to gather and to save without delay the scattered remants of the ancient language of the Isle of Man, this noble symbol of its old civilisation.
   In taking this unusual step to offer to a member of a foreign community the support of our scientific funds, they are of the opinion that the time has passed for arguing to whom this task rightly belongs. They are also convinced that you are eminently qualified for the work in question and they wish to express to you their gratitude for the work done by you in your field of studies, so creditable to yourself and the Isle of Man and so important to your fellow-workers in all countries. Neither can they forget that the population of the Island is to a great extent of Norwegian origin, that for centuries the Isle of Man was held and cultivated by our ancestors and that even at the present day the place-names of every parish bear testimony to this ancient chapter of our common history (Letter Marstrander-Kneen 16.10.1929, J. J. Kneen Papers, MM.).

Mona Douglas, a rural librarian and journalist by profession, was also involved in the 'First Phase'. As a protégée of Sophia Morrison, she collected folksong and folkdance material at a time (particularly in the 1920s) when scant attention was apparently being paid to things Manx, collecting from ca.1912 to ca.1930 from some of the last bearers of the relevant traditions (see Douglas & Foster 1928, 1929, 1957; Cubbon 1933, 1939; also Speers 1997). Mona Douglas was also a poetess and romantic, and some of her poetry about Man was inspired by the 1916 Rebellion in Ireland (Douglas 1916). In 1931 she (with others) founded the Manx youth movement *Aeglagh Vannin* 'youth-band of Man' (with resonances of *Óglaigh na hÉireann* 'warriors of Ireland', i.e. the IRA)[6] (Douglas 1932), at a time when such movements were in vogue, and was active in YCG and the Celtic Congress right up until the Second World War and after. Douglas was evidently equally vigorous in pursuing her interests in Manx nationalist politics, and from personal enquiry and interviews with surviving members (ca.1990) she seemingly played a central role in the seemingy shadowy organisation *Ny Manninee Dooie* 'the true Manx' at the outbreak of war or shortly before. This group evidently advocated a neutral stance for the Isle of Man, as taken by the then Irish Taoiseach Éamonn de Valéra for Ireland and advocated also by the Welsh nationalist party *Plaid Cymru* for Wales, and was apparently looked upon by the Manx authorities as being pro-German.[7] After the war Mona Douglas's overt interests in Manx politics appeared to have evaporated (cf. Broderick fc/b).

From the beginning and even today, interest in and enthusiasm for matters Manx, particularly the language, is linked in the minds of many Manx people with pride in 'Manxness' and the Manx national identity, hence the YCG motto *gyn chengey, gyn cheer* 'no language, no country'. The striving for individual national consciousness in Man, but also in other Celtic countries during the first half of the 20th century, attracted interest from Germany where 'exaltation of the native thing' was a fundamental aspect of government policy, particularly after 1933.

The Nazis took a keen interest in matters Celtic (including Manx), especially the SS-Wissenschaftsamt *Ahnenerbe* 'ancestors' heritage' (in 1942 renamed 'Amt A' within the Hauptamt of the personal staff of the Reichsführer-SS Heinrich Himmler), set up in 1935 by Himmler and two others. The purpose evidently was to attract specialists in a number of fields of study that could also serve the political interests of the state (cf. Simon 1985a, 1985b, Lerchenmüller 1997: 265, note 88). One such field was devoted to matters Celtic headed by Prof. Dr. Ludwig Mühlhausen (1888-1956) who became Professor of Celtic in Berlin in 1936 on the enforced resignation of his Jewish predecessor Julius Pokorny. Mühlhausen joined the NSDAP in 1932 and the SA in 1933, and in 1943 transferred to the SS. In December 1936 Mühlhausen with others, set up in Berlin the *Deutsche Gesellschaft für keltische Studien* 'German Society for Celtic Studies' (DGKS) which had as its Geschäftsführer the West Prussian Celticist Gerhard von Tevenar (1912-1943) and the renowned Celtic scholar Rudolf Thurneysen (d. 1940) as its honorary president; Mühlhausen was president. By 1942 through Mühlhausen's endeavours the DGKS (as well as the Celtic

---

[6] For details of the impact of the Irish Rising of 1916 on Manx nationalist aspirations, cf. Broderick 1991-92.

[7] For an analysis of Mona Douglas's world view of and engagement in the Manx cultural revival, cf. Broderick fc/b, Speers 1997. A comprehensive, judicious and balanced assessment of Mona Douglas's activities and contribution to the 'Manx cause', as she saw it, still needs to be written.

studies periodical *Zeitschrift für celtische Philologie*, with vols. 22 (1941) and 23 (1943) entitled *Zeitschrift für keltische Philologie und Volksforschung* under Mühlhausen's editorship) had come under SS control (BDC/Akte Mühlhausen M/32 (courtesy of Gerd Simon, Tübingen); Lerchenmüller 1997).

In addition to his duties as Geschäftsführer of the DGKS Tevenar evidently had an interest Celtic fringe matters (Lerchenmüller 1997: 387), including Manx; it could be said that he was the DGKS's 'specialist' for Manx. In September 1941 he delivered a lecture on the Isle of Man, its history, constitution, traditions, language, etc, at a joint symposium of the DGKS and a science ministry sponsored initiative (primarily directed against England) styling itself *Kriegseinsatz der Geisteswissenschaften* 'deployment of the Humanities in war' at Wernigerode, Sachsen-Anhalt (Tevenar 1941a). It is clear from the contents of the published version of the lecture that, in spite of one or two minor slips, Tevenar was fairly *au fait* with the Manx situation. It is also clear that he had made contact in Man with J. J. Kneen, possibly in a letter from the DGKS via the Manx Museum and passed on to Kneen (who could handle German from his time as censor at the Knockaloe Internment Camp just south of Peel during the First World War), if not through a personal visit, since it is Kneen's unpublished language map of Man (drawn in 1910 and recently discovered in his papers at the Manx Museum) which appears with one or two modifications in Tevenar's article.

The Irish Rising of 1916 and its aftermath had made clear to the Nazis that it was possible for a Celtic country to detach itself from its dominant neighbour, and SS interests in matters Celtic evidently had as an aim, in a British Isles context, to fragment English control through support for political and cultural movements in the Celtic countries. Tevenar was also the author of an obituary and *laudatio* of J. J. Kneen after the latter's death in November 1938 (Tevenar 1941b).

5.4. The Third Phase (1945-1990s)

After the Second World War language enthusiasts and nationalists turned their attention once more to matters Manx. On 30 September 1952 Douglas C. Fargher (1926-1987), then secretary of YCG and one of the 'giants' of the language movement, together with Joe Woods, secretary of the Manx Branch of the Celtic Congress, printed an appeal in the *Mona's Herald* to 'Support the Manx Language' (Fargher & Woods 1952). This came at a time when YCG, following the examples of the Irish Folklore Commission (1948) and the Manx Museum Folklife Survey (1949-52), was making a series of sound-recordings of the last dozen or so of the native Manx Gaelic speakers (1951-53; cf. Section 3.5.3.4. & 3.6.5; also HLSM/I & III Intro.), and felt that it had a sufficient corpus of material to get things going once more. As with the founding of *Yn Cheshaght Ghailckagh* in 1899 (cf. §5.2. above), the appeal linked language with patriotism and nationality.

> In this Island are hundreds of people who are members of one or more of the various patriotic societies; in addition there are many thousands of Manx men and women who [...] have a great fund of knowledge of their beloved home and its traditions, and an instinctive pride in their nationality and heritage. We appeal to members of this legion of Manx people to come forward with a practical demonstration of their nationality by enrolling in a Manx language class [...] (Fargher and Woods 1952).

At the end of Fargher's and Woods' appeal a call is made to

> throw off apathy and disinterestedness and take part in another crusade which can harm no one, but which will strengthen us as individuals and as a nation. We refer to the crusade for maintaining and using the Manx Language. Join an Evening Class, Manxmen, and bring a friend with you (Fargher & Woods 1952).

At that time a number of Manx enthusiasts had learned the language direct from the then surviving native speakers. Interest in native Manx speech had evidently been sparked off in the 1930s by Marstrander's visits (Marstrander 1929-33b), and by April 1946 C. W. Loch, a visitor to Man, interviewed some of the enthusiasts and was able to report a number of twenty surviving speakers whose names and addresses were printed by A. S. B. Davies of Mochdre, Colwyn Bay, in 1948 (Loch 1946, Davies 1948; cf. also Section 3, §3.5.3.). Fargher had at that time opened a wholesale fruiterer's business in Douglas with close friend and Manx enthusiast Leslie Quirk, and the duo, according to themselves, conducted all their business together in Manx. In 1956 the business folded and Fargher took off for Zambia (then Northern Rhodesia) for a six-year stint in the copper-mines, as a result of which YCG for a while lost an active secretary. Fargher returned to Man in 1962. In September 1965 Douglas Fargher and Leslie Quirk received *An Fáinne* 'the Ring', the Irish award for proficiency in Gaelic, in recognition of their fluency in Manx. This was apparently the first time that such an award had been made to persons outside Ireland. It was only a few days later that the Fáinne-awarding body in Ireland *Caomhnóirí an tSuaitheantais* ('keepers of the badge') decided that the Fáinne, in Manx *fainey* [fɛːnjə], could be awarded generally for proficiency in spoken Manx. Later that same month (Sept. 1965) the *Bing ny Fainey* ('the Fainey Committee') was set up under the chairmanship of Brian Stowell. To date (1997) some 108 Gold Faineys have been awarded and it has proved a great incentive for people to gain proficiency in spoken Manx.[8] The numbers in the 1971 Census would reflect this (cf. Section 2.5. above). In 1970 Douglas Fargher was once again at the helm of YCG, now injected with fresh blood, and he set things in motion once more.

Over the next few years Fargher and his dynamic team set in train a series of publications: reprints of older editions, such as Kneen's *Place-Names* (1925-28), or new material produced by YCG or similar undertakings, e.g. books (Jerry 1978, 1980, Kelly 1993), language courses (Stowell 1970, 1986, 1992-96), dictionaries (Fargher 1979, Kelly 1991), etc. Such material is still being produced.

Around 1973 and for some time after that a weekly Manx column in the now defunct newspaper *Manx Star* appeared. In the early 1970s YCG organised on a rota basis a 15-minute news programme in Manx Gaelic on Manx Radio, which in 1976-77 became an hour in length and ran under the title *Claare ny Gaeil* ('programme of/for the Gaels'). This programme is still running, but under the slightly modified title *Claare ny Gael*.

From 1983 to 1986 a local amateur film unit *Foillan Films* produced four documentary films entirely in Manx and one bilingual Manx-English film for public consumption. The

---

[8] A Silver Fainey is also awarded for semi-proficiency as a means of encouraging people to gain the Gold Fainey. The awarding of a Gold Fainey is made solely on the basis of oral proficiency in the language, decided upon during an informal gathering, and of necessity involves a certain amount of subjectivity. It cannot, and is not intended to replace a formal oral and written examination, but essentially serves to indicate support for the language.

subject matter covered ranged from folksongs to the Manx Language and its native speakers to Steam Packet ships and modern day poets.

In 1985 YCG instituted the Ned Maddrell Memorial Lecture in honour of the last known native Manx speaker. The lecture is held annually, usually nowadays in November (see below), delivered by an invited academic in the field of Celtic Studies. In 1997 YCG instituted *Leeaght y Ghaaue* 'the Gaaue Lecture' in honour of John Kneen ('the Gaaue' 1852-1958), the last known native Manx speaker from the north of Man who plied his trade there as a blacksmith. The lecture is delivered in Manx and, as with the Ned Maddrell Memorial Lecture, forms part of the *Feailley Ghailckagh* 'Manx Gaelic Week', set up in 1995 and held in November as a celebration of Manx language, music, and song.

During the course of 1970s, in order to promote an active competence in the spoken language, YCG held *Oieghyn Gailckagh* 'Manx-speaking evenings' once a month in a local bar, changing in venue from month to month. This had the effect of inspiring confidence in speaking Manx and presenting an opportunity to learners to acquire it directly from those who had obtained their Manx from the old native speakers themselves. In that respect, at any rate, the tradition of spoken Manx could be said to be unbroken. After a period of inactivity *Oieghyn Gailckagh* are held fairly regularly at present in Castletown, and more recently in Ramsey.[9]

As an offshoot of this, regular Saturday night Manx music and song sessions began to take place from late 1974 onwards at which quite a bit of Manx was, and still is spoken. The 'Central' bar in Peel served at the focal point until 1989, when the session transferred to the 'White House' bar, also in Peel. Emphasis nowadays is laid on music rather than on song, but the sessions have encouraged many musicians into the musical aspect of Manx tradition. Other such music sessions are held in various bars throughout the Island on different nights of the week. At present Manx music and dance enjoys considerable popular support in Man (more so than that for the language, primarily due to easier acquisition), and recently the various folksong collections have once more been made available for general use (Jerry 1987, 1991).[10]

With regard to church services, four such services, organised by YCG in conjunction with a local Manx speaking chaplain or with the relevant church vicar, are held annually in Manx. They take place around Easter, Tynwald Fair Day (5 July), Harvest Home, and Christmas. A Manx-English service is held at Malew parish church on 2 January as part of the Illiam Dhone Commemoration.[11]

---

[9] However, as the memory of the old native speakers now fades into the background and as the first generation of learners who obtained their Manx directly from them gradually passes away, and given the interim change in population in Man since the 1970s with its various dialects of English, present-day Manx (residual in existence anyway) in its pronunciation at any rate is, perhaps unavoidably, growing further and further away from that of the old native speakers, with additional anglicisation. Given the circumstances this development is perhaps to be expected.

[10] For an assessment and application of material used in the present Manx traditional music and dance 'revival', see Speers 1997.

[11] A commemoration, organised since 1979 by the Manx branch of the Celtic League and the Manx nationalist party *Mec Vannin* ('sons of Man'), to mark the execution by firing squad of William Christian (*Illiam Dhone* 'brown-haired William'; 1608-1663) is held every 2 January at Hango Hill, Castletown, the place of execution.- (on 02.01.1662/3 Christian was executed for alleged 'disloyality' to the Royalist Derby régime in Man during the English Civil War pe-

5.5. Manx in education

There has always been in Manx schools a recognition that, despite the use of the 'English Code' from the 1872 Act (see Section 3 above) in the Manx education system, there was a strong flavour of 'Manxness' about the whole arrangement. Most of the pupils then bore Manx names: forenames (male) Juan, Ffynlo, Orree, Gilnoe, Juan, etc; (female) Kirree, Joney, etc; surnames: Cowle, Clague, Corlett, Kelly, Mylechreest, Quine, etc - the list goes on. They spoke a Manx English dialect, lived in places bearing Manx names, e.g. Ballacannell, Magher y Kew, etc, and their teachers used the occasional greeting of *moghrey mie* [mɔrə 'maːi] 'good morning' or *fastyr mie* [faːstə 'maːi] 'good afternoon/evening' (cf. also Peter 1984: 50-51). Efforts to have Manx taught in Island schools, which failed in the early years of the century, did not begin to bear fruit until 1974 when a new Director of Education, Mr. Alun Davies, a native Welsh speaker from Dolgellau, was appointed. He was sympathetic to the idea, provided that there were people capable of teaching Manx. The situation then was that there were a number of individuals, usually YCG members, competent in Manx, but not trained teachers, and a few trained teachers (about a dozen at the outside) both competent in Manx and able to teach it. The latter were mainly concentrated in the (then) thirty-two primary schools, and were given the opportunity of introducing Manx into the classroom as and when they saw fit. In the five secondary schools at that time there was, so far as was then known, no teacher on the staff able in Manx. To remedy this the Director of Education sanctioned the use of 'laymen/laywomen' to teach Manx once a week during the lunchtime break as a 'club' activity. The first of such clubs was set up in the Easter term 1976 at Ballakermeen High School, Douglas, and lasted till the end of the summer term of the same year.

In 1982 a GCE (General Certificate of Education) Ordinary or 'O'-Level examination in Manx was instituted, preparation for which took place at evening classes initially for adults at the College of Further Education (now the Isle of Man College) in Douglas. The idea was that teachers with an 'O'-Level qualification would be in a position to teach Manx formally in the schools to 'O'-Level standard. One or two secondary-school teachers took up this option. However, a lack of 'takers' for the examination led to its suspension four years later.[12] Its replacement by a GCSE (General Certificate of Secondary Education) examination, with more emphasis on the spoken language, is now being taught in Manx schools as part of the present (1997) scheme (see next).

---

riod, having come to an arrangement with Cromwell's forces in 1651 to spare the Manx community unnecessary bloodshed) - at which speeches, usually political in content, in Manx and English are delivered. In the last few years the commemoration has been followed by a church service, in both Manx and English, at Malew parish church (burial place of Illiam Dhone), organised by the vicar. The solemnities are then followed by an adjournment to a local hostelry where Manx traditional music and songs are played and sung.

After long years of indifference the Isle of Man Government has recently recognised William Christian as a national hero, dedicating a new Government building to his name and installing a portrait of him in a stained glass window in the newly erected Tynwald Court Building (cf. König 1996: 101).

For details of the circumstances of the Manx 'Rebellion' of 1651 and Illiam Dhone's execution and its attendant ballad, cf. Section 3, Note 8.

[12] Robert L. Thomson was responsible for the 'O'-Level examinations in Manx at the time (GB discussions with RLT over the period).

Its replacement by a GCSE (General Certificate of Secondary Education) examination, with more emphasis on the spoken language, is now being taught in Manx schools as part of the present (1997) scheme (see next).

In recent years, in line with the general trend in the European Union to favour minority rights and cultures, there has been a move to have Manx taught on a regular basis in all the Island's schools. This 'demand', evidently emanating from pressure groups such as the Celtic League and from a Gallup Poll of January 1991 showing that 36 per cent of those asked were in favour of Manx as an *optional* subject in schools. This resulted in the Manx Heritage Foundation (a Manx Government 'quango') setting up the position of *Oaseir Gailckagh* 'Manx Language Officer' under the aegis of the Department of Education in 1992. The initial task was to set up syllabuses in Manx for pupils in the schools, eventually covering the full age range from 5 to 19. Dr. Brian Stowell, the first incumbent of that post, took up his duties on 2 January 1992, assisted by two peripatetic teachers, Phil Kelly (Kirk Michael) and Paaie Carswell (Douglas), seconded from the teaching pool, in the implementation of what must be an historic undertaking in the history of education in the Isle of Man. In September 1996 Dr Stowell retired as Manx Language Officer and was replaced by Phil Kelly; he in turn was replaced by Ms. Katreeney Craine of Ramsey. It remains to be seen what the future holds for the maintenance and promotion of Manx Gaelic in the Isle of Man.

For additional details see König (1996: 56-111).

5.6. 1991 Census figures regarding Manx

In contrast to the 1981 census, where no questions regarding Manx were asked, the census of 1991 sought information about those who could read, write, and/or speak Manx in various contexts. They are as follows:

Table 4: *Place of Residence of Speakers, Writers, and Readers of Manx*

Area of residence:	Speaks Manx	Writes Manx	Reads Manx
Town or District:			
Douglas (capital)	166	65	103
Ramsey	65	39	48
Peel	53	32	46
Castletown	43	24	27
Port Erin	13	12	15
Port St. Mary	21	8	11
Laxey	10	6	8
Onchan	57	26	42
Parish:			
Andreas	19	11	13
Arbory	20	12	17
Ballaugh	12	10	14

Jurby	12	4	5
Lezayre	15	6	8
Lonan	10	10	11
Malew	11	5	11
Marown	13	6	13
Maughold	8	5	8
Michael	15	11	13
Patrick	16	14	17
Rushen	19	16	17
Santan	3	2	5
Total	*643*	*343*	*479*

Source: 1991 Isle of Man Population Census.
Analysis: Economic Affairs Division, Isle of Man Government.

Table 5: *Breakdown of those with a knowledge of Manx Gaelic (persons who can speak and/or read and/or write Manx Gaelic) by age.*

Age Group:	Knowledge of Manx Gaelic
Under 5 yrs.	13
5 - 9	23
10 - 14	64
15 - 19	47
20 - 24	41
25 - 34	124
35 - 44	136
45 - 54	96
55 - 64	77
65 - 74	60
75 - 84	37
85 - 94	21
95+	2
Total	*741*

Source: 1991 Isle of Man Population Census.
Analysis: Economic Affairs Division, Isle of Man Government.

Table 6: *Breakdown of Manx Gaelic Speakers, Readers, and Writers by Age.*

Age Group	Speaks Manx	Reads Manx	Writes Manx
Under 5 yrs.	12	5	4
5 - 9	20	8	0
10 - 14	57	36	27

15 - 19	43	27	15
20 - 24	37	25	17
25 - 34	107	83	61
35 - 44	119	100	74
45 - 54	81	62	46
55 - 64	66	54	42
65 - 74	51	44	29
75 - 84	33	23	19
85 - 94	16	12	9
95+	1		
Total	*643*	*479*	*343*

Source: 1991 Isle of Man Population Census.
Analysis: Economic Affairs Division, Isle of Man Government.

Table 7: *Breakdown of Manx Gaelic Speakers, Readers and Writers by Place of Birth*

Place of birth	Speaks Manx	Reads Manx	Writes Manx
Isle of Man	476	336	242
England	126	106	84
Wales	2	5	2
Scotland	12	12	7
Northern Ireland	8	2	0
Republic of Ireland	11	10	2
Other EU Country	2	3	2
Channel Islands	1	0	0
North America	1	2	1
Far East	4	3	3
Total	*643*	*479*	*343*

Source: 1991 Isle of Man Population Census.
Analysis: Economic Affairs Division, Isle of Man Government.

Table 8: *Breakdown of Manx Gaelic Speakers, Readers, and Writers by Occupation*

Occupation	Speaks Manx	Reads Manx	Writes Manx
- Managers & Administrators	53	45	36
- Professional Occ.	53	48	35
- Associate Professional & Technical Occ.	30	26	19
- Clerical & Secretarial			

Occupations - Craft & Related	44	40	26
Occupations - Personal & Protective	70	51	44
Service Occupations	30	18	14
- Sales Occupations	14	8	5
- Plant & Machine Operatives	21	13	10
- Other Occupations	32	26	20
Total in Work	*347*	*275*	*209*

Source: 1991 Isle of Man Population Census.
Analysis: Economic Affairs Division, Isle of Man Government.

5.6.1. Comment

1. The first thing to note is that without exception all persons who can speak, read, or write Manx today are learners of the language, and that the foregoing is a consequence of the latest imput into the Revival over the past 20 years or so, i.e. *before* the introduction of Manx into the Island's schools (1992). So far as is known, there are *no native speakers* in the ordinary sense of that term, i.e. there is no one at present who is brought up in Manx in an all-Manx speaking household, simply because Manx is no longer the community language of the Isle of Man. There are, however, some children who are spoken to partially in Manx at home and elsewhere by their parents (and perhaps others) some of the time.
2. These figures include the full range of competence in Manx, from those who could be regarded as fluent speakers to those who would have a few phrases only.

Table 4
1. As can be seen from the table, the larger numbers lie with those who can speak Manx. This would reflect the main emphasis of the Revival over the years on the spoken language, especially fostered by *Oieghyn Gailckagh* in an informal public house atmosphere.
2. The figures for those who write and read Manx, which would naturally overlap with some of those who speak it, and vice versa, would reflect those who have learned Manx in the more formal surroundings of the evening class.
3. Douglas, being the capital and largest settlement area, might be expected to, and does record the highest figures in all three columns.The high figures in Onchan and Braddan would be due to the fact that both areas adjoin, and serve as overspills for Douglas.

Table 5
1. It is noticeable that the larger figures are found in the age-ranges 25 - 74. This would reflect the numbers who have learned Manx over the last 20 or so years as part of the Third Phase.

2. Those in the age-ranges 5 - 14 would have learned their Manx, either in a Kindergarten, or in a school where Manx was on offer (i.e. before the general inclusion of 1992 when Manx became available throughout the education system as a whole), or perhaps at home.
3. Those in the age-range of ca. 60+ would include, but not be limited to those who had learned their Manx from the old native speakers.

Table 6

1. As with Table 1, the largest figures are found among the Manx speakers, reflecting the main emphasis of the Revival.
2. As with Table 2, the largest numbers are found in the age-range 25 - 74, i.e. those forming part of the Revival over the past 20 or so years.
3. The figure 12 for those under 5 who reflect those few families who occasionally speak to their children in Manx at home, or those children who have learned some Manx in a Kindergarten.
4. The figures of 5 and 4 in the under 5 range would reflect those who perhaps can write their name, or read an write the odd sentence or rhyme.

Table 7

1. As is to be expected, the main area of derivation or place of birth of Manx speakers outside the Island is England, simply because England was and is the chief area of immigration of Manx people within the British Isles, and many of those whose place of birth is England would include many of Manx extraction and ethnicity. Much less so in the other areas.
2. In the other areas the numbers likely reflect interest in Manx by nationals from those areas, rather than persons of Manx extraction from the same. The high number from Ireland probably reflects those drawn into Man to service the finance sector.
3. The relatively high number from the Far East may reflect British expatriate interest in Manx, though interest in matters Celtic from Japan in general terms is not insignificant.

Table 8

1. As is perhaps to be expected, the greatest number of speakers is to be found among those with expertise in craft, probably meaning traditional occupations, such as stone-walling, or manual occupations associated with the Revival.
2. The relatively high numbers in the first two aforementioned occupations would include teachers, among whom a knowledge of Manx is to be expected, but also those servicing the finance sector. The latter would include the figure of 44 for the clerical and secretarial occupations.
3. The mechanical and sales professions seem to attract the smallest numbers. Many native born Manx people find employment in this sector. This would indicate, if accurate, that the bulk of this section of the community, i.e. the native born Manx people, shows very little interest in Manx or its revival. In other words, the Revival depends very much on the support of those who have come to settle in the Island within the last twenty years or so.

5.7. Conclusion

Although much active and worthwhile work and energy has been ploughed into promoting Manx and diffusing a knowledge of it for long years by societies, such as *Yn Cheshaght Ghailckagh*, and the tireless efforts of a number of individuals over a similar period, nevertheless, it is my view that the future of Manx must lie primarily with the Department of Education and the professional teaching body.

Since the introduction of Manx as an optional subject into the Island's schools with the appointment in 1992 of a Manx Language Officer and two peripatetic school teachers the status of Manx within the public perception, now that it has official backing, has risen dramatically and is now becoming accepted as one of those things that happens, and its greater acceptability, or otherwise, within the Manx community will determine its future progress within the Manx education system. Although the Dept. of Education's efforts in this respect may serve the interests of the Revival, promoting the Revival is not the Department's business. Its function is to ensure that those taking Manx are given a sound grounding in the subject, just as those are who opt for French or German, or any other subject.

I understand that work is now in progress to producing a Manx GCSE, and that an Advanced Level course in Manx is in prospect. Given the realities of the Manx situation as outlined above (Sections 1-4), the literary tradition has to be allotted a significant role in the whole process, if a sound knowledge of Manx among those who study it at school is to be guaranteed. This will especially need to be the case for Advanced Level where a deep and substantial understanding of the subject is required.

Though an enjoyment of Manx today may be associated with good earthy songs and catchy Manx tunes at evening music sessions in local bars, nevertheless the future of Manx and its acceptability within the community in my view must lie primarily with the school system and ultimately with the children themselves. It is they who will decide whether they wish to speak or use Manx or not in times to come, and thereby determine the future of Manx. The task in hand must surely be to make certain that the best possible provision is made in materials and manpower for the development of Manx as a credible subject of study at school and to ensure that the children are not at all disadvantaged in acquiring a sound knowledge of *Chengey ny Mayrey Ellan Vannin* 'the mother tongue of the Isle of Man'.

Bibliography

Ackerley, F. G. (1928): Manx Marginalia. Y Cymmrodor 39: 20-38.

Adelaar, Willem F. H. (1991): The endangered languages problem: South America. In: Robins & Uhlenbeck (eds.) 1991: 45-92.

Akutagawa, Michie (1987): A Linguistic Minority under the Protection of its own Ethnic State: a Case Study in an Irish Gaeltacht. In: MacEoin, Ahlqvist, Ó hAodha (eds.) 1987: 125-146.

Andersen, Per Sveas (1983): To what extent did the balley/baile names in the Isle of Man supplant place-names of Norse origin? In: Fell, Foote, Graham-Campbell, Thomson (eds.) 1983: 147-168.

Andersen, R. W. (ed.) (1983): Pidginization and Creolization as Language Acquisition. Rowley MA: Newbury House.

Anderson, J. (ed.) (1982): Papers Dedicated to Angus McIntosh: Current Issues in Linguistic Theory 15. Amsterdam: John Benyamins.

Annual Reports of the Manx Museum and Ancient Momument Trustees: Year ending 31 March 1948 and Year ending 31 March 1949.

Bailey, Richard, and Görlach, Manfred (eds.) (1982): English as a World Language. Cambridge: Cambridge University Press.

Ball, Martin, J. W. (ed.) (1993): The Celtic Languages. London: Routledge.

Ball, Martin J., Fife, J., Poppe, E., Rowland, J. (eds.) (1990): Celtic Linguistics. Ieithyddiaeth Geltaidd. Readings in the Brythonic Languages. Festschrift for T. Arwyn Watkins. Amsterdam: Benjamins.

Barry, Michael V. (1984). Manx English. In: Trudgill (ed.) 1984: 167-177.

Berger, Marianne (1988): Sprachkontakt in der Bretagne. Sprachloyalität versus Sprachwechsel. Beihefte zur Zeitschrift für Romanische Philologie Vol. 220. Tübingen: Niemeyer.

Berlin Document Centre (1941-44). Personalakte Mühlhausen M32 (courtesy of Dr. Gerd Simon, University of Tübingen).

Birch, J. W. (1964): Isle of Man: an economic geography. Cambridge.

Bird, Hinton, n.d. [1991]: An Island that Led - The History of Manx Education. Vol. 1. Port St. Mary, Isle of Man: private publication.

— (1995): An Island that Led - The History of Manx Education. Vol. 2. Port St. Mary, Isle of Man; private publication.

Borgstrøm, Carl Hj. (1937): The Dialect of Barra in the Outer Hebrides. NTS VIII: 71-242.

— (1940): The Dialects of the Outer Hebrides NTS Supplementary Volume 1. Oslo.

— (1941): The Dialects of Skye and Ross-shire NTS Supplementary Volume II. Oslo.

— (1967): Carl Marstrander. NTS XXI: 7-10. Obituary.

Breatnach, R. A . (1956): Revival or survival: an examination of the Irish language policy of the State. Studies 45: 129-45.

Breatnach, Risteard B. (1947): The Irish of Ring, Co. Waterford. Dublin: DIAS.

— (1964): Characteristics of Irish Dialects in Process of Extinction. Communications et rapports du Premier Congrès de Dialectologie Générale: 141-45. Louvain: Centre International de Dialectologie Générale.

Brenzinger, Matthias (1982): Language Death: Factual and Theoretical Explorations with Reference to East Africa. Contributions to the Sociology of Language - ed. Joshua A. Fishman. Berlin: Mouton-de Gruyter.

Breu, Walter, (1991): Zur aktuellen Situation in den nördlichen italoalbanischen Kolonien. In: Breu, Ködderitzsch, Sasse (eds.) 1991: 1-16.

Breu, Walter, Ködderitzsch, Rolf, Sasse, Hans-Jürgen (eds.) (1991): Aspekte der Albanologie. Akten des Kongresses Stand und Aufgabe der Albanologie heute, Köln 1988. Wiesbaden: Harrassowitz.

Broderick, George (1978): *Baile* in Manx Nomenclature. BUPS Ser. 2, Vol. 1: 16-18.

— (1979a): *Ceall, cill* in Manx Place-Names. BUPS Ser. 2, Vol. 2: 20-23.

— (1979b): Millennium of Tynwald. An historical assessment. Douglas: Mec Vannin.

190

— (1980): Irish and Welsh strands in the genealogy of Godred Crovan. JMM VIII 89: 32-38.
— (1980-81a): *Arddae Huimnonn* - a Manx Place-Name?. BUPS Ser. 2, Vol. 3: 13-15.
— (1980-81b): Manx Traditional Songs and Song Fragments I. Béaloideas 48-49: 9-29. The Clucas Coll.
— (1981a): Review of: The Manx National Song-Book Vol. 1. Anglo-Welsh Review 68: 131-34.
— (1981b): Manx Stories and Reminiscences of Ned Beg Hom Ruy. ZCP 38: 113-178. Introduction and Texts.
— (1981c): Secular Settlement Terms in Manx Place-Names. BUPS Ser. 2, Vol. 3: 40-41.
— (1981-82): The Baronial Possessions of Bangor and Saul in Man. BUPS Ser. 2 Vol. 4: 24-26.
— (1982a): Manx Stories and Reminiscences of Ned Beg Hom Ruy. ZCP 39: 117-194. Translation and Notes.
— (1982b): Baase Illiam Dhone. Celtica XIV (1982): 105-23.
— (1982c): Manx Traditional Songs and Song Fragments II. Béaloideas 50: 1-41. The Clague Coll.
— (1984a): A Handbook of Late Spoken Manx. Vol. 1: Grammar and Texts, Vol. 2: Dictionary. Tübingen: Niemeyer (Buchreihe der ZCP, Bd. 3, 4).
— (1984b): Berrey Dhone - a Manx Caillech Bérri ?. ZCP 40 (1984): 193-210.
— (1984c): Ec ny Fiddleryn. ZCP 40 (1984): 211-27.
— (1984d): Ny Kirree fo Niaghtey. Celtica XVI (1984): 157-68.
— (1984e) (as Shorys y Creayrie): Recording Native Manx Speech. In: Ó Luain (ed.) nd. [1984]: 308-20.
— (1986): A Handbook of Late Spoken Manx. Vol. 3: Phonology. Tübingen: Niemeyer (Buchreihe der ZCP, Bd. 5).
— (1987): *Creag* and *Carraig* in Manx Place-Names. Ainm II: 141-143.
— (1990): Fin as Oshin. Celtica XXI: 51-60.
— (1991): The Decline and Death of Manx Gaelic In: Ureland and Broderick (eds.) 1991: 63-125.
— (1991-92) (as Shorys y Creayrie). 1916 the ripples in the Celtic tide: Mannin. Carn 76 (Winter 1991-92) Supplement: 11-12.
— (1993a): Manx. In: Ball (ed.) (1993): 228-286.
— (1993b): Revived Manx. In: Ball (ed.) (1993): 654-60.
— (1993c): Sprachkontakt und Sprachgeschichte der Insel Man im Rahmen ihrer Ortsnamen. In: Rockel & Zimmer (eds.) 1993: 57-65.
— (1994): Place-Names of the Isle of Man I (Sheading of Glenfaba). Tübingen: Niemeyer.
— (1995): Place-Names of the Isle of Man 2 (Sheading of Michael). Tübingen: Niemeyer.
— (1997a): Place-Names of the Isle of Man 3 (Sheading of Ayre). Tübingen: Niemeyer.
— (1997b): Manx-English. An overview. In: Tristram (ed.) 1997: 123-34.
— (fc/a). Language decline and language revival in the Isle of Man. Ned Maddrell Memorial Lecture 28.11.1996, Douglas, Isle of Man.
— (fc/b). Under the 'Three-Legged-Swastika': Celtic Studies and Celtic Revival in the Isle of Man in the context of the 'National Socialist Idea'. In: Heinz (ed.) 1999.
Bruce, J. R. and Cubbon, Wm. (1930): Cronk yn How. "An early Christian and Viking site, at Lezayre, Isle of Man". Archaelogia Cambrensis (Dec. 1930): 267-308. Reprinted under the same title (but omitting Isle of Man) in Proc. IOMNHAS III/4 (1931): 282-97.
Bullock, H. A (1816): History of the Isle of Man. London.
Butler, W. (1799): Memoirs of Mark Hildesley, DD. London.
Camden, William (1586): Britannia. London.
Campbell, D. (1886): The Isle of Man, its history and language. TGSI XII.
Campbell, Lyle & Muntzel, Martha C. (1989): The structural consequences of language death. In: Dorian (ed.) 1989: 181-196.
Carlisle, N. (1813): A topographical dictionary of Scotland and of the islands in the British Seas. London (unpaginated, v.s. Isle of Man).
Carmody, Francis J. (1947): Manx Gaelic Sentence Structure. Publications in Linguistics I, No. 8: 297ff. University of California at Berkeley.
— (1953): Spoken Manx. ZCP 24: 58-80.

Carney, James, and Greene, David (eds.) (1969): Celtic Studies: Essays in Memory of Angus Matheson 1912-1962. London.

Cashen, William (1912): Manx Folklore. Douglas: Johnson.

Christian, Robert E, nd. [ca.1880]: Lessons on the Manx Language.

Chronique V (248) nd. [ca. 1930]: Letter from Carl Marstrander, VIII (356-57) Letter from J. Cubbon. MM.MS. H140/lx/151.

Clague, John (1893-98): [Collection of Folktunes]. Manx Museum MSS.448A, 449B in Archdeacon Kewley Coll.

— (1911): Cooinaghtyn Manninagh. Manx Reminiscences. Castletown: Blackwell.

Clamp, Peter (1988a): English schooling in the Isle of Man 1660-1700: the Barrovian Design. Journal of Educational Administration and History XX/2 (July 1988): 10-21.

— (1988b): The struggle for the Common School System in the Isle of Man: a compulsory Education Bill for Mona! History of Education Society Bulletin No. 42 (Autumn 1988): 18-33.

— (1988c): Bishop Wilson's Discipline: Language schooling and confrontation in the Isle of Man 1698-1755. Journal of Religious History 15/2: 185-98.

Coiste Comhairleach Pleanála (1988): The Irish Language in a Changing Society. Dublin: Bord na Gaeilge.

Commins, P. (1988): Socioeconomic development and language maintenance in the Gaeltacht. In: Ó Riagáin (ed.) 1988: 11-28.

Cooper, R. L. (ed.) (1982): Language Spread: Studies in Diffusion and Social Change. Bloomington: Indiana University Press.

Cregeen, Archibald (1835): A Dictionary of the Manks Language... Douglas: Quiggin.

Cubbon, William (1924): A Bibliographical Account of the Literature translated into the Manx Language; compiled from the Manx Library of Mr. G. W. Wood in the Manx Museum. Douglas: Manx Society.

— (1933 & 1939): A Bibliographical Account of Works relating to the Isle of Man. Oxford: OUP. 2 volumes.

Cumming, J[oseph] G[eorge] (1848): The Isle of Man: its History, Physical, Ecclesiastical, Civil, and Legendary. London: Van Voorst.

— (1861): A Guide to the Isle of Man. London.

— (ed.) (1859): Wm. Sacheverell (1702): An account of the Isle of Man. Douglas: Manx Soc. I.

— (ed.) (1864): J. Chaloner (1656): A short treatise of the Isle of Man. Douglas: Manx Soc. X.

Daily Mail: 12.07.1930. Island's Dying Tongue. Only 2,000 Speakers. Holiday "Invasion" Blamed.

Darlington, T. (1900): Some dialectal boundaries in Mid-Wales. Transactions of the Honourable Society of Cymmrodorion, 13-39.

Davey, Peter (ed.) (1978): Man and the Environment in the Isle of Man. British Archaeological Reports. Ser. LIV. Liverpool: UP.

Davies, A. S. B. (1948): Cyflwr Presennol Iaith Geltaidd Ynys Manaw. BBCS 12 (1946 (1948)): 89-91.

de Bhaldraithe, Tomás (1945): The Irish of Cois Fhairrge, Co. Galway: a Phonetic Study. Dublin: DIAS.

— (1953): Gaeilge Chois Fhairrge: An Deilbhíocht. Dublin: DIAS.

— (1959): English-Irish Dictionary. Baile Átha Cliath: Oifig an t-Soláthair.

de Búrca, Seán (1958): The Irish of Tourmakeady, Co. Mayo: a Phonemic Study. Dublin: DIAS.

Denison, Norman (1977): Language Death or Language Suicide. In: Dressler and Wodak-Leodolter (eds.) 1977: 13-22.

Dimmendaal, Gerrit J. (1989): On language death in eastern Africa. In: Dorian (ed.) 1989: 13-31.

Dolley, Michael (1977): Procurator extraordinary - Sir Wadsworth Busk (1730-1811). Proc. IOM NHAS VIII/3: 207-45.

Dorian, Nancy C. (1973): Grammatical Change in a Dying Dialect. Language 49: 413-38.

— (1976): Gender in a Terminal Gaelic Dialect. SGS 12: 279-82.

— (1977a): A Hierarchy of Morphophonemic Decay in Scottish Gaelic Language Death: the Differential Failure of Lenition. Word 28: 96-109.

192

— (1977b): The Problem of the Semi-Speaker in Language Death. In: Dressler and Wodak-Leodolter (eds.) 1977: 23-32.
— (1978a): The Preservation of the Vocative in a Dying Gaelic Dialect. SGS 13: 98-102.
— (1978b): The Fate of Morphological Complexity in Language Death. Language 54: 590-609.
— (1978c): East Sutherland Gaelic: the Dialect of Brora, Golspie, and Embo Fishing Communities. Dublin: DIAS.
— (1980a): Linguistic Lag as an Ethnic Marker. Language in Society 9: 33-41.
— (1980b): Maintenance and Loss of Same-Meaning Structures in Language Death. Word 31: 39-45.
— (1981a): The Valuation of Gaelic by Different Mother Tongue Groups Resident in the Highlands. SGS 13(2): 169-82.
— (1981b): Language Death. The Life Cycle of a Scottish Gaelic Dialect. Philadelphia.
— (1982a): Language Loss and Maintenance in Language Contact Situations. In: Lambert and Freed (eds.) 1982: 44-59.
— (1982b): Linguistic Models and Language Death Evidence. In: Obler and Menn (eds.) 1982.
— (1983): Natural Second Language Acquisition from the Perspective of the Study of Language Death. In: Andersen (ed.) 1983.
— (1985): Radical Asymmetries in the Skills of Speakers of Obsolescent Languages. Invited paper presented at the Centre for Franco-Ontarian Studies. The Ontario Institute for Studies in Education, Toronto, May 1.
— (1986a): Abrupt Transmission Failure in Obsolescing Languages: How sudden the 'tip' to the Dominant Language in Communities and Families? In: Nikiforidu, van Clay, Niepokuj, Feder (eds.) 1986.
— (1986b): Making do with Less: Some Surprises along the Language Death Proficiency Continuum. Applied Psycholinguistics 7: 257-76.
— (1989): Investigating obsolescence. Studies in language contraction and death. Cambridge: University Press.
— (1994): Varieties of variation in a very small place: Social homogenity, prestige norms, and linguistic variation. Language 70: 631-96.
Douglas, Mona, nd. [1916]. A Manx Call to Arms. Douglas.
— (1924): Letter to the Editor. The Observer 01.02.1924. London.
— (1932): Manx Nationalism and Aeglagh Vannin. Yn Lioar Aeglagh Vannin: 5-6.
— (ed.) (1935): Beginning Manx Gaelic. A Manx Primer. Douglas: YCG.
— (1981): Rallying Song. Peel, Isle of Man: Mansk-Svenska.
Douglas, Mona and Foster, Arnold (eds.) (1928): Twelve Manx Folksongs. Set 1. London: Stainer & Bell.
— (1929): Twelve Manx Folksongs. Set 2. London: Stainer & Bell.
— (1957): Twelve Manx Folksongs. Set 3. London: Stainer & Bell.
Dressler, Wolfgang (1972a): Allegroregeln rechtfertigen Lentoregeln. Sekundäre Phoneme des Bretonischen. IBS 9: 9-10. Innsbruck: Institut für Sprachwissenschaft. English Summary: Fast Speech Rules Justify Slow Speech Rules.
— (1972b): On the Phonology of Language Death. Papers from the Eighth Regional Meeting of the Chicago Linguistics Society: 448-57. Chicago: Chicago Linguistics Society.
— (1981): Language Shift and Language Death - a Protean Challenge for the Linguist. Folia Linguistica 15: 5-27.
— (1982): Acceleration, Retardation, and Reversal in Language Decay. In: Cooper (ed.) 1982.
Dressler, Wolfgang and Wodak-Leodolter, Ruth W. (1973): Sprachbewahrung und Sprachtod in der Bretagne. Wiener Linguistische Gazette 3: 45-58.
— (1977): Language Preservation and Language Death in Brittany. In: Dressler and Wodak-Leodolter (eds.) 1977: 33-44.
— (1977): Language Death. International Journal of the Sociology of Language 12.
Durkacz, Victor E. (1983): The Decline of the Celtic Languages: a Study of Linguistic and Cultural Conflict in Scotland, Wales and Ireland. Edinburgh: John Donald.

Excerpts from Journals. A Collection of Extracts from various early periodicals, bound in two volumes (I: 1754-1879, II: 1880-1918). From the Collection of George William Wood, London (cf. Cubbon 1939: 1307-16). MM.L8.F.

Fargher, Douglas C. (1979): Fargher's English-Manx Dictionary. Onchan: Shearwater.

Fargher, Douglas C. and Woods, Joseph (1952): Support the Manx Language. Mona's Herald 30.09.1952.

Farquar [Faragher], Edward (1901): Skeealyn Æsop: a selection of Æsop's Fables translated into Manx-Gaelic, together with a few poems... Douglas: SKB & Co.

Farrant Family Papers. MM.MS.9257.

Fell, Christine, Foote, Peter, Graham-Campbell, James, and Thomson, Robert L. (eds.) (1983): The Viking Age in the Isle of Man. London: University College. Viking Society for Northern Research.

Fellows-Jensen, Gillian (1980): Common Gaelic *áirge*, Old Scandinavian *ærgi* or *erg* ? Nomina 4: 67-74.

— (1983): Scandinavian Settlement in the Isle of Man and Northwest England: the Place-Name Evidence. In: Fell, Foote, Graham-Campbell, Thomson (eds.) 1983: 37-52.

— (1985): Scandinavian Settlement Names in the North-West. Copenhagen: Reitzels Forlag.

— (1987): The Vikings Relationship with Christianity in the British Isles: the evidence of place-names containing the element kirkja. Proc. of the Tenth Viking Congress, Larkollen, Norway, 1985. Universitetets Oldsaksamlings Skrifter, Ny rekke. No. 9 Oslo: 295-307.

— (1993): Tingwall, Dingwall, and Thingwall. Nowele [North-Western European Language Evolution] 21/22 (April 1993): 53-67.

Feltham, John (1798): A Tour through the Isle of Man in 1797 & 1798. Bath: Crutwell.

Fennell, Desmond (1980): The last days of the Gaeltacht. Irish Times, 3 June.

— (1981): Can a Shrinking Minority be Saved? Lessons from the Irish Experience In: Haugen, McClure, Thomson (eds.) 1981: 32-39.

Finck, Franz Nikolaus (1899): Die Araner Mundart. Marburg: Elwert.

Fisher, J. (1929): Two Welsh-Manx Christmas customs. Archaeologia Cambrensis 84: 308-16.

Fishman, Joshua A. (1965): Who speaks what language to whom and when? La Linguistique 2: 67-88.

— (ed.) (1978): Advances in the Study of Societal Multilingualism. The Hague: Mouton.

Fitzgerald, G. (1984): Estimates for Baronies of minimum level of Irish-speaking amongst successive decennial cohorts, 1771-1781 to 1861-1871. Proc. RIA 84C: 117-55.

Fynes-Clinton, O. H. (1913): The Welsh vocabulary of the Bangor district. Oxford: OUP.

Gell, Juan (1977): Conversational Manx. Douglas: YCG.

Gelling, Margaret (1970): The Place-Names of the Isle of Man. JMM VII (86): 130-139.

— (1971): The Place-Names of the Isle of Man. JMM VII (87): 168-75.

— (1991): The Place-Names of the Isle of Man. In: Ureland and Broderick (eds.) (1991): 141-156.

Gibson, Edmund (1695): Camden's Britannia. London (Facsimile repr. 1971. Newton Abbot: David & Charles.

Gilchrist, Anne G (ed.) (1924-26): [Manx Traditional Songs]. Journal of the Folksong Society VII (28-30). These three issues are devoted to the Clague Coll.

Gill, W. Walter (1929): A Manx Scrapbook. London: Arrowsmith.

— (1934): Manx Dialect Words and Phrases. London: Arrowsmith.

— (1963): A Third Manx Scrapbook. London: Arrowsmith.

Gill, William (ed.) (1859): John Kelly. A practical grammar of the Antient Gaelic, or language of the Isle of Man, usually called Manks. Douglas: Manx Soc. II. First published in 1804.

Gillies, William (1993): Scottish Gaelic. In: Ball (ed.) (1993): 145-227.

Goodwin, Edmund (1901): Lessoonyn ayns Chengey ny Mayrey Ellan Vannin. Douglas: The Celtic Association and The Manx Society. Repr. 1947 as First Lessons in Manx (Lessoonyn ayns Chengey ny Mayrey Ellan Vannin). Douglas: YCG. Repr. 1966 and 1974 in several reprints; revised by Robert L. Thomson.

Gleasure, James W (1987): Gaelic dialects, principal divisions. In: Thomson (ed.) 1987.

194

Greene, David (1981): †he Atlantic group: neo-Celtic and Faroese. In: Haugen, McClure, Thomson (eds.): 1-9.

Hale, Ken, et al. (1992): Endangered languages. Language 68: 1-42.

Hamilton, Noel (1974): The Irish of Tory Island. Belfast: Institute of Irish Studies. SILL Vol. 3.

Hamm, J. (ed.) (1967): Phonologie der Gegenwart. Graz: Böhlau.

Hamp, Eric, P. (1968): Acculturation as a Late Rule. Papers from The Fourth Regional Meeting, Chicago Linguistics Society: 103-10.

— (1989): On Signs of Health and Death. In: Dorian (ed.) 1989: 197-210.

Haugen, Einar, McClure, J. Derrick, Thomson, Derick (eds.) (1981): Minority Languages Today. Edinburgh: University Press.

Heinz, Sabina (ed.) (unter Mitarbeit von Karsten Braun) (1999): Die Deutsche Keltologie und ihre Berliner Gelehrten bis 1945. Beiträge zur internationalen Fachtagung *Keltologie an der Friedrich-Wilhelms-Universität vor und während des Nationalsozialismus* vom 27.-28.03.1998 an der Humboldt-Universität Berlin. Berlin: Peter Lang Verlag.

Hennessey, J. S. (1990): Spirantization to Lenition in Breton: Interpretation of Morphophonological Variability. In: Ball, Fife, et al. 1990: 209-24.

Hill, J. H. (1978): Language death, language contact, and language function. In: McCormack & Wurm (eds.) 1978.

— (1983): Language death in Uto-Aztecan. International Journal of American Linguistics 49: 258-76.

Hill, J. H. & Hill, K. C. (1977): Language death and relexification in Tlaxcalan Nahuatl. IJSL 12: 55-69.

— (1980): Mixed grammar, purist grammar and language attitudes in modern Nahuatl. Language in Society 9: 321-48.

Hill, Thomas (ed.) (1849): Letters and Memoir of the late Walter Augustus Shirley, DD, Lord Bishop of Sodor and Man. London.

Hindley, Reg. (1984): The Decline of the Manx Language: a Study in Linguistic Geography. Bradford Occasional Papers. No. 6 (Autumn 1984): 15-39.

— (1990): The Death of the Irish Language. A Qualified Obituary. London: Routledge.

Holmer, Nils (1938): Studies on Argyllshire Gaelic. Uppsala: Almquist & Wiksell.

— (1940): On Some Relics of the Irish Dialect spoken in the Glens of Antrim. Universitets Aarskrift. Uppsala: University of Uppsala.

— (1942): The Irish Language in Rathlin Island, Co. Antrim. Dublin: Hodges Figgis.

— (1957): The Gaelic of Arran. Dublin: DIAS.

— (1962a): The Dialects of County Clare, Part. 1. Dublin: RIA.

— (1962b): The Gaelic of Kintyre. Dublin: DIAS.

— (1965): The Dialects of County Clare, Part 2. Dublin: RIA.

Hughes, John P. (1952): A Phonemic Description of the Aran Dialect of Modern Irish with a Detailed Consideration of Problems of Palatalisation. Unpubl. diss. Columbia University.

Hymes, D. (ed.) (1971): Pidginization and Creolization of Languages. Cambridge: UP.

Ifans, Dafydd and Thomson, Robert L. (1979-80): Edward Lhuyd's Geirieu Manaweg (c. 1700). Studia Celtica XIV-XV: 129-67.

Ingram, David (1989): First language acquisition. Method, description and explanation. Cambridge: Cambridge University Press.

Jackson, Kenneth H. (1951): Common Gaelic. The Evolution of the Goidelic Languages. The Sir John Rhys Memorial Lecture. Proceedings of the British Academy 37 (1951): 71-97. London.

— (1955): Contributions to the Study of Manx Phonology. Edinburgh: Nelson.

— (1960): The Phonology of the Breton dialect of Plougrescant. Études Celtiques 9: 327-99.

— (1967): Palatalisation of Labials in the Gaelic Languages. In: Meid (ed.): 179-92.

— (1990): Aislinge Meic Con Ghlinne. Dublin: DIAS (Linguistic Appendix 72-140).

Januschek, Franz (ed.) (1985): Politische Sprachwissenschaft. Opladen: Westdeutsche Verlag.

Jenner, Henry (1875): The Manx Language: its Grammar, Literature, and Present State. Transactions of the Philological Society 1-29.

Jerry, Colin W. P. (1978): Kiaull yn Theay. Manx Music and Song for Folk Instruments. Douglas: YCG.

— (1980): Kiaull yn Theay II. Manx Music and Songs for Folk Instruments. Douglas: YCG.

— (1987): Kiaull Vannin. A Source Book for Manx Tunes. Transcribed from the the Collections of Dr. J. Clague and Others [incl. A. W. Moore & Mona Douglas]. Peel, Isle of Man: priv. publ. Revised edition 1991.

Jones, Bedwyr Lewis (1981): Welsh: Linguistic Conservatism and Shifting Bilingualism. In: Haugen, McClure, Thomson (eds.) 1981: 40-52.

Kaye, K. (1980): Why don't we talk 'baby talk' to babies? Journal of Child Language 7: 489-507.

Keller, R. E. (1968): Der Umwandlungsprozess eines mundartlichen Lautsystems. Verhandlungen des 2. Internationalen Dialectologenkongresses. Wiesbaden: Steiner: 446-51.

Kelly, Henry Percy (1914): Lessoonyn Beggey Gailckagh I. Manx Reading Lessons translated from the Irish of Norma Borthwick. Douglas: Meyer.

Kelly, John (1804): A Practical Grammar of the Ancient Gaelc or Language of the Isle of Mann, usually called Manks... London: John Nichols & Son. Reprinted by the Manx Society (Vol. II) in 1859.

— (1866): Fockleyr Gailckagh as Baarlagh [Manx-English & English-Manx Dictionary]. Douglas: Manx Society Vol. VIII. Prepared by Kelly in 1805. Manx-English section reprinted by YCG 1977.

Kelly, Phil (ed.) (1991): Fockleyr Gaelg-Baarle. Manx-English Dictionary. Kirk Michael, Isle of Man: priv. publ.

— (ed.) (1993): Manx Usage. Rheynn Cullen, Isle of Man: priv. publ. 2 vols.

Kermode, R. D. (1954): The Annals of Kirk Christ Lezayre some time known as Trinity Ayre. Douglas: Norris Modern Press.

Kerruish, W. S. (1881): Manx Gaelic. A paper read at the 13th Annual Session of the American Philological Association, Cleveland, Ohio, July 1881. Unpublished.

Kewley-Draskau, Jennifer (fc).Gaelic influences in Anglo-Manx. Liverpool: Institute of Irish Studies.

Killip, Margaret (1975): The Folklore of the Isle of Man.London: Batsford. Repr. 1986.

Kinvig, R. H. (1975): The Isle of Man: a Social, Cultural, and Political History. Liverpool: UP.

Kneen, J[ohn] J[oseph] (1890): Simple Lessons in Manx. In: Isle of Man Examiner 1890ff.

— (1901a): Lessons in the Manx Language. In: Celtia, June 1901, w. Eng. trans.

— nd. [1901b]: Lessoonyn ayns Gailck. Douglas: SKB.

— (1911): Yn Saase Jeeragh (The Direct Method of Teaching Manx). Douglas: SKB.

— (1925-28): The Place-Names of the Isle of Man with their Origin and History. Douglas: YCG. 6 vols. Reprinted in one volume 1970.

— (1926-27): Lessoonyn Gailckagh Aashagh (Easy Manx Lessons). In: Ellan Vannin Magazine for 05.01.1926, 06.08.1926, 07.01.1927, 08.06.1927.

— (1931): A Grammar of the Manx Language. Oxford: University Press. Prepared by Kneen 1910. Reprinted by YCG 1973.

— (1938): English-Manx Pronouncing Dictionary. Douglas: Mona's Herald. Reprinted by YCG 1970.

Kneen, J. J. Papers. MM. Unaccessioned.

König, Claudia (1996): The Manx Language - Past and Present. A Sociolinguistic Study. Wissenschaftliche Prüfungsarbeit zur Ersten Staatsprüfung für das Lehramt an Gymnasien, Universität Mainz. Unpublished.

Krauss, Michael (1992): The World's Languages in Crisis. Language 68: 4-10.

Kürschner, Wilfried and VOGT, Rüdiger (eds.) (1985): Sprachtheorie, Pragmatik, Interdiziplinares. Akten des 19. Linguistischen Kolloquiums, Vechta 1984, II. Tübingen: Niemeyer.

Ladefoged, Peter (1992): Another view of endangered languages. Language 68: 809-11.

Lambert, R. D. and Freed, B. F. (eds.) (1982): The Loss of Language Skills. Rowley MA: Newbury House.

Leo, Heinrich (1847): Ferienschriften. Vermischte Abhandlungen zur Geschichte der Deutschen und Keltischen Sprachen. Halle: Eduard Anton. Vol. 1 contains (pp.117-242): Grammatik des auf der Insel Man gesprochenen Dialectes der gaelischen Sprache oder des Manxischen.

Lerchenmüller, Joachim (1997): Keltischer Sprengstoff: Eine wissenschaftsgeschichtliche Studie über die Deutsch-Keltologie 1900-1945. Tübingen: Niemeyer.

Lewis, Glyn (1978): Migration and Decline of the Welsh Language. In: Fishman (ed.) 1978.

Lhuyd, Edward (1707): Archaeologia Britannica... Oxford. Manx section pp. 290-298.

Loch, Charles W. (1946): Some Notes on the Present State of the Manx Language. April 1946. Manx Museum MS.5134B. Unpublished. But see Davies 1948.

Lucas, Leslie W. (1979): Grammar of Ros Goill Irish, Co. Donegall. Belfast: Institute of Irish Studies. SILL Vol. 5.

Mac an Fhailigh, Éamonn (1968): The Irish of Erris, Co. Mayo. Dublin: DIAS.

MacAulay, Donald (1966): Palatalization of labials in Scottish Gaelic. SGS 11: 72-84.

— (1978): Intra-Dialectal Variation as an Area of Gaelic Linguistic Research. SGS 13: 81-97.

— (1982a): Borrow, Calque and Switch: the Law of the English Frontier. In: Anderson (ed.) 1982: 205-37.

— (1982b): Register, Range and Choice in Scottish Gaelic. International Journal of the Sociology of Language 35: 25-48.

— (1992): The Celtic Languages. Cambridge Language Surveys. Cambridge: CUP.

MacBain, A. (1894): The Gaelic Dialect of Badenoch. TGSI 18: 79-86.

MacEoin, Gearóid, Ahlqvist, Anders, Ó hAodha, Donncha (eds.) (1987): Third International Conference on Minority Languages: Celtic Papers. June 1986, Galway, Ireland. No. 32. Celvedon, Avon: Mulilingual Matters.

McCormack, W. C. & Wurm, S. A. (eds.) (1978): Approaches to language: Anthropological issues. The Hague: Mouton.

MacKinnon, Kenneth (1977): Language Education and Social Processes in a Gaelic Community. London: Routledge and Kegan Paul.

— (1978): Gaelic in Scotland 1971: Some Sociological and Demographic Considerations of the Census Report for Gaelic. Hatfield: The Hatfield Polytechnic.

— (1981): Scottish Opinion on Gaelic: a Report on a National Attitude Survey for An Comunn Gàidhealach undertaken in 1981. Hatfield: The Hatfield Polytechnic.

— (1984): Scottish Gaelic and English in the Highlands. In: Trudgill (ed.) 1984: 499-516.

— (1987): Occupation, Migration, and Language Maintenance in Gaelic Communities. Hatfield Polytechnic Business and Social Science Occasional Papers Series No. DSS 15. Hatfield: Herts.

— (1988a): Gaelic Language-Maintenance and Viability in the Isle of Skye - A Report to ESRC. Hatfield: Hertis Publications.

— (1988b): Language-maintenance and viability in contemporary Gaelic communities: Skye and the Western Isles today. In: Ureland and Broderick (eds.) 1991: 495-533.

— (1991): Scottish Gaelic Today: Social History and Contemporary Status. In: Ball (ed.) (1993): 491-535.

Maclennan (Mac Gill-Fhinnein), Gordon (1966): Gàidhlig Uidhist a Deas. Baile Átha Cliath: Institiúid Árd-Léinn Bhaile Átha Cliath (DIAS).

— (1988): Proceedings of the First North American Congress of Celtic Studies. Ottawa: University of Ottawa.

McKenna, Malachy (1988): A Handbook of Modern Spoken Breton. Tübingen: Niemeyer. (Buchreihe der ZCP, Bd. 6).

Manchester Guardian (27.09.1913): The Manx Revival. Mona's New Aspirations.

Manx Language Society (1899-1931): The Manx Language Society - Annual Meeting (reprinted from The Isle of Man Examiner 18.11.1899) Manx Museum, Douglas, Isle of Man: 1-7.

Manx Sun (20.12.1845): Vanninee Ghooghyssagh, as ooilley shiuish yoareeyn feudagh, ta cummal aynes Thalloo Vannin. Manx Museum.

Marstrander, Carl J. S. (1929-33a): Defunctae Linguae Manniae Specimina quae collegit Carolus Marstrander. Manx Museum MSS.5354-57B (4 vols.). Bound mss.

— (1929-1933b): Dagbok ('Diary'). Manx Museum MS. 5357B. See Appendix A.

— (1932): Det Norske Landnåm på Man. NTS VI (1932): 40-386. With English summary. English trans. of whole by John Farrington 1956-59, with linguistic material dealt with by Robert L. Thomson 1960. Unpublished. Manx Museum F64/106a.

— (1934): Remarks on the Place-Names of the Isle of Man. NTS VII: 287-334.

— (1937): Treen og Keeill. NTS VIII: 287-500. With English summary.

Megaw, Basil R. S. (1976): Norseman and Native in the Kingdom of the Isles: a reassessment of the Manx evidence. Scottish Studies 20: 1-44. Revised version in Davey (ed.) (1978): 265-314.

Megaw, Eleanor (1978): The Manx eary and its significance. In: Davey (ed.) 1978: 327-345.

Meid, Wolfgang (ed.) (1967): Beiträge zur Indogermanistik und Keltologie. Julius Pokorny zum 80. Geburtstag gewidmet. Innsbruck: Institut für Sprachwissenschaft der Universität Innsbruck. (IBS 13).

Menn, Lise (1989): Some people who don't talk right: Universal and particular in child language, aphasia, and language obsolescence. In: Dorian (ed.) 1989: 335-45.

Miller, Stephen (ed.) (1994): Manx Folk Song, Folk Dance, Folklore. Collected Writings. Isle of Man: Chiollagh Books.

Monas' Herald: (27.12.1833): Pledeilys eddyr daa Vanninagh Dooie. Full text in Appendix E.

— (21.02.1834): Pledeilys eddyr daa Vanninagh Dooie (cited as 1834a).

— (06.06.1834): Dys Chaghter Kiauleaght Vannin (cited as 1834b).

— (08.08.1834): Dys Editor yn Mona[s] Herald (cited as 1834c).

— (06.02.1835): Coyrle da Manninee.

Moore, Arthur W. (ed.) (1887): The Manx Note Book III. Douglas.

— (1889-92): An Historical Sketch of the Manx Language, with an Account of the Sources from which a Knowledge of it can be Aquired. Yn Lioar Manninagh 1: 129-34.

— (1891a): Folklore of the Isle of Man. London.

— (1891b): Carvallyn Gailckagh. Douglas.

— (1896): Manx Ballads and Music. Douglas.

— (1900): A History of the Isle of Man. London: Unwin. Repr. 1977 for the Manx Museum and National Trust. 2 vols.

Moore, Arthur W, Morrison, Sophia, and Goodwin, Edmund (1924): A Vocabulary of the Anglo-Manx Dialect. London: OUP. Repr. 1991 YCG.

Moore, Arthur W. and Rhys, John (eds.) (1893-94): The Book of Common Prayer in Manx Gaelic. London. 2 vols. Manx Soc. 32 & 33. Oxford: UP.

Mühlhaäuler, Peter (1982): Tok Pisin in Papua New Guinea. In: Bailey and Görlach (eds.) 1982: 439-66.

— (1996): Linguistic Ecology: Language change and linguistic imperialism in the Pacific Region. London: Routledge.

Munch, P. A. (1860): Chronica Regum Manniae et Insularum. The Chronicle of Man and the Sudreys, with English translation and historical notes. Christiania. Revised version of Munch's edition by Rev. Goss (1874). Douglas: Manx Society 22, 23.

Nikiforidu, V., Van Clay, M., Niepokujn, M., and Feder, D. (eds.) (1986): Proceedings of the Twelfth Annual Meeting of the Berkeley Linguistics Society. Berkeley CA: Berkeley Linguistics Society.

Ó Baoill, Dónall P. (1979): Occasional Papers in Linguistics and Language Learning. No. 6 Papers in Celtic Phonology. Coleraine: The New University of Ulster.

Ó Cuív, Brian (1944): The Irish of West Muskerry, Co. Cork: a Phonetic Study. Dublin: DIAS.

— (1951): Irish Dialects and Irish-Speaking Districts. Dublin.

— (1957): A poem in praise of Raghnall, King of Man. Éigse VIII/4: 283-301.

— (1969): A View of the Irish Language. Dublin: Stationery Office.

— (1985): The Irish Language. Dublin: Department of Foreign Affairs and Bord na Gaeilge.

Ó Dochartaigh, Cathair (1976): The Rathlin Catechism. ZCP 35: 175-233.

— (1987): Dialects of Ulster Irish. Belfast: Institute of Irish Studies.

O'Driscoll, Robert (1982): The Celtic Consciousness. Portlaoise/Edinburgh.

Ó Luain, Cathal (ed.), nd. [1984]: For a Celtic Future. A Tribute to Alan Heusaff. Dublin: Celtic League.

Ó Murchú, Máirtín (1989): East Perthshire Gaelic. Dublin: DIAS.

— (1993): Aspects of the Societal Status of Modern Irish. In: Ball (ed.) 1993: 471-90.

O'Rahilly, T. F. (1932): Irish Dialects Past and Present. Dublin: Browne and Nolan. Reprint 1972 DIAS.

Ó Riagáin, P. (1988): Language Planning in Ireland. International Journal of the Sociology of Language 70.

Ó Sé, Diarmuid (1991): Prosodic Change in Manx and Lexical Diffusion. In: Ureland and Broderick (eds.) (1991): 157-180.

Ó Síothcháin, Conchobhar (1940): Seanchas Chléire. Baile Átha Cliath: Oifig an tSoláthair. New edition 1970.

Ó Súillebháin, Mícheál (ed.) (1982): The Roche Collection of Traditional Irish Music. Cork: Ossian.

Obler, L. and Menn, L. (eds.) (1982): Exceptional Language and Linguistic Theory. New York: Academic Press.

Oftedal, Magne (1956): The Gaelic of Leurbost, Isle of Lewis. Supplementary Volume No. 4. NTS. Oslo.

— (1963): On 'Palatalised' Labials in Scottish Gaelic. SGS 10: 71-81.

— (1969): Notes on Leurbost Gaelic: a Supplement. Lochlann IV: 270-78.

— (1982): Professor Carl Marstrander and his work in the Isle of Man. Proc. IOMNHAS IX/1 (Apr. 1980-Mar. 1982): 11-19.

Peter, Anne (1984): Diachronische und synchronische Überlegungen zur Sprachsituation auf der Insel Man. Zulassungsarbeit für die wissenschaftliche Prüfung für das Lehramt an Gymnasien, Universität Mannheim. Unpublished.

Petrovici, Emil (1967): Le modèle serbo-croate du système phonématique istro-roumain. In: Hamm (ed.): 262-72.

Pool, P. A. S. (1982): The Death of Cornish (1600-1800). Saltash: Cornish Language Board. 2nd ed.

Price, Glanville (1984): The Languages of Britain. London: Arnold.

— (1992): The Celtic Connection. Colin Smythe (Princess Grace Irish Library 6).

Pryce, W. T. R (1978): Welsh and English in Wales 1750-1971: a Spatial Analysis based on the Linguistic Affiliation of Parochial Communities. BBCS XXVIII: 1-36.

Quiggin, E. C. (1906): A Dialect of Donegal, being the Speech of Meenawannia in [...] Glenties. Cambridge: Cambridge University Press.

— (1911): Manx Language and Literature. In: Encyclopaedia Britannica, s.v. 'Celt'.

Ravenstein, E. G. (1879): On the Celtic Languages in the British Isles: a Statistical Survey. Proceedings of the 45th Annual Meeting of the Statistical Society. London.

Révue Celtique XLIV (1927) Section VII ['l'état linguistique de l'île de Man']: 466-68.

Rhys, John (1894): The Outlines of the Phonology of Manx Gaelic. In: Moore and Rhys (eds.) 1894 II appended.

Robertson, Charles M. (1897): The Gaelic dialect of Arran. TGSI XXI: 229-65.

— (1900): Perthshire Gaelic. TGSI XXII: 4-42.

— (1901-03): Sutherland Gaelic. TGSI XXV: 84-125.

Robins, Robert H. and Uhlenbeck, Eugenius M. (eds.) (1991): Endangered Languages. Oxford/New York: Berg.

Rockel, Martin, & Zimmer, Stefan (eds.) (1993): Akten des ersten Symposiums deutschsprachiger Keltologen (Gosen bei Berlin, 8-10 April 1992). Tübingen: Niemeyer (Buchreihe der ZCP, Vol. 11).

Roeder, Charles (1904): Manx Notes and Queries. Douglas: SKB.

Rosser, James (1849): The history of Wesleyan Methodism in the Isle of Man. Douglas.

Russell, Paul (1995): An Introduction to the Celtic Languages. London: Longman.

Sacheverell, William (1702): An Account of the Isle of Man, its Inhabitants, Language... London: Hartley.

Sasse, Hans-Jürgen (1991): Arvanítika. Die albanischen Sprachreste in Griechenland. Teil 1. Wiesbaden: Harrasowitz (and forthcomimg).
— (1992a): Theory of Language Death. In: Brenzinger (ed.) (1992): 7-30.
— (1992b): Language Decay and Contact-Induced Change: Similarities and Differences. In: Brenzinger (ed.) 1992: 59-80.
Schmidt, Annette (1985): Young people's Dyirbad: An example of language death from Australia. Cambridge: Cambridge University Press.
Shaw, William (1780): Galic and English Dictionary. 2 vols. London: Strahan.
Sherwood Richard (1882): The Constitution of the Isle of Man... Manx Society 31. Douglas: James Brown.
Silverstein, M. (1971): Language contact and the problem of convergent generative systems: Chinook Jargon. In: Hymes (ed.): 191-92.
Simon, Gerd (1982): Zündschnur zum Sprengstoff: Leo Weisgerbers keltologische Forschungen und seine Tätigkeit als Zensuroffizier in Rennes während des 2. Weltkriegs. Linguistische Berichte 79/82: 30-52 (Thurneysen quote p.40).
— (1985a): Sprachwissenschaft im Dritten Reich. Ein Überblick. In: Januschek 1985: 97-141.
— (1985b): Die Sprachsoziologische Abteilung der SS. In: Kürschner & Vogt (eds.) 1985: 375-96.
Sjoestadt, M. L. (1931): Phonétique d'un parler irlandais de Kerry. Paris: Ernest Leroux.
Sjoestadt-Jonval, M. L. (1938): Description d'un parler irlandais de Kerry. Paris: Champion.
Sommerfelt, Alf (1920): Le breton parlé à Saint-Pol-de-Léon. Rennes: Imprimeries Reunies. New edn. by Falc'hun F. & Oftedal M. Oslo: Universitetsforlaget (1978).
— (1922): The Dialect of Torr, Co. Donegal. Christiania: Dybwad.
— (1925): Studies in Cyfeiliog Welsh: a contribution to Welsh dialectology. Oslo: 1 Kommission Hos Jacob Dybwad.
— (1929): South Armagh Irish. NTS II: 107-91.
— (1965): The phonemic structure of the dialect of Torr, Co. Donegal. Lochlann 3: 237-254.
Speed, John (1611): Theatre of the Empire of Great Britaine. London.
Speers, David (1997): The historical references to Manx traditional music, song and dance: a reappraisal and a chronology. Béaloideas 64-65 (1996-97): 225-77.
Stenning, E. H. (1942-56): The original lands of Bishop Barrow's trustees. Proc. IOMNHAS V: 122-45.
Stenson, Nancy, and Ó Ciardha, Pádhraic (1986): The Irish of Ráth Cairn. A Supplement to Linguistic Atlas and Survey of Irish Dialects (Part I). ZCP 41: 66-115.
— (1987): The Irish of Ráth Cairn. A Supplement to Linguistic Atlas and Survey of Irish Dialects (Part 2). ZCP 42: 116-137.
Stern, Ludwig Christian (1909): Die Manx-Literatur. In: Die Romanischen Literaturen und Sprachen mit Einschluss des Keltischen. Berlin: Teubner.
Stockman, Gearóid (1974): The Irish of Achill. Belfast: Institute of Irish Studies. SILL Vol. 2.
— (1988): Linguistic Trends in the Terminal Stages of Q-Celtic Dialects. In: Maclennan (ed.) 1988: 387-96.
Stowell, Brian (1968): Gaelg Trooid Jallooghyn. Castletown: YCG.
— (1970): Bunneydys. A Course in Spoken Manx. Douglas: YCG.
— (in co-operation with Douglas C. Fargher) (1986): Abbyr Shen. Say That. Starting to Speak Manx. Douglas: Manx Radio. With 3 accompanying cassettes.
— (1996): Bun Noa. Douglas: Dept. of Education, Isle of Man Government. 4 vols.
Stowell, Brian, and Ó Breasláin, Diarmuid (1996): A Short History of Manx. Belfast.
Stowell, Hugh (1808): Lessons and Stories for Good Children. Douglas: Jefferson.
— (1818): Yn Chied Lioar gailckagh; ny Cooney dy ynsaghey Chengey ny Mayrey Ellan Vannin ('the First Manx Gaelic Book; or a help to learn the Mother-Tongue of the Isle of Man'). London.
Strachan, John (1897): A Manx folksong. ZCP 1: 54-58.
Telford, John (1931): The letters of Rev. John Wesley. London. 8 vols.
Ternes, Elmar (1970): Grammaire structurale du Breton de l'Ile de Groix. Heidelberg: Winter.

— (1973): The Phonology of Scottish Gaelic. Hamburg: Buske.

Terrien Christoll (1861): Les huit Dialectes Caledonec Vivants en 1861. Anthologie Caledonec. Études de linguistique Indo-Celtique comparée. Shrewsbury.

Tevenar, Gerhard von (1941a): Die völkische Eigenart der Insel Man. Volksforschung (begründet als Auslandsdeutsche Volksforschung), ed. Heinz Kloss. Stuttgart: Enke, 1942 Vol. 5: 279-90.

— (1941b): Nekrolog: J. J. Kneen (1872-1938). Zeitschrift für keltische Philologie und Volksforschung 22: 445-46.

Thomas, Alan R. (1973): The Linguistic Geography of Wales. Cardiff: University of Wales Press.

Thomas, C. H. (1993): Tafodiaith Nantgarw. Astudiaeth Gymraeg Llafar Nantgarw yng Nghwm Taf, Morgannwg. Cardiff: University of Wales Press. 2 vols.

Thomson, Derrick S. (ed.) (1987): The Companion to Gaelic Scotland. Oxford: Blackwell.

Thomson, Robert L (1950-51): Syntax of the verb in Manx Gaelic. Études Celtiques 5: 260-292.

— (1954-57): A Glossary of Early Manx (1610). ZCP 24: 272-307; 25: 100-40, 264-308; 27: 79-160.

— (1960): Svarabhakti and Some Associated Changes in Manx. Celtica V: 116-126.

— (1960-63): The Manx Traditionary Ballad. Études Celtiques 9 (1960-61): 521-548, 10 (1962-63): 60-87.

— (1965): Norse Loan Words in Manx. SGS 10: 65-68.

— (1969a.): The Study of Manx Gaelic. Sir John Rhys Memorial Lecture. Proc. of the British Academy, Vol. LV: 177-210. London: OUP.

— (1969b): Edward Lhuyd in the Isle of Man? In: Carney and Greene (eds.) (1969): 170-82.

— (1976): The stressed vowel phonemes of a Manx idiolect. Celtica XI: 255-63.

— (1977): Kelly's Manx-English Dictionary (reprint): Foreword. Douglas: YCG.

— (1978): The interpretation of some Manx place-names. In: Davey (ed.) (1978): 319-325.

— (1979): Bible Chasherick yn Lught-thie. The Manx Family Bible. Onchan: Shearwater. Introduction. Reprint of 1819 edition.

— (1981): Lessoonyn sodjey 'sy Ghailck Vanninagh. A linguistic commentary on the translations of St. John's Gospel. Douglas: YCG.

— (1983): The Continuity of Manx. In: Fell, Foote, Graham-Campbell, and Thomson (eds.) (1983): 169-174.

— (1984a): The history of the Celtic languages in the British Isles. In: Trudgill (ed.) (1984): 241-58.

— (1984b): Manx. In: Trudgill (ed.) (1984): 306-17.

— (1984c): Aspects of the Gaelic-Norse controversy: Manx personal names and general vocabulary. Proc. IOMNHAS IX: 145-55.

— (1987): The Revd. Dr. John Kelly as a lexicographer. Proc. IOMNHAS IX: 443-58.

— (1991a): Foreign Elements in the Manx Vocabulary. In: Ureland and Broderick (eds.) (1991): 127-140.

— (1991b): Notes: Borraine again. Proc. IOMNHAS X, 1 (April 1989-March 1991): 161-62.

— (1992a: The Manx Language. In: MacAulay 1992: 100-36.

— (1992b): Manx Language and Literature. In: Price 1992: 154-70.

— (1995): Pargys Caillit & Parnell's 'Hermit'. Douglas: CMS Research Report 3.

— (1997): Paart dy Homileeyn ny Sharmaneyn Oikoil Agglish Hostyn. Douglas: Yn Cheshaght Ghailckagh.

Thomson, Robert L, and Pilgrim, Adrian (1988): Outlines of Manx Language and Literature. Douglas: YCG.

Thurneysen, Rudolf (1946): A Grammar of Old Irish. Dublin: DIAS. Repr. 1970.

Timm, Leonora A. (1980): Bilingualism, Diglossia, and Language Shift in Brittany. International Journal of the Sociology of Language 25: 29-41.

— (1984): The Segmental Phonology of Carhaisien Breton. ZCP 40: 118-192.

Tovey, H. (1988): The State of the Irish language: the role of Bord na Gaeilge. In: Ó Riagáin (ed.) 1988: 53-68.

Trudgill, Peter (ed.) (1984): Language in the British Isles. Cambridge: University Press.

Tristram, Hildegard L. C (ed.), (1997): The Celtic Englishes. Heidelberg: Winter. Anglistische Forschungen Band 247.

Tsitsipis, Lukas D (1981): Language Change and Language Death in Albanian Speech Communities in Greece: a Sociolinguistic Study. Unpubl. PhD diss. University of Wisconsin, Madison.

— (1983): Narrative performance in a dying language: Evidence from Albanian in Greece. Word 34: 25-36.

Ureland, P. Sture and Broderick, George (eds.) (1991): Language Contact in the British Isles. Proceedings of the Eighth International Symposium on Language Contact in Europe, Douglas, Isle of Man, 1988. Tübingen: Niemeyer.

Vallancy, Dr. (1782): A Grammar of the Iberno-Celtic, or Irish Language. Dublin. References to Manx on pp. 61, 115, 118, 119, 122 (cf. Cubbon 1939: 815).

Vetter, Eva (1997): Nicht mehr Bretonisch? Sprachkonflikt in der ländlichen Bretange. Frankfurt-Main: Peter Lang. Series: Sprache im Kontext. Vol. 2.

Wagner, Heinrich (1956): Review of Kenneth H. Jackson, 1955. Contributions to the Study of Manx Phonology. Edinburgh. In: The Modern Language Review 51 (1956): 107-109.

— (1958-69): Linguistic Atlas and Survey of Irish Dialects. Dublin:DIAS. 4 vols. Vol. 1 repr. 1981 by DIAS.

— (1959a): Das Verbum in den Sprachen der Britischen Inseln. Tübingen: Niemeyer [Charakteristik des manxischen Verbums 88-94].

— (1959b): Gaeilge Theilinn. Dublin: DIAS.

— (1962): Nordeuropäische Lautgeographie. ZCP 29: 225-298 (IV. Bemerkungen zur Phonesis des Manxischen 293-94).

— (1982): Near Eastern and African Connections with the Celtic World. In: O'Driscoll (ed.) 1982: 53ff.

Wakelin, Martyn (1975): Language and History in Cornwall. Leicester: University Press.

Watson, Seosamh (1974): A Gaelic Dialect of N. E. Ross-shire: the Vowel System and General Remarks. Lochlann VI (1974): 9-90, Index ibid.: 207-217.

— (1984): Séamus Ó Duilearga's Antrim Notebooks - I: Texts. ZCP 40: 74-117.

— (1986): The sounds of Easter Ross Gaelic: Historical development. SGS 14(2): 51-93.

— (1987): Séamus Ó Duilearga's Antrim Notebooks - II: Language. ZCP 42: 138-218.

— (1989): Scottish and Irish Gaelic: the giant's bed-fellows. In: Dorian (ed.) 1989: 41-59.

Weinreich, Uriel (1967): Languages in Contact. The Hague/Paris: Mouton.

Weisgerber, Leo (1941): Die keltischen Völker im Umkreis von England. Marburg (Marburger Universitätsreden 7).

Wilks, [James] (1777): The Inhabitants of the Isle of Mann and their Language. In: Moore (ed.) (1887): 178-80.

Wilson, Thomas (1707): The principles and duties of Christianity [Mx. *Coyrle Sodjey*]. London. Bilingual. Repr. Menston 1972.

— (1783): Sharmaneyn, liorish Thomas Wilson DD Chiarn Aspick Sodor as Vannin dy Kiaralagh chyndait veih Bayrl gys Gailck. Lioar I (all published). Bath: Cruttwell. Known as 'Wilson's Sermons'.

Withers, Charles W. J. (1984): Gaelic in Scotland 1698-1981. The Geographical History of a Language. Edinburgh: John Donald.

Wolfram, Walt, and Schilling-Estes, Natalie (1995): Moribund Dialects and the Endangerment Canon: the Case of the Ocracoke Brogue. Language 71: 696-721.

Appendix A

Dagbok

Carl J. S. Marstrander's diary of his visits to the Isle of Man 1929, 1930, and 1933 (translation and text)

Introduction

This is an English translation of a diary in Norwegian kept by Carl J. S. Marstrander (1883-1965), Professor of Celtic Studies at the University of Oslo, of his visit to the Isle of Man for the purpose of collecting samples of native Manx Gaelic speech, from June to September 1929, with short entries of visits there in August and September 1930, and January and February 1933. The original text is also provided for reference. The text was transcribed at my request by Anne Fevang, Sandefjord, and Lars Anders Ruden, Roa, Norway, in May 1998. Also at my request, it was translated by Knut Janson, a Norwegian national living in Dublin, in 1983, with minor revisions by Bo Almqvist, Professor of Irish Folklore at University College Dublin, and Mícheál Ó Siadhail, Dublin Institute for Advanced Studies. Additional notes were supplied for this edition by Robert L. Thomson, Isle of Man, and Máirtín Ó Murchú, Dublin Institute for Advanced Studies.

Housed in the Manx Museum Archive under the archive reference MM.MS.5358B, the diary text is found in an exercise book measuring some 21 x 16.5 cms. and extends to 87 pages of manuscript, with 23 pages left blank at the end. Inside the back cover are some names and addresses of informants. The front cover bears the pencilled title *Man Dagbok* with the subtitle *Dagbok av en reise til Man juni 1929. C. Marstrander*. The text itself bears no title.

The diary is found among an assortment of items which go to form Vol. 5 of Marstrander's *Defunctae Linguae Manniae Specimina quae collegit Carolus Marstrander* (Marstrander 1929-33b), a series of exercise books bound together in red leather with gilt tooling into five volumes (the last or box volume containing loose items) and containing essenitally a collection of material in phonetic script drawn from native Manx Gaelic speech during that period. Spanning some 2630 pages this collection was presented to the Manx Museum by Marstrander himself on behalf of the Norwegian Government on 2 July 1951 as part of the Festival of Britain celebrations, in which the Isle of Man took part (cf. also Section 3.5.2. & §§3.6.2.1-2.).

Except for the last few pages and some interlinear insertions, the handwriting of the diary is in ink, and in places it is not all that easy to read. In fact in some places it was found almost impossible to make out the text, and here the transcription and translation is only tentative. Difficult readings in the text are marked [?]. The odd-numbered pages only are enumerated, each double-page receiving the number in the top right-hand corner. However, the third double-page is marked with the numeral 6, which has resulted in the left side of this and the following double-page being numbered 5A and 6A respectively for the purposes of this translation. Though spanning 87 sides the numbers extend, therefore, only to 85. In addition pages 42-51 inclusive are lettered 'a' to 'i' which, to judge from the position of the numbering, seem to have preceded the page-enumeration of the entire diary. All page enumeration from the diary is given here in both text transcription and translation in square brackets following two strokes, viz. //[1], which indicate where each new page begins.

During the course of the text the occasional English word or phrase occurs within the Norwegian text, e.g. *en god Manks speaker* (p. 18 and elsewhere), *en splendid te* (p. 17), *set mig om after lodgings* (p. 53), etc. The test sentences for his informants are all given in English, as are most, but not all, the individual lexical items. Interlinear comments on informants' answers are generally in Norwegian. Replies in Manx from his informants to test sentences or words, or individual pieces, e.g. the Lord's Prayer, verses of songs, etc, are recorded by Marstrander in phonetic script. In addition Marstrander often for his own benefit writes some personal or place-names, or parts of names, in phonetic script, e.g. pp. 35-36. His idiosyncratic use of capitals in personal and place-names is reproduced here; the rest is rendered in accordance with the system used elsewhere in this book. In the transscription all renderings in phonetic script are given in square brackets. In the translation the same is accompanied by the text in standard Manx orthography, also set in italics within square brackets. Irish examples or equivalents of Manx forms appear in the text in Irish script. In both transcription and translation they are rendered in italicised roman script.

Marstrander's slightly irregular renderings of some of the place and personal names, e.g. *Kewaige* (p. 9) for Kewaigue, *Waterson* (p. 20) for Watterson, *Waid* (p. 39) for Wade, *Djurby* (p. 56) for Jurby, etc, are given in the transcription as written, but in the translation are followed on the first occurrence by the standard form in square brackets. Thereafter the standard forms only are given. Marstrander enumerates (in a circle) his informants (whether names or unnamed) as he goes along. The sequence runs from 1 to 36. The same enumeration is supplied here in round brackets in both the transcription and translation.

For the sake of his own easy reference Marstrander has generally underlined names and examples (whether or not in phonetic script), especially where they occur in the middle of a piece of text. This practice has not been followed in the translation, unless it is felt to be relevant, in which case M's underlining is italicised and attributed to M as such. In the transcription all underlinings appear in italics.

In a number of places, to facilitate comprehension, initials in some personal names have been expanded and thus are given in the translation in square brackets, and first names or initials to surnames have been supplied in square brackets. Explanatory notes, or the standard literary forms of names following those supplied only in phonetic script, etc, are given in square brackets; enclosures in round brackets are as in the original. In the transcription such names, whether abbreviated or written out in full, are given as in the text.

Marstrander's footnotes are indicated with an asterisk(s) or dagger(s) or the like followed in the translation by the remark [M's note]. Other footnotes are enumerated. In the transcription only Marstrander's own footnotes appear.

In both transcription and translation the punctuation follows present day convention. In the transcription Marstrander's <ö> is rendered <ø>.

The translation is presented first, then followed by the original text.

G.B.

The Translation

//[1] June 1929

4th June: left on the Bergen train at 11-00; I was accompanied by Audh. and Sverdrup to the station.

5th June: left Bergen on the 'Leda'; nice boat, good cuisine.

6th June: arrived Newcastle where I just about managed to catch the train to London; left at 14.54. Arrived London at approx. 8-00pm; had to book into a small B & B place in Liverpool Street [no.] 26 (near King's Cross Station).

7th June: got a room at Euston Hotel. Went to see [Robin] Flower in the British Museum and spent the afternoon and evening with him partly in London, partly in Croydon. Flower is an excellent man. He is attempting to sketch the main strata in the development of Irish literature, something that no one has done before. His studies of Irish mss. and the centres of Irish writing seem to have given him a new perspective on Irish literature and the origins and dissemination of the saga-cycles.

//[2] He was very interested in [Reidar Th.] Christiansen's work on Fenian literature which hopefully will be published this year.[1] It appears that Flower is not persona grata in Dublin (an impression I also got from [J. G.] O'Keeffe). I should think that he would do better work than any of the Irish scholars in Dublin.

Spent the evening in Croydon, approx. 20 min. by train from London, where Flower has rented a little house, and he lives there with his wife, his mother, and 3 children - 2 girls and a boy. My god-daughter Barbara turned out to be a sweet little girl. She is, according to Flower, quite gifted at languages, and Flower wants her to become a scholar. She has the devil of a temper, he says, and will not be suitable for marriage.

Mrs. Flower is a pleasant lady, but //[3] gives the impression of being very tired and worn out.

Flower told me that he had been offered a job as professor in Irish at Oxford, which Frazer, however, got, but he was unable to take it because the salary (£600)* was not enough. He seems now to regret his decision, for his work in the British Museum will not give him much time for Irish studies, when the catalogue he is working on is ready next year. He was rather irritated over a review - a typical [Osborn] Bergin review - where Flower was criticised for putting more into a catalogue than Bergin thought necessary. I think I must review the catalogue in detail (together with Christiansen) in vol. V of the *Tidsskrift* [i.e. NTS, founded by M. in 1928].

8th June: moved to the Gower Hotel, a short distance from Euston; cheap and clean.

9th June: a pleasant trip up the Thames (alone) to Richmond. Returned by bus.

10th June: met Flower in the Museum and looked at the Celtic coin collection. It wasn't very //[4] impressive. The best place for Celtic coins is probably Paris. One coin was interesting which in Latin letters read BIRACO..: cf. the Lepontic coins.

---

[1] viz. Christiansen 1931 (qv).

* [M's note] Aug. 1930: Flower's salary would be as Director of [the British] Museum £1100, according to his own account.

2 M. probably has *Táin Bó Cuailnge* in mind here, where Aillil and Medb are king and queen of Connacht. In TBC Aillil plays very much second fiddle to Medb.

3 Probably a reference to *Anecdota from Irish Manuscripts*.

Had lunch together with Flower and O'Keeffe whom I was pleased to see again after all these years. He was the same nice outspoken man I've always known. He has a son who is 21, the same son that was born during my first stay in Dublin, and whom I was so unfortunate as to refer to as Ailill.[2] Poor Medb is dead, which I didn't know.

O'Keeffe was very sharp in his criticism of the people in Dublin, and very bitter that the School of Irish Learning [founded 1911] was discontinued and *Ériu* taken over by the Academy and that *Anecdota*[3] had folded up. The criticism of Bergin was particularly strong. He completely lacks initiative, cannot //[5] form a school, cannot educate new students. He is slack and inactive in a situation in which a man with initiative could work wonders. In his defence one has to say that he is overworked with university work. His Irish courses are attended by 300 students who all will have to take their exams at the end, and he has to correct all their papers. [T. F.] O'Rahilly, who for some time was in Trinity College where, however, he didn't seem to get on well with the others, has gone to Cork; and when [Douglas] Hyde retires in a short while, one fears that Mrs. [Agnes] O'Farrel[l]y will get the job as professor in Modern Irish in the National University. Good expectations seem to be had of [Séamas Ó] Duilearga. But I have strong doubts whether Irish linguistics and philology will ever grow strong on Irish soil without *outside* [M's italics] organisation. [Kuno] Meyer kept things together from Liverpool, and he thinks that [Alf] Sommerfelt and I could do a lot //[5A] from Oslo. But our interests are not like Meyer's limited to Irish or Celtic alone. Energetic work in creating a scholarly atmosphere in Dublin would mean that for many years - perhaps for ever - we would have to put all other work aside. Maybe we would serve scholarship best if we did this and carried Celtic studies over the slump which it now seems to be going down into with threatening speed. When [Rudolf] Thurneysen dies - and I don't think we can expect to keep him for many years[4] - Germany will not have a Celtic scholar any more; I don't think we can take J[ulius] P[okorny] seriously.[5] And when [J.] Loth retires next year (if I'm not mistaken) from the Sorbonne, there is no one to step forward to take his place. And [J.] Vendryes is also advanced in years and Mlle. [M. L.] Sjoestedt [later Sjoestedt-Jonval] //[6] is supposed to be very ill. The prospects everywhere are dark. Best, perhaps, in Norway where Celtic studies are done by relatively young people and where we will make sure that it is not given up.

11th June: left for Liverpool. Booked into the Adelphi Hotel which has been completely rebuilt since I was last there (in 1914).

12th June: to Man! The sea flat-calm. Arrived Douglas approx. 2-30pm. Booked into British Hotel near the old Market Place. A Danish ship was, so to say, anchored outside the windows; it had brought timber from Riga and was now taking on ballast.

13th June: paid a visit to the [Manx] Museum (a red-brick building originally built as a hospital). Met [P. M. C.] Kermode,[6] a pleasant and talkative old gentleman who introduced me to //[6A] the librarian Mr. [William] Cubbon and to J[ohn] J[oseph] Kneen, the author of the excellent work on Manx placenames; both were particularly nice people.

Cubbon offered the [Oslo] University Library a copy of the Manx Bible (1st edition [1771-75]) as a gift, and he also offered to sell 1 copy of the 1819 edition. I had found two

---

4   died August 1940.
5   For an assessment of German Celtology in the service of Irish and Breton nationalism ca. 1900-45 and in the politics of the Third Reich, cf. Lerchenmüller 1997.
6   Manx Museum Director 1922-32, followed by Wm. Cubbon to 1940.

copies of the 1819 edition in Simpson's antique shop in Douglas. I took one of the copies for myself and reserved the other one for Sommerfelt.

P. A. Munch's work[7] is not forgotten here. A framed picture of him hangs in the library.

That afternoon Kneen and myself had a pleasant trip on Braddan Church where several runic crosses are placed. Kneen's information about the condition under which scholarly work is carried out here was particularly sad to hear. The English [?Manx] //[7] government couldn't care less. Kneen's own work is on a part-time basis. His book has given me a strong impression of the strength of the Norse settlement here. In some places all the names of the larger farms seem to be Norse, e.g. in Garf; furthermore, one meets Norse names along the whole coastline. Kneen's collection is hardly complete; he admits himself that it is only on the south-west coast that his collection of coast-names, place-names, and names on small islands is more or less complete. I have a feeling that there is a rich field here for a place-names scholar with a knowledge of history. The Norse names are so numerous here on Man that one could read from them whole chapters of the history of Norse settlement [there]. Kneen's work is so important from a Norwegian point of view that it would be reasonable if the Nansen Fund acknowledged his work with a grant of £100 towards //[8] further collection of material.[8]

That evening tea at Cubbon's place together with Kneen. Mrs. Cubbon, whom we didn't see much of, appeared to be a pleasant lady. We sat talking till after 11-00pm and talked about different things. Of particular interest was Kneen's interpretation of Smeale as *smiða ból*,[*] an interpretation of particular interest because of the finding of a ship-burial there which contained among other things a blacksmith's tongs. From the same place there is named in later sources a Patrick Crowe and one... Teare (*an t-Saoir*). In this instance, consequently, archaeology and linguistics together draw a continuous line from the 10th to the 15th centuries.

The Museum also contains several ogham stones and runic crosses (originals and plaster-casts), but cannot be said to be especially rich.

//[9] 15th June: a short visit to the Museum and exchanged part 3 of my copy of Kneen's [place-names] book where a gathering was missing. I happened to land in on a board meeting and was presented to "Mr. Chairman" and to the Norwegian consul in Douglas, Mr. Oates, who both seemed to be pleasant gentlemen.

Started that afternoon on my *Cuairt Manan[n]* ('tour of Man') with Castletown as the first point.

(1) My first victim was a 60 year old man from the farm Kewaige [Kewaigue], 1-2 km. from Douglas. The old people in those parts didn't speak Manx any longer, he said. His old parents spoke a little Manx, but they preferred English, and refused to have their children speak Manx. His grandparents, however, spoke mainly Manx and spoke English with an accent.

(2) A man in Baconsfield (not on the map, but not too far from Kewaigue) ca. 55 yrs. old. Said //[10] one did not hear Manx any longer. His own father and mother spoke only English. Apart from that he was rather vague and not very precise in his statements.

Rather a lot of rain on the east side, and I was rather wet when I arrived in Castletown where I booked a room in the Union Hotel. Later on that evening I had a pleasant conversa-

---

[7]   Particularly known for his edition of the Chronicles of Man (cf. Munch 1860 & 1874).
[8]   See Section 5, Note 4 above.
[*]   [M's note] better *smiðju-holl* [but see PNIM/III: 166-67 s.v. *Smeale* - GB].

tion with the older and younger people from Castletown and the surrounding area. However, none of them spoke Manx. There was one exception, however, in a relatively young man whom I estimated to be in his forties; he had learned a little Manx, typically enough, from his grandfather.When I took a random sample and asked him what was "it is a cold day" in Manx, his reply was quite correct. I amused myself by throwing 'darts' with a very young man from the place. He won at last after approximately sixty throws //[11] and afterwards I had to buy him a glass of beer. A cheap and reasonable hotel.

16th June: left Castletown around 11-00am for Grenaby. Good weather, even though rather windy.

(3) Just outside Castletown I had a chat with a 70 yr. old man. He was from Derbyhaven (born there) and did *not* [M's italics] speak Manx; neither did his father, but his mother who was significantly from Ballabeg near Grenaby[†] did speak it, however. Someone who spoke good Manx, according to him, was "[kᵘe:l] [Quayle] the Gardener". He is a man of over 80 yrs. born in Arbory[††] and he lives just north of Castletown. Turned off to Derbyhaven. Met here 2 younger and 1 older Manxman. They gave me as good Manx speakers Thomas Taggart, the tailor in Grenaby, 80-85 yrs. old, born, according to //[12] them, in [kæriki:l] [Kerrookeil] (near Castletown). Further they mentioned Tom Harrison in Ballasalla; he was well over 80 yrs. old. Then they mentioned Archdeacon [kju:li] [Kewley] who in turn mentioned Thomas Taggart. He [Kewley] was a man in his 70s, born of poor parents in Castletown parish. My rambling led me to Ballasalla where I paid a short visit to Rushen Abbey which is situated quite near. Several 'Norse' kings are supposed to be buried here, according to what the boards say. One of them was Magnus, one Reginald, and another Olaf.[9] A lid from one of these coffins had been found, according to the guidebook, during excavations in recent years and is now housed in the museum which was closed when I was there; (it only opens on Sundays from 3 o'clock on).

//[13] (4) 1/2 km west of Ballasalla at "Cross Four Ways" (I've marked this in the Manx guide, but is not on the Ordnance Survey [map]). A woman of 40 declared that no one in the neighbourhood could speak Manx, but further on in the direction of Grenaby one could find "lots of them". This was an exaggeration, however.

(5) A little north from here and before the side-road turns off for Grenaby from the main road (to Peel) I had a chat with a man in his 50s. He was born in Ballasalla. The father understood Manx, but ordinarily spoke English. His grandfather, however, preferred to speak Manx, but understood English nevertheless. As good speakers he mentioned two old women Mrs Wade and Mrs Johnson, both ca. 90 yrs. and living quite near. In addition, he mentioned the tailor Taggart in Grenaby and a shoemaker in the same place William Preston who was over 80; he thought it was useless to go to him, as he would //[14] probably "slam the door in my face if I called on him".

From this man I also heard the first bit of Manx. He was familiar with some ordinary greetings and some other phrases and had often heard about [dˈɔk ən ˈdɔrəs] [*jough yn dorrys* 'drink at the door'], he said, the last drink before one leaves (Ir. *deoch an doruis*). 'How do you do' he repeated to me something that sounded to me at the time like [kænəs ˈtɒ ʃu]

[†] [M's note] near Grenaby is my own comment. There is a Ballabeg close to Arbory which is probably meant here as a bigger place; see the map.

[††] [M's note] approx. 3 km east of Colby on the road to Port Erin.

[9] For details regarding the genealogy of the kings of Man in the Scandinavian period, cf. Broderick 1980.

[*kynys ta shiu*]. 'How are you today' as [kænəs tɒɡə læː] [*kynys t'ou gy (sic) laa*].[10] The answer is [tɒ brou, tɒ brou, kænəs ta (or kæˈnes tɒ) hiːn] [*ta braew, ta braew, kynys ta hene*] 'how's yourself'. 'Time enough yet' (no hurry) he translated as [trei də ˈluɒ][*traa dy liooar*] and 'goodbye' with [iː ˈvɒːi] [*oie vie*] (apparently [in fact is] 'good night'. His knowledge doesn't go any further).

It was this man, however, who //[15] told me about William Kneen as a good spea-ker. This Kneen is over 70 yrs, born in Croit-e-Caley* (somewhat south-west of Colby) where he now lives.

Another speaker is [Bænŏken Regg] [?Ben Kinrade] (so written according to its pronunciation), ca. 76 yrs. probably born in Arbory. But I cannot remember from whom I got this information.

(6) William Kenne [i.e. Kennah] from [Bɑlə Dugən] [Balladuggan] just south of Grenaby, 62 yrs. old; he says he can express himself using ordinary sentences in Manx. A random sample 'I am going to Castletown' he translated correctly. His father and mother both spoke Manx, but also a bit of English. When they spoke to each other they used Manx in preference, and especially when there was something they did not wish the children to understand (this trait I have heard emphasised from many other quarters).

As a good speaker he mentioned [Tomɒs Liːs] [Thomas Leece] (so written according to its pronunciation) from [Kærə ˈMuːᵊr] [Kerroomooar], Grenaby, ca. 70 yrs. old.

//[16] (7) Thomas Taggart turned out to be a jolly old man with a great apostolic beard, and quite a talkative man with a brilliant sense of humour. His pronunciation appears to me to be inarticulate, not only in Manx but also in English (which, however, doesn't say much, because my knowledge of Manx is practically nil). He lisps a little bit; certainly he doesn't have all his teeth, and some of the words appear to stick in his beard. But as far as I can see his Manx is impeccable. He told me that he also knew several Manx songs of the sort you couldn't repeat in public [e.g. HLSM/I: 390-91]. I'm quite sure I can use the man; I have to keep him in mind, but at the moment I have to carry on my round.

//[17] Was offered a splendid tea and afterwards cycled down to Port Erin where I booked in at the Falcon's Nest, where I have written this (15 [i.e. 16] /6/29).

@ conger (eel) is in Manx [ɒstən] [*astan*] or something like ([G.] *eascon*) according to him [see also below].

17th June: Glorious weather. Started walking to the south to get a glimpse of the Calf of Man.

(8) In the village of [Krɛdˊneːⁱʃ] (Cregneish) I had a chat with a 69 yr. old man [kærən] [Karran]. He was from [Hɔu] [Howe]* (on the map Howe) just north of Cregneish, but his father was born in Cregneish. He was able to express himself in Manx, as long as the sentence wasn't too complicated. A sentence like 'I would not have beaten him if he were not a bad man' neither he nor another older man could translate. But a sentence like 'I shall go to the fair tomorrow', 'I went to the fair yesterday, but bought nothing' they both managed without any difficulty. Calf of Man is in //[18] Manx [kɒːlu] [Colloo], they said (orig.

---

[10] i.e. *kynys t'ou jiu* [dʒøu]. The forms *gy laa* would seem to be from English 'today', suggesting that the Manx of M's informant was suspect.

* [M's note] (pr. [kroitikeːli]). [This is a spelling pronunciation of the sort recorded 1989-92 by MPNS (qv). Expected would have been something like [krɔtˊə ˈkeːli/keːli] - GB].

* [M's note on left side] *Haugr* is more like Hofuŏ, a village not situated by the sea.

Kalfr). Also met [Kærəns] [Karran's] somewhat younger brother (55 yrs.), a sailor. His father spoke good Manx; he even preferred it to English and was well able to read it. Both recommended as a good Manx speaker

(9) Harry Kelly, 77 yrs. old, who lives at the bottom of the village on the right hand (south) side of the road. A nice old man with a clear pronunciation. The few sentences I gave him to translate - they were quite simple - he managed without any difficulty. His father spoke practically only Manx. Kelly has a Manx Bible which also [Kærən] has (he's the oldest of them), but none of them wanted to part with it. Taggart in Grenaby also has a Bible from 1819, the 'Manx Soc.' [Vol. 8] dictionary and the quarto edition of the Prayer-Book.

//[19] Kelly knows the names of all the small islands and skerries outside here. A skerry is known as [krɛg ə lˊɛmən] [Creg y Lhieman] ([lˊɛm] 'a jump', he said; Ir. léim), the exact form I couldn't be quite sure of. 'How many horses have you?' is [kwɔd kævəl tæd] [c'woad cabbyl t'ayd?] or something like it. (Correct! Aug. 1930).

Kelly can be used without doubt.

Excellent oysters in a little shop close by the hotel (down at the beach). They are served at the place; cider is also available there. They go really well together.

Peel 17th June:

Before I left Port Erin I went to see Joseph Woodworth, an old fisherman whose name was mentioned to me in Douglas as one who was a good Manx speaker. He was out fishing and his daughter said that that he was not expected back //[20] before 3 o'clock, so I spent the time walking all over the peninsula south of Port Erin.

(10) An old man in the village of [Feʃtər[d]] [Fistard] who was about 70 told me that his father spoke only Manx; his mother, however, spoke both. He was himself only able to manage a simple sentence in Manx. As a good Manx speaker he mentioned (11) Waterson [Watterson] in Glen ['tʃas] [Glenchass] near Howe, ca. 65 yrs. I called on this man; he didn't live more than a few hundred metres away (he told me he had seen me from the window speaking to the other man). Watterson said that the place where he lived was known as [Fisˌtər[d]], but that many called it Glen ['tʃas].

Watterson gave me the impression that he was able to hold a conversation in Manx, although his knowledge of the language probably wasn't //[21] perfect judging from several examples. He gave me several forms of numerals which I noted in a hurry:

[nɛːn] [1]	['nɛn dʒɛg] [11]	['nɛnəsˈfigˊ] [21]	[dɑːgˊ] "40"
[dʒiːs] [2]	[gɑi ɛg] [12]	['dʒiːsəsfigˊ] [22]	[dʒɑiəsdɑːgˊ] "50"
[triː] [3]	['triːdʒɛg] [13]	[dʒɑiəsfigˊ] "30"	[triːfidˊ] "60"
[kɛːr] [4]	[kɛːrdʒɛg] [14]	['nindʒɛgəsˈfigˊ] "31"	[triːfidˊ əsdʒɑi] "70"
[fᵘɛg] "5" (sic)	[fᵘɛgdʒɛg] [15]	[gɑiɛgəsfigˊ] [32]	[kɛːrfidˊ] "80"
[ʃeː] [6]	['ʃeːdʒɛg] [16]	[triːdʒɛgəsfigˊ] [33]	[kɛːrfidˊ əsdʒɑi] "90"
[ʃæːx] [7]	[ʃæːxdʒɛg] [17]	[kɛːr ......] [34]	[kiːd] "100"
[hɑːx] [8]	[hɑːxtʒɛg] [18]	[fᵘɛg .....] [35]	
[niː] [9]	[niːdʒɛg] [19]	[ʃeː ......] [36]	
[dʒɑi] [10]	[figˊ], [fidˊ] "20"	[ʃaxtʃɛgəsfigˊ] [37]	
		[hɑːxt ......] [38]	
		[niːdʒɛg ....] [39]	

Watterson was, however, not quite certain when he exceeded 40. He mentioned 60 as //[22] [triː ˈkiːd] [tree keead] which has to be 300, but he corrected himself later.

'I was born at the Howe' is [vɑ mi ˈrɔgəd ɛgən ɔu] [*va mee ruggit ec yn Howe*], he said. From words he gave me I have noted:

[strɛin] [*stroin*] 'nose'

[mɔnəl] [*mwannal*] 'neck'

[biːl] [*beeal*] 'mouth'

[læu] [*laue*] 'hand'

[kæːb] [*cab*] 'chin'

[kaːs] [*cass*] 'foot' (western [æː])

[klⁱiːʃ] [*cleaysh*] 'ear'.

[suːlʹ] [*sooill*] 'eye' (which he, however, couldn't remember immediately, and it was only after I mentioned the Irish word for it that he did remember it).

[lurəgə] [*lurgey*] 'leg' (*u*-sound perhaps not quite correctly written down).

[riː] [*roih*] '(fore)arm'.

[drⁱiːm] [*dreeym*] 'back'.

Manx speakers one could find at [Bɔləkⁱilˈfɛrikʹ] [Ballakilpheric] and in [Lɛn Gig] [Linguage], both near Colby, says Watterson.

Howe must be Haugr. It suits excellently the farms that are situated //[23] on top of a "hill".

(12) Joseph Woodworth is 75 yrs. old and appears really to know a good deal of Manx. He is a fisherman and his day much depends on the weather. 'I would like to go to Douglas tomorrow' he translates: [lʹak lʹum ðə ˈgɔl gɔs Duːliʃ meːrɑx] [*liack lhiam dy goll gys Doolish mairagh*].[11] 'If he hadn't been a bad man (I *would* not have beaten him) he translates: [mɑnɑx ˈbɛxɛ ə ˈveː drɑxˈgɔnəʹə] [*mannagh beagh eh er ve drogh ghooinney*]. He was willing to talk Manx with me if I came back to Port Erin. As another good speaker he named

(13) [Tɔmɑs ˈKrɛbən] [Thomas Crebbin] in Bradda Village just near Port Erin and he showed me his house from his window. This [Krɛbən] whom I visited before I made my way to Peel made a very good impression. He is supposed to be over //[24] 80 yrs. The sentence 'I would like to go...' he immediately translated like Woodworth. The man seems to have a better grasp on the language than most others. Off his own bat he gave me all the expressions in Manx for wind and weather, the names of stars; (the stars he called [reːltən] [*realtyn*] or something like it, similar to Irish). He was quite willing to speak Irish [i.e. Manx] if I came back to Port Erin.

From Port Erin I followed the road to Douglas into Ballasalla where I took the opportunity of paying a visit to the museum in Rushen Abbey. In the last few years there have been quite a few stone coffins and skeletons dug up, and most of them are assumed to date from early Norman [i.e. Norse] times. The coffin lid appeared to //[25] belong to one of the Norse kings' graves and was very well preserved. It shows two swords in relief and a lot of ornaments, but I am not competent to say whether the type of swords and ornaments date back to the 13th century. The man who is normally the "guide" was not present when I arrived, but another man in the "office" showed me around, and I had to promise him that I would let them know when I visited the place again, so I could meet the man in charge of the excavation. This had to stop because of the war [1914-18], but is soon to be started up again.

---

[11] Here W. has omitted the (past) of the copula before *liack* (< Eng. 'like'), viz. *by*, *b'*, and follows *lhiam* w. the infin. *dy g(h)oll* instead of the expected verb-noun *goll*, viz. *b'liack lhiam goll gys Doolish mairagh*.

From Rushen Abbey back to Four Cross Ways [i.e. Cross Four Ways] where I took the main road northwards to Peel. The steep hill [i.e. Ballamodha Straight] was very difficult because of the heavy load on the back of the bike. On the top near [Bɑˈruːl] [Barrule] Farm (on the Peel road) I met a 53 yr. old man,

(14) William Keggan, who himself doesn't speak Manx. //[26] No one spoke Manx in the district, he said. The only one, if any, had to be Taggart in Grenaby (which he mentioned without being prompted); but his father spoke Manx (and English). He informed me that he had a Bible in Manx from his father. I gave him 2 shillings for it without even having seen it (he would, however, have given it to me for nothing). It turned out to be in a bad state, but I took it all the same. He didn't have (a copy of) the Prayer Book.

(15) A short distance from Peel - ca. 3 miles - I met two men in their 60s. Manx wasn't spoken there, they said. The old ones who once spoke it were all gone. Their parents spoke Manx, they admitted, especially when the children were not to know what was talked about.

In the same direction, said the younger man who was in his 50s, and a short distance from Peel (ca. //[27] 2 miles from there). He mentioned as excellent speakers of Manx Advocate [Henry Percy] Kelly in Douglas and Archdeacon Kewley in Andreas.

Arrived at Peel around 9-00pm and booked into the Marine Hotel just by the beach.

18th June: Mitre Hotel, Kirk Michael (good but expensive; 7/6 bed and breakfast). Before I left Peel I called to see the chemist C[harles] H[enry] Cowley [1874-1944, a *Heitmatarchae-ologe*], who had been recommended to me in Douglas. One cannot say he is a native speaker, although he has often heard Manx spoken in his childhood and has learned a great deal later on. He recommended Caesar Cashen and William Quane, the same as Cubbon and Kneen had mentioned In Douglas.

(16) Quane lives in St. German's Place together with his sister. He is 79 yrs. old (born 1850) and gives the impression of being able to speak Manx quite well. He quite often speaks it with Caesar Cashen at the Market Place. But I notice //[28] he doesn't get much practice, which is understandable. His pronunciation was quite clear. He has, if my memory serves me rightly, 2 copies of the 1819 Bible (Cashen too had at least one copy). Words and expressions which I noted in my conversation with Quane:

[fæˈstər mɑːi] [*fastyr mie*] 'good evening'.

[ˈiː ˈvɑːi] [*oie vie*] 'good night'.

[mɑːri (a deep [ɑ]) mɑːi] or [mɑxri mɑːi] [*moghree mie*] 'good morning' (*moch-éirghe?* CM).

[ən ˈfamən] [*yn famman*] 'the tail'.

[ˈɛlɑn nuː ˈPærⁱkˊ] [Ellan Noo Perick] 'St. Patrick's Island'.

[Pɔrt nə ˈhiːnʃə] [Purt ny Hinshey] 'Peel'.

[hæ ˈdʒɛn mi ˈgɔl gǫs ən ˈkiːdən ˈmɑːri meⁱ vis iː ˈstɛrəmɑx (ˈsterᵊmɑx)] [*cha jean mee goll gys yn keayn moghree my vees ee sterrymagh* 'I will not be going to sea tomorrow if it is stormy'].

(I shan't go, probably the verb *deinim* 'do' CM [yes, as auxiliary of the future - GB]).

[kiːdən] [*keayn*] 'sea' (*cuan*? CM [yes - GB])

'sea' also [ən øːrkə] [*yn aarkey*] (*fairrge*, Irish).

//[29] 12. Nov. to be held a [kruːnɑx] [*cruinnaght*] 'a gathering' in Douglas.

Numerals:

[nɛːn], [dʒiːs], [triː], [kiːr], [kᵘɛg], [ʃeː], [ʃæːx], [hɑːx] (deep [ɑː], [nei], [dʒei], [ˈnendʒigˊ] ([hæ nel im ɑs ...] 'I have not but eleven'; *vel* = [Ir.] *ní fhuil* CM), [dɛịigˊ], [triːdʒigˊ], [kiːr ...], [fid´] 20, [ˈneːnəsfid´] 21, [ˈdʒei əs ˈfid´] 30, [dɑid´], [dɑid´] 40, [ˈdʒeiəsˈdɑid´] 50, [ˈtriːˈfid´] 60, [...... ɛs dʒei] 70, [ˈkiːr fid´] 80, [...... əs dʒei] 90, [kid] 100, [töuˈzɛːn] 1000 (open e̩̯).

Wind:

[tæ n ˈgiːə ɛg ɪn njæːr] [*ta yn geay ec yn niar*] '(the wind is) from the east'.

[................. niːr] [....................*neear*] '......................... west'.

[.................tuːi] [....................*twoaie*] '.........................north'.

[.................dʒæːs] [...................*jiass*] '..........................south'.

[.................njæːr huːi] [........*niar hwoaie*] '....................north-east'.

[.................niːr huːi] [..........*neear hwoaie*] '...................north-west'.

[.................niːr ɛs] [..........*neear ass*] '........................south-west'.

[.................ˈnjæːr ɛs] [..........*niar ass*] '.......................south-east'.

//[30] [ɑ nɛl mi ˈfaːxin ɛs ɔːn rɔˈlɛːg] [*cha nel mee fakin agh un rollage*] 'I do not see but one star'.

[ɑ ˈnɛl ʃu̥] [*cha nel shiu*] (close *u*) 'you are not'.

[tæ mi ˈfaːxin ˈɛru rɔˈlɛgən] [*ta mee fakin earroo rollageyn*] 'I see many stars'.[12]

Fish:

[æːstən] [*astan*] 'conger', pl. [æːstənən] [*astanyn*].

[ˈskɑdɑn] [*scaddan*] (*ɑ*-sound) 'herring'.

[brɛk] [*breck*] 'mackerel'; [rɛn mi ˈkɛnɑx ɛru də brɛk] [*ren mee kiannagh earroo dy breck*] 'I bought a lot of mackerel'.

Birds:

[lɔn] [*lhon*] 'blackbird'.

[trɛslən] [*treshlan*] 'the big thrush'.

[ˈspɪru] [*spirroo*, i.e. *sparroo*] 'sparrow' [*sperriu* is the pl. form - GB].

[ˈɔʒɑg] [*ushag*] 'bird' (all kinds); [ɛru də ˈɔʒɑgən] [*earroo dy ushagyn* 'many birds'].

[ˈɔʒɑg ˈhæpɑx] [*ushag happagh*] 'lark'.

[ən ˈkoːg, k âːg] [*yn cooag*] 'cuckoo'.

Domestic animals:

[kæːbəl] [*cabbyl*] 'horse'; [tæ ˈrɛm kæːbəl ɛgi] [*ta ram cabbil echey*] 'he has many horses'. This word [rɛm] [*ram*] which is used quite a lot is //[31] according to Quane not in any of the dictionaries [not in Kelly or Cregeen (qv) - GB].

[ta ˈrɛm ˈɑ̆lɑx (ɑ-) ĕgi] [*ta ram ollagh echey*] 'he has a lot of cattle'.

[buːə] [*booa*] 'cow'

[mɑːdə] (dark [ɑː]) [*moddey*] 'dog'.

[muk] (Europ. *u*) [*muck*] 'pig'.

[kæt] [*kayt*] 'cat'.

[Lɔx] (a broad *l* clearly heard) [*lugh*] 'mouse'.

[rɑ̆dɑn] ([ɑ] - sound) [*roddan*] 'rat'.

[əˈnɛsɑg] [*yn assag*] 'weasel'.

[tæ ˈdʒiːs buːꜰ ɛki] [*ta jees booa echey*] 'he has (two cows)'.

[oːn buː ˈtækə] [*un booa t'echey*] 'he has got one cow'.

[tæ ˈrɛm ˌɛrgəd ɛka] [*ta ram argid echey*] 'he has got lots of money'.

---

[12] One would expect here something like [...raːm rɔˈlɛːgən] ...*ram rollageyn* 'a lot of, many stars'. The use of *earroo* 'number, a number of' here and elsewhere seems to derive from Eng. idiom.

[............... ɛgən ˈbɛdən ʃɔ (open)] [........ *ec yn bedn shoh*] 'this woman has got lots of money.

[.................ɛk] [...........*eck*] 'she has got...'.

But Quane in fast speech doesn't seem to distinguish between *aige* and *aice*, as in Irish. However, more examples would obviously make clearer the Manx forms.

Varia:

[mɔˈrædən] [*mooarane*] 'much' ([G.] *mórán*).[13]

[ˈɪmədi ʃlei] [*ymmodee sleih*] 'a lot of people'.

[ʃẹː] = Irish *'s eadh* has clearly a close ẹ, but [vɛː] [*va*] 'was' clearly open.

//[32] [kis ˈtɛʂu] or [ˈkɪnəs ˈtɛʂu] [*kynys ta shiu*] 'how are you?' [kɪs] is enough, says Quane.

Together with Quane I walked down to the Market Place and here met Caesar Cashen (ca. 70 yrs.). He remembered Rhys quite well whom he had often spoken to when he came to consult his [Quane's] older brother. Cashen seems to speak quite good Manx. The sentence 'I would like to go to Douglas' he repeated immediately like Woodworth, but Quane used a different expression ([tæ mi buʃ...] [*ta mee bwooish...*] 'I am wishing...') which doesn't appear to be very idiomatic.[14] Both Quane and Cashen were extremely pleasant. It is very likely that with help from them it should be possible to outline the main features of the Peel dialect - phonetic and grammatical.

Without being asked Cashen mentioned as a good speaker 'Quayle the Gardner', the same as I'd heard mentioned in Castletown, and the //[33] same one as Mr Cubbon in a later letter from Castletown had brought to my attention (Quayle's address is Shore Road; he is, writes Cubbon, the "most fluent speaker in this town").

Both Cashen and Quane would like me to come to the annual ceremony at Tynwald on 5th July and to the Manx church service on 7th July at [merðun] [Marown] Church. The Archdeacon in Andreas would no doubt get me a ticket.

Left Peel at 6-00pm in the afternoon and came to Kirk Michael on the western road (the coast road) at 8-00pm. Booked into the Mitre Hotel.

Saw Peel Castle on Patrick's Island in the forenoon before I visited Quane. In the middle of the island (and inside the castle walls) there was a rectangularly built mound which reminds one a little bit of Tynwald. 4 workers were busy excavating it //[34] when I arrived.They had made a cut into the centre and dug all the way down to the bottom layer of sand, but no grave was found - to the disappointment of the archaeologist, who told me that they had got £100 from the English government for these excavations and who had hoped if there was a sensational find it would enable them to get a bigger grant. The workers, however, showed me a whole collection of flint-stones which had been found in the mound, and told me that there had been found two fragments of bronze. All signs are that the mound is prehistoric. Maybe Tynwald is too?[15]

Mrs Corkill, Peel, who Cubbon told me was a good speaker, was not at home, neither was Mrs Taubman (c/o Mr Kennaugh, grocer), Port Erin (she is of course mentioned by [John] Rhys [cf. Rhys 1894]). But first of all it is important that I find an individual whose

---

[13] A literary word, hardly used in the spoken language; cf. HLSM/II: 305, s.v. *mooarane*.

[14] But is nevertheless found (< E. 'wish'), cf. HLSM/II: 53 s.v. *bwooishagh*; also Strachan 1897: 54-58 *cha wishym...* 'I do, will not wish...'. Cregeen (C.21 s.v. *bwooish, bwooishal*) regards this as "an Anglicism".

[15] For a discussion of this name, cf. Broderick 1979b, Fellows-Jensen 1993.

speech I can make daily notes //[35] of, who is patient and co-operative - and women are hardly suitable for that.

19th June: In Kirk Michael one can say that Manx is completely dead. No one was able to name even a single old man around here who spoke it. Vicar Cannan here is supposed to be quite knowledgable in the language, it is said. It is he who is to preach at St. John's on 7th July. But Cashen said that his Manx and his pronunciation appeared to be somewhat strange, and that he didn't understand what he said all the time [yes - GB]. Cannan's father lives near Ballaugh (pr. [Bɑˈlɑf]), "Alpine House".

Kirk Michael lies a few hundred metres from the sea. The old harbour must have lain at the opening of Glen Wyllin (i.e. *Mölledalen* ['the mill dale']), somewhat south-west from the built-up area. It is a place that can give shelter on this part of the coast.

As a joke I carved x ⍓Ⲕ:ⲔⲀRⲣ:ⱤⲀⳡ'⳩⳽'⳩ⲭ⳽⳩:ⲣⲭ⳩R x 'I Karl erected this stone' on a gatepost whose flat even surface was much too tempting. I hope that no one will find it and take it seriously.

[top p. 37 but indicated to be placed here] P.S. Kirk Michael: John [Kisik [Kissack] in [Bale Krink] [Ballachrink] on the Douglas road just on the outskirts of Kirk Michael; he is a man of over 70 yrs. He knows amongst others things the Our Father in Manx - but appears strangely enough not to be able to count to 10. As a good Manx speaker he mentioned Daniel Cain in Little London, 2-3 miles further south on the Douglas road (the place is marked on the map). But the place was too far off my route.

//[36] 20th June: Sulby Glen Hotel.

The carpenter William [Kåːlet] [Corlett], ca. 80 yrs. old from what I've heard was from Kirk Michael. He was not at home when I enquired about him. I did not visit Mrs [Kɔləster] [Collister], the Dolly, near the station at Kirk Michael.

Route 19th June: Kirk Michael-Ballaugh-Jurby-Sulby. At Bishop's Court between Kirk Michael and Ballaugh I met a (17) man around 50. He was born in Ballaugh parish and could count from 1-20 (12: [deidʒɛg]). But apart from that he hadn't a lot more knowledge of Manx.

A good speaker is:

(18) Mr. Gawne, W. Nappin just south of Jurby Church. He is about 70 yrs. old and has quite a good pronunciation. The man gives you the impression of being somewhat older. I bought a nice copy of the Bible (of 1819) from him for 10 shillings. I think Gawne is fairly usable and given some time would be able to squeeze the complete Manx system out of him. He is extremely //[37] willing to co-operate. Here are a couple of words and expressions which I noted (in insufficient phonetic script):

[hɑ rou ə mi hɑ bulə eː na bi e drox dunˈə] [*cha row mee er bwoailley eh [man]nagh bee eh drogh dooinney*] 'I w[oul]d not have beaten him if he were not a bad man'. [kən ˈaʃtou friːl] [*cren aght t'ou freayl*] (dark *k*, 'how are you keeping'. This is Gawne's own) [cf. §4.6.3.- GB] [tɑ mi ˈmɑːï gurǫ ˈmɑːï ɔːt] [*ta mee mie gura mie ayd*] 'I am well thank you'. [mɔːri mɑːï, ˈfɑstə(*sic*) mɑːï, ˈiː ˈvɑï] [*moghree mie, fastyr mie, oie vie* 'good morning, good evening, good night']. [tou gɔl dəˈkirɑx əˈnɑːïl ɑs kɔ ˈgiːl eː] [*t'ou goll dy kerragh yn aile as cur geayl er*] '[you] go to mend (i.e. make up) the fire and put coal ([gil] = [G.] *gual*) on'. [kidən] [*keayn*] 'the sea', [nəˈfɑːkə] [*ny faarkey*] 'the waves' ? CM (seem to remember that the quality of *a*- vowel is rather doubtful). [tæ ən dˈigˈigˊ ɛm maru as ɔ̃ŋlikˊ ɑs tɑ n moir //[38] ɛm blˈɔː fɔːs (ɔː Norsk [åː])] [*ta yn jishig aym marroo as oanluckit, agh ta yn moir aym bio foast*] 'my father is dead and buried, but my mother is still alive'. [hɑi mi dɔsnə 'mör´g´ə lɛʃ raːm (soft [aː]) 'n´ɑlax] [*hie mee dys ny margey lesh ram nollagh*] 'I went to the market with lots of cattle'.[16] [buːə] [*booa* 'cow'], [muc] (Europ. *u*) [*muck* 'pig'], [g´uːï] [*gioee*] 'geese', [tæ raːm g´uï ɛ ɛs tæ nə 'smuː də kaːkən ɛm ɑs raːm 'tɔnɑg] (ducks) [*ta ram gioee er as ta ny smoo dy kiarkyn aym as ram thunnag*] 'he has lots of geese, but I have more ([G.] *ní as mó*) hens and ducks'. ([G.] *cearc*!!). [kaːvəl] [*cabbyl*] 'horse'. [mɔdə], plur. [mɔdi]: [tæ nə 'mɔdi ɛm kal´t´] [*ta ny moddee aym caillt*] 'my dogs are lost', [tæ ən mɔdə ɛm kal´t´] [*ta yn moddey aym caillt*] 'my dog is lost'. But there was a little bit of uncertainty here, and I did not have time to entice the forms out of him during ordinary conversation. [lɔi] [*lheiy*] 'calf', ['kɔlbax] [*colbagh*] 'heifer', [taru] [*tarroo*] 'bull', [tæ raːm taru ɛm] [*ta ram tarroo aym*] 'I have a lot of bulls', [vɛl raːm 'taru ɔuiʃ] [*vel ram tarroo euish?*] 'have you got, etc'.

From there I called on //[39] carpenter Wilfred Waid [Wade], Sandygate, Jurby, who is hardly much of a number. His pronunciation seems quite clear. He can read quite a lot of the Manx Bible (which he has at least one copy of), which one notices in all his conversation. Provided I can manage to work with Gawne, Wade might be useful.

[klɔx 'ɒndin] [*clagh undin*] 'foundation stone'. [finnə ən gɔlæːn] [*finney yn giaullane*] 'ringing the bells' [cf. *kiaullane* 'bell' (C.109), Ir. *ceolán* 'little bell' (Di.186)] (but [finnə] is apparently very incomplete. Wade was extremely dissatisfied with my pronunciation). [dʒiːr´ax] [*jeeragh*] 'straight', opp. [kæm] [*cam*] 'crooked'.

As a good speaker he mentioned to me
(20) John Cain, Ballamoar [a small sketch map is drawn].

//[40] He gave me Cain's age as 80-odd yrs, but he didn't give me the impression of being more than 70-odd. He unfortunately had visitors when I came (one was in a colourful waist-coat who was irritating as he was always asking questions), but I got the impression that he knew a bit of Manx. Nevertheless, he recited *stante pede* a good deal of Manx poems.[17] His pronunciation seemed to be clear and correct. He would probably be of some help if I settled down here to work with Gawne.

As a good speaker he mentioned a young man at the Railway Hotel in Ballaugh, a John [Kɛləp] [Killip], Sulby Glen. The same man was also recommended by Fayle. He lives about 200 metres from the railway station.

(21) Mr. Fayle (pr. [Fɛl], Stauard (my hostess pronounced [Stouərd], a farm-name?) is 76 yrs. old. He lives a few hundred metres from the hotel on a line which goes from it and across to the chapel or a little bit to the right //[41] of it. His father spoke only Manx and spoke in a thick accent when speaking English. His mother spoke both Manx and English. He gives the impression of being quite knowledgable in Manx, but lacks practice. The sentence 'I would not have beaten him, if he hadn't been a bad man' he hesitated for a while; for 'beat' he used [betɑl] [*beatal*] or something like it, which has to be the English word [yes - GB]. He did not know of any Manx for Sulby.[18] *Glen* is here not pronounced with *dn*.[19] Without doubt he would be quite useful, but I think rather difficult to work with.

Up Sulby Glen.
(22) A man of 64 (his name was [Farəkəl (*sic*)] [?Faragher]) born "at the bottom of the glen" said that his father spoke Manx and his grandfather only Manx. But his own knowledge

---

[16] For comment on this see Section 4.6.3.
[17] For texts of these see HLSM/I: 312-15.
[18] There is none - GB; cf. PNIM/III: 468, s.v. *Sulby*.
[19] For preocclusion in Mx. cf. HLSM/III: 28-34.

of the language was rather fragmentary. He recommended as a good speaker Mrs. Craine, ca. 55 yrs. old (whose grandfather spoke only Manx); she lives on the road to Ballaugh (Cool Ben [i.e. Cooilbane] Cottage).

[ɑ 'nɛl 'tɛgɑl 'gᵘɛlˊik´] [*cha nel [mee] toiggal Gailck*] '[I] can't understand Manx', he says; 'naked' is called [ruːʃ] according to him.

Numerals:

[nɛːn] (open), [dʒiːs], [triː], [kᵘɛg], [ʃeː], [ʃax], [hɔx] (*sic*), [nɛi], [dʒɛi], [arəndʒɛg] (*sic*) [*annan jeig*, 11].

[up left side of page] 1933. Mr. Killip, Sulby, has forgottem everything. His parents spoke Manx. 1933: 2/2 took two cylinders with me to Fayle; almost impossible.

//[42] But the man was very careful and told me that his pronunciation was not quite idiomatic.

Lunch in Tholt y Will. From there up a steep road to the south; ca. 1 mile up there is a side-road to the left. It leads to ['Krɛgən] [Creggan] (pl. of [Krɛg]) 'rocks' where (23) Cowley (Mac Ólaibh) lives. He is now 85 yrs. old, almost blind and rather rheumatic, but his pronunciation is quite clear. His memory seems somewhat weakened. Even when he speaks English he hesitates and seems to be rooting for the words. It was impossible for him to remember what 'head' was in Manx. It wasn't until I mentioned the southern Manx [kˊɔːn] [*kione*] that he gave his pronunciation of it as [kˊɔun]. He also had problems differentiating between 'with him' and 'with her', but things like that will hopefully diminish fairly naturally in more connected speech.

Numerals:

[nɛːn], [dʒiːs], [triː] (not esp. palatal), [kɛ̣ːr], [kᵘɛg], [ʃeː], [ʃax] (clearly [a]), [hɑx] (dark [ɑ]), [nei], [dʒei],

//[43] [arəndʒɛg], ['dɛijɛg], ['triːjɛg], ['kɛːrdʒɛg], [kᵘɛgdʒɛg], [ʃeːdʒɛg], [ʃaxdʒɛg], [hɑxdʒɛg], [neidʒɛg], [fidˊ], [nɛnəfidˊ], [dʒeiəsfidˊ], [da-idˊ], [dʒeiəs'dɑ-idˊ], [kɛ̣ːd] (*sic*, clearly, but a very closed /e/).

[dei keːd buə ɛm] [[*ta*] *daa keead booa aym*] 'I have 200 cows'.

[ta/tæ ən tɑi ɛm muːˀ / ən tɑi ɛmis muːˀ] [*ta yn thie aym/aym's mooar*] 'my house is big'.

[kaːbəl ɛm] [*yn cabbyl aym*] 'my horse'.

[" ɛməs] [.......... *aym's*]

[ən kaːbəl ɔs] [*yn cabbyl euish*] 'your horse'.

[tæ ən kaːbəl ɛkə 'maːru] [*ta yn cabbyl echey marroo*] 'his horse is dead'.

[ta ən .... ɛk maru] [*ta yn .... eck marroo*] 'her ....' ?CM cp.p. c [45], line 2 below! (.m

[tæ-i 'fɔrɑxtən ɛgən 'tai ɛm / ɛməs] [*ta ee fuirraghtyn ec yn thie aym / aym's*] 'she is staying in my house', [...ɛgən tɑi ɛin] [...*ec yn thie ain*] '...in our house'.

[tæ-i 'beˀxə...] [*ta ee baghey...*] 'she is living...'

But Cowley cannot really make the difference between 'with him' and 'with her' ([G.] *aige* : *aice*).

[nim 'bulˊəxu -?? 2. per. pn. ? CM - mɛ 'dʒin ʃu 'ʃen] [*neeym bwoailley hoo my jean shiu shen*] 'I shall strike you if you do that'.[20]

---

[20] *bwoailley hoo* palat. form by contamination with the stem [G.] *buail*-, w. *x*- for *h*-; for ex. of *hoo* (G. *thú*), cf. HLSM/II: 340-41 s.v. *oo*; for 2. sg. & pl. for same person, cf. §4.5.1. below.

//[44] [pɪn] [*pian*] 'pain', [tæ 'pɪn (open [i]) əns mə kˊǫun] [*ta pian ayns my kione* 'I have a pain in my head'].

[tæ 'ræm 'ɑlɑx (very deep [ɑ]) ɛkɛ] [*ta ram ollagh echey*] 'he has got a lot of cattle'.

['Krɛgən] [Creggan] 'rocks' [*rectius* 'rocky place', cf. ScG. *creagan*], name of farm.

[Snˊeːl] [*Sniaul*] 'Snaefell', said in Sulby Glen, but on the south side of the mountain they say [Snˊǫːl], [Snjɔːl],

[Baruːl] [Barrule (mtn)],

[Kǫuli] [Cowley] pers. n.

[kræməg] [Crammag] 'snail'

[mɑːdə] [*moddey* 'dog'],

[gei] pl. [gˊɔːi], [ɡjɔːi] [*guiy, gioee*] 'goose, geese'

[famən kaːbəl] [*famman cabbyl*] 'horse's tail'

[kaːθ] 'foot' (*sic*) (Cowley spells it *c + a +th*!!) [?back formation from *cassyn* 'feet', *cassan* 'footpath' - RLT].

As a good speaker Cowley mentioned Christian in [Lörgɪrɛnən] (on the map Lhergyrhenny south-east of Creggan). But he is almost deaf. He also has a brother.

(24) John Christian, carpenter, 84 yrs. old (several years older than the brother). He lives a short distance from the chapel near the Sulby Glen road. [Farəkəl] [?Faragher] also //[45] recommended him and he seems really to be one of the best.

Our Father

[ən 'æːr ein tɔns 'nˊou 'kɑʃərikˊ dərou dəˈɛnim də dʒɛg də rəˈriɛx ən aːrdnˊǫu də rou dʒent ərˊə 'tɑlu mǫːr əs dʒent ǫs 'nˊou 'kǫr dǫȋn narɑn dʒu as dɑx (*sic*) Læː (broad *l*) ɑs lei dǫȋn 'lɔxtən mǫr tɑ 'ʃɪnˊˊlei 'doəsen də dʒɛnu 'lɔxtənə nei as nə 'lɪdʒ ʃin ɔs mi ǫːləs lɪ've; ʃin wɑi ən 'ɔlk sɔn ʃeː 'lɑts ən rəˈriːᵒx ən fuːər ɑs ən 'lǫːr (*sic*) sɔn dəˈbrɛx as də 'brɛx 'ɛːˈmeːn].

[pɛːn nəs mə xˊɔun] [*pian ayns my chione*] 'a pain in my head'.

[maː dˊɛgəˈsɔː (short for dʒɛgə ?), tʃötˢesǫː] in here) [*manna jig oo aynshoh, cheet aynshoh*] 'if you don't come here' [i.e. *mannagh jig oo aynshoh* or (w. aux.) *mannagh jean oo cheet aynshoh* (cf. HLSM/I: 103-04) - GB].

[tæ dæː kaːbəl ɛgə 'ʃɔː] [*ta daa cabbyl echey shoh*] 'he has two horses'.

[ta 'ram 'kabəlˊ (*sic*) ɛm] [*ta ram cabbil aym*] 'I have lots of horses'.

[ən 'vɛːn ʃɔː] [*yn ven shoh*] 'this woman'.

[ta raːm öˊᶠgəd ɛk] [*ta ram argid eck*] 'she has got lots of money'. He uses [ɛk] quite naturally here.

//[46] [ən ɛːr vᵘiː] [*yn airh vwee*] 'the yellow gold' (Chr. pronounces 'yellow' [jalou]).[21]

21st June: Ramsey, Saddle Hotel. I called on Mr. Killip before I left Sulby. He lives on the Ballaugh road a couple of hundred metres from Sulby railway station. He turned out to be identical with a man I had stopped the previous night and asked directions to the Sulby Glen Hotel. The man was quite sure of himself and spoke a little about his knowledge of Manx, which in fact was deficient. He couldn't even recite the Our Father and naturally got stuck rather quickly when I gave him the ordinary test sentences. He had an 1819 Bible, a Manx

---

[21] If M's phonetic rendering is to be relied upon, it is clear that Christian had access to more traditional Manx. He has a) palatal velar fricative [xˊ] after *my* 'my' in *my chione* 'my head' and b) the attenuated pl. form (w. palatalisation) in *ram cabbil* 'a lot of horses', viz. [kabəlˊ], G. *capuill*.

Soc. dictionary together with an old edition of the Old Testament in the same volume (of the same thickness as the 1819 Bible). He wouldn't give away the dictionary.

['beːn 'vɑnᵃnᵃx] [ben Vanninagh] 'a Manx woman'.

['mɑnᵃnᵃx] [Manninagh] 'a Manxman'.

//[47] Left Sulby in the afternoon to go to Andreas, which appeared to be an excellent starting point for my excursion to the flat northerly part of the island. I met a young man a couple of miles from Andreas. He didn't know of any Manx speakers in the district. He had heard Manx in his childhood, he told me, and the old ones spoke it when it was something they didn't want the younger ones to understand. The hotel in Andreas (Grosvenor) was fully booked, therefore I continued to Ramsey, Saddle Hotel, Market Place. The cafe was full of a jolly party of solely young people from Douglas; 7-8 young girls were standing and kissing a young man of 17 summers on the mouth, eyes, neck. He received all these passionate advances with an aloof expression and downcast eyes.

(26) Thomas Christian whom I visited today lives in College Street quite near the hotel. He is an excellent old man, a Nordic type through and through. Here I seem finally to have found the man to work with. His pronunciation is clear; //[48] the man is intelligent, patient, and understands that he can be of great service to scholarship by making himself available. He answers small test examples quickly and idiomatically. He has an 1819 Bible and an old Hymnbook* probably from the 18th century. I cycled to Maughold and took a taxi to Douglas and returned here later. I can investigate the northern part of the country from Ramsey.

22nd June: Ramsey, Saddle Hotel. Left Ramsey yesterday around 2-00pm. Made for Douglas which I reached just before 8-00pm just in time to get my letters and papers at the post office.

Stopped at Maughold Church to have a look at the Celtic cross and the runic crosses which are collected under a half-roof in the churchyard. This collection is extremely interesting. The interpretation of no. 144 which is given on the plaque is hardly correct. All the runes //[49] appear to be quite clear:

I seem to see two dots here

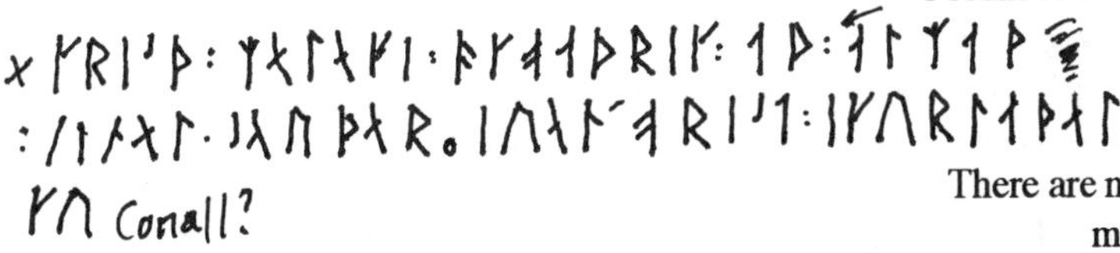

ᚷ ᚠᚱᛁ'ᚦ : �ᚴᛅᚠᛁ · ᛒᚱᚨᛁᚦᚱᛁᚴ᛬ ᛁᚦ᛬ᛏᛁ ᚤᛁ ᚦ

᛬ᛁᛏᚨᛏ · ᛃᚴᚿ ᛒᚴᚱᵒ ᛁᚿᛅᚠᚨ ᚱᛁ'ᛏ᛬ᛁᚠᚿᚱᛗᚦᚨᛏ

ᚠᚿ Conall?

There are no traces of any more runes here.

On cross no. 142 there are some inscribed runes which are smaller and which are not mentioned on the plaque. One of them quite clearly gives a man's name - guðr (ᛁᛁᚠᚿᛒᚱ) another ᚿᚠᛁᛚᛏ Lifilt, probably ᛚᛁᚠ a woman's name. The ᛚᛁᚠ is followed by a missing piece. I wonder if Lifhild was written there originally? A third inscription is difficult to see. I seem to see ᚿᚦᚱᛁ (but it's quite uncertain).

(27) A digger at the churchyard gave me Tom ['Luːni] [Looney] ca. 75 yrs. as one who spoke Manx. He lives quite close to the churchyard. He was not at home when I came, but

---

* [M's note up left side of page] Kneen in Douglas has a copy of it.

his brother's son said he had only heard "an odd word of Manx" from him. So he can probably be erased from my //[50] list of Manx speakers.

In Ballaskeig Beg [Baləskeːg bɛg] on the road from Maughold to Ballaglass I met a man of 74 yrs. with the well-known (28) name [Mɒləkriːs] [Mylchreest]. His father and mother spoke only Manx. He appeared to have a good grasp of the language. "Good subject" my notes tell me. Words and expressions from him:

['kʹɔːn] [kione] 'head', [kæːs] [cass] foot'.

[ɛrə 'mʉlʹən] [er y ?meeillyn] 'upon your knees' (your is of course wrong [as is 'knees'; it is not certain what [milʹən] is -GB]),

[ta mi smaːᵊxin də gɔl də Duːliʃ meːrᵃx] [ta mee smooinaghtyn dy goll dy Doolish mairagh] 'I'm thinking to..[i.e. of going to Douglas tomorrow]'.

[mɒnɒx hu dʒɛnu ʃɛdən i̯ou vi 'gɔtʹ] [mannagh [jean] oo jannoo shen yiow ve goit] '[if you do not do that] she will be talk' (I think he says) [in fact '...you will be 'took', i.e. 'taken'; this sentences as it stands is a nonsense, and probably a clear articulation was not forthcoming - GB].

[tæ dæː buːə ɛgən dᵘꞮnə ʃɛdən] [ta daa booa ec yn dooinney shen 'that man has two cows'].

[nɛːn buːə ɛgən bɛdn ʃɛdən] [nane booa ec yn ben shen 'that woman [has] one cow'].

[tæ nɛːn buːə ɛk] (feminine) [ta nane booa eck 'she has one cow'].[22]

[Mɒləkriːs] [Mylchreest] lives alone; his wife has a bed and breakfast place in Douglas. He seems to be excellent and I think it would be useful to have a chat with him later on when I've got //[51] a better grasp of the language.

(29) As a Manx speaker he gave me a Robert ['Djɔkən] [Joughin], Dhoon Church, a man over 70; but I didn't manage to get a hold of him.

My next victim was

(30) James Kewley ([kʹuːli]), 79 yrs. old (b. 1850) the youngest and only surviving one of 10 brothers. Born in [Lizeːr] [Lezayre], but brought up in Lonan parish (south of Laxey). He had also lived for some time in Maughold. Met him on the island somewhat south of Laxey and had a long chat with him. He certainly knows a lot of Manx.

[gɔu] [gow [i.e. dow]] 'bullock' ([margin] damh CM. 1933).

['kɔlbɒx] [colbagh] 'heifer',

[gei], [gʹɔʹꞮ] [guiy, gioee] 'goose, geese'

[mɒk] [muck 'pig'], but [dæː vɒk] [daa vuck] 'two pigs', [triː mɒgən] [tree muckyn 'three pigs'] (sic. Also I seem to remember hearing a g where I expected a k. Was it a mistake?) [No. - GB].

[lei] [lheiy] 'calf', [tæ dæː vuːᵊ ɛgə] [ta daa vooa echey] 'he has two cows' (my notes have correctly [vuːᵊr]) [w. Eng. svarabhakti r in hiatus? - RLT]

[kɛnəs tɔu] [kynys t'ou] 'how are you?'

[ei vɒːi] [oie vie] ([ei] sic).

[in bottom right-hand corner] (I have often heard these forms later in different places, such as Kennah, Baile Cleary [Ballacleary], and also further south on the island. CM Aug. 1930).

//[52] He recited some verses he had heard from an older brother:

[kɛn sörtʃ də rɛk də hɒi krɔg ʒɛk	[cre'n sorch dy wreck dy hie chrog Jack
ən öröxə mɛx ɔn gʹɔurə	yn orraghey magh un geurey

---

[22] In contrast to Christian above Mylechreest's Manx shows an absence of lenition: daa booa for daa vooa 'two cows', nane booa for nane vooa 'one cow', etc.

vi dʒɛnt mə gæːïˡ ɔs kˊuːn ə væːïˡ   *v'eh jeant myr gaih erskyn y vaie*
sɔn foːsi ənsə tɔurə] (in the summer)   *son phoosee ayns y tourey*].

[margin] I do not understand this CM 1933.

['what sort of a wreck of a house did Jack build during one winter. It was built as a folly (lit. 'toy') above the bay for a wedding in the summer']²³

There were several verses, but I only remember this one. A nice man and quite informative.

Booked into the British Hotel in Douglas. Today I bought a couple of old books amongst others, a Bible that was in bad condition and a Manx prayerbook, or something like it, but the beginning of the book was missing. I called on Kneen whom I met later on in the afternoon. He gave me his manuscript of his devotions in Manx which is not obtainable any longer from the bookshops. Kneen has a small sweetshop in Douglas. He sits in a small room at the back of the shop, which has to do as his dining room, and makes sugar-//[53] sticks (Manx rock). The man who ought to be a professor in Manx at a university. Life is very hard for some.

23rd June (Sunday): Went out to look for lodgings. I'll probably book into the Bridge Inn, 30s. a week (bed and breakfast).

25th June: Had my first lesson with Christian today. Manx is going to be a complicated study when it comes to phonetics. It is not possible at this stage to make detailed phonetic notes. I'll have to work my way into the language first and then check details later on when my ear is more attuned to it. The phonetic system is much different from Irish, and I will have to orientate myself from scratch.

31st [*sic*] June: Have now worked with Christian for appr. a week (from ca. 10-12 and from 2-4), and beginning //[54] to get the hang of the system. Chr. without doubt knows a lot of Manx. But it is quite clear that even he is a long time without practice at speaking the language. He often neglects the ordinary rules of mutation (aspiration [i.e. lenition], eclipsis), but maybe that is part of the development of the dialect he is speaking [yes, of the language as a whole - RLT/GB].

29th June: Saturday afternoon I went to see Christian* in order to meet the headmaster at one of the secondary schools in Ramsey, Mr. Killey, who is very interested in Manx. We practised by reading chapters of the Old and New Testaments and Killey also sang a couple of songs in Manx, which are very reminiscent of the Irish. His pronunciation is much affected by his English. Gave me the loan of Edmund Goodwin's *Lessoonyn ayns Chengey ny Mayrey Ellan Vannin*, Douglas (S.K. Broadbent & Co. Ltd, Printers, Examiner Office, Victoria Street) 1901. It appears to be an excellent book, which I have //[55] to get. Killey is a good friend of Norway. He visited the western part of the country about 30 yrs. ago; an excellent photograph of one of the fjords hangs in his sitting room.

Sunday in Wesleyan Chapel with Christian. A farmer from the neighbourhood spoke simply and appealingly about the lesson of that day. Later in the afternoon I went to Jurby Church to have a look at some of the runic crosses. But the cross that interested me most

---

²³ This is a satirical song on the building of the Castle Mona Hotel on Douglas Promenade in 1804, formerly the residence of John Murray, Fourth Duke of Athol and Governor of Man (1793-1830). For a fuller text (4 stanzas) see Broderick 1982c: 11-12.

* [M's note up left side] Christian died in 1930(31?) [in fact Feb. 1930 - GB]. Killey gave a graveside oration in Manx, - and died a short while after (1931?) of lung cancer [1933] [CM's square brackets - GB].

(the one M[agnus] O[lsen] thinks has the name *Fair Tur* **) was not there. Inside the church wall lies what appears to be an old gravemound, and 1 km. or so north of the church a big tumulus is seen against the sky.

(31) On the Jurby Road some miles or so from Ramsey I had a chat with John Joseph Corrin (['Kɔrən]), 71 yrs. old, born in Ballaugh parish in [Bɑlə Krɔʃə] [Ballacroshey], now lives in Jurby in [Bɑlə'Kɔri] [Ballacurry] (on Jurby Road). Fifty years ago when he //[56] came to Djurby [Jurby] Manx was in extensive use. He appears to have quite some proficiency in spoken Manx. The test sentence 'if you don't come at once, I shall beat you' he managed quite well (with the exception of 'at once' which he did not translate); the weekdays he rattled off at a surprising rate (Christian got stuck on 'Tuesday', which can be attributed to his lack of memory in general. Even in English he seemed sometimes to hesitate). 'sickle' he translated as ['kɔrɑn] [*corran*]. I'll have to call on him later. He is more than willing to receive me again. North of Jurby Church I got some more information from S[ɑ:]tfield [Sartfield] farm from a man in his 50s. He gave me as a good Manx speaker
//[57] (32) John [Se:l] (i.e. Sayle) in [Bɑlə'tɔːnə] [Ballathona] about 3 miles north of Jurby, North Road (Shore-road), ca. 70-80 yrs. old. Furthermore

(33) Mr. Kneen, Lane [i.e. Lhen]²⁴ (a short distance from S[ɑ:]tfield and

(34) Mrs. Killip (also in Lhen judging from my notes). Her husband died more than 40 yrs. ago. She is different from the Mrs. Killip I met in Sulby whose husband is still alive. [The] World Manx Association are sending me an invitation to the 19th annual gathering at the Nunnery near Douglas on Tynwald Day, the Manx National Day. The committee wants me to make a speech, which I would like to do, if not... It is difficult for an obscure professor from Oslo to travel unnoticed. A newspaper in Ramsey had a note about my visit to the island. It is probably taken from a paper in Douglas.
//[58] Letter from Gwynne²⁵ who invites me to Ireland. If I go over there it is above all to see him again.

Knight of the Arslegion [*Chevalier de la Legion d'Honneur*] "for services rendered to French language and culture". The beginning is not to my taste. Orders on the whole are an abomination. But I'm indifferent to the whole affair and my French colleagues would no doubt be offended if I declined to receive it. So let me in God's name keep it - in silence.

8th July: Arrived too late at Tynwald on 5th July. The service had been held and the laws read when I arrived around 12-00. The national gathering at the Nunnery was in many ways very interesting. But we didn't hear a word of Manx with the exception of a telegram from the London branch of the World Manx Association, which the author //[59] read out. But it is rather significant that of the work that is going on to save whatever can be saved of the old traditions here on the island, only one speaker, Archdeacon Kewley from Andreas, said in a spirited speech that Manx should be brought back at least as a subject for studies, and asked and exhorted them all to hand over to the Museum all old things of value. All the other

---

** [M's note up left side] PS. Feb. 1930 (Oslo) the word is to be found on the north wall of the church, but *fairþur* and the following words are knocked off.

²⁴ This turned out to be John Kneen (the Gaaue; 1852-1958, b. St. Jude's, Kirk Andreas) recorded later by IFC, MM, YCG, as well as interviewed by Carmody, Wagner, and Jackson; cf. HLSM/I: 230-69). Marstrander apparently did not visit Kneen.

²⁵ Almost certainly E. J. Gwynne, by then Provost of Trinity College Dublin. He is known for his work and notes on Irish mss, incl. a catalogue of Irish mss. in Trinity College Dublin and the *Metrical Dindshenchas*.

speeches seemed more about telling jokes and suggestive stories. It is here about the same as in Dublin. There is a lack of organisation; everything seems to be going its own way. Had a chat with the archdeacon who seemed a nice and pleasant man. Met Cubbon (Kneen and Kermode were in Liverpool to receive an MA degree) and went to his place for tea. Long discussion about *treen* (Scandinavian or Celtic?). He suddenly appeared yesterday at Christian's and we had decided Wednesday to see some fat sheep at Billown, near Ballabeg, on Mr. T. G. Moore's estate.

//[60] Yesterday went on a long tour with Mr. Killey to Cronc Noo (or Now) [i.e. Cronk yn Howe], a burial mound a short distance from Ramsey, which had been excavated a short time ago[26] and where they had found a piece of amber which was declared by the British Museum to be Scandinavian. The grave lies on a hill, the ground below is known in Manx as 'Lough'.[27] so it was probably under water years ago. In the grave they had found a stone with some figures on, which is now in the Museum in Douglas. Some of the other stones were probably later taken and used as gateposts. We examined several of them, but there was nothing on any of them.

11th July: With Cubbon to Billown, near Ballabeg. The owner T. G. Moore drove us himself to Skibrich [i.e. Skibrick] (the mound here has the shape of an upturned boat [small drawing given], so it is not //[61] impossible that the name at least contains the word *skip* as Kneen thinks. Investigated several "standing stones" and "white stones" on the side of a small pond. The stone circle near the houses is very interesting. It is very near a circle and its diameter is about 10 metres which almost without exception is formed of round white blocks of stone, which at least in one place seem to form a burial-chamber (without a roof). The two stones in the middle were without doubt in early times rolled down from a somewhat higher plateau where two round white stones are standing and seem to have formed a chamber together with these. The inside of the circle was completely free of obstruction. In this area they found a whole lot of roughly cut flint, and in addition to that a finely cut piece of flint in the shape I have drawn [thumbnail sketch given]. Furthermore, a few fragments of pottery had been found. Consequently we are dealing here //[62] with an old monument from the Neolithic period or the Bronze Age. Here we are without doubt dealing with a burial place or an old centre of culture - the white stones without doubt have their own meaning and are unconnected with the few isolated stones in the bottom layer.

Mrs. Moore was divinely beautiful, but we saw little of her.

An evening meal at Cubbon's in Douglas. Kneen was asked, but couldn't come. He [Cubbon] gave me a couple of Manx books. As a good Manx speaker he mentioned

(35) Mr. J. Kelly, Laxey, on the Ramsey side of the glen and at the mines. He is over 80 yrs. old. The information is Cubbon's.

15th July: In Douglas yesterday to see the tailor Larsen (Danish and married here). //[63] Visited Kneen who was ill. Kneen has made the same observations as me, that the mutations are not adhered to and that there is a tendency to cut them out. Also the genitive forms are replaced by the nominative. As a good Manx speaker in Port Erin he mentioned

(36) Edmond Maddrell, a tailor, ca. 80 yrs. old, Athol Park. Invited to lunch at the Rotary Club, Douglas, Wednesday 17th July by T. R. Radcliffe, editor of the *Examiner*, Douglas.

---

[26] It was excavated by J. R. Bruce and Wm. Cubbon in 1928; cf. Bruce & Cubbon 1930 & 1931.
[27] i.e. Lough Mollow. For a discussion of this name, cf. PNIM/III: 429-30, s.v. *Lough Mollow*.

8th Sept: Will travel tomorrow morning to Douglas and afterwards on the 4-30pm boat to Liverpool-Newcastle-Oslo ("Bessheim").

I am quite satisfied with my stay here. The material I have collected will without doubt have significant value when Celtic speech has completely disappeared from the island in 5-10 yrs. time, even though the phonetic interpretations on several points are naturally only tentative.

//[64] I have really got the hang of Manx and I hope that when I return next year I can start on the southern dialect, which in my opinion differs to a significantly greater degree than is generally throught from that in the northern part of the island.

My plan for next summer is: to investigate the southern dialect and to excavate and old *kol* [i.e. *keeill*] in a very Norse district, and perhaps find a few new runic crosses. Hopefully I will be able to get a little bit of financial help for this purpose from some fund in Norway.

We ought to get Kneen a grant for two years so that he can continue recording the place-names. This work has to be done within the next few years, because it would not be possible to obtain the Celtic pronunciation in a few years' time. For some of the places //[65] a phonetic notation is probably now already impossible.

Cubbon, Kneen, and Killey are excellent types and good friends. Had Killey to dinner last night in the Prince of Wales Hotel. Cubbon has got a whole pile of Manx literature for me, and has furthermore been a great help to me. He also found an old missing piece of a runic stone from Jurby (the Odin's Stone) which completely refutes a certain *fairthur* and proves that the readings I suggested in *Révue Celtique* some 10-15 years ago are correct. I think I have a good grip on the writing on the cross slab found earlier from Bride.

Prof. [Alan] Maw[e]r[28] from Liverpool (from Jan. London) is a pleasant and affable man. Have visited him twice in Ballasalla where he has rented a small picturesque house //[66] for the summer. But he is tied to old ways of doing things. I suggested to him that he should try to get Kneen a scholarship, but I have some doubts that he would do anything in that direction. From the English Historical Musuem he is allocated £150 yearly.

A young student from Trinity College, [?Cosslett] Quin, has visited me several times at the Bridge Inn. He is intelligent, interesting, and has wide views. He is very interested in Irish, will spend some weeks next year in an Irish speaking area in Donegal - but will they ever get off the ground in Ireland? I gave him all the help I could.

My trip to Ireland will have to wait until next year.[29]
//[67]

1930

On 'Bessheim" to Newcastle on one of the first days in August. Stopped for some days in London (Euston and Gower Hotels). Met Flower who was talking about sending my god-

---

[28] Professor Alan Mawer was Hon. Secretary of the English Place-Name Society and Director of the Survey of English Place-Names.

[29] M was apparently *persona non grata* in Ireland owing to difficulties with Irish sholars concerning the RIA Contributions; M. edited the first fascicle D-*degóir* which came out in 1913. The next fascicle to appear was E, edited by Maud Joynt and Eleanor Knott, published in 1932. The Contributions were completed in 1976. As an act of reconciliation M. was invited by Irish scholars to take part in the first Congress of Celtic Studies held in Dublin in 1959. This was apparently his first visit back in Ireland since his departure in 1913. Marstrander died on 23.12.1965, aged 83 years.

daughter to Oslo in order to perfect her in comparative linguistics. He appears to have plans to get her in as Fraser's successor in Oxford.

Through Liverpool to Douglas. Cubbon so nice as always. Kneen married; met them at Cubbon's one evening for tea. Mrs. Kneen did not impress me much. Heard nothing from Kneen, although I have about 10-12 days left in Man. Now working with Taggart in Grenaby. He is a bit of a disappointment; he's very overrated. He has forgotten most of his Manx; he does not remember the most ordinary of words like 'shoulder', 'knee', etc, and this is probably not because of his //[68] great age. I will probably give him up shortly.

Edward Kennah from Ballacleary, a short distnace from Grenaby, is better. The man is from the Port Erin area. He is an absolutely trustworthy man. But he doesn't speak Manx with ease.

The best is Jos. Woodworth, Port Erin, with whom I am now writing down the story of Joseph. He is clear and certain, and his Manx seems to be with him something more than just memories.

A letter from W. Cubbon on 14th Aug. in which he sends the following document [in English]:

A5

14th August 1930.

Sir,

I am directed by the Manx Museum and Ancient Monument Trustees //[69] to request the favour of an Advance on Imprest of £20 (twenty pounds) in accordance with the following resolution of the Ancient Monuments Committee, 12th August 1930.

145. 'Resolved, that while Professor Marstrander of Oslo University is on the Island, an examination of the Knocksharry tumulus be undertaken on behalf of the Museum, and that in order to pay for the labour in connection therewith, the Treasurer of the Isle of Man be requested to grant an Advance on Imprest of a sum not exceeding twenty pounds".

I am, Sir,
Your obedient servant,
W.C.
Secretary.

The Treasurer of the Isle of Man
Government Office
ISLE OF MAN

//[70] Port Erin 28/8/30. Moved from Old Abbey Hotel today. Gave the burnt Bible I found in the chimney in Grenaby to Mr. and Mrs. Witham (the owners of the hotel). The poor man has been confined to bed for two years, and seems to think that this Bible will bring him luck.

Taggart is a very difficult subject to put it mildly. First of all he's deaf and a continuous conversation with him is almost impossible. His memory is also weakened to a considerable degree. All his information will have to be checked and used with the greatest care. False associations with synonyms or similar sounding English or Manx words would often lead him to produce completely mad forms, such as [æː-kəl] 'lime-kiln' (under the influence of Eng. 'kiln' for [iːl] = [G.] aoil!!). I'll have to arrange some phonetic system //[71] of what he has explained. Yesterday we were shouting for a full 41/2 hours, which I'm sure could be heard all over the parish - and we were both completely knackered when we were finished.

Woodw. sick today; for that reason I took a trip to Cregneish and met old Kelly. He makes a very good impression. He grew up in a home where the parents spoke Manx to each other. He has always understood Manx himself - even as a small boy he was able to speak a little. He only achieved complete mastery of the language when, as with Woodw, he went fishing with the older men when he was around 15 yrs. old. It was most interesting to observe that K. did not have a broad fronted *l*, as in *laa* 'day'.[30] There is a question here whether we are up against a change in the old Manx dialect in the Port Erin district, or the loss of this feature could be that W. and K. grew up with English as their main language. The problem will have to be solved. It is of considerable general interest.

Station Hotel (proprietor Chadwick) seems //[72] OK. For the room and breakfast and 1 meal I pay 71/2 shillings, which is quite reasonable.

30/8. Took a trip to Cregneish yesterday evening and paid a visit to Harry Kelly. Arranged to meet him tomorrow morning at 9 o'clock and have just arrived back from my first session with him. He will be 79 next year. He appears to have an extraordinarily good knowledge of Manx. I've still not been able to get to know him well at all. but it would not surprise me that of all the speakers I have met he is the one who speaks best and most idiomatically. Made him tell me his "Life" in English; I'll take it down in Manx tomorrow morning about 9 o'clock. Kelly is supposed to be very unapproachable - a fishmonger who passed by was surprised that I ever got Kelly to speak Manx.

//[73] The English dialect on Man is very interesting and will have to be investigated. For 'Chasms' Woodw. says [kæːsəms] (placename). The first part of a diphthong which is so common in Manx, also in Anglo-Manx, is longer. I heard from a passer-by in Ballasalla: [taːim] 'time', ['laːisəns] 'licence'.

1/9/30. My impression of Kelly is confirmed. He appears to be an excellent speaker considering the position of Manx. I noted down his *vita* yesterday, which contained many interesting pieces of information about manners and customs in the old days. But he is a difficult man to handle. When I called in this morning at 9 o'clock as we had agreed he had no time to spare. I'll have to come to a permanent arrangement with him.

Called on Thomas Crebbin in Bradda Village today, and am going to meet him tomorrow or the day after tomorrow. He appears to have a clear pronunciation. A palatal *n* came very clearly from him. He was born in //[74] Port Erin (half way between P. Er. and Bradda Village). Like his father and grandfather he has spoken Manx from early childhood. He appears to pronounce *laa* 'day' with a broad fronted *l*. In other words Woodw. and Kelly's pronunciation is flavoured by the dialect from which they learned Manx. Odd words: [tʃeb] 'offer' (so and so much for an article), [nˊaːr] 'east', [nˊˊiːr] 'west' [i.e. from the E, W], [dʒaːs] 'south' [kˊeːʳ] 'four', etc.

Koht's article in *Tid. Tegn* of the 23rd Aug. on the Manx language came just in time and will most likely turn out to be excellent support for further work.[31]

20/9. Finished off my work in Grenaby and P[ort] E[rin]. Kelly is an excellent subject and I must come back another year and make further use of him. Woodw. is reliable, but his Manx does not seem to be as genuine (vernacular) as Kelly's or //[75] Crebbin's. The latter is the one I can probably do nothing much with, because he is quite ill. It is rather doubtful

---

[30] For comment on Kelly's Ls see Section 3.5.2.

[31] Most of the linguistic periodicals were then best known by the name of their current editor, not their proper titles. In this case probably *Tidsskrift Tegner*.

whether I will find him alive in another year. He has forgotten the most part of his Manx, but the little he has gives the same genuine impression as Kelly's.

I will have to get hold of Maddrell before I leave and will have to throw some light on Crebbin's [palatal] [l] (same as Kelly's?). I'll also have to arrange it that I get a few days in Peel, in other words tomorrow Sunday: Taggart; Monday: Woodw. (for the last time) and Maddrell; Tuesday and Wednesday: Peel; Thursday: farewell to Douglas; Friday to Liverpool.

Station Hotel good and reasonable.

30/9/30. Home again. Finished the work with Kelly and Woodworth. Visited Crebbin in Bradda Village and got all the 32 points of the compass from him. T. Maddrell in Glenchass was an //[76] uncongenial man between 70 and 80 and did not appear to be much worthwhile as a subject. He told me himself that he could not speak Manx before he was 18, when from that time he learned it from the old people. But he couldn't keep up a conversation nor speak it fluently. The same evening paid a visit to Percy Kelly the Manx teacher, T. Crebbin at Four Roads near Port Erin. He is an old man of around 80. His knowledge of Manx is rather limited from several angles. I did not miss much by not visiting him earlier.

//[77] Worked in Peel with Quane Wednesday afternoon and Thursday morning and managed to get some fairly good material during the short time. Characteristic of Peel Manx is amongst other things the *a*-sounds. I hope to get the opportunity to come back to Peel to spend a week or two another year.

Thursday afternoon in Douglas; Cubbon, Oates, Quilliam, Kneen, and a pupil of his, a rather young congenial man. Cubbon gave me his map of treen-names which turned out to be extremely useful. He deserves to get an award for his work from Norway.

Saturday 27th: from Newcastle on Bessheim; travelled with Dr. Christiansen whom I met on the station in Liverpool. Terrible weather on //[78] the coast of England, but calm sea on the Norwegian coast and up the Oslo Fjord.

Port Erin 29th Jan. 1933

1933

Phonographic Recordings

From Oslo Saturday 12 o'clock 7th Jan. (Vippetangen) on "Blendheim". Good crossing. Pibbe with us, a little seasick at the beginning, but managed better that I did later. One of the group was Hans Kittelsen;[32] played bridge on board with two Norwegian ladies, Misses Glörsun and Kristiansen. The first one continued with us to London, but the other one remained with Kittelsen in Newcastle to get a later train south. Your man Hans turned out to be a bit of a womaniser.

//[79] London, Euston Station Hotel 1st night; 15s. for a room only, too expensive. Moved over to the Gower Hotel in Euston Road, 10s. for a double room and breakfast for the two of us.

Went to the zoo with Pibbe who was very interested. Got myself kitted up in Rim[m]el and Alsop's - I really needed it. To Liverpool 14th Jan. Adelphi was looking for 18s. for room only. A policeman recommended a boarding house near the station, At-lantic Hotel (ca. 12s. B & B), a sleasy place, will probably never come here again.

Monday at 10-45am on the "Peel Castle" to Douglas, excellent weather. Kneen on the pier. Tea at Cubbon's Wednesday, later on with Kneen. Tea with the Deputy Governor,

---

[32] An entertainer and celebrity in Norway of the period, acc. to Knut Janson.

Deemster La Mothe, a pleasant man. He lives //[80] a little way out of Douglas (Balla na Brooie [Ballabrooie]) on the road to Braddan if I remember correctly - with his daughter Mrs. McGay (?) [?McGee]. Asked me to bring Pibbe the next time I came back to Douglas.

Cubbon got ca. 10-11 copies of my book [viz. Marstrander 1932]. They were given (with a dedication) to:

Dep. Gov. La Mothe	Canon Quine
Deemster Farrant	Mr [P. G.] Ralfe
Att. Gen. [R. B.] Moore	Rev. [E. H.] Stenning
Archdeacon Cowley [?Kewley]	

Prideaux, postmaster in Port Erin, got one later on. The book has been well received here, and has been mentioned in the press. There was a long article yesterday in the Manx *Examiner* (?).[33]

When in London I had a meeting with the general manager of the Gramophone Company. //[81] He was a helpful young man who gave me the impression of being very interested in the project. He promises to be available the moment I arrive in London with Harry Kelly.

Brought with me part 1 of the phonographic recordings which Selmer and Leip had used in America. Selmer pointed out that there was something wrong with the stylus, and that this was a great handicap here. It is a pity, because at least 1/5 of the wax cylinder cannot be used, and the whole thing could have been easily fixed by changing the stylus only. It has to be done as soon as I get back home. Apart from that the recording apparatus is functioning well. I cannot use it when the temperature is less than 20 degrees which is what Selmer prefers. It is cold here and practically impossible to get the temperature up in the rooms. I tried to get in contact with Kelly on 24th Jan; walked over the hill from Port Erin (Station Hotel as in 1930), and started the recordings here in the hotel on 25th. My impression is that the recordings are rather uneven. Kelly's voice is somewhat hoarse, //[82] is a bit squeaky and not very sonorous, but the result improves when he speaks relatively softly and has his mouth well close to the horn. Have worked with him for four days now; will probably finish tomorrow morning the 30th Jan. (2) The second apparatus I brought with me is a graph by which I can determine the sonority, nasality, consonant and vowel sounds, pitch, and as far as I can see it is not functioning very satisfactorily and I cannot compare it with the French apparatus I used in Brittany. It is very difficult to get the oscillations to show on the paper here. Maybe it could be improved if I changed the nibs; it is probably there that the fault lies. Have not yet used the apparatus here, but will try it tomorrow morning with Kelly.

//[83] 29/1/33. Visited Quane yesterday. Recorded the Lord's Prayer, some verses of a hymn (see Peel material) together with a couple of small sentences. Quane's voice didn't turn out to be very good either for the recordings, and his knowledge of Manx is probably rather limited. He is not like Kelly and Cashen born with Manx, but has leanred it, as he says himself, by listening to the old people when he was a boy. His pronunciation often varies for the same words, it seems to me.

30/1/33. Finished my work with Harry Kelly today, 29 cylinders for "metalisation". I also tried the other apparatus on him. The oscillations were more visible when I used a *short* arm. The main result: faintly voiced media [x], [ɣ] in *dorcha* are voiced; *p, t, k* considerably weaker aspiration than in Norwegian; [ɒunˊ] 'river', [dɒunˊ] 'deep' have a non-nasal vowel.

---

[33] *Isle of Man Examiner* for 20.01.1933, p.2, 'Recording the Manx Langauge'.

//[84] 5/2/33. Recorded several cylinders in Peel with Quane and Cashen. 12 long cylinders from Liverpool. Came in handy. I have to mention that the 18cm. cylinders which Selmer mentions in his letter as quite useful cannot be cut, as they are cone-shaped.

3/2. To Sulby where I used a couple of cylinders on Fayle. He was an impossible subject, hoarse and had a squeaky voice, and barked the words into the horn - and his memory of Manx was rather limited.

4/2. To Jurby. John Cain //[85] confirmed completely the good impression I got of him in 1929. Used the two last cylinders on him. It is a pity I hadn't met him before. He would have been one of my main informants together with Christian, Woodworth, and Kelly.

[inside back cover]
Edmond Maddrell, tailor, P[ort] E[rin], no. 36 Athol Park. Mrs. Taubman, P. Erin. Mrs. Corkil[l], Peel. Gawne, no. 18 Jurby. Kane [Cain], no. 20 Sulby.

* * * * * * * * * *

The Transcription

Man Dagbok

Dette er en dagbok av Prof. Carl J. S. Marstrander. Han besøkte Isle of Man fra juni til september 1929, august til september 1930 og januar til februar 1933.
Under sitt opphold på øya forsøkte ham å kartlegge det gamle Manske språket og de forskjellige dialektene.
Dagboken ble renskrevet fra orginalversonen våren 1998.

Sogndal 24.05.1998
Anne Fevang   Lars Anders Ruden

//[1] JUNI 1929

4. juni:
kl. 11 aften avreise med Bergenstoget. Audh. Og Sverdrup fulgte til stasjonen.

5. juni:
avr. Bergen med "Leda". Bra båt, eksellent og rikelig kjøkken.

6. juni:
ankomst Newcastle, hvor jeg såvidt nådde Londontoget kl. 14^{54}. Ankomst London ved 8 tiden. Måtte ta inn i en liten pensjon i Liverpool Str. 26. (ved Kings Cross station).

7. juni:

fik værelse på Euston Hotel. Opsøkte Flower i British Museum og tilbrakte eftermiddagen og aftenen med ham, dels i London, dels i Croydon. Flower er en utmerket mann. Han søker å trekke linjer i irsk litteratur, hvad ingen før ham har gjort. Hans studier av irske håndskriftarter syns å ha ført ham til nye synsmåter ang. den irske litteratur og sagncyklers oprinnelse og //[2] utbredelse. Han var meget interessert i Christiansens arbeider om Finndiktningen, som forhåbentlig kommer iår. Det syns som Fl. Ikke er persona grata i Dublin (det forsto jeg også av O`Keeffe). Jeg skulde tro han vil gjøre bedre arbeide enn noen av irdagene i Dublin. Aftenen tilbraktes i Croydon, en 20 min. vei med toget fra Lond., hvor Fl. har leiet et litet hus og har med kone, mor og 3 barn, 2 piker og en gutt. Min guddatter Barbra viste sig å være en søt pike. Hun skal efter hvad Fl. sier være en sprogelig begavelse og Fl. vil gjerne hun skal bli *a scholar*, hun har the devil of a temper, sier han og vil ikke passe for ekteskapet.

Mrs Flower en elskverdig dame, men //[3] virker noe slitt og gammel. Flow. forteller at han var tilbudt professorat i Oxford i irsk, som Frazer fikk, men at han ikke kunde motta det, da salæret £600[*] var for litet.

Han syns nu å angre på det, for hans arbeider i British Mus. vil ikke gi ham større tid til irske studier når katalogen blir ferdig til neste år. Han var temmelig irritert over en anmeldelse som Bergin hadde skrevet, en typisk Bergin anmeldelse, hvor Fl. bebreides for å si mer enn hvad en katalog efter B`s mening bør inneholde. Tenker jeg får anmelde katalogen utførlig (sammen med Christiansen) i bind 5 av tidsskriftet.

8. juni:

Flyttet over til Gower Hotel (billig og renslig), kort fra Euston.

9. juni:

en prektig tur op Themsen (alene) til Richmond. Tilbake med buss.

10. juni:

Møtte Fl. i museet og så på den keltiske myntsamling. Den var ikke særlig //[4] imponerende. Det rette sted for kelt. mynter er sikkert Paris. Interessant var en mynt som i latinske bokstaver leste BIRACO ..., trul. de "lepontiske" myntene. Lunchte sammen med Fl. og O`Keeffe som det var en glede å se igjen efter alle disse år. Han var samme hyggelige, frittalende menneske som før og har holt seg udmerket. Han har en søn på 21 år, den samme som blir ført under mit første ophol i Dublin og som jeg var så uheldig å [referere] til som Ailill ! Medb, stakkars, er død, det viste jeg ikke. O`K. var meget skarp i sin kritikk over Dublinfolket og meget bitter over at School of Irish Learning var nedlagt og Ériu overtats av Akademiet og at Anecdota var gått inn. Kritikken over Bergin [særlig] sterk. Han mangler komplett initiativ, kan ikke //[5] skape skole, ikke opdra nye elever, han står slapp og virkeløs i et miljø hvor en initiativrik mann kunde gjøre underverker. Til hans unskyldning tjener at han er overlesset med univ. arbeider. Hans irskkurser frekventeres av 300 tilhørere som alle skal ha sin eksamen og hvis skriftlige besvarelser han formod. må lese igjennom. O`Rahilly som en tid var i Trinity College, hvor han ikke syns å ha kunnet gjort ut av med herrene der, er gått til Cork og når Hyde går om kort tid frykter man for at Mrs. O`Farrely

---

[*] Aug. 1930: Flow. salær er i Br. Mus. 1100£ ! efter egen opgave.

rykker op til prof. i nyirsk; Nat. Univ. Duilearga syns man å ha godt håb til. Men jeg har sterke tvil om irsk lingvistikk og filologi noensinne vil vokse seg sterk på irsk grunn uten organisasjon *utenfra*. Meyer holdt det hele sammen fra Liverpool av. Sommerfelt og jeg kunde gjøre adskillig //[5A] fra Oslo av; men våre interesser er ikke som Meyers begrenset til irsk eller keltisk alene. Et energisk arbeid på å skape et videnskapelig miljø i Dublin vilde si at vi for mange år - måske for alltid - måtte legge annet arbeid tilside. Kan hende vilde vi tjene videnskapen best om vi gjorde det og således bar keltologien over den bølgdal, som den nu med truende fart syns å gå ned i. Når Thurneysen dør - og mange år kan vi ikke vente å beholde ham - har Tyskland ingen keltolog mer; ti J.P. kan ikke tas alvorlig og når Loth til neste år (om jeg ikke tar feil) går av ved Sorbonne, står det formod. ingen ferdig til å ta hans plass. Også Vendryes er oppe i årene og Mlle Sjoestedt //[6] skal være meget syk. Utsiktene er overalt mørke. Best måske i Norge, hvor de keltiske studier drives av forholdsvis unge folk og hvor vi nok skal sørge for at det ikke blir gitt op.

11. juni:
Avreise til Liverpool. Tok inn på Adelphi hotel, som (i 1914) er blitt fullstendig ombygget siden jeg var der sist.

12. juni:
Til Man ! Sjøen blikkstille. Ankom Douglas ved $2^{1/2}$ tiden. Tok inn på British Hotel ved den gamle Market Place. En dansk skute lå så å si utenfor vinduene; den hadde bragt tømmer fra Riga og tok nu inn ballast.

13. juni:
Avla visitt i museet (en rød mursteinsbyggning, oprinnelig bygget til hospital). Traf Kermode, en hyggelig og snaksom gammel herre, som presenterte meg for //[6A] bibliotekaren, Mr. Cubbon og for J.J Kneen, forfatteren av det udmerkede arbeide over manske stedsnavn, begge overordentlige hyggelige folk.
Cubbon tilbø seg å overlade Univ. biblioteket et eks. av den manske bibelovers. (1. utgaven) som gave og at selge det 1. eks. av utgaven av 1819. Jeg sel hadde i Simpsons Antikvariat i Douglas funnet 2 eks. av 1819 utgaven hvor jeg tok det ene sel og reserverte det annet for Sommerfelt. P.A. Munchs arbeider er ikke glemt her. I biblioteket henger hans billeder i ramme. Om eftermiddagen en prektig tur med Kneen til Braddan Church, hvor flere runekors er stillet op. Kneens oplysninger om de betingelser hvorunder det videnskabelige arbeidet her foregår, var i høieste grad mistrøstige. Den engelske regering //[7] gir det hele en god dag. Kneens eget arbeid er leilighetsarbeide. Hans bok har gitt meg et sterkt inntrykk av styrken av den norske bosettelse her. Enkelte steder syns navnene på alle større gårder norske, således i Garf; de norske navn møter en desuten langs hele kysten. Kneens samling er neppe fullstendig, han medgir sel at en noenlunde fullstendig saml. av kystnavn og skjer og holmenavn har han bare vært i stand til å samle for sydkysten. Jeg har en levende følelse at her er et rikt felt for en stedsnavnforsker med historisk skjøn. Så talrike som de norske navnene er her på Man, må man liketil kunne lese hele kapitler av den norske bosettelseshistorie ut av dem. Så viktig som Kneens arbeider er også fra et norsk synspunkt, vilde det bare være rimelig om Nansenfondet påskjønnet hans arbeid med en bevilning på £100 - til //[8] fortsatt innsamling av materiale. Om aftenen te hos Cubbon sammen med Kneen. Mrs. Cubbon, som ikke viste sig meget, syntes en sympatisk dame. Vi ble sittende til over 11 og prate om de forskjellig-

ste temaer. Av særlig interesse var Kneens tyding av Smeal som *smiða ból* *, en tyding som får en betydelig interesse ved det skipsgravfunn som er gjort der og som b.a. også rummet en smietang. Fra samme sted nevnes i senere kilder en Patrick Gowe (Crowe) og en ...Teare (*an t-Saoir*). Her trekker altså arkeologi og sprogvid. i forening en sammenhengende kulturhistorisk linje fra det 15. årh. Museet inneholder flere ogamstener og runekors (originaler og avstøpninger) men kan ikke ellers sies å være rikholdig.

//[9]

15. juni:

Kort besøk i museet for å bytte hefte 3 av mit eks. av Kneens bok, hvor et ark manglet. Råket midt oppe i et direksjonsmøte ble presentert for "Mr. Chairman" og for den norske konsul i Douglas Mr. Oates, som begge lot til å være gemyttelige menn. Startet så om eftermiddagen på min *Cuairt Manan[n]* ('tour of Man') med Castletown som første mål.

(1)

Mit 1. Offer var en ca. 60 år gammel mand fra gården *Kewaige*, 1- 2 km. fra Douglas. Det gamle folk der i egnen talte ikke lenger mansk, sa han. Hans egne foreldre talte riktignok mansk, men de foretrakk engelsk og forbø barna å snakke mansk. Hans besteforeldre talte fortrinnsvis mansk og "brøt" på engelsken.

(2)

En mann i Baconsfield (ikke på kartet, men ikke så langt fra Kewaige) ca. 55 år gl. sa //[10] mansk ikke lenger hørtes der i egnen. Hans egen far og mor talte bare engelsk. Han var forøvrig nokså vag i sine uttalelser.

Nokså meget regn på veien og nokså våt ved fremkomsten til Castletown, hvor jeg tok inn på Union Hotel. Her hadde jeg senere på aftenen en hyggelig prat med en del eldre og yngre folk fra Castletown og omegn, hvorav dog ingen talte mansk. En undtagelse dannet dog en forholdsvis ung mann, som jeg anslog til å være i 40 - årene; men hadde betegnende nok lært mansk av sin bestefar. Da jeg tok en stikkprøve og spurte han hvad "it`s a cold day" hette på mansk, svart han ganske riktig.

Moret mig forøvrig med å kaste "darts" med en meget ung mann på stedet. Han vant tilslutt efter noen og seksti kast //[11] hvad der hadde tilfølge at jeg måtte rive i et glass øl på ham. Renslig og rimelig hotel.

16. juni:

drog fra Castletown ved 11 - tiden til Grenaby. Fint veir, skjønt ordentlig vind.

(3)

Like utenfor Castletown hadde jeg en prat med en ca. 70 år gammel mann. Han var fra Derby Haven (født der) og talte *ikke* mansk. Faren heller ikke, men moren, som betegnende nok var fra Ballabeg nær Grenaby**, gjorde det derimot. Godt mansk taler ifølge ham "[kᵘe:l] the Gardener". Han er en mann på over 80 år, født i *Arbory* * og bor like nord for Castletown. Bøiet ned til Derby Haven. Traf her 2 unge og 1 eldre manskmann. De opgav som gode mansktalende Tomas Taggart, skredder i Grenaby, 80- 85 år gl., født efter hvad //[12] de sa i [kæriki:l] (nær Castletown). Videre *Tom Harrison* i Ballasalla godt og vel 80 år gammel. En-

---

* bedre *smiðju-holl*

** nær Grenby er min egen bemerkning. Der er et Ballabeg kloss til Arbory som vel er ment her, da det er et større sted. Se kartet.

* En 3 km. øst for Kolby ved veien til Port Erin.

delig nevnte de også (som senere også Tomas Taggart) archdeacon [kju:li], en mann på godt og vel 70 år, født av fattige foreldre i Parish Castletown.

Min vei førte mig nù til Ballasalla hvor jeg avla et kort besøk i Rushen Abbey som ligger like ved. Her skal flere norske konger være begravet efter hvad de opstilte tavler forteller, således en Magnus, en Ragnald og en Olav. Låkket på en av disse kister skal være funnet sier guiden meden utgravinger i de senere år og opbevares nù i museet som var stengt da jeg var der. (Det åpnes om søndagen først kl. 3)

//[13]

(4)

1/2 - 1 km. vest for Ballasalla ved "Cross Four Wags" (avsatt merkelig nokk på kartet i Manks guiden, men ikke på Ordnance turveg) erklærte en kone på ca. 40 at ingen her i egnen talte mansk, men lenger oppe i retning av Grenaby kunde man finne "lots of them". Dette var dog en overdrivelse.

(5)

Noe nord herfor og før sideveien tar av til Grenaby fra hovedveien (til Peel) hadde jeg en prat med en mann i 50 årene. Han var født i Ballasalla. Faren forstod mansk, men talte almindelig engelsk. Bestefaren derimot talte fortrinsvis mansk, sjønt han nok forstod engelsk. Som gode speakers nevnte han 2 gamle koner Mrs. *Wade* og Mrs. *Johnsen*, begge ca.90 år og boende like i nærheten. Videre nevnte han også skredder Taggart i Grenaby og en skomaker sammstedts *William Preston* på over 80, som han forøvrig mente det var nytteløst å henvende seg til, da han formodentlig //[14] "vilde smelle døren igjen i nesen på en".

Fra denne mann fikk jeg også høre de første brokker av mansk. Han var fortrolig med de almindelige hilsningsformularer og enkelte andre strålende vendinger jeg vilde ofte hørs tale om [dˊɔk ən 'dɔrəs] sa han, den siste drikk før man bryter op.(irsk *deoch an doruis*). 'How do you do' gjenga han med noe som for mig i farten hørtes ut som [kænəs 'tɑ ʃu]. 'How are you to-day' med [kænəs tɤgə læ:] svaret er [tɑ brou, tɑ brou, kænəs ta (eller kæ'nes tɑ) hi:n] hvordan har du det selv). 'Time enough yet' (no hurry) gjenga han med [trei də 'luɑ] og 'good by' med [i: 'vɑːi] (å brukbart *good night* ! dypere stikker altså hans kunnskaper ikke).

Det var formodentlig denne mann, som //[15] også opgav mig William Kneen som en god speaker. Denne Kneen er over 70 år, født i Croitecaley[*] (noe sydvest for Colby), hvor han også bor.

En annen speaker er *Bændken Regg* (så skrevet efter uttalen), ca. 76 år, født i Arbory sansyn-ligvis. Men jeg husker ikke nù fra hvem jeg har denne oplysning.

(6)

William Kenne fra [Bɑlə Dugən] like før Grenaby, 62 år gl., sier han kan uttrykke almin-delige setninger i mansk. En stikprøve: 'I am going to Casteltown' oversatte han riktig. Faren og moren talte begge mansk, men også engelsk. Sig imellom talte de mansk fremfor alt når det var noe de ikke vilde barna skulde forstå (dette trekk har jeg hørt fremholdt fra mange andre hold). Som god speaker nevnte han *Tomas Lis* (så stavet efter uttalen) fra [Kærə 'Muːªr], Grenaby, ca. 70 år gl. //[16]

(7)

Tomas Taggart viste sig å være en munter olding med et veldig apostolisk skjegg, en meget talende mann med et glimrende humør. Hans uttale forekom mig dog utydelig ikke bare av mansk (hvad der sier litet, da jeg ennu praktisk talt ingenting forstår derav) men også av en-

---

[*] Utt. Kroitikèli

gelsk. Han lesper litt, har sikkert ikke alle sine tenner og lyden ble lissom hengende igjen i skjegget hans. Men hans mansk er visst upåklagelig. Han betrodde mig også at han kjente flere manske sanger av den art, at de ikke godt kunne foredras offentlig. Jeg tror nok mannen kan brukes, jeg får ha ham i mente, men får iallefall foreløbig fortsette min rundtur. //[17] Ble budt på en splendid te og cyklet så ned til Port Erin, hvor jeg tok inn på Falcons Nest, hvor dette er skrevet (15/6.29)

\# Congre (ål) het på manks [ɑstən] eller lign. (eascon) ifølge ham.

17. juni:
Strålende veir. La ivei til fots sydover for å få et glimt av The Calf of Man.

(8)
I landsbyen [Krɛd´neːiʃ] (Cregneish) hadde jeg en prat med en 69 år gl. mann [Kærən]. Han var fra [Hɔu]* (kartets Howe) straks nord for Creigneish, men faren født i Cregneish. Han var istand til å uttrykke sig på manks, bare komplikasjonene ikke var for innviklet. En setning som 'I would`nt have beaten him if he were not a bad man' klarte hverken han eller en noe eldre mann# på stedet mens vendinger som 'I shall go to the fair to morrow', 'I went to the fair yesterday but bought nothing' klarte de uten hovedbry. Calf of Man het på //[18] manks [kɑːlu] sa de (orig. *Kalfr*). Traf også [Kærəns] noe yngre bror (55 år), en sjømann. Faren talte godt manks, foretrakk det enn også for engelsk og var også i stand til å lese det. Begge anbefalte som en god manks speaker

(9)
Harry Kelly skrevet Kelly, Aug. (1930], 77 år gl., som bor nederst i landsbyen på høire (syd) side av veien. En hyggelig gammel mand med tydelig uttale. De få setninger jeg gav ham å oversette - de var ganske enkle - klarte han uten vanskelighet. Hans far talte praktisk talt bare manks. Kelly har en manks bibel, det samme har [Kærən] (den eldste av dem), men ingen av dem vil skille sig ved den. Også Taggart i Grenaby har bibelversjonen av 1819 (og Manx Soc. ordboken og kvarto- utgaven av boken).

//[19]
Kelly kjenner navnene på alle holmer og skjer her utenfor. Et skjer heter således [krɛg ə l´ɛmən] ([l´ɛm] 'a jump', sa han irsk *léim*), den nøiaktige form innestår jeg ikke for. 'How many horses have you' heter [kwɔd kævəl tæd] eller lignende. (Riktig ! aug. 1930)
Kelly kan uten tvil brukes.
Glimrende østers i en liten shop rett ved hotellet (ned mot stranden). De serveres på stedet, cider er også å få der. Det går ganske bra sammen.

Peel 17. juni:
Før jeg forlot Port Erin gik jeg for å hilse på Joseph *Woodworth*, en gammel fisker, som man i Douglas hadde nevnt for mig som en god manks speaker. Han var ute på fiske og datteren sa han var ikke ventendes tilbake //[20] før kl. 3, så jeg benyttet tiden til en tur på halvøen syd for Port Erin.

(10)
En gammel mann i landsbyen [Feʃtər[d]] på vel 70 sier at hans far talte bare manks, hans mor derimot begge deler. Sel var han nok istand til å klare enkle setninger i manks. Som en god manks speaker nevnte han

(11)

---

* Vel *Haugr* snarere enn Hofuð, da landsbyen ikke ligger ved sjøen.

Waterson i *Glen Càs* nær Howe ca. 65 år. Denne mann opsøkte jeg, han bodde ikke mange hundre meterne borte (han hadde som han fortalte mig fra vinduet set mig samtale med den andre !). Waterson sa at stedet han bodde i hette [Fistər[d]], men at mange kalte det Glen Càs.

Waterson gjorde inntrykk av å kunne føre en konversasjon på manks, skjønt hans kjenskap til sproget sikkert ikke er //[21] fullkommen efter flere merker å dømme. Han gav mig flj. former av taleordene, som jeg nedskrev i al hast.

[nɛːn] [1]	['nɛn dʒɛg] [11]	['nɛnəsˈfigˊ] [21]	[daːgˊ] "40"
[dʒiːs] [2]	[gɑi ɛg] [12]	['dʒiːsəsfigˊ] [22]	[dʒɑiəsdaːgˊ] "50"
[triː] [3]	['triːdʒɛg] [13]	[dʒɑiəsfigˊ] "30"	[triːfidˊ] "60"
[kɛːr] [4]	[keːrdʒɛg] [14]	['nindʒɛgəsˈfigˊ] "31"	[triːfidˊ əsdʒɑi] "70"
[fᵘɛg] "5" (*sic*)	[fᵘɛgdʒɛg] [15]	[gɑiɛgəsfigˊ] [32]	[keːrfidˊ] "80"
[ʃeː] [6]	['ʃeːdʒɛg] [16]	[triːdʒɛgəsfigˊ] [33]	[keːrfidˊ əsdʒɑi] "90"
[ʃæːx] [7]	[ʃæːxdʒɛg] [17]	[kɛːr ......] [34]	[kiːd] "100"
[hɑːx] [8](mørkt à)[hɑːxtʒɛg] [18]		[fᵘɛg .....] [35]	
[niː] [9]	[niːdʒɛg] [19]	[ʃeː ......] [36]	
[dʒɑi] [10]	[figˊ], [fidˊ] "20"	[ʃaxtʃɛgəsfigˊ] [37]	
		[hɑːxt ......] [38]	
		[niːdʒɛg] ....] [39]	

Dog var W. usikker straks han kom over 40. Han sa således at 60 hette //[22] [triː ˈkiːd]*, som dog må bety 300, men rettet det dog sel senere.

'I was born at the Howe' het [vɑ mi ˈrɔgəd ɛgən ɔu], sa han.

Av ord han opgav noterte jeg.

[strɛin] nese
[mɔnəl] hals
[biːl] mund
[læu] hånd
[kæːb] hake
[kaːs] fot (nesten [æː])
[kliːʃ] øre
[suːlˊ] øie (som han forøvrig måtte betenke sig på og først gav da jeg nevnte det irske ekvivalent)
[lurəgə] legg (u -lyden kanskje ikke riktig notert).
[riː] arm
[drîːm] rygg

Manks speakers vil man finne i [Bɑləkilˈfɛrikˊ] og i [Lɛn Gig], begge nær Colby, sier Waterson.

Howe må være Haugr. Det passer udmerket til gårdens beliggenhet //[23] på toppen av en 'hill'.

(12)

---

* Vel sammenblanding med *trí fichid* !!

Joseph Woodworth er 75 år gammel og synes virkelig å kunne adskillig manks. Han er fisker og hans dag avhenger ganske mye av veiret. 'I wd like to go to Douglas tomorrow' oversatte han: [l´ak l´um ðə ˈgɔl gɔs Duːliʃ meːrɑx]. 'If he had`nt been a bad man (I wd not have beaten him) oversatte han: [mɑnɑx ˈbɛxɛ ə'veː drɑxˈgɑnə]. Han var villig til å prate manks med mig, om jeg kom tilbake til Port Erin.

Som god speaker nevnte han

(13)

[Tomɑs 'Krebən] i Bradda Village like ved Port Erin og hvis hus han viste mig fra vinduet sit. Denne [Krebən] som jeg opsøkte før jeg gav mig i vei til Peel, gjorde et meget godt inntrykk. Han skal være over //[24] 80 år. Setningen 'I would like to go' oversatte han straks som Woodworth. Mannen syntes å ha et ganske annet overblikk enn de fleste andre. Således kjente han til sa han helt av sig sel alle mankske uttrykk for vind og veir, navnene på stjernene osv. (stjerne kalte han [reːltən] eller noe lignende, sml. irsk).

Han var fult villig til å prate irsk med mig om jeg kom tilbake til Port Erin.

Fra Port Erin fulgte jeg nù veien til Douglas inntil Ballasalla, hvor jeg benyttet anledningen til å avlegge et besøk i museet i Rushen Abbey. Her er det i de siste år gravet op en hel del stenkister med skeletter, hvorav de fleste antogs å stamme fra tidlig normannisk tid. Kistelåket, som antogs å ha //[25] hørt til en av de norske kongegraven, var meget smukt. Det viser to sverd i relieff og endel ornamenter - men om sverdtypen og ornamentene kan tilsies det 13. årh. savner jeg forutsetninger til å kunne avgjøre. Den egentlige "omviser" var fraværende da jeg kom, men en annen mann i "office" viste mig elskverdig omkring og jeg måtte love ham å la dem vite når jeg atter kom på de kanter for å møte den, som hadde med utgavningene å gjøre. Dette ble avbrutt med krigen, men skal nù tas op igjen.

Fra Rushen Abbey tilbake til Four Cross Ways, hvor jeg tok den regulære vei til Peel nordover. Den sterke stigning var meget besværlig med den tunge oppakning bak på cyklen. På toppen, ved [Bɑˈruːl] Farm (på Peel veien) traf jeg en mann på 53 år.

(14)

William *Keggen*, som ikke sel taler mansk. //[26] Ingen talte manksk sa han der i distriktet, den eneste måtte være *Taggàrt i Grenaby* (som han nevnte helt av sig sel). Men faren hans talte manks (og engelsk). Han oplyste at han hadde en manks bibel efter faren. Jeg gav 2 skilling for den uten å ha sett den (han vilde forøvrig ha gitt mig den for ingenting). Den viste sig å være i en horibel forfatning, men jeg tok den nå med likevel. Book of Prayer hadde han ikke.

(15)

Kort fra Peel - en ca. 3 miles- traf jeg 2 menn i 60 årsalderen. Manks var ikke talt der i egnen sa de. De gamle, som kunde tale det, var borte. Foreldrene deres talte manks, medga de, særlig når ikke barna skulde vite hva de snakket om.

I samme setning uttalte også en mann i 50 årene - sig kort fra Peel (ca. //[27] 2 miles derfra). Han nevnte som fremragende kjender av manks advok. Kelly i Douglas og archdeacon Kewley i Andreas.

Kom til Peel først ved 9- tiden. Tok inn på Hotel Marine like ved stranden.

18. juni:

Mitre Hotel, Kirk Michael (godt, men dyrt 7/6 bed & breakf.) Opsøkte apoteker *C. H. Cowley*, som man hadde anbefalet mig i Douglas, før jeg forlot Peel. Han kan ikke kalles a native speaker, skjønt han ofte hørte manks i sin barndom og senere har lagt sig adskillig efter det. Han anbefalte *Caesar Cashin* og *William Quane*, det samme som Cubbon og Kneen hadde nevnt i Douglas.

(16)

Quane bor i St. Germans Place sammen med sin søster. Han er 79 år gl. (født 1850) og gjør inntrykk av å tale manks ganske bra. Han taler det ofte sammen med Caesar Cashin på Market Place. Men jeg syntes å //[28] merke at han manglet øvelse, som rimelig kan være. Uttalen hans var tydelig. Han har om jeg husker rett 2 eks. av bibelen av 1819 (også Cashin har iallefall 1 eks.). Ord og vendinger som jeg tok med i samtale med Quane:

[fæstər mɑːi] 'good evening'

['iː 'vɑːi] 'good night'

[mɑːri (dypt a) eller [mɑːxri mɑːi] 'good morning' (*moch éirghe?* C.M.)

[ən 'famən] 'Tail' (hale)

[ɛlɑn nuː 'Pærⁱk´] = St. Patricks Island

[Pɔrt nə 'hiːnʃə] = Peel.

[hæ "ikke" 'dʒɛn mi 'gɔl gɔs ən 'kiːdən 'mɑːri meⁱ vis iː 'stɛrəmɑx ('sterᵊmɑx)] ('I shan`t go', vel verbet *deinim* 'gjøre' CM)

[kiːdən] 'sea' [*cuan?* C.M.] "sea" også [ən 'øːrkə] sier han (*fairgge* irsk).

//[29]

12 nov. holdes en [kruːnɑx] 'a gathering' i Douglas.

Talord:

[nɛːn], [dʒiːs], [triː], [kiːr], [kᵘɛg], [ʃeː], [ʃæx], [hɑːx] (dypt a), [nei], [dʒei], ['nendʒig´] ([hæ nel im ɑs ...] 'I have not but eleven'; *vel* = *ní fhuil* CM), [dɛįig´], [triːdʒig´], [kiːr ...], [fid´] 20, ['neːnəsfid´] 21, ['dʒei əs 'fid´] 30, [dɑid´], [dɑïd´] 40, ['dʒeiəs'dɑid´] 50, ['triː'fid´] 60, [...... ɛs dʒei] 70, ['kiːr fid´] 80, [...... əs dʒei] 90, [kid] 100, [töu'zɛːn] 1000 (open è).

VIND:

[tæ n 'giːə ɛg ın njæːr] '[the wind is] fra øst'.

[................niːr] 'vest'.

[................tuːi] 'nord'.

[................dʒæːs] 'syd'.

[................njæːr huːi] 'nordøst'.

[................niːr huːi] 'nordvest'.

[................niːr ɛs] 'sydvest'.

[................'njæːr ɛs] 'sydøst'.

//[30]

[ɑ nɛl mi 'faːxin ɛs ɔːn rɔ'lɛːg] 'I do not see but one star'

[ɑ 'nɛl ʃu] (lukket ù) 'you do not'

[tæ mi 'fɑːxin 'ɛru rɔ'lɛgən] 'I see many stars'

FISK:

[æːstən] 'congre', pl. [æːstənən].

['skɑdɑn] (a-slyd) 'sild'.

[brɛk] 'makrel'

[rɛn mi 'kɛnɑx ɛru də brɛk] 'eg kjøpte mange m.'

FUGL:

[lɔn] 'blackbird'.

[trɛslən] 'the big trust'.

['spɪru] 'sparrow' .

['ɔʒɑg] ['fugl' (i almind); [ɛru də 'ɔʒɑgən] [*earroo dy ushagyn* 'many birds'].

['ɔʒɑg 'hæpɑx] ['lille stær'.

[ən 'koːg, k âːg] 'gjøk'.

HUSDYR etc.

[kæˑbəl] 'hest'; [tæ 'rɛm kæːbəl ɛgi]'he has many horses'. Dette ordet [rɛm] som er meget i bruk, skal //[31] ifølge Quane ikke finnes i ordbøkene.

[ta 'rɛm 'ɑ̌lɑx (ɑ-) ɛ̌gi] (mørkt a) 'he has a lot of cattle'.

[buːə] [*booa*] 'cow'

[mɑːdə] (mørkt a) 'hund'.

[muk] (europ. *u*) 'gris'.

[kæt] 'katt'.

[Lɔx] 'mus' (det brede <u>l</u> høres tydelig).

[rǎdɑn] (a - lyd) 'rotte'.

[ə'nɛsɑg] 'weasal'.

[tæ 'dʒiːs buːʳ ɛki] (hos ham?).

[oːn buː 'tækə] 'he has got one cow'.

[tæ 'rɛm ˌɛrgəd ɛka] 'he has got lots of money'.

[.............. ɛgən 'bɛdən ʃɔ (åpent)] 'this woman has got lots of money.

[................ɛk] [..........*eck*] 'she has got...'.

Men Quane syns i farten ikke å skelne skarpt mellom *aige* og *aice* som i irsk. Noen få videre eksempler vilde naturligvis ha klarlagt de manskske formene.

VARIA:

[mɔ'rædən] 'much' (*mórán*).

['ɪmədi ʃlei] 'a lot of people'.

[ʃḛ:] = irsk '*s eadh* har tydelig lukket è, men [vɛː] [*va*] 'var' tydelig åpent.

//[32] [kis 'tɛʂu] eller ['kɪnəs 'tɛʂu] ['How are you?' [kɪs] ier nok, siger Quane.

Sammen med Quane gik jeg ned til Market Place og traf her Caesar Cashin (ca. 70 år). Han husket godt Rhys, som han ofte hadde pratet med når han kom for å konferere med hans eldre bror. Cashin synes å tale et godt manks. Setningen 'I w*d* like to go to Dougl.' gjenga han øieblikkelig som Woodworth, mens Quane brukte en omskrivning ([tæ mi buʃ...] 'I am wishing...') som syntes litet idiomatisk. Både Quane og Cashin var overordentlig elskverdige. Det er neppe tvilsomt at det ved hjelp av dem vilde kunne lykkes å trekke op hovedlinjene i Peeldialekten fonetisk og grammatisk.

Cashin nevnte av sig sel som en god speaker "Quayle the Gardener", den samme som jeg hørte omtalt i Casteltown og den //[33] samme som Mr. Cubbon i et senere brev fra Castletown gjør mig opmerksom på (Quale`s adr. er Shore Road, han er skriver Cubbon "the most fluent speaker in this town").

Både Cashin og Quane vilde gjerne jeg skulde komme til den årlige høitidelighet på Thinwall den 5. juli og til den mankske gudstjeneste den 7 juli i [merõun] Church. Archdeaconen i Andreas vilde uten tvil skaffe mig en billet.

Forlot Peel ved 6 tiden om eftermiddagen og kom til Kirk Michael ad den vestre vei (kystveien) ved 8 -tiden. Tok inn på Mitre Hotel.

Beså Peel Castle på Parick Island i formiddag før jeg opsøkte Quane. Midt på øen (og innenfor slottets område) ligger en rektang. opbygget vold som minner noe om Thinwall. 4 arbeidere var beskjeftiget med å grave den ut //[34] da jeg kom. Der var laget et snitt inn mot centrum og gravet helt ned til underste sandlag, men ingen grav var funnet - til skuffelse for arkeologen, som av den eng. regjering hadde fått 100£ til disse utgravningene og som hadde håpet ved et sensasjonelt funn å bane veien for en ny og større bevilgning. Derimot viste arbeiderne mig en hel del flintsteiner som var funnet i haugen og de fortalte også at der var funnet 2 fragmenter av bronse. Altså syns haugen førkeltisk. Skulde Thinwall også være det? *Mrs. Corkill,* Peel, som Cubbon opga som god speaker, fikk jeg ikke hilse på, heller ikke på *Mrs. Taubmann* (c/o Mr. Kennaugh, grocer), Port Erin (hun nevnes vist av Rhys). Men det er mig i første rekke om å gjøre å finne et individ, hvis sprog jeg kan nedtegne i //[35] dagstødt , tålmodig samarbeide - og kvinner egner sig neppe for det.

19. juni:

I *Kirk Michael* må manksen sies å være helt utdød. Ingen har vært i stand til å nevne mig en eneste gammel mann her, som taler det. Vicar Cannon her på stedet skal være ganske kyndig i sproget sier man. Det er han som den 7 juli besørger gudstjenesten i St. Johns. Men Cashin sa om hans manx at uttalen virket noe fremmed og at han ikke altid forsto hvad han sa. Cannons far bor nærmere Ballaugh (utt. Balaf), "Alpine House".

Kirk M. Ligger noen hundre meter fra sjøen. Den gamle havn må ha ligget ved åpningen av Glen Wyllin (ved "Mølledalen") noe sydvest for bebyggelsen. Det er det eneste sted som kan gi ly på denne kyststrekning.

Ristet for spøk ᚷ ᛁᚢ᛬ ᛘᛅᚱᛏ᛬ ᚱᛅᛁᛏᛁ᛬ ᛏᛅᛁᚼ᛫ᛒᛚᛅᛏᛘ᛫ᚱi en grindstø, hvis pene flate var altfor fristende. Bare ikke noen finner den og tar den alvorlig. //[36]

[top p. 37 but indicated to be placed here]
P.S. *Kirk Michael*: John [Kisik] i Bale Krink på Douglas- veien like i utkanten av Kirk Mich., er en mann på over 70 år. Han kan som så mange andre fadervor på manx - men syntes merkelig nok ikke å kunne telle til 10. Som god manx speaker opgav han *Daniel Caine* i Little London 2-3 miles lenger syd på Douglasveien (stedet er avsatt på kartet). Men stedet lå for langt unda min rute.

20. juni: Sulby Glen Hotel.

Snekker William Kålet, ca. 80 år gl. efter hvad det ble sagt, i Kirk Michael var ikke hjemme da jeg spurgte efter ham. Mrs.[Kɔləster], the Dolly, nær stasjonen, Kirk Michael, opsøkte jeg ikke.

Rute 19. juni: Kirk Michael - Ballaugh- Jurby - Sulby.

(17)

Ved Bishops Court mellom Kirk M. og Ballaugh traf jeg en mann på ca. 50. Han var født Ballaugh Parish og kunde telle fra 1 -20 (12: [deidʒeg]). Men ellers var det smått bevart med hans kunnskaper i manx.

En god manx speaker er

240

(18)

Mr. Gawne, W. Nappin straks syd for Jurby Church. Han er ca. 70 år gammel og har en ganske bra uttale. Konen gjør et noe eldre inntrykk. Kjøpte et pent eks. av bibelen (av 1819) av ham for 10 skillings. Jeg tror Gawne er ganske brukbar og at man med tiden vilde kunne få presset hele det mankske sytem ut av ham. Han er meget //[37] villig til å samarbeide. Her er en del ord og vendinger som jeg tok med (i mangelfull fonet. skrift.)

[hɑ rou ə mi hɑ bulə eː na bi e drɑx dunˊə] 'I w[oul]d not have beaten him if he were not a bad man'. [kən ˈaʃtɔu friːl] (mørkt k) 'how are you keeping' (Denne overs. er Gawnes egen) [tɑ mi ˈmɑï gurǫ ˈmɑï ǫːt] 'I am well thank you'. [mɔːri mɑːi, ˈfɑstə mɑːï, ïː ˈvɑːï] 'good morning, good evening, good night']. [tou gɔl dəˈkirɑx əˈnɑːïl ɑs kɔ ˈgiːl eː] '[you] go to mend (i.e. make up) the fire and put coal ([gil] = *gual*) on'. [kidən] [*keayn*] 'the sea', [nəˈfɑːkə] [*ny faarkey*] 'the waves' ? CM (synts å minnes at a vokalens kvalitet forekom mig tvilsom). [tæ ən dˊigˊigˊ ɛm maru as ȝŋlikˊ ɑs tɑ n moir //[38] ɛm blˊǫː fɔːs (ǫː norsk [åː])] 'my father is dead and buried, but my mother is still alive'. [hɑi mi dosnə ˈmörˊgˊə leʃ raːm (blødt à) ˈnˊɑlɑx] 'I went to the market with lots of cattle'. [buːə], [muc] (europ. *u*), [gˊuːï] 'geese', [tæ raːm gˊuːï ɛ ɛs tæ nə ˈsmuː də kaːkən ɛm ɑs raːm ˈtɔnɑg] (ducks) 'he has more of geese, but I have more (*ní as mó*) hens and ducks'. (*cearc*!!). [kaːvəl] 'horse'. [mɔdə], plur. [mɔdi]: [tæ nə ˈmɔdi ɛm kalˊtˊ] 'I have lost my dogs', [tæ ən mɔdə ɛm kalˊtˊ] 'I have lost my dog'. Men der var litt usikkerhet her og jeg hadde ikke tid til å lure formene ut av ham i almindelig konversasjon. [lȫi] 'calf', [ˈkɔlbax] 'heifer', [taru] 'bull', [tæ raːm taru ɛm] 'I have a lot of bulls', [vɛl raːm ˈtaru ɔuiʃ] 'have you got, etc'.

Derefter opsøkte jeg //[39]

(19)

Snekker *Wilfred Waid*, Sandy Gate, Jurby, som neppe er noe stort nummer. Uttalen hans syns dog tydelig, han har også lest en hel del i den mankske bibel (som han har iallefall 1 eks. av), det merker man på hele hans konversasjon. Under forutsetning av at jeg kommer til å arbeide med Gawne, kan dog Waid tenkes å komme til nytte.

[klɔx ˈǫndin] 'foundation stone'.

[finnə ən gɔlæːn] 'ringing the bells' (min gjengivelse [finnə] er vist meget ufullkommen, Waid var ytterst misfornøiet med min uttale).

[dȝiːrˊax] 'straight', opp. [kæm] [*cam*] 'crooked'.

Som god speaker opgav han mig

(20)

John Kane, Ballamoar //[40] [small sketch map]

Kanes alder blev opgitt til noen og åtti år, men han gav ikke inntrykk av å være mer enn noen og sytti. Han hadde desverre besøk da jeg kom (en sprade i broget vest og som irriterte en med sine nærgående spørsmål), men jeg fikk inntrykk av at han kunde en hel del manks. *Han citerte iallefall stante pede en hel del manx poem: Hans uttale hørtes klar og grei ut. Han vil sikkert bli til god* hjelp om jeg slår mig ned her og arbeider med Gawne.

Som god speaker opgav han en ung mann på Railway hotellet i Ballaugh en John [Keləp], Sulby Glen. Samme mann ble også anbefalet her av Fayle. Han bor ca. 200 m. fra jernbanes-tasjonen.

(21)

Mr. *Fayle* (utt. [Fɛl]), Steward (min vertinne uttalte [Stouərd], et gard- navn?) er 76 år gl. Han bor et par hundre meter fra hotellet på en linje som går fra dette og over kapellet eller litt til høire //[41] derfra. Hans far talte bare manx og brøt fryktelig på engelsken, moren talte både manx og engelsk. Han gir inntrykk av å kunne en hel del manx men å være nokså uøvet. Setningen 'I would not have beaten him if he hadn`t been a bad man' betenkte han sig lenge på; for *beat* brukte han [betal] ell. lign. som jo må være det engelske ord. For Sulby kjente han ingen manx form. *Glen* uttales her med *dn*. Han vil uten tvil være til nytte, men jeg tror nokså vanskelig å arbeide med.

Op Sulby Glen.

(22)

En mann på 64 (hans navn var [Fɑrəkəl]) født "at the bottom of the glen" sa at hans far talte manx og bestefaren bare manx. Men hans eget kjennskap til sproget var nokså fragmentarisk. Han anbefalte som god speaker Mrs. Crane, ca. 55 år gl. (hvis bestefar bare talte manx); hun bor ved veien til Ballaugh (Cool Ben Cottage).

[ɑ 'nɛl 'tɛgɑl 'gᵘɛlˊⁱkˊ] '[I] can't understand Manx', sier han.'naked' heter [ru:ʃ] ifølge ham.

Talord: [nɛːn] (åpent), [dʒiːs], [t̮riː], [kᵘɛg], [ʃeː], [ʃax], [hɔx], [nei], [dʒei], [arəndʒɛg].

[Up left page]

1933: Mr Killəp, Sulby, glemt alting. Foreldrene mansk.

//[42]

1933: 2/2 tok ned to ruller med Fayle, nokså umulig.

Men mannen er meget forsiktig og gjør opmerksom på at hans uttale vist ikke er helt idiomatisk.

Lunch i Tholt y Will. Derfra op den bratte vei i syd, ca. 1 mil op går en sidevei til venstre. Den fører til [Krɛgən] (plur. av [Krɛg] 'rocks') hvor

(23)

Cowley (Mac. Ólaibh) bor. Han er nu 85 år gl., nesten blind og meget rheumatisk, men hans uttale er tydelig. Hans hukommelse syns noe svekket. Også når han taler engelsk, står han stundom fast og leter efter ordet. Det var ham umulig å komme på hvad "hode" hette på manx. Først da jeg nevnte det sydmankske [kˊɔːn] gav han som sin uttale [kˊɔun]. Han hadde også vanskelig for å skilne mellom "hos ham" og "hos hende" - men slike ting vil vel gi sig ganske naturlig under mere sammenhengende samtale.

TALORD:

[nɛːn], [dʒiːs], [t̮riː] (ikke utpreg. palat), [kɛːr], kᵘɛg], [ʃeː], [ʃax] (tydelig a), [hɔx] (mørkt a), [nei], [dʒei], //[43] [arəndʒɛg], ['dɛiɟɛg], ['t̮riɟɛg], ['kɛːrdʒɛg], [kᵘɛgdʒɛg], [ʃeːdʒɛg], [ʃaxdʒɛg], [hɔxdʒɛg], [neidʒɛg], [fidˊ], [nɛnəfidˊ], [dʒeiəsfidˊ], [da-ĭdˊ], [dʒeiəs'dɑ-ĭd], [kɛːd] tydelig med meget lukket e.

[[tœ]dei keːd buə ɛm] 'I have 200 cows'.

[ta/tæ ən tɑi ɛm muːᵊ / ən tɑi ɛmis muːᵊ] 'my house is big'.

[kaːbəl ɛm] 'my horse'.

["   ɛməs]

[ən kaːbəl ɔs] 'your horse'.

[tæ ən kaːbəl ɛkə 'maːru] 'his horse is dead'.

[ta ən .... ɛk maru] 'her ....'   ? C.M. cp.p.c, line 2 below ! C.M.

[tæ-ĭ 'fɔrɑxtən ɛgən 'tai ɛm / ɛməs] 'she is staying in my house', [...ɛgən tɑi ein] '...in our house'.

[tæ-ĭ 'beᵊxə...] ['she is living...'

Men Cowley kan ikke riktig gjøre rede på forskjellen mellom "hos ham" og "hos hende" (*aige : aice*).

242

[nim 'bul´əxu - må være 2. pers. pron. ? C.M - mɛ 'dʒin ʃu 'ʃen] 'I shall strike you if you do that'. . //[44]

[pin] 'paine': [tæ 'pin (åpent i) əns mək´ɔun] 'I have a pain in my head'.

[tæ 'ræm 'ɑlɑx (meget dypt a) ɛke] 'he has got lot of cattle'

[Krɛgən] 'Rocks', navnet på gården

[Sn´e:l] Snefjell, så i Sulby Glen, men på sydsiden av fjellet sies [Sn´o:l], [Snjɔ:l].

[Baru:l], n.l.

[Kɔuli], n. pr.

[kræməg] 'snail'

[mɑ:də]

[gei]: pl. [g´ɔ:i], [gjɔ:i] 'goose : geese'

[famən ka:bəl] 'hestehale'

[ka:θ] 'foot' sic ("stav det *c* + *a* + *th*" sier Cowley !!).

Som god speaker nevner Cowley Christian i [Lörgi'rɛnən]. Men han er nesten døv (Kartets Lhergyrhenny, sydøst for Kregen). Videre en bror av denne

(24)

John Christian, snekker, 84 år gammel (flere år eldre enn broren). Han bor kort fra Kapellet ved Sulby Glen veien. Også [Farəkəl] //[45] anbefalte ham og han syns i virkeligheten å være en av de bedre.

Fader - Vor:

[ən 'æːr ein tɔns 'n´ou 'kɑʃərik´ dərɔu də'ɛnim dədʒeg də rə'riəx ən aːrdn´ɔu də rɔu dʒɛnt ər´ə 'tɑlu mɔːr əs dʒɛnt ɔs 'n´ou 'kɔr dɔ̃in narɑn dʒu as dɑx (*sic*) læ: (broad *l*) ɑs ɫei dɔ̃in 'lɔxtən mɔr tɑ 'ʃin´ ɫei 'dɔəsen də dʒɛnu 'lɔxtənə nei as nə 'lɪdʒ ʃin ɔs mi ɔ̃:ɫəs lɪ've: ʃin wɑi ən 'ɔlk sɔn ʃeː 'lɑts ən rə'riːⁿx ən fuːər ɑs ən 'lɔːr (*sic*) sɔn də'brɛx as də 'brɛx 'ɛː'meːn].

[pɛːn nəs mə x´ɔun] 'a pain in my head'.

[ma: d´ɛgə'sɔ: ([?] fa dʒɛgə ?), tʃötˢesɔ:] inn here) 'if you don'.t come here'.

[tæ dæ: ka:bəl ɛgə 'ʃɔ:] 'he has 2 horses'.

[ta 'ram 'kabəl´ (*sic*) ɛm] 'I have lots of horses'.

[ən 'vɛːn ʃɔ:] 'this woman'.

[ta ra:m ö:ʳgəd ɛk] 'she has got lots of money'. Her kom, [ɛk] ganske av sig selv. //[46]

[ən ɛːr vᵘiː]'the yellow gold' (Chr. Uttaler yellow: [jalɔu]).

21. Juni:

(25)

Ramsey, Saddle Hotel. - Opsøkte før jeg forlot Sulby Mr. Kilip. Han bor på Ballaugh - veien et par hundre meter fra jernb.stasjonen. Han viste sig å være identisk med en mann jeg hadde stanset op aftenen i forveien og spurgte efter Sulby Glen Hotel. Mannen er meget sel-sikker og prater litt av sit kjennskap til manks, som igrunneren meget mangelfullt. Han kunde ikke engang fadervor og stod naturligvis fast på de alminnelige prøvesetningene jeg gav ham. Han har bibelen av 1819, Manx Soc. ordbok samt en åbenbart eldre utgave av det gamle testamentet i et bind (av samme tykkelse som bibelutg. av 1819). Ordboken vilde han ikke skille sig ved.

[bɛːn 'vɑnᵃnᵃx] 'Kvinde fra Man'

['mɑnᵃnᵃx] 'en manxmann'

//[47] Forlot Sulby ut på aftenen for å dra til Andreas, som syns et udmerket utgangspunkt for ekskursjonen i det flate nordlige slettepartiet av øen. En ung mann jeg mødte et par miles fra Andreas kjente ingen manxspeakere i distriktet. Han hadde hørt manx i sin barndom sa han, da de gamle talte det, når det var noe de ikke ville de yngre skulde forstå. Hotellet i Andreas (Grovernor) var optatt, hvorfra jeg fortsatte til Ramsey, Saddle Hotel, Market Place. Kafeen var optatt av et lystighets-selskap fra Douglas av pene unge mennesker; 7-8 unge piker stod og stormkysset en ung spire av en mann på 17 somre - munn, øine, hals. Han mottok disse voldsomme kjertegn alvorlig og med nedslagende øine.

(26)

Thomas Christian som jeg opsøkte i dag bor i College Strect, ganske nær hotellet. Det er en prektig gammel mann, en nordisk type helt igjennom. Her tror jeg endelig å ha funnet en mann å arbeide med. Hans uttale er tydelig, //[48] mannen er intelligent, tålmodig og forstår at han kan gjøre videnskapen en tjeneste ved å stille seg til disposisjon. Små prøvesetninger besvarte han raskt og ideomatisk. Han har bibelen av 1819 og en gammel Book of Hymns*, sikkert fra 18. årh. Jeg cyklet nu til Maughold og tok drosje til Douglas, vender så tilbake her. Nordlandet kan meget godt undersøkes videre her fra Ramsey.

22.Juni:

Ramsey, Saddle Hotel. - Forlot Ramsey igår ved 2 tiden. Dro med kurs for Douglas, som jeg nådde litt før 8, så vidt at jeg fikk mine brev og aviser på postkontoret.

Stanset ved Maughold Church for å se på det keltiske kors og runekorsene som er samlet under et halvtak på kirkegården. Denne samlingen er overordentlig interessant. Tydningen av no. 144 som den gis i opslaget, er vel neppe sikker.

Runene //[49] er nesten alle tydelige: jeg synes å se to prikker her

[runic inscription]

[runic inscription]

[runic] Conall?   ikke spor av flere

runer her.

På kors no. 142 er et par runeinnskrifter med mindre runer, som ikke nevnes i opslaget. Den ene gir tydelig et mannsnavn på [runic] , den annen [runic] *Lifilt*, antagelig kvindenavn. Dette (R) følges umiddelbart av en avskalling. Stod det oprinnelig *Lifhild* ?. En 3. innskr. er mer utydelig. Jeg synts å skimte [runic] (men ganske usikker)

(27)

En graver på kirkegården opgav mig Tom [Lu:ni], ca. 75 år, som en der talte manks. Han bor like ved kirkegården. Var ikke hjemme da jeg kom, men en brorsøn sa han aldri hadde hørt annet enn «odd words of manx» fra ham. Så han kan formodelig strykes av //[50] listen over manks speakers.

I Balla Skeg Beg [Bɔləskeːg bɛg] på veien fra Maughold til Ballaglas traf jeg en mann på

(28)

74 år med det velkjente navn [Mɔləkriːs]. Faren og moren talte bare manks. Han synts å ha et ganske bra kjennskap til sproget. "Godt objekt" sier notatene mine. Ord og vendinger fra ham:

[kˊɔːn] hode, [kæːs] fot

---

* Kneen, Douglas, har et eksemplar av den.

244

[εrə'mil´ən] 'upon your knees' (*you* er vel galt).

[ta mi smaːᵊxin də gɔl də Duːliʃ meːrᵃx] 'I am thinking to....'

[mɑnɑx hu dʒenu ʃedən ɉou vi 'gɔt´] 'she will be talk' (synes jeg han sa)

[neːn buːæɡən dᵘinəʃedən]

[neːn buːæɡən bɛdn ʃedən] (feminin)

[Mɑləkriːs] bor alene, hans kone har et pensjonat i Douglas. Han var meget forekommende og jeg tror det kunde lønne sig å ha en prat med ham senere når jeg har fått //[51] et bedre innblikk i sproget.

(29)

Som manks speaker ble mig også opgitt en Robert [Djɔkən], Dhoon Church, en mann på over 70; men jeg fikk ikke tak i ham. Mit neste offer var

(30)

James Kewly, ([k´uːli]),79 år gl. (f. 1850) den yngste og eneste gjenlevende av 10 brødre. Født i Lizer, men vokset op i Lonan Parish (syd for Laxey), har også levet en tid i Maughold. Traf han på veien noe syd for Laxey og hadde en lang prat med ham. Han kan sikkert adskillig manks.

[gɔu] 'A bullock' *damh* CM.1933

[kɔlbɑx] a heifer

[gei], [g´ɔi] 'goose, geese'

[mɒk], men [dæː vɒk] '2 griser'

[triː mɒɡən]

(sic: også ellers synes jej å minnes å ha hørt en g vor jej ventet *k*. Feilhørsel ?

[lei] 'calf'

[tæ dæː vuːᵊ ɛɡə] 'han har 2 kjør' (mine notater har riktignok vuːᵊr])

[kɛnəs tɔu] how are you

[ei vɑːi] 'god natt'

(Denne formen har jeg senere ofte hørt på forskjellige steder som Kennah, Baile Cleary, og også videre sør på øya. CM. Aug. 1930) //[52]

Av noen vers han hadde hørt av en eldre bror citerte han :

> [kɛn sörtʃ də rɛk də hɑi krɔg ʒɛk
> ən örəxə mɛx ɔn g´ɔurə
> vi dʒɛnt mə gæːï ɔs k´uːn ə væːï
> sɔn foːsi ənsə tɔurə] (in the summer)

(Dette skjønner jeg ikke ! C.M 1933.)

Det var flere vers men han erindret bare dette. En hyggelig mann og meget meddelsom.

Tok i Douglas inn på British Hotell. Kjøpte i dag en del gamle bøker (b.a. en skotsk gal. bibel og en Manks Prayerbook, ell. lign. hvorav begynnelsen riktignok manglet.) Opsøkte så Kneen som jeg endelig traf ut på eftermiddagen. Han forærte mig manuskript til sine øvelser i manks, som forlengst er ute av bokhandelen. Kneer har en liten sjokolade og godteri-forretning i Douglas. Her sitter han sel i et litet rum bak butikken som også tjener som spisestue, og lager

sukker //[53] stenger (manx rock), denne mann som burde ha vært professor i manks ved et universitet. Det er noen livet ikke fører det bra for.

23. Juni:
(Søndag). Vært ute og set mig om efter lodgings Kommer antagelig til å leie mig inn i
Bridge Inn, 30 sk. uken (bead and breakf.)

25. juni:
Hadde min først time med Christian i dag. Manks tegner til å bli et innviklet kapitel-fonetisk
sett. En hårfin fonetisk nedtegning kan det ikke være tale om på dette stadium. Jeg får arbeide
mig inn i sproget først og så fiksere lydene senere når mit øre er blitt mere vant til dem. Det
fonetiske system er meget forskjellig fra irsk, man må orientere sig helt fra nytt av.

31. [*sic*] juni:
Har nå arbeidet med Chr. en ukes tid (fra ca. 10-12, en. ca. 2-4), og begynner //[54]
å komme inn i systemet. Chr. kan uten tvil en masse manks. Men det merkes tydelig sel på
han at han i lang tid har vært uten øvelse i å tale sproget. Han neglisjerer som oftest de
alminneligste mutasjonsregler (aspirasjon, eklipse), men det kan jo tenkes at dette er et
trekk i utviklingen av den dialekt han taler.

29. juni:
Lørdag aften, var jeg hos Chr.* for å møte bestyreren av en høiere skole i Ramsey, Mr. Killey, som er meget interessert i manks. Vi øvet oss i å lese kapitler av det gamle og nye tes-
tamente og Killey ssang dessuten et par manske sanger, som minner sterk om de irske. Hans
uttale er sterkt engelskfarvet. Lånte mig Edmund Goodwin`s: Lessoonyn ayns Chengey ny
Mayrey Ellan Vannin, Douglas (S:K Broadbent & Co. Ltd, Printers, Examiner office, Victoria street) 1901. Det synes å være en fortreffelig bok, som jeg må se å //[55] skaffe meg. Killey er en god norgesvenn. Besøkte vestkysten for en 30 år siden, et udmerket fotografi fra en
av våre fjorder henger i dagligstuen hans.
Søndag i Wesleyan Church med Christian. En bonde fra omegnen talte enkelt og tiltalende
om dagens tekst. Utpå aftenen cyklet jeg til Djurby Church for å se på runekorsene. Men det
kors som interesserte mig mest (det som M.O. mener bærer navnet Fair Tur**) var ikke der.
Innenfor kirkemuren ligger hvad der synes å være en gammel gravhaug og 1 km. eller så
nord for kirken tegner en stor tumulus sig mot himmelen.
(31)
På Djurby Road noen miles eller så fra Ramsey hadde jeg en prat med John Joseph *Corrin*
([Kɔrən]) 71 år gl., født i Parish of Ballaugh i [Bɑlə Krɔʃə], bor nå i Djurby i [Bɑlə Kǫri]
(på Djurby Road). For 50 år siden, da han //[56] kom til Djurby var manks i full bruk. Han
syns å ha adskillig ferdighet i å tale manks. Prøvesetning: 'If you don`t come at once, I shall
beat you', klarte han bra (når undtas at han lot 'at once' uoversatt), ukedagene ramset han op
med forbløffende fart (Christian stod fast på 'Tirsdag', hvad der dog kan henge sammen med
hans sviktende hukommelse i sin alminnelighet, også i engelsk leter han ofte efter ordene),
"sigd" oversatte han med [kɔrɑn]. Får opsøke ham senere. Han var mer enn villig til å ta i
mot meg.

---

* [left margin] *Christian* døde i 1930 (31?) *Killey* hadde gravtaler over ham på Mansk - og døde
  sel kort tid efter (1931 ?) av lungekreft. (1933).
** P.S Feb. 1930 (Oslo) : [?] det står der i nordveggen av kirken men *fairþur* og det [?] er slått
  vekk.

Nord for Djurby Church fikk jeg andre oplysninger på gården *Sātfield* av en mann i 50 års alderen. Han opgav som mankskyndig

//[57] (32)

John [Se:l] (*d.e. Sayle*) i [Bɑləˈtoːnə] ca. 3 miles nord for Djurby, North Road (shore-road), ca. 70-80 år gl. Videre

(33)

Mr. *Kneen*, Lane (kort fra Sātfield) og

(34)

Mrs. *Killip* (også i Lane å dømme efter mine notater). Hendes mann døde for en 40 år siden, hun er altså forskjellig fra den Mrs. Killip jeg traf i Sulby og hvis mann lever.

World Manx Association sender mig innbydelse til the 19th annual gathring at the Nunnery ved Douglas på Tynwald Day, den mankske nasjonaldag. Komiteen vil [?] at jeg skal holde en tale, hvad jeg gjerne skulde ha gjort, hvis ikke......
Det er uvanelig selv for en obskun Osloprofessor å reise ubemerket. Et blad i Ramsey hadde en notis om mit ophold på øen. Den må formod. være tatt fra et blad i Douglas. //[58]

Brev fra Gwynne, som inviterte mig til Irland. Reiser jeg over er det i første rekke for å se ham igjen.
Ridder av Æreslegionen "for fortjeneste av fransk sprog og kultur" Begrunnelsen smaker mig ikke riktig og ordensvesenet i det hele er mig en vederstyggelighet. Men det hele er jo en hvitt likegyldig ting og mine franske kolleger vild uten tvil bli stødt om jeg avslog å motta den. Så la meg i Guds navn beholde den - i stillhet !

8.juli:
Kom forsent til Tinwall den 5 juli. Messen var holt og lovene lest da jeg kom der ved 12-tiden. Nasjonalfesten i The Nunnery var i mange måter ganske interessant. Men manks hørtes det ikke et ord av- når jeg motar et telegram fra Londonavdelingen Manx World association, som forfatteren //[59] sel leste op.
Men det er nokså betegnende at arbeide for å redde hvad ennu reddes kan i gammel tradisjon her på øen, bare nevnes av en taler, Archeacon Kewley fra Andreas som i et varmt innlegg talte for å bevare manks, iallefall som emne for studie og undervisning og kraftig opfordret alle til å overlate museet gamle saker av verdi. Ellers syntes talerne nærmest å løpe ut i vitser og pikante historier. Det er her omtrent som i Dublin: De mangler plan og organisasjon, man lar alting skure. Hadde en prat med archeaconen som syntes en hyggelig og gemyttelig mann. Traf Cubbon (Kneer og Kermad var i Liverpool for å motta degrees som M.A) og ble med ham hjem til te. Lang diskusjon om *treen* (skandinavisk eller keltisk?). I går dukket han plutselig op hos Christian og bad mig bli med på Onsdag og se på noen fat sheep i Billown, nær Ballabeg, på Mr. T.G. Moors grund.
//[60]
I går søndag en lang tur med Mr Killey til *Cronc noo* (eller now?), en gravhaug kort fra Ramsey, som ble utgravet for kort tid siden og hvor der ble funnet et stykke rav som av Brit. Mus. ble erklært for skandinavisk. Graven ligger på en haug, terrenget nedenfor bærer navnet Lough, så det har vel engang stått under vann. I graven ble også funnet en sten med noen figurer på som nå er i museet i Douglas. Enkelte av de andre stenene ble tatt til grindstolper. Vi undersøkte flere av dem, men de var intet på dem.

11. juli:
Med Cubbon til Billown nær Ballabeg. Eieren T.G. Moore kjørte os sel om - til Skibrick (haugen har virkelig en form av en hvelvet båt, så det er ikke //[61] umulig at navnet iallefall inneholder også skip som Kneen mente). Beså flere "standing stones" og white stones på siden av dammen. Stensetningen nær huset er meget interessant. Den er så og si i vinkelform med en diameter på ca. 10 m. og nesten utenlukkende dannet av svære hvite stenblokker, som iallefall på ett sted synes å danne et gravkammer (uten tak). De to stener i midten er uten tvil i tidlig tid veltet ned fra det noe høiereliggende platå hvor 2 svære hvite stener står å synes å ha dannet et kammmer sammen med disse, således at cirkelens indre oprinnelig var helt fritt. På feltet ble funnet en mengde rått tilhugget flint, samt et fint tilhugget stykke flint av denne form og størrelse. Videre noen få fragmenter av keramik, som Cubbon og mener kan skrives fra en høiereliggende mound like ved, hvor der tidligere er funnet keramik. Under enhver omstendighet viser //[62] funnet at vi står ovenfor et gammelt minnesmerke fra realistisk tid eller bronsealderen, hvad enten det dreier seg om en gravplass eller et gammelt kultsted- de hvite stener har uten tvil sin egen betydning og uforbundet med de isolerte endereiste stener i nabolaget. Mrs. Moore var guddommelig vakker, men vi så litet til hende. Spiste Aftens hos Cubbon i Douglas. Kneen var ventet, men kom ikke. Cubbon uventet? mig endel bøker på manx. Enbra manks speaker skal være
(35)
Mr. *J. Kelly*, Laxey på Ramsey siden av glennen og ved minene. Han er over 80 år gl. Opplysningene er Cubbons.

15. juli:
I Douglas i går hos skredder Larsen (dansk, gift her). Besøkte Kneen som //[63] var dårlig. Kneen har gjort samme erfaring som mig at mutasjonene ikke overholdes og at der er en tendens til å erstatte gen. former med nominativ. Som god manx speaker i Port Erin nevnte han
(36)
Edmond Maddrell, en skredder ca. 80 år gl, Athol Park.
Innbydelse til lunch fra Rotary club, Douglas, onsdag 17. juli gjennom T.R. Radcliffe, red. av the Examiner, Douglas.

8. sept:
Reiser i morgen tidlig til Douglas og videre med 4.30 båten til Liverpool-Newcastle-Oslo ("Bessheim")
I det hele velfornøid med opholdet her. Det materialet jeg har samlet vil uten tvil ha betydelig verdi videre når keltisk sprog om en 5-10 år er totalt forsvunnet fra øen- selv om den fonetiske gjengivelse naturligvis på flere punkter bare tilnærmelsesvis treffer det rette. //[64] Jeg har virkelig fått grep på manksken og håber til neste år å kunne ta fatt på den sydlige dialekt, som efter mitt inntrykk å dømme udskiller sig fra den nordlige i betydelig høiere grad enn alminndelig antatt.
Min plan for neste sommer er: undersøkelse av den sydlige dialekt og utgravning av en gammel *kol* i et godt norsk distrikt for om mulig å finne nye runekors. En mindre bevilgning må vel kunne fås for dette formål av et eller annet norsk fond. Kneen bør skaffes en bevilgning over 2 år for å fastsette nedtegningen av stedsnavnene. Dette arbeid må gjøres i løpet av de nærmeste kommende år, da den *keltiske* uttale om få år ikke lenger er å oppdrive.

248

For enkelte steder //[65] er en fonetisk nedtegn. formodelig ellers nu umulig. Cubbon, Kneen og Killey er prektige typer og gode venner. Hadde Kelly til middag i går aftens på Hotel Prince of Wales. Cubbon har skaffet mig en hel del manks litteratur, og også ellers vært mig megen til nytte.Han fant således frem et gammelt hittil ukjent fot. av runestenen fra Jurby (Odinstenen), som fullstendig gjenspeiler bestemte *fair þur* og godkjenner at den lesingen jeg foreslo i Revue Celtique for en 10-15 år siden er riktig. Innskriften på den siste funden cross slab fra Bride tror jeg jeg har fått ganske bra tak på.

Prof. Mawr fra Liverpool (fra Jan. London) er en hyggelig omgjengelig mann. Har besøkt ham 2 ganger i Ballasalla hvor han hadde leiet et fasjonabelt litet hus //[66] for sommeren. Men han er bunnet i gamle former. Jeg foreslo ham å prøve å skaffe Kneen et *Scholarship*, men har liten tro på at han vil foreta noe i den anledning.

En ung student fra Trinity College, Quin, har besøkt mig flere ganger i Bridge Inn. Han er intelligent, interessant og har utsyn. Han er meget interessert i Irsk, vil til neste år tilbringe noen uker i et irsk talende distrikt i Donegal- men vil de noensinne få noe gjort fra Irland ? Jeg stivet ham op så godt jeg kunde.

Min Irlandstur må nok utsettes til neste år.
//[67]

1930

Med "Bessheim" over til Newcastle en av de siste dagene i August. Noen dagers ophol i London (Euston og Gower Hotels) Traf Flower, som talte om å sende min guddatter til Oslo for å perfeksjonere i sml. sprogforskning. Tenkte visst på å få henne inn som Frasers efterfølger i Oxford.

Over Liverpool til Douglas. Cubbon som elskverdig mann som altid. Kneen gift, møtte dem hos Cubbon en aftens til te. Ikke noe bestemt inntrykk av Mrs. Kneen. Intet hørs fra Kneen - skjønt jeg nu vel [?] en 10-12 dager på Man.

Arbeider nå med Taggert i Grenaby. Han er nærmest en skuffelse, veldig overvurdert, har glemt nesten al sin mansk, husker ikke de alminnelige ord som "skulder", "kne" osv. og dette skyldes vel ikke bare //[68] hans alder. Jeg kommer sannsynligvis til å gi ham op innen kort tid.

Bedre er Edward Kennah på Ballacleary, kort fra Grenaby. Konen er fra Port-Erin kanten. Han er et absolutt pålitelig menneske. Men han taler ikke mansk lett.

Best er Jos. Wodwork, PortErin, med hvem jeg nå tar ned Joseph-historien. Han er klar og bestemt og mansken syns hos han å være noe mere enn en blot og bar erindring.

Brev fra W.Cubbon av 14.aug. hvori han oversendte fl. skriveri

A5   14th August, 1930
Sir,
    I am directed by the Manx Museum & and Ancient Monument Trustees //[69] to request the favour of an Advance on Imprest og £20 (twenty pounds) in accordance with the following resolution of the Ancient Monument Committee, 12th August 1930.
    145. "Resolved, that while Professor Marstrander og Oslo University is on the Island, an examination of the Knocsharry tumulus be undertaken on behalf of the Museum, and that in

order to pay for the labour in connection therewith, the Treasurer of the Isle of Man be requested to grant av Advance on Imprest of a sum not exceeding twenty pounds"

I am, Sir,
Your obedient sevant,
W.C
Secretary

The Treasurer of the Isle og Man
Goverment Office
ISLE OF MAN

//[70]
Port Erin 28/8.30:
Flyttet fra old Abbey Hotel i dag. Forærte den svidde bibelen jeg fant i skorsteinen i Grenaby
til Mr. & Mrs. Witham (indehaverne av hotellet). Den arme mann har vært sengeliggende i
2 år og tror vist, denne bibelen vil bringe ham lykke.
Taggart er et meget vanskelig objekt for å bruke et mildt uttrykk. For det første er han så
døv, at en sammenhengende konversasjon nesten er umulig. Dernest er hans hukommelse
svekket i en uhyggelig grad. Alle hans oplysninger må kontrolleres og brukes med den
største forsiktighet. Falske assosiasjoner med synomymene eller likelydene engelske eller
manske ord leder han ikke sjelden til å opgi ravruskende gale pentamutasjonsformer, som [æː-
kəl] 'lime-kiln' (under inflydelse av eng. 'kiln' for [iːl] = *aoil* !!).
Jeg får dog se å få det fonetiske system //[71] han har klarlagt. I går skreks vi om kapp sam-
fulle 4¹/² timer, det måtte kunne høres over hele sognet og vi var begge utkjørte da vi sluttet.
Woodw. syk i dag, hvorfor jeg tok mig en trip til Cregneish og traf gamle Kelly. Han gjør et
meget godt inntrykk. Vokset opp i et hjem hvor foreldrene snakket mansk sig imellom. Sel
har han alltid forstått mansk - også som smågutt, var også i stand til å snakke litt. Men fullt
herredømme over sproget fikk ham - som Woodw. først, da han drog på fiske med de gamle i
15 års alderen. Meget interessant var det å fastslå at heller ikke K. har det brede, framskutte *l*
i *laa* 'dag'. Spørsmålet er om vi her står ovenfor en mer eller mindre gammel nydannelse i
Port-Erin strøkets mansk - eller om tapet av [?] W. og K. skal forklares derav at de vokset op
med engelsk som deres [?] sprog. Spørsmålet må kunne løses. Det har adskillig generell in-
tresse.
Station Hotel (proper Chadwich) ser bra //[72] ut. Jeg betaler for værelse + frokost + 1 mål
7 ¹/² skilling, hva der er ganske rimelig.

30/8.
Tok en tur til Cregnish ut på aftenen og hilste på Harry Kelly. Avtalte å møtes her i morgen
ved 9 tiden og er netopp kommet tilbake fra min første time hos ham. Han blir 79 år i nov. i
år. Han synes å ha et ualminnelig godt kjenskap til mansk. Er ennu ikke kommet ham riktig
inn på livet, men det skulle ikke undre mig om han av alle speakers jeg har truffet er den
som taler best og mest idiomatisk. Lot ham fortelle sitt "liv" i engelsk, tar det med på
mansk i morgentidlig ved 9-tiden. Kelly skal være meget utilgjengelig, - en fiskeselger som
kom forbi undret sig [?] over at jeg i det hele fikk Kelly til å snakke mansk. //[73]

Den eng.dial. på Man er meget interessant og må undersøkes. For *Chasms* sier Woodw. [kæːsəms] (stedsnavn). Forlengelse av diftongers 1. ledd som i sin alm. i mansk, også i anglo-eng. Jeg hørte av forbipasserende i Ballasalla: [tɑːim] 'time'; ['lɑːisəns] 'licence'.

1/9.30.
Mit inntrykk av Kelly bekreftes. Han synes en fortreffelig speaker i betraktning av manskens hele stilling. Tok ned hans viten igår med mange interessante oplysninger om skikk og bruk i gamle dager. Men han er en vanskelig mann å ha med å gjøre. Da jeg presenterte mig i morges kl. 9 efter avtale, hadde han ingen tid å avse. Jeg må komme til en fast avtale med ham. Hilste på Tomas Creben i Bradda Village i dag og skal [?] nærmere på tennene i morgen efter i overmorgen. Han synes å ha en tydelig uttale. Det palatale *n* kom meget tydelig frem hos ham. Han er født //[74] i Port Erin (half way between P. Er. og Bradda Village). Likeså hans far og bestefar talte og mansk fra barndommen av. Han syns å uttale *laa* 'dag' med bredt fremskudt *l*. Altså skyldes Woodw. og Kellys uttale vel de [?] frahvor de lærte mansk.

Tilf. ord : [tʃɛb] 'tilby', 'by' (så og så meget for en vane) [nˊaːr] 'øst', [nˊiːr] 'vest', [dʒaːs] 'syd', [kˊeːʳ] '4', osv.
Kohtˋs artikler i Tid.Tegn fra 23. aug. om Mansk-sproget. Kom i rett til og skal nok vise sig å være en udmerket støtte for vårt arbeide.

20/9.
Ved avslutningen av mit arbeide i Grenby og P.-E. Kelly er et funn. Jeg bør se å komme tilbake og utnytte ham videre et annet år. Woodw. pålitelig - men hans mansk gjør ikke det samme ekte (vernacular) inntrykk som Kelly eller //[75] Crebbin. Den siste er det formod. lite å gjøre med, da han er meget svakelig. Det er vel meget tvilsomt om jeg finner ham i live et annet år. Han har dessuten glemt størsteparten av sit manks; men det han har, gir det sammme ekte genuine intrykk som Kelly.
Bør vel se å få tak i Maddrell før jeg reiser og vil også bringe på det rene artikelen palatale *l* fra Crebbin (som Kellys ?). Så må jeg ordne mig slik at jeg får et-par dager i Peel. Altså: i morgen søndag Taggart, mandag, : Woodw. (for siste gang) og Maddrell tirsdag og onsdag : Peel, torsdag farvel. Douglas, Fredag til Liverpool.
Station Hotel godt og rimelig.

30/9.30.
Hjemme igjen. Avsluttet arbeidet med Kelly og Woodworth. Besøkte T. Crebbin i Bradda Village og fikk alle kompassets 32 points av ham. T. Maddrell i Glenn chass var en //[76] usympatisk herre på mellom 70 og 80 år og åpenbart av liten verdi som objekt. Han fortalte sel at han ikke kunde noe manx fra han var 18 år; da han efterhvert lært det av de gamle. Men en sammenhengende konversasjon var han ikke i stand til å føre. Avla samme aften et besøk hos Percy Kellys manske lærer *T. Cubbon* i Four Road ved Port Erin. Han er en gammel mann på henover 80. Hans kjenskap til manx er temmelig begrenset efter flere merker å dømme. Ingen større skade skedd er at jeg ikke har opsøkt han tidligere. //[77]
Arbeidet i Peel med Quane Onsdag em. og Torsdag morgen og fikk tatt ned et bra materiale i løpet av denne korte tid. Eiendommelig for Peel manxen er b.a *a*-lydene. Jeg håber jeg får anled. til å komme tilbake til Peel for en uke eller to et annet år.

Torsdag efter middag i Douglas: Cubbon, Oats, Quilliam, Kneen og en elev av ham, en ganske sympatisk mann. Cubbon overrakte mig sit kart av Treennavnene som synes overmåtelig nyttig. Han fortjener en påskjønnelse for dette arbeide fra norsk hold.

Lørdag 27 fra Newcastle med Bessheim, følge med Dr. Christiansen som jeg traf på stasjonen i Liverpool. Felt vier ved //[78] Englandskysten, men stille, fin sjø ved norskekysten og op Oslofjorden.

Port Erin 29.jan.1933

1933

Fonografiske optagelser.

Fra Oslo lørdag kl. 12 d. 7. jan. (Vippetangen) med "Blendheim". Bra overreise. Pibble med, litt sjøsyk til å begynne med, men klarte sig ellers bedre enn jeg. Følge med Idas sønn *Hans Kittelsen*, bridge ombord med 2 norske damer frk. Glørsun og Kristiansen. Den første fortsatte med over til London, den siste ble igjen med Kittelsen i Newcastle for å ta et senere tog sydover. Hansemann godt anlegg som kurfisør. //[79]

London, *Euston St. Hot.* 1ste natten, 15 s. for bare værelset. For dyrt. Flyttet over til Gower Hot. i Euston Road, 10 s.døgnet værelse + frokost for os begge to.

Zoologisk have med Pibbe, som var veldig interessert. Kledde meg op hos Rimel og Alsop - det trengtes sandelig.

Til Liverpool 14.jan. Adelphi forlangte 18 s. for bare værelset. En politikonstabel anbefalte et boardinghouse ved stationen, Atlantic Hotel (ca. 12 s. vær. + frok.), et uappetittelig sted, som jeg forhåbentlig aldri ser igjen.

Mandag kl. 10.45 med "Peel Castle" til Douglas, nydelig veir. Kneen på bryggen. Te hos Cubbon Onsdag, senere hos Kneen. Te hos the Deputy Governor, en sympatisk dus mann. Han bor //[80] litt utenfor Douglas (Balla na Brooie) på veien til Braddon om jeg husker rett - med sin datter Mrs. McGay (?). Bad mig komme igjen med Pibbe når jeg kommer tilbake fra Dougl.

Cubbon fikk ca. 10-11 eks. av min bok. De fikk (med dedikasjon) til Dep.

Dep. Gov. La Mothe	Mr Ralfe
Deemster Farrant	Rev. Stenning osv.
Att. Gen. Moore	
Archdeacon Cowley	
Canon Quine	

Prideaux, postmester i Port Erin, ga jeg et eks. senere. Boken har slått godt an her - og har ofte vært omtalt i pressen, vier i en lang artikkel igår i Manx Examiner. (?)

Konferert i London med General manager i Gramaphone Company, //[81] en ung elskverdig mann, som jeg fikk inntrykk av var nokså interessert i prosjektet. Han lover å stå til disposisjon øieblikkelig jeg kommer til London med Harry Kelly.

Medbringer (1) Det fonogr. optagerapparatet som Selmer og Leip brukte i Amerika. Selmer gjorde opmerksom på at der var noe galt med skruen, og det har vært til stor [?] her. Synd, da iallefall 1/5 av voksrullen ikke kan brukes og det hele lett kunne vært rettet på ved å bytte skrue. Det må gjøres straks jeg kommer hjem. Ellers fungerer app. bra. Jeg kan ikke ta op i en temperatur av noen og tyve grader som Sehue helst vil, det er kaldt her og praktisk talt umulig å få en jevn temperatur i værelsene. Men det går likevel. Satte mig i forbindelse med Kelly den 24.jan., spaserte over åsen fra Port Erin (Station Hotel. som i 1930), og begynte optakene her på hotellet den 25. Mit inntrykk er at optgelsene er nokså ujevne. Kellys stemme er noe hes, //[82] blir lett skrikende, den er litet sonar. Best blir resultatet når han taler forholdsvis lavt med munnen meget nær traktåpningen. Har arbeidet med ham nu i 4 dager, avslutter formod. i morgen den 30 jan.

(2) Det andre apparat jeg bringer med mig er en [?] graf for bestemmelse av sonoritet, nasalitet, konsonant og vokallyder, tonehøyder osv. Det fungerer så vidt jeg kan se lite tilfredsstillende og kan ikke sammenlignes med det franske apparat jeg brukte i Bretagne. Det er meget vanskelig å få svingningene frem på papiret her. Kan hende dette kan endres ved en forbedring av pennene; det er sikkert der feilen ligger. Har ennu ikke brukt dette apparatet her; men vil prøve det i morgen med Kelly. //[83]

29/1.33.
Hos Quane i går. Tok med LordsPrager, noen vers av en hymne (se Peel materialet), samt enkeltord og småsetninger. Heller ikke Quanes stemme synes mig å ligge godt ann for optagelse, og hans kjenskap til mansk er vel nokså begrenset. Han er ikke som Kelly og Cashen født med mansk, men har lært det, som han sel sier, ved å høre på de gamle da han var gutt. Hans uttale varierer ofte i samme ord forekommer det mig.

30/1.33.
Avsluttet arbeidet med Harry Kelly idag, 29 ruller for "metallisering" Prøvde også det andre apparatet med ham. Svingningene kom betydelig bedre fram når jeg brukte *kort* slange. Hovedres: Medien svakt stemte, [x], [ɣ] i dorcha er stemt, *p t k.* betydelig svakere aspektet enn i norsk, [ɑun´] 'elv', [dɑun´] 'dyp' har unasalnet vokal. //[84]

5/2.33.
Fikk tatt flere ruller i Peel med Quane og Cashin. 12 langeruller fra Liverpool kom godt med; det er å [?] de 18 cm. ruller som Selmer nevner som brukelige i sit brev. De kan ikke parteres, sylindrene er konisk.

3/2
Til Sulby hvor jeg brukte et par ruller på Fayle; han var et umulig objekt, hes og skrikende stemme, bjeffet ordene inn i trakten og hans erindring av mansk var åbenbart nokså utvisket.

4/2
Til Jurby; John Caine //[85] bekreftet tilfulle det gode inntrykk jeg fikk av ham i 1929. Brukte de to siste rullene på ham, shade jeg ikke traff ham før. Han vilde lett ha blitt en av mine hovedkjennelsesmenn ved siden av Christian, Woodworth og Kelly.

Appendix B

Letters (1-5) for and against the use of Manx

1. *MANKS ADVERTISER*, 18.01.1821.

To the Editor of the Manks Advertiser.

Sir. It is obvious that when tribes of men are intermixed, who speak different languages, a great part of the advantages which man should afford his neighbour, must be diminished or lost. The Magistrate cannot address his subjects, the Pastor his flock, but by the imperfect medium of an interpreter. Lawyers, Divines, Physicians, Merchants, Manufacturers, and Farmers, all feel more or less this inconvenience, when they have to do with those with whom they have no common language.

To remedy such evils, Schools have been established for a century in the Highlands of Scotland, where the Erse, a dialect very much resembling the Manks, is spoken; and in these schools English books were the first put into the scholar's hands; but the result was, that the scholar, although taught to read English, did not understand it, in a great proportion of cases. The failure arose from supposing that every person who could read a language, understood it of course.

Effectual education must be commenced in the language of the scholar. Suppose an English child, who had not learned his letters, put under a Greek tutor, who should begin with teaching him the Greek alphabet, to spell and read in Greek, but not to translate, to get by rote passages of Greek authors, how would such a scheme of tuition be approved of? Yet, if you will suppose the scholar the son of a Highland peasant, and for Greek substitute English, you have a picture of the mode of education whose defect Scotland has but lately discovered after an hundred years' trial, and this Island has yet to learn.

Some may fear, that any encouragement to the revival of the Manks language may be injurious, by delaying its decline and the consequent extension of the English; to me this decline does not appear so rapid as it may to many others. - But with respect to the extension of the English language, it appears likely to be promoted at present, by the cultivation of the Manks. This will open an easy path to the first rudiments of knowledge. When these are obtained, emulation and interest will soon excite him to the acquisition of the English language, on which his hopes depend, and he will speedily outstrip the scholar, who has been taught, like a parrot, to pronounce by signal, words which convey to his mind no meaning whatever.

A revival of the Manks language does not infer a depression of the English; but it is so much to be wished, that many of those who speak but one of those languages, should learn to speak both. Nor is this difficult for the young. Nor is the state of a country, where a considerable proportion of the population use two languages, unusual. The maritime towns of Europe, some of the smaller states of Germany, Switzerland, and Italy, speak two languages.

Let us then diminish the inconvenience of distinct languages by multiplying interpreters. All the intercourse of society will be conducted with more facility, and the tribes so long separated may at length begin to blend into one nation.

January 16, 1821.   A MANXMAN.

2. *MANX ADVERTISER*, Thurs. 13th December 1821.

Dys Robin Briw, na quoierbee ehhene ta shirrey chur lesh stiagh y ghailck reesht.

Doolish, Jecrean, yn unlaa-yeig
jeh Meeveanagh y yeuree 1821.

Cha sayms nee Robin, na Thom, na Juan t'ort; agh dy veeit mee rish yn ennym Robin Briw 'sy phabyr, as dyn ennym elley; agh ta mee ourryssagh ny yei dy vel shiu myr y chenn legion roish nish, as dy vel shiu ymmodee; son cheayll mee jiu roie. Ta mee goaill yindys cre ta jannoo ort, solla ta! Va mee dy slane karail loayrt rhyt roish nish, agh duirree mee orrym tammylt, jerkal rish tooilliu ommijys voïd. Te jeeaghyn nish myr dy row 'er nghoaill fea; agh ta mee dooteilagh dy bee oo ec obbyr reesht, cha leah's yiow caa. Cre wooishagh oo? Nee dy chur lesh gailck reesht er e toshiaght, as myr shen dooney magh schleï, as soiljey as tushtey veih Manninee? Tou steetagh dy lioor, raad tou gra nagh vel oo shirrey liettal y vaarle, - ec y traa cheddin dy vel oo moylley gailck! Vel oo sheiltyn ayns dty chree, dy re blebbinyn sleih? Verryms fys dhyt er, nee blebbinyn Manninee, mannagh nee! Manninagh, tou fagin mish, chamma rhyts:- agh yoin nearey moylley meehushtey as lhagynsagh da my gheiney cheerey. Shinney lhiam ad foddey roa vie dy chraiddey mou myr shen, na dy chur lheid y vranlaadee ayns nyn ghing, as cheumooie jeh shen cur shiaghrynys er y cheeloghe aeg ta girree. Wooishin ad heet myr cheernyn elley - ynsit - as gêyrit, as coamrit lesh schleï; chouds t'ou uss, ta laick, son freayll ad sheese dys nyn shaan oayll, nagh loayr ad dys earishyn foddey, brenneein dy ghlaare agh gailck. Gow coyrle, leh, as bee fêagh.

MANNINAGH DOOIE

('To Robin Brew, or whoever he is who seeks to bring back Manx.

Douglas, Wednesday, 11th [*recte* 12th]
of the mid-month of winter [December] 1821.

I don't know whether your name is Robin, Thom or Juan; but Robin Brew is the only name I came across in the paper. However, I suspect that you are like the old legion of long ago, i.e. that you are numerous; for I have heard of you before. I wonder what is wrong with you, I do indeed! I fully intended speaking to you before today, but I held back for a while, expecting more silliness from you. It now seems that you have quietened down; but I have no doubt that you will be at it again, as soon as you get a chance. What do you want? Is it to promote Manx again, and so exclude skill, enlightenment and understanding from Manx people? You are very disingenuous when you say that you do not seek to hinder the English language, - (while) at the same time you praise Manx!. Do you really think that people are fools? I'll tell you whether Manxmen are fools or not! You see that I am a Manxman, like yourself; but I would be ashamed to recommend ignorance and lack of education to my countrymen. I am far too fond of them to mock them like that, or to put such delusions into their heads, and apart from that to lead the coming generation astray. I would want them to become like other countries - educated - and developed, and provided with skills; while you, it seems, want to restrict them to their old ways, so that they do not speak any jot of language other than Manx for ages to come. Take my advice, man, and keep quiet').

TRUE MANXMAN.

3. *MANKS ADVERTISER*, Thurs. 6 June 1822.

To the Editor of the Manks Advertiser.

Sir,

I have often heard it observed by Manksmen, that is, my own countrymen, that we should keep up the Manx. They argue that many old persons know no other language, and that, therefore, they ought to be spoken to in that language from the pulpit; that many of the country people do not understand English, and that the lawyers should speak for them and examine them as witnesses in the Manx. Now, Mr Editor, I contend for it that this is quite a wrong view of the subject. The plea, that old persons know nothing but Manx, is the very argument of all others which is most against encouraging that tongue, or dialect - for language it deserves not to be called. Mankind ought to improve, and not remain in their pristine barbarism. There was a time, no doubt, when our ancestors were savages, and could understand each other by nods, and signs, and inarticulate sounds. But those times are past and gone. Wherefore, then, should we recal[l] them? What better is the gibberish called Manx than an uncouth mouthful of course (*sic*) savage expressions, as distant from any degree of civilized sound as that of the Kamskatcadales (*sic*) is from the classic beauty of one of the orations which grace the first orators of the British senate? Such a jargon is Manx. Unless for the purpose of preaching to very old people indeed, it is quite useless; and in this view it is very right that our country clergy should know Manx; and in order the better to promote litigation, our young lawyers ought to study the lingo. But when we speak of civilization, of refinement, of the paramount excellence of cultivated society above savage nature and harsh barbarism, can it be endured? We know that civilization is promoted best by letters, by books, by reading; but what literature, what books, what reading does the Manx dialect afford? None, save an old translation of the Bible, which cost a great deal, and which cost had far better been expended on English Bibles and Testaments, and prayer books. Abolish the Manx; I would say then, as fast as ye can, ye learned of the country. Judges, Lawyers, Clergy, crush it. Allow no one, not even one of your servants or neighbours to speak one word of Manx; and thus, by degrees annihilate it. Several years ago Bishop Hildesley ordered the schoolmaster of his diocese not to allow Manx to be spoken in his school; and, as a penalty on boys who ventured to express their thoughts in the language they best understood, they were marked with a brand of infamy, called the *sign of Manx* [writer's italics] - and were punished, and justly, for having it upon them. Had this been continued, almost all the rising generations would have been regenerated, and we should have the pleasure of seeing a civilized nation arising in the place and stead of the old one - a nation not wearing karanes [sandals of untanned hide], but shoes and boots. Indeed, in spite of the pains that I see on all sides taken to bring in the Manx again, I see some of my countrymen wear as decent boots and boot-tops as men of any other nation. And, Mr Editor, I do not know of a much better test of moral refinement and the good taste and fancy of a nation, than that individuals who a century ago would inevitably be condemned to karanes, are now wearing boots, well polished with Day and Martin's best, and tops of the genuine Dandy kind. - Your's (*sic*), &c.

May 26, 1822.   A NATIVE.

4. *MANKS ADVERTISER*, 13.06.1822. A reply to the foregoing.

Sir. Your correspondent, A Native, deserves to be thrashed, for writing such stuff, and you are not much better for taking it in your pepar. He is an ennemy to this Isle. For every one knoweth, and you know as well as any body I am sure that manx is the very palladium of the country. If you put the manx down, our nation will be no longer manx - it will be english or scotch or irish - it will be mungrel at least. Put manx down and where is the keys - put manx down and where is our clergy - put manx down and where is our judges? - You say they may do all their duty in english, put let me ask you will the peeple undar- [next half-line lost] - you will say. I say the peeple is the peeple, and the peeple is manx; [two words obscure] a please argumint. Native says it is a savage dialect, and yet you know it is as good a language as any other. - The manks translation of the Bible is reckoned very good, and it sound[s] well in reeding. And our clergy write there sarmans - Will you say that they are not any thing but gibberish? The peeple understands them at any rate, and what is better every one in the congrigation understand them. What then will you say to the Law? At Cammon law we all knows that the jury understands manx better then English, and the lawyer that speak to them is better for his clyent if he is understood surely. And how could they understand the witnesses without manx? - In short words, Mr. Editor, it is very necessary that manks should be spoke and understood in this Island, and the man who signeth himself a Native is no true Manxman if he says other. He is one of those men who would trimble [i.e. trample] on the rites of his country. And as for talking of karranes and boots and saying they be testes of civilazation, it is plean he knoweth little of civilazation for one. Let him shew me what is civilazation. Let him point out to me the difference there is betwixt an english speech and a manks speech any more then that the one is english and the other manx. Do you think Mr. Editor that I count any thing of a man for wearing boots with yellow tops to them? And that a man's sense is better for the leather on his legs is polished with Day and Martin's blacking? It is true enough, when a man gets rich his words goes farther than when he was poor - and money buys leather as well as hide - but it will never buy sense. It may pay for schoollin sure enough, but it will not give disernment. Now common sense Mr. Editor is all that I lies stress upon. And what common sense is there in speaking to a people in a language which they do not understand? Can Native shew me that there is common sense in this eh?

I am your humble Servant,

9th June 1822.   A MANKSMAN.

5. *MANX PATRIOT*, 07.07.1824.

Letter to the Editor.

No man blames national prejudices more than I do, and yet there is not one who ardently cherishes a love of country and admires it in others. Your Englishman, for instances, despite his acknowledged goodness of character, has his faults and follies, his failings and weaknesses - but just hint to him that any one of them are national, and *John Bull's* [writer' sitalics] ire is soon drawn upon you; your Scotchman is well known to spurn at and

resent every insult offered to his country or countrymen, and to bind close to every northern brother, - an insult offered to him or any of them, sinks deep, and rankles long before it is smothered or forgotten; your red-hot off-hand son of Hibernia, is all-fire and tow the moment he hears his country reflected upon, in the slightest degree, or a general odium thrown upon it, or its buoyant natives. I am a Manxman, and we Manxmen are often doomed to hear with patience the worst epithets bestowed upon us, without daring to resent the insult in any way [...] We are blown up and bullied on all sides for want of knowledge and information, and our native language is ridiculed by those who cannot comprehend or understand it; and yet I think before we are stigmatized and abused in this way, we ought to be *taught* [writer's italics] the language they wish us to speak, whether English, Scotch, or Irish, and not kicked or cuffed into obedience like spaniel dogs - such ruling and such doctrines may be tolerated amongst the Hottentots, or practised in Turkey, or Algiers, but it will not do here. - Yours & c.
Kirk Santan, June 19th, 1824.   A MANXMAN.

Appendix C

(Table 9)

CENSUS FIGURES FOR THE TOWNS AND PARISHES 1726-1891

	1726	1757	1784	1792	1821	1831	1841	1851	1861	1871	1881	1891
Douglas	810	1,814	2,850	3,625	6,054	6,776	8,647	9,880	12,511	13,972	15,719	19,525
Castletown ...	785	915	1,318	1,423	2,036	2,062	2,283	2,531	2,373	2,320	2,243	2,178
Ramsey.........	460	882	894	920	1,523	1,754	2,104	2,701	2,891	3,934	4,025	4,866
Peel	475	805	1,254	1,269	1,909	1,722	2,133	2,342	2,848	3,513	3,829	3,631
Patrick	745	954	1,452	2,153	2,031	2,195	2,768	2,925	2,778	2,888	2,626	2,228
German.........	510	925	1,220	1,236	1,849	1,791	1,896	2,168	1,924	1,762	1,691	1,467
Marown*	499	658	841	842	1,201	1,216	1,318	1,364	1,161	1,123	990	961
Michael.........	643	826	980	1,003	1,427	1,317	1,376	1,416	1,314	1,231	1,101	1,005
Ballaugh	806	773	871	1,015	1,467	1,416	1,516	1,392	1,228	1,076	970	830
Jurby...........	483	467	637	713	1,108	1,097	1,063	985	911	788	661	543
Lezayre.........	1,309	1,481	1,080	1,721	2,209	2,657	2,323	2,468	2,520	1,620	1,486	1,412
Andreas.........	967	1,067	1,390	1,555	2,229	2,217	2,332	2,165	1,955	1,759	1,482	1,239
Bride	612	629	652	678	1,001	1,039	1,153	1,053	919	880	741	640
Maughold	525	759	1,079	1,087	1,514	1,341	1,585	1,762	1,654	1,432	1,147	982
Lonan	547	869	1,219	1,408	1,846	1,923	2,230	2,607	2,909	3,740	3,277	2,970
Conchan	370	434	560	690	1,451	1,482	2,589¶	3,400¶	2,177	1,621	1,508	1,890
Braddan.........	780	1,121	1,214	1,420	1,754	1,927	2,122	2,405	2,301	2,214	2,071	2,041
Santon	1,250	507	589	512	800	798	769	714	693	628	593	510
Malew	376	1,466	1,861	1,910	2,649	2,778	3,085	3,260	2,692	2,467	2,597	2,275
Arbory	661	785	912	1,143	1,455	1,511	1,615	1,593	1,410	1,355	1,274	1,000
Rushen	813	1,007	1,451	1,590	2,568	2,732	3,079	3,256	3,300	3,719	3,527	3,415
Totals.........	14,426†	19,144‡	24,924	27,913§	40,081‖	41,751	47,986	52,387	52,469	54,042	53,558	55,608

	1726	1757	1784	1792	1821	1831	1841	1851	1861	1871	1881	1891
Towns	2,530	4,416	6,316	7,237	11,522	12,314	15,167	17,454	20,623	23,739	25,816	30,200
Country	11,896	14,728	18,608	20,676	28,559	29,437	32,819	34,933	31,846	30,303	27,742	25,408
Total.........	14,426	19,144	24,924	27,913	40,081	41,751	47,986	52,387	52,469	54,042	53,558	55,608

Source: Moore (1900: 646-47).

* for Marown an estimate only.

¶ increase mainly due to the extension of Douglas.

†14426 (1726) from a paper in Bishop Wilson's hand (cf. Sherwood 1882: 284, quoted after Moore *ibid.*).

‡19114 (1757) return by clergy (Sherwood 1882: 285, quoted after Moore *ibid.*).

§ 27913 (1792) return by the clergy at the request of Governor Smith (Sherwood 1882: 286, quoted after Moore *ibid.*).

‖ Year 1821 was the first official census in the Isle of Man.

Appendix D

MAP 1: Percentage of population able to speak Manx 1874 (according to Jenner 1875)

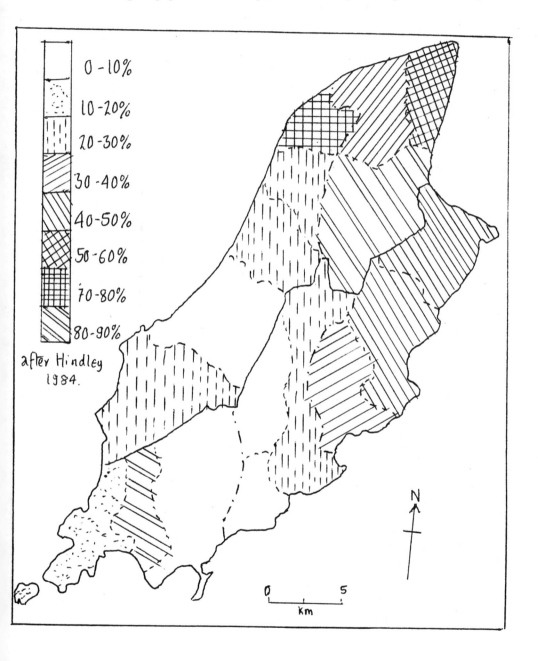

0 - 10%

10 - 20%

20 - 30%

30 - 40%

40 - 50%

50 - 60%

70 - 80%

80 - 90%

after Hindley
1984.

N

0   5
km

260

MAP 2: Areas where Manx was spoken 1874 - ca.1900 (according to Jenner 1875 and later information)

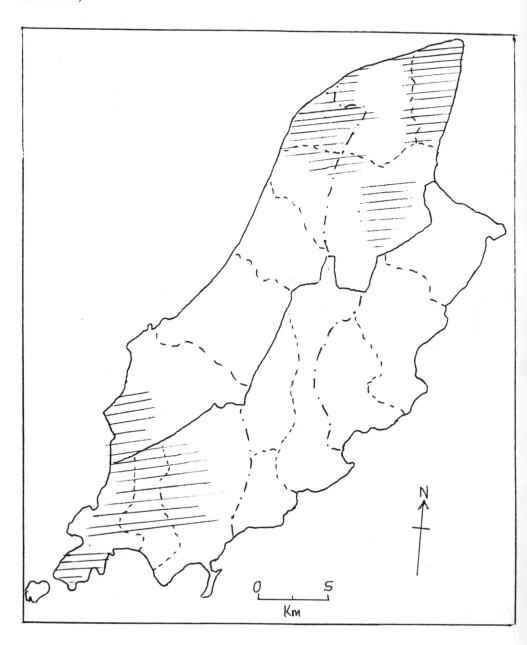

MAP 3: Marstrander's 'Tour of Man' 1929

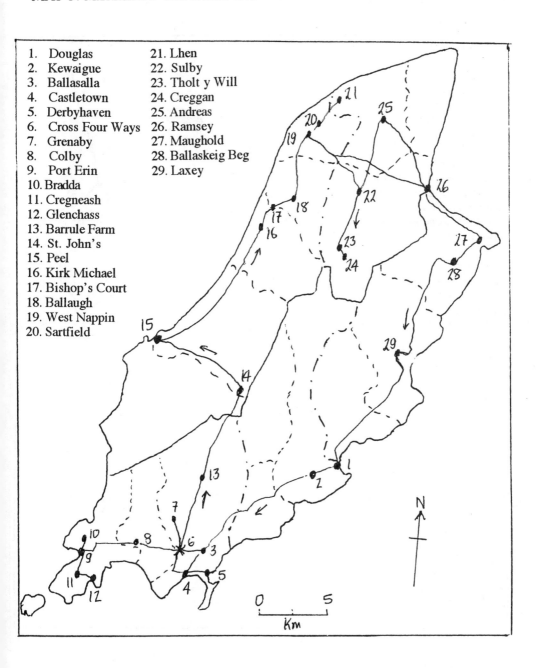

1. Douglas
2. Kewaigue
3. Ballasalla
4. Castletown
5. Derbyhaven
6. Cross Four Ways
7. Grenaby
8. Colby
9. Port Erin
10. Bradda
11. Cregneash
12. Glenchass
13. Barrule Farm
14. St. John's
15. Peel
16. Kirk Michael
17. Bishop's Court
18. Ballaugh
19. West Nappin
20. Sartfield
21. Lhen
22. Sulby
23. Tholt y Will
24. Creggan
25. Andreas
26. Ramsey
27. Maughold
28. Ballaskeig Beg
29. Laxey

MAP 4: Birthplaces of the last native speakers

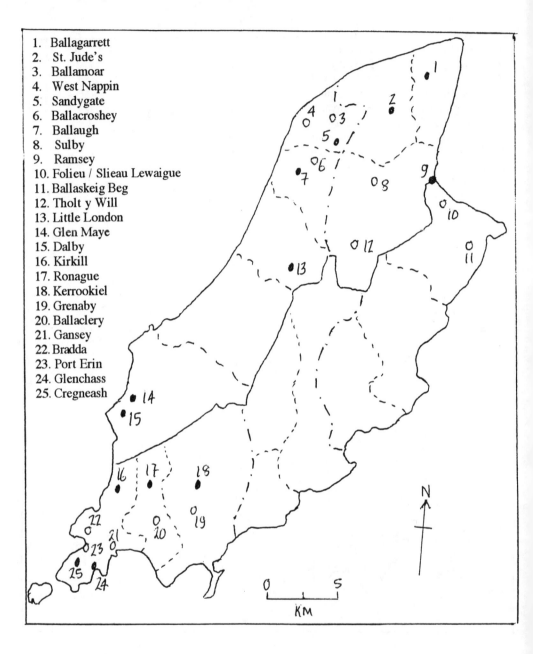

1. Ballagarrett
2. St. Jude's
3. Ballamoar
4. West Nappin
5. Sandygate
6. Ballacroshey
7. Ballaugh
8. Sulby
9. Ramsey
10. Folieu / Slieau Lewaigue
11. Ballaskeig Beg
12. Tholt y Will
13. Little London
14. Glen Maye
15. Dalby
16. Kirkill
17. Ronague
18. Kerrookiel
19. Grenaby
20. Ballaclery
21. Gansey
22. Bradda
23. Port Erin
24. Glenchass
25. Cregneash

• acc. to Loch 1946
o additional places acc. to Marstrander 1929-33b

Appendix E

Texts

An example of spoken Manx 1833

MONA'S HERALD AND GENERAL ADVERTISER
27.12.1833
ORIGINAL COMMUNICATIONS

PLEDEILYS EDDYR DAA VANNINAGH DOOIE
[Juan as Illiam meeteil.]

[Editorial: reproduced as printed].

Juan. - Tou cheet.

Illiam. - Ta. Tou uss cheet neesht.

J. - Ta moghree fihn ayn.

I. - Ta shen ayn, agh ta tra mie ras-tagh harrish ain.

J. - Ta dy jarroo. Geayll oo jehn lhong va trait laa chaiee mooie jeh kione Yerby?

I. - De ve shicker, - nagh row eh sy fabyr.

J. - Cren pabyr tou us goaill?

I. - Ta ga na three jin goaill yn Heral eddyr shin; as shimmey oor plesal te cur orrin ceau; te cur shiaghe[y] yn traa, chouds te ginsh jeh ny reddyn ta goll.

J. - Ta Juan Bowyr as mee hene goaill y Sun eddyr shin. Taa wite pleat jeant ayn er y gherrid shoh my-chione y Chiare-as-feed - wite jin-glerys.

I. - Hoh! Ommijys leh - jus ryd dy lieeneyn duillag.

J. - Ta ny smoo na shen ayn. Vell oo toiggal ad?

I. - Tad mie doillee lhiam ny cheayr-tyn, fooast strow hene dy vel me laanvie.

J. - Insh dou cre tan fogle lhiauyr shen meanal, Rebrezentashyn. Tad

gusal mennic eh, agh cha vel y cheeall my chione cre te meanal.

I. - Cha sayd cre Rebrezentashyn! Tou dty voght glen ny yei, mannagh sayd cre Rebrezentashyn. Jeeagh sy Dicksinerry, ghooinney, as yiow jeeragh eh. Vel Dicksinerry ayd - foddee nagh vel - yeeaseeyms nane dhyt.

J. O ta shann unnane aym ny lhie er y latt ayns shen sthie, agh ta ny duillaggyn eic faagys ooilliu reabit assjee; agh yioym un ogle aynjee fooast - nee un duillag shen.*

I. - Cre shiu dhyt boirey? Injyms mee hene dhyt, ghooinney - Reb-rezentashyn - ta shen fer shassoo ayns ynnyd fer elley. Tan Heral shas-soo er dy lhisagh sleih jannoo leighyn dy phlesal ad hene, cha nee fagail dan Kiare-as-feed ad. As dy jarroo ta mish me hene goaill toshi-aght dy leaystey red beg bentyn daue. Nagh beagh eh foddey share dooin stroak ve ain ayns ny coonseilyn oc? Shen myr tadyr ayns Sosthyn. Ta dagh skeerey cur stiagh dooinney ayns yn ynnyd oc; dooinney rheit lioroo hene. As nagh mie veagh eh dy voghe shin kied voish y Ree dy

264

rei dooinney ayns y skeerey ain, fer veagh toiggal feme y skeerey, as myr shen veagh fondagh dy charail leighyn fondagh dooin.

J. - Cha vel mee gobbal. Nish hene tad taggloo jeh gobbal kied da ny hirrinee ta shin ayn cur pudaasyn ass cheer; as ta fys mie ain ooilliu er dy vel shoh ryd feer neuchreeney; son cren phrice yiow nish er yn arroo? As cren aght nee yn Thennys y maal? Er son feme cha bee ayn; yiow main palchey voish Nolbin, as shen ayns tra giare, lhig da gennid ve ayn na dyn; agh ta fys ain er un rgd [ryd], bee curnaght voish ny cheer-nyn mooie lieeney stiagh orrin, as freayll sheese price yn arroo myr boallagh eh. Myr shan nagh bee chynce eddyr faagit dooin.

I. - Tan irrin ayd. Craad yiow sleih argid ec y tra tayn dy eek ny fee-aghyn bleeaney oc? Agh bee eh ny share da ny leighdaryn.

J. - Wahll, wahll, cha vel shoh agh un ryd ny yei, agh shimmey ryd tayn.

I. - Shohn whashtyn, vel eh lowal dan Chaire-as-feed janoo leigh erbee fegooish consent y theay? Ernonney lhig aue ve rheit liorish y theay, as eisht veagh dagh skeerey as chynce eikey son cairys; son oddagh ad eisht janoo stiagh rish y dooinney mooar oc hene er dy choilliu oyr jeh egin foshlit na feme erbee oddagh ve reaghit liorish leigh noa.

J. - Veagh shoh resoonagh, dy ghra yn chooid sloo jeh. Agh cre shiu taggloo? Cha vow mayd nyn aigney!

I. - Kys sayds son shen? Foddie dy now.

J. - Beggan! Tan Kiare-as-feed as sneih currit orroo, as tad gra dy vel ad corree, as dy vel paart jeu hene

scrieu ayns y Sun cha keoi as dy beagh ad dy feer baanrit.

I. - Cha voddyms credjal shen - ta sins smoo ayndoo na dy ghoaill olk rish yn irriney, shickyr. Ta fys mie oc er nagh re noi oc hene myr deiney erlheh tan chooish bentyn, agh daue myr Khingleeidee yn theay, as shenyfa cha vel eh agh quashtyn ta bentyn da resoon chadjin, chamoo vel eh madyr erbee daue-syn agh dys vondeish y cheer; cheu-mooie jeh shen, dy beagh ad currit ass oik mairagh veagh eh dys y vondeish oc hene, son haueagh eh cost daue cha nee beggan, goll dys Balleychashtal myr whilleen goar dys bwoaillee. Ec y chooid smessey veagh ad myr vadyr - as eer bentyn da nyn oashley oddagh eh ve ny share, son oddagh ad, whillin as ta feiu, ve rheit ass y noa. As lurg ooilliu quoi s'fondagh veagh son y visnis nad hene.

J. - Cha sayms bwo, agh hee main cre jir yn Heral tra hig eh. Ta mish coondey lane jehn Heral. Ta mee treeall goaill eh son y nah raie. Yeeasee oo dou eh, as yeeasyms y Sun dhyts. Bee plea dewil goll son shiaghtinyn.

I. - Dyn dood cha vod ad ve feeagh.

J. - Tou us er cheu yn Heral.

I. - Ta mee goaillrish dy vel, as cha nee fegooish resoon. Ta ooilliun sleih son eckey. Eie stiagh myr tou goll shiaghey, as jeeaghyms dhyt ee.

J. - Feer vie, my vees tra aym neem gyllagh er raad bac.

[*TRANSLATION*

Juan - 'You're coming.
Illiam - Yes. You're coming as well.
J. - There's a fine morning in.
I. - Yes, there is that, but we've a very blustery spell behind us.

J. - Yes, indeed. Did you hear about the ship that was stranded the other day out from Jurby Head?

I. - To be sure; wasn't it in the paper?

J. - What paper do *you* take?

I. - Two or three of us take the *Herald* between us; and many a pleasant hour it has given us; it passes the time, while it tells about what's going on.

J. - Juan Bouyr (Deaf John) and myself take the *Sun* between us. There's been a great deal of dis-cussion recently in it about the House of Keys - a good deal of heated discussion.

I. - Hoh, tomfoolery, lah - just something to fill the page.

J. - There's more than that in it. Do you understand them (the arguments)?

I. - They're quite difficult for me to follow at times, still I think I'm quite good (at it).

J. - Tell me, what does this long word Representation mean? They often use it, but I've no idea at all what it means.

I. - You don't know what Representation is! You're a right poor thing if you don't know what Representation is. Look it up in the dictionary, man, and you'll have it right away. Do you have a dictionary - perhaps not - I'll lend you one.

J. - Oh, I have an old one lying on the shelf there at home, but its pages are nearly all torn out; but I'll find the word in it yet - that page will do.

I. - You needn't bother? I'll tell you myself, man - Representation - that is one standing in place of another. The *Herald* maintains that people should make laws to please themselves, not leave it to the House of Keys. And indeed I myself am starting to swing a wee bit as far as they are concerned. Wouldn't it be far better for us to have a say in their deliberations? That's how they are in England. Each parish sends in a man to represent them (lit. in their place); a man elected by themselves. And wouldn't it be good if we got leave from the king to choose a man in our parish, one who would understand the needs of the parish, and so would be certain to ensure adequate laws for us.

J. - I don't deny it. At present they talk of refusing permission to us farmers to send potatoes abroad; and we all know very well that this is an unwise thing, for what price will you now get for corn? And how will the tenants make up rent? As for shortage there won't be any; we'll get plenty from Scotland, and in a short time at that; let there be a scarcity or no. But we know one thing, wheat from countries outside will flood in on us and keep down the price of corn as usual. And so we won't have any chance at all.

I. - You're right. Where do people get money from at present to pay their yearly debts? But it will be better for the lawyers.

J. - Well, well, that's only one issue after all, but there are many issues.

I. - This is the question, whether it is lawful for the House of Keys to make any law without the people's consent? Otherwise they should be elected by the people, and then every parish would have a chance to get justice; for then they would be able to influence their representatives on every case of public necessity or any want that could be remedied by (the passing of) a new law.

266

J. - That would be reasonable. to say the least of it. But what do you say? We'll not get our own way!

I. - How do you know that? Perhaps we will.

J. - Not much! The House of Keys is vexed, and they say they are angry, and that some of them write in the *Sun* as wildly as if they were quite mad.

I. - I can't believe that - they have more sense than to take offence at the truth, surely. They know very well that it does not affect them as private individuals, but as leaders of the people, and therefore it is only a question that relates to common reason, and is not at all a matter for them but for the benefit of the country; apart from that, if they were put out of office tomorrow it would be to their own advantage, for it would save them not a little, going to Castletown like so many goats to a fold. At worst they would be as they were - and even as regards their standing (in society) they could, as many as are worthy, be chosen afresh (under the new system). And after all who would be more competent for the business (of governing) than themselves.

J. - I don't know, bhoy, but we'll see what the *Herald* says when it comes. I think a lot of the *Herald*. I'm thinking of taking it for the next quarter-year. If you lend me it I'll lend you the *Sun*. There'll be a severe debate underway for weeks.

I. - No doubt, they can't be quiet.

J. - You're on the side of the *Herald*.

I. - I admit I am, and not without reason. All the people are for it. Call in when you're passing and I'll show you it.

J. - All right, if I have time I'll call in on the way back'.]

*Juan may shortly avail himself of purchasing a new Dictionary, as we understand Mr. [Archibald] Cregeen is making arrangements for the publication of his forthcoming volume, - in which undertaking we heartily wish him success.

The following texts are taken as samples of recorded native Manx speech, three from both North and South. The first from each area was taken down by Marstrander (M) (cf. §3.6.2.2.), the second and third recorded by the Manx Museum (MM) and *Yn Cheshaght Ghailckagh* (YCG) (for details see Section 3.5.). In each case the year of recording is given in brackets. The texts are given here for convenience in phonemic script, then in standard Manx orthography plus English translation, and are taken from HLSM/I. The following and additional texts can be found there, but in phonetic script.

FROM THE NORTH

1. THOMAS CHRISTIAN (the Carter), Ramsey
(M/II: 949-51(1929), HLSM/I: 200-01)

[The Buggane of Gob ny Scuit]

/keːrtə reu ve 'dunˊə as ve nenəm egə bil 'kˊenisˊ. vi 'komǝl egǝ korǝni skilǝ 'maːl; ve tai beg tuːtˊ egǝ. vi tˊsˊǝt gǝs rum'seː menikˊ dǝ mǝ'deːl 'kaːrdˊǝn astǝ 'gedin dˊoːx as erǝ toːr. ha reu e 'gobǝl 'dˊox tre er'biː, vi gˊalǝtˊ de. ǝi dǝ reu vi gol 'taːi ek ba'lˊuːr, ax ve 'reur dˊoːx egǝ as rin e klasˊtˊǝn ko're: 'muːr ǝǝǝu tˊsˊǝt nus vei ǝn klˊuː. ha rǝu e aglax geː dǝ 'reu e er klasˊtˊǝn mǝkˊeun bo'geːdn muːr gob nǝ 'skut. foːdǝ vei rei er'suːl hai e sus geːdǝr ǝn 'sˊiːdn. geː nax vak e 'veg ve ŋ 'sˊiːdn nǝ smelˊǝ as nǝ 'smelˊǝ as vi gol 'aːgǝl nax 'biː e son 'dˊenu veg. sai e sˊiːsˊ er kreg as vi 'pudǝ max nǝ lǝrgaxǝn egǝ as ren neːn dˊeu 'taːrtǝn er 'kreg vuːr ve foː as ren ǝ 'kreg gol 'todˊǝx dǝ rǝulǝl, as mǝr 'harax e rin e 'todˊǝm uns tǝul ve ǝdǝr deː kreg as rin e liǝnǝ e 'suːs. axa reu sˊidn sodˊǝ rǝ klasˊtˊǝn. vi 'harisˊ gorisˊ sˊedn as ve ŋ sˊidn sˊedn 'enmǝsǝtˊ bo'geːdn 'muːr 'gob ne 'skut. vi 'soilsˊǝtˊ deu nǝ lǝrg sˊedǝn ve faːslǝ muːr unsǝn oxtax erǝ tˊsˊeu sˊedn as faːslǝ beg erǝ tˊsˊeu elǝ. ax treː ve ŋ 'gᵘiːǝ 'sˊeːdˊǝ vei ǝn 'aːrn sˊedn vi 'liǝnǝ ǝn teul 'muːr as 'vi gol 'maːx asǝn teul 'beg as dˊenu ǝ fair 'muːr/

Keayrt dy row va dooiney as va'n ennym echey Bill Kennish. V'eh cummal ec y Corrany Skylley Maghal; va thie beg thooit echey. V'eh cheet gys Rhumsaa mennick dy meeiteil caarjyn as dy geddyn jough as er y thoyr. Cha row eh gobbal jough traa erbee; v'eh giallit da. Oie dy row v'eh goll thie ec Ballure, agh va rouyr jough echey as ren eh clashtyn coraa mooar - oooh cheet neose veih yn clieau. Cha row eh agglagh ge dy row eh er clashtyn mychione Buggane Mooar Gob ny Scuit. Foddey veih roie ersooyl hie eh seose geiyrt er yn sheean. Ge nagh vaik eh veg va yn sheean [gaase] ny s'melley as ny s'melley, as v'eh goaill aggle nagh bee eh son jannoo veg. Soie eh sheese er creg as v'eh puttey magh ny lurgaghyn echey, as ren nane jeu tayrtyn er creg vooar va fo, as ren y creg goaill toshiaght dy rollal. As myr haghyragh eh ren eh tuittym ayns towl va eddyr daa creg as ren eh lhieeney eh seose as cha row sheean sodjey ry clashtyn. V'eh harrish gollrish shen as va yn sheean shen enmyssit Buggane Mooar Gob ny Scuit. V'eh soilshit dou ny lurg shen; va fosley mooar ayns yn ughtagh er y cheu shen as fosley beg er y cheu elley, agh tra va yn geay sheidey veih yn ayrn shen v'eh lhieeney yn towl mooar as v'eh goll magh ass yn towl beg as jannoo y feiyr mooar.

'Once there was a man and his name was Bill Kennish. He was living at the Corrany in Kirk Maughold and he had a wee thatched house. He would often come to Ramsey to meet friends and to get a drink and 'go on the tear'. He'd never refuse a drink at any time; he was given to it. One night he was going home via Ballure. He had too much drink taken and he heard a loud voice - oooh coming down from the mountain. He was not afraid even though he had heard about the Great Buggane of Gob ny Scuit. Far from running away he went up after the noise. Although he saw nothing the noise was (getting) worse and worse, and he was afraid that he'd be unable to do anything. He sat down on a rock and was stretching out his legs. One of them caught on a large rock that was under it and the rock began to roll. And as it would happen it fell into a hole that was between two rocks and blocked it. The sound was to be heard no longer. It was over just like that, and that noise was called the Great Buggane of Gob ny Scuit. It was shown to me afterwards that there was a large opening in the hillside on that side and a small one on the other. When the wind would blow from that part it would fill the large hole and go out via the small one and make a loud noise'.

2. JOHN KNEEN (the Gaaue), Ballaugh Curragh, Ballaugh
(YCG/4(1952), HLSM/I: 248-51)

['Took' by the Fairies]

/oː va misˊ ˈgoit egˊə ˈfeːrisˊən nisˊ. renˊ ad ˈkurarəm ˈsˊuːl rid gorisˊ dˊai ˈviːlˊə ... sˊen ə ˈnei va mi os rumˈseː əs rən mi tˊət ˈtaːi lˊesˊ hari ˈkriŋ as ren e ˈgˋiːsˊ dum, vaim gedn ˈmaːkax ˈtaːi lˊesˊa. as tre rensˊin ˈgedn tai rena korən sailˊsˊə ˈsterəm dum son də gol ˈtaːi. ha ˈrau fiː ˈfodə em də ˈgol, bət rən me ˈgol ˈtruːdˊən lˊiniən a sən treː va mi sˊiːsˊ egə lˊini, oː rid gorisˊ kid stənˈdaːt əː beː ˈbeg, as va ˈdeː doilisˊ, ˈdeː ˈgjap egə kˊodn ən ˈveː, as va mi ˈlaːl goilˊən ˈneːn osə lˊini as ren mi goilˊə neːn osə ˈveːə, as va mi sˊuːl məˈgit ən ˈvaː as ren mi tˊit dusə bol ren mi ˈgoilˊ wusˊ, as ren mi goilˊən ..., əˈnaːsˊ ren me tˊit, ən ˈaːsˊ ren mi goilˊ ˈmaːx dəsən veː ˈvuːə.., as va ˈrid sˊen gorəsˊ miːlˊə, as ren mi tˊit dusə beːə ˈvuːə əs rən mi ˈgoːilˊən lau ˈkˊedax em, wŭnˊə, as lˊigəm gulˊ ən ˈleu kˊeːdax, as ren mi ˈsˊuːl son deː ˈmiːlˊədus skilˊ anˈdreːəs, as vamə faːgən ulˊu əˈtaːiən erə ˈraːd, as va mi greː dus miˈhiːn - ta ˈsˊoː ən tai dˊudn, as ən ˈtaːi elˊə dˊem, as ən ˈtaːiən sˊaːən tˊabal əs va mi greː dəs miˈhiːn - te ˈsˊoː ən tˊabal, as ha ˈrau mi ˈeːbəl ˈsaː su minid, wŭnˊə, as ren mi ˈgol as ren mi ˈgol wusˊ ˈsˊen, wusˊ skilˊən ˈdreːs ˈsˊiːs dus sən ˈdˊuds, as rən mə faːgən ə kiːlˊ əs ren mi tˊənˈdeː eː məlau ˈkˊeːdax əs rin mi tˊit ˈsˊaː usən ˈraːd va ˈgol dus ˈdˊəːbi, as rən mi ˈsˊuːl rid gorisˊ miːlˊə ərəˈraːd sˊen, as va məˈkˊaː sən esˊ gedn soːː. rin mi ˈsai erə kreg as tre ren mi ˈsai gaː nətriː də ˈminidən ren mi gol də dˊenu toiagən dəgol taːi, as va ˈkˊaːsən eməs ˈsoː, wŭnˊə, ha ˈrau mi ˈeːbəl ˈsˊuːl, as ren mi ˈgoːilˊ ən breːgən dˊem as kurəd erə ˈdribm em as rin mi ˈsuːl ən deː ˈviːlˊə ˈtaːi us məˈoːiərən. əsən ˈvoːri, rən mi ˈgiri osə ˈvoːri, ad ulˊu eˈsuːl də ˈlai ən ˈtreː ren mi gedn ˈtaːi. as ren mi goːilˊ mə ˈsˊiber əs ren mi ˈgol dəsə lˊaːvi as unsə ˈvoːri va ˈdeː vlistə ˈvuːr erə ˈbaunən em gorisˊ, oː gorisˊ lˊeː ˈjau. as treː va mə ve ˈfoːs ˈgˋaːrə ən ˈbaun dˊe ən deː ˈkˊaːs as ən vreg, as gol məˈgit moˈsen əs ren mi tˊit.., və mi gobər ulˊu ən ˈleː əs ren mi tˊit ˈtai əs gol də ˈiaːi əs unsən ˈvoːri van ˈblistərən olˊu əˈsuːl, wŭnˊə; ha ˈrau u ˈruː ə ˈfaːgən, as ha ˈrau u ˈruː əˈsmunˊaːn də rau ridəˈbiː ˊer, as va ˈsˊen ridən kwaːx də lˊuːə/

Oh, va mish goit ec y ferrishyn neesht. Ren ad cur orrym shooyll red gollrish jeih veeilley.., shen yn oie va mee ayns Rhumsaa as ren mee cheet thie lesh Harry Kring as ren eh ginsh dum, vaim geddyn markiagh thie lesh-eh, as tra ren shin geddyn thie ren eh cur yn soilshey sterrym dum son dy goll thie. Cha row eh feer foddey aym dy goll, *but* ren mee goll trooid yn lheeanneeyn, as yn traa va mee sheese ec y lheeannee, oh red gollrish keead stundayrt er bayr beg, as va daa doarlish, daa *gap* ec y kione yn vayr, as va mee laccal goaill yn nane ayns y lheeannee as ren mee goaill yn nane ayns y vagher, as va mee shooyll mygeayrt yn vagher as ren mee cheet dys y boayl ren mee goll woish, as ren mee goaill yn.., yn aght ren mee cheet, yn aght ren mee goll magh dys yn vayr vooar, as va y red shen gollrish meeilley, as ren mee cheet dys y bayr vooar as ren mee goaill yn laue kiuttagh aym, wooinney, as lhig ym goll yn laue kiuttagh, as ren mee shooyll son daa meeilley dys Skyll Andreays, as va mee fakin ooilley y thieyn er y raad, as va mee gra dys mee hene, 'Ta shoh yn Thie Juan, as yn thie elley Jem, as yn thieyn shaghey yn chabbal'. As va mee gra dys mee hene, 'Ta shoh yn chabbal', as cha row mee abyl shassoo minnid, wooinney, as ren mee goll as ren mee goll woish shen, woish Skyll Andreays sheese dys St. Jude's, as ren mee fakin yn keeill as ren mee chyndaa er my laue kiuttagh as ren mee cheet shaghey ayns yn raad va goll dys Jurby, as ren mee shooyll red gollrish meeilley er y raad shen, as va my cassyn eisht geddyn *sore*. Ren mee soie er y creg as tra ren mee soie gaa ny tree dy minnidyn ren mee goll dy jannoo toshiaghtyn dy goll thie, as va cassyn aym's *sore*, wooinney; cha row mee abyl shooyll, as ren mee goaill yn braagyn jeem as cur ad er y dreeym aym, as ren mee shooyll yn daa veeilley thie ayns my oashyryn. Ayns yn voghree, ren mee girree ayns y voghree, v'ad ooilley ersooyl dy lhie yn traa ren mee geddyn thie. As ren mee goaill my shibbyr as ren mee goll dys y lhiabbee, as ayns y voghree va daa vlister vooar er y boynyn aym gollrish, oh, gollrish lieh-ooh. As tra va mee [er] ve foarst giarrey yn boyn jeh yn daa cass ass yn vraag as goll mygeayrt myr shen, as ren mee cheet..,va mee gobbyr ooilley yn laa, as ren mee cheet thie as goll dy thie as ayns y voghree va'n blisteryn ooilley ersooyl, wooinney; cha row oo rieau er fakin, as cha row oo rieau er smooinaghtyn dy row red erbee er, as va shen reddyn quaagh dy liooar.

'Oh, I was took by the fairies too. They made me walk something like ten miles.., that's the night I was in Ramsey and I came home with Harry Kneen and he told me, I was getting a lift home with him, and when we got (to his) house he gave me the storm-light for to go home. It wasn't very far for me to go, but I went through the meadows and when I was down at the meadow, oh something like a hundred yards along a wee road, there were two gaps at the end of the road, and I wanted to take the one into the meadow, and I took the one into the field. I was walking about the field and I came to the place I went from, and I took the way I came, the way I went out to the main road, and that was something like a mile, and I came to the main road and I turned to my left, man, and I took the left turn and I walked for two miles to Andreas, and I was seeing all the houses on the road, and I was saying to myself, 'This is Juan's house and the other house Jem's and the houses past the chapel', and I was saying to myself, 'This is the chapel', and I wasn't able to stand for a minute, man, and I went and I went from there, from Andreas, down to St. Jude's, and I saw the church and I turned to my left and I came by on the road that was going to Jurby, and I walked for about a mile along that road, and my feet were then getting sore. I sat on the Rock*, and when I had sat for two or three minutes I went to start off for home, and my feet were sore, man; I wasn't able to walk, and I took off my shoes and put them on my back, and I walked the two miles home in my stockings. In the morning, I got up in the morning - they were all away to bed when I got home. And I took my supper and went to my bed, and in the morning there were two big blisters on my heels like, oh, like a half-egg. And when, I had to cut the heel of my two feet out of the shoe and I was going about like that, and I came.., I was working all the day, and I came home and went to bed, and in the morning the blisters were all gone, man; you'd never have seen it, and you'd never have thought that there had been anything on it (?on them), and that was queer enough'.

* i.e. the Craig, a large rock on the corner of the Loop Road (to West Craig and Close y Kewin) and the Jurby Road west of St. Jude's, removed ca. 1900 by the then Highway Board. It gave its name

to *Bayr ny Cregga* 'road of/by the rock', the older name on that part of the Jurby Road from St. Jude's crossroads westward to Ballaugh Cronk, cf. PNIM/III: 93.

3. JOHN TOM KAIGHIN, Ballagarrett, Bride
(MM22(1950), HLSM/I: 290-93)

[The Parson and the Pig]

/wel, van sˊaːn ben as sˊaːn dunˊə as vad 'bəː a 'kodsˊax, as vad freːl 'buːə as va triː 'maːrən ok, as vad friːl ə 'buːə as muk, oːn muk vad 'friːl as vad ... olˊu ə treː van 'muk 'genzax ok də tˊsˊit 'sˊtˊaːx də gedn ən 'viː ek də holˊə 'treː. vad 'kuntəs 'xwiːsˊ dˊen muk, son vad 'fetˊsˊən 'muk sˊtˊaːx də gˊednˊ viː ek ən uːn treː as vad 'hiːn gen di, as ulˊə sˊaːx əhoːx erə klag 'moːri van 'muk egə dorəs də 'gedn ən 'brekfəs ek niːsˊ. esˊ ved 'goːil ə vrekfəs as vad ko 'brekfəs egə 'muk əs sˊaːn pot, as va piːs aːs ə 'pot as van 'muk 'giː aːsə as vad 'sˊen goːil ən brekfəs ok, as vai tˊsˊit də hulˊə 'moːri, hulˊə dˊe'neːə as tˊsˊet də 'gedn e 'sˊiberek, aːs van sˊaːn 'ven uːn, ha 'rau ən 'dunˊə uːn ən leː sˊen edə, van tˊsˊaːn 'ven uːn as van 'muk gedn in dˊe'neːrek as van tˊsˊaːn 'vedn gedn ə dˊə'neːrek. kweː rin tˊsˊit dəsə dorəs əsə 'saːgət, feː ved 'goːil saːgət 'kwaltərax risˊ, son vi son 'loːrt gilkˊ as prə'dˊeːl gilkˊ 'niːsˊ, as renˊ e tˊsˊit 'sˊtˊaːx as ren ən sˊaːn 'ven greː dəsə 'saːgət - sai 'sˊiːs. - ha 'dˊin mi sei sˊiːs me'teː. - ked ta dˊenu 'oːrt - korə muk sˊən 'maːx hojax. - ha 'dˊen mi kərə muk 'maːx mə'teː. -wel, ha 'dˊen mi sei esˊ. -wel, imi sˊu maːx esˊ main 'dˊindˊi sˊu 'sai. - korə 'muk sˊen 'maːx hosˊax. - ha 'dˊin mi kərə muk 'maːx hosˊax. man sˊu 'laːl 'sei imi sˊu 'maːx esˊt, son ha 'dˊin mi kərə muk 'maːx, son tan muk 'fetˊsˊ en 'eːgid 'hum as ta 'sˊusˊ goːil 'eːgid 'vum, as ha 'dˊin mi kərə muk 'maːx/

Well, va'n shenn ben as shenn dooinney as v'ad baghey cooidjagh, as v'ad freayll booa, as va tree magheryn oc, as v'ad freayll y booa as muc, un muc v'ad freayll, as v'ad, ooilley y traa va'n muc gynsaght oc dy cheet stiagh dy geddyn yn vee eck dy chooilley traa. V'ad coontey cho wheesh jeh'n muc, son v'ad *fetch* yn muc stiagh dy geddyn y vee eck yn un traa as v'ad hene geddyn vee, as ooilley shiaght or hoght er y clag moghree va'n muc ec y dorrys dy geddyn yn brekfys eck neesht. Eisht v'ad goaill y vrekfys as v'ad cur brekfys ec y muc ayns shenn poht, as va peesh ass y poht, as va'n muc gee ass y poht, as v'ad shen goaill yn brekfys oc, as v'ee cheet dy chooilley moghree, [dy] chooilley jinnair as cheet dy geddyn y shibber eck, as va'n shenn ven ayn - cha row row yn dooinney ayn yn laa shen eddyr - va'n chenn ven ayn as va'n muc geddyn yn jinnair eck as va'n chenn ven gedyn y jinnair eck. Quoi ren cheet dys y dorrys agh y saggyrt, fer v'ad goaill Saggyrt Qualteragh rish, son v'eh son loayrt Gailck as preacheil Gailck neesht, as ren eh cheet stiagh as ren yn shenn ven gra dys y saggyrt, Soie sheese. - Cha jean mee soie sheese, my te. - C'red ta jannoo ort? - Cur y muc shen magh hoshiaght. - Cha jean mee cur y muc magh, my te. - Well, cha jean mee soie eisht. - Well, immee shiu magh eisht mannagh jean-jee shiu soie. - Cur y muc shen magh hoshiaght. - Cha jean mee cur y muc magh hoshiaght. - Man[nagh vel] shiu laccal soie immee shiu magh eisht, son cha jean mee cur y muc magh, son ta'n muc *fetch* yn argid hym as ta shiuish goaill argid voym, as cha jean mee cur y muc magh!

'Well, there was an old woman and an old man and they were living together, and they were keeping a cow, and they had three fields, and they used to keep a cow and a pig, one pig they were keeping, and they were, all the time the pig was taught by them to come in to get its food every time. They thought so much of the pig, for they'd fetch the pig in to get its food the same time as they themselves would get their food, and each time at seven or eight o'clock of a morning the pig was at the door to get its breakfast too. Then they'd take their breakfast and they would give breakfast to the pig in an old pot, and there was a piece out of the pot, and the pig would eat out of the pot and they would take their breakfast, and it would come every morning, every dinner (time), and would come to get its supper. And the old woman was there - the husband wasn't there that day at all - the old woman was there, and the pig was getting its dinner and the old woman was getting her dinner. Who came to the door but the parson, one they were calling Parson Qualtrough to, for he was able to speak Manx and preach (in) Manx as well, and he came in and the old woman said to the parson, - Sit down. - I'll not sit down so. - What's the matter with you? - Put that pig out first. - I'll not put the pig out so. - Well, I'll not sit then. - Well, get out then if you won't sit. - Put that pig out first. - I'll not put the pig out first. If you don't want to sit get out then, for I'll not put the pig out, for the pig fetches me money (in) and you take money from me, and I'll not put the pig out!'

FROM THE SOUTH

4. HARRY KELLY, Cregneash, Rushen
(M/III: 1807-35(1930), HLSM/I: 328-31)

[Fishing customs and practices]

/uns nəsˊedn 'laːγən ve ən slei kreial uns 'butˊsˊərax. a dˊenax beːdə erˈbiː 'gol 'maːx ən triːu beːdə da bi 'nˊaːrt ok 'er. uz boːlˊ enax veːx ad kur sˊeː nə sˊaːxtə veːdən 'mui eg kyːrt. tad kreial də dˊen 'kroːs dˊen 'bilˊə 'koːrn kur lˊesˊ luk 'maːi dədə beːdə as 'jiːstax 'fiːr 'vuːr. te 'kuːnˊaxtən ebm er sˊedn 'slei [as] bolaxad 'gˊaːrə banagən dˊen bilˊə 'koːrn. vad 'kˊoːlə ad kujax də jenu 'kroːsˊən dˊeu as vad kˊoːl ad uns 'famən ə nˊalax də freːlˊ ən 'butˊsˊərax erˈsuːl. vad treinˊə 'krau 'kolax 'kaːbəl uns də hwulˊə voːl as pəːrtə xyːrtən unsnə beːdən. viːx a 'foːs ve 'krau 'kalax; arou 'kraːu 'leːr 'veg də 'eməd. ha 'bloːs dətˊ enəm 'keːt nə radan ə 'greː er 'boːrd treː viːxu egə xydn. bala sˊin 'gilax ən 'keːt skreːbərə as ən radan seˈkoːtə. as ən red 'smadə 'fodax ad 'greː erə xyːdn 'enəm ə 'saːgərt. fodax ad gilax a 'skaːi 'paːilət. ma 'jenax feːr taxərt də 'emnə 'enəm dˊe neːnak 'sˊoː viːx a 'foːs grãmə 'piːstə 'jaːrn ədə 'fiːklən, nəkyːrtən 'smuː 'sˊeː ən poːga viːxa 'foːs 'grãmə. a reu 'lout hwislol er 'boːrd ə 'beːdə egə xyːdn. ve nəˈgilˊən 'eːgəhwislol san 'spoːrt nə 'sˊedn 'geːnˊə də 'gedən 'giːə. vad 'klˊaːxtə kur 'skedn ədə xradn gurə 'hoi-i, dəˈdˊenax 'pərt dˊe 'sˊedn jəˈsteːrən gedən 'hoːlt dˊe ən skedn as 'kˊeu a 'harisˊ 'boːrd sə xyːdn. uns 'erisˊ 'əːlən a reu ad lout də 'jenu a san vad smuːnˊax də 'dˊenax ə skˊedˊn 'kur lˊesˊ sterəm. ma 'beːx ən erisˊ stirəmax vad 'klˊaxtə 'roːbə ən 'kradn gurə 'hoːi-i gedən 'kˊuːnˊədˊ ə 'vaːrə. ma 'jenax gˊilə eːg tˊsˊənˈde: slaːdˊ ən 'xrodn tˊsˊeu 'hoːs siːs, marə ren a 'kur er ə 'naːx 'keːar mar veː 'er 'roːi treː veːn krodn 'oːdn, esˊ 'jenax ən 'sˊedn 'geːnˊə greː - kaːn redn sˊu sˊedn, təu er vilˊəˈnisˊ. mar 'teː sˊin er γreː: 'a rou 'lout də 'enmax pəːrt də emnaxən treː te sˊin egə 'xiːdn, ax te sˊin 'lout də 'emnax enəm ə dˊoul. veː 'enmən 'foːlsə erə 'naːrn 'smuː dˊe ən sˊoijax as ve də hwulˊə nẽːn 'geːbm nə emnən 'sˊedn er boːrd ə 'beːdə/

Ayns ny shenn laghyn va yn sleih credjal ayns buitcheraght. Cha jinnagh baatey erbee goll magh yn treeoo baatey dy beagh niart oc er. Ayns buill ennagh veagh ad cur shey ny shiaght dy vaatyn mooie ec keayrt. T'ad credjal dy jean crosh jeh'n billey cuirn cur lesh *luck* mie dys y baatey as eeastagh feer vooar. Ta cooinaghtyn ayn er shen sleih [as] boallagh ad giarrey banganyn jeh'n billey cuirn. V'ad kiangley ad cooidjagh dy yannoo croshyn jeu as v'ad kiangley ad ayns famman yn ollagh dy freayll yn buitcheraght ersooyl. V'ad treiney crou collagh cabbyl ayns dy chooilley voayl as paart dy cheayrtyn ayns ny baatyn. Veagh eh foarst ve crou collagh; cha row crou laair veg dy ymmyd. Cha b'loys dhyt ennym kayt ny roddan y gra er boayrd tra veagh oo ec y cheayn. Boallagh shin gyllagh yn kayt 'scraberey' as yn roddan 'sacote'. As yn red smessey foddagh ad gra er y cheayn ennym y saggyrt. Foddagh ad gyllagh eh 'sky pilot'. My yinnagh fer taghyrt dy enmey ennym jeh nane oc shoh veagh eh foarst greimey *piece* dy yiarn ayns e feeakleyn; ny keayrtyn smoo she yn poagey veagh eh foarst greimey. Cha row oo lowit whistlal er boayrd y baatey ec y cheayn. Va ny guillyn aegey whistlal son sport ny shenn geiney dy geddyn geay. V'ad cliaghtey cur skynn ayns y chroan gour-e-hoshee, dy jinnagh paart jeh shenn eeasteyryn geddyn holt jeh yn skynn as ceau eh harrish boayrd sy cheayn. Ayns earish aalin cha row ad lowit dy yannoo eh son v'ad smooinaght dy jinnagh y skynn cur lesh sterrym. My beagh yn earish sterrymagh v'ad cliaghtey rubbey yn croan gour-e-hoshee geddyn kiunid y varrey. My yinnagh guilley aeg chyndaa slatt yn chroan cheu heose sheese, mannagh ren eh cur er yn aght cair myr v'eh er roie tra va'n croan ayn, eisht yinnagh yn shenn geiney gra, - Cre'n (sic) ren shiu shen? T'ou er villey eh nish. Myr ta shin er ghra, cha row oo lowit dy enmagh paart dy enmaghyn tra ta shin ec y cheayn, agh ta shin lowit dy enmagh ennym y jouyl. Va enmyn foalsey er yn ayrn smoo jeh yn sheshaght as va dy chooilley nane geam ny enmyn shen er boayrd y baatey.

'In the old days the people believed in superstition. No boat would go out the third boat if they could help it. In some places they'd send six or seven boats out at the same time. They believe that a cross from the rowan tree brings good luck to the boat and a big catch. I remember the old people (and) they used to cut branches off the rowan tree. They'd bind them together to make crosses of them and they'd tie them in the tails of the cattle to keep the evil spirits away. They's nail a stallion's shoe everywhere and sometimes in the boats. It had to be a stallion's shoe; a mair's shoe was of no use. You dared not mention a cat or a rat by name on board when you'd be at sea. We used to call the cat *scraberey* ('scraper') and the rat *sacote*. And the worst thing they could say at sea was the name of the parson. They could call him 'Sky Pilot'. If a man happened to mention one of these by name, he'd have to grip a piece of iron in his teeth; more often it'd be the bag he'd have to grip. You weren't allowed to whistle on board the boat at sea. The young lads would whistle to rild the old men to get wind. They used to put a knife on the forward side of the mast, so that some of the old fishermen would get hold of it and throw it overboard into the sea. In fine weather they weren't allowed to do it, for they were thinking that the knife would bring a storm. If the weather was stormy they would rub the forward side of the mast to get a calm sea. If a young lad turned the mast-beam upside down, if he didn't put it right as it was before when the mast was up, the old men would then say, - Why did you do that? You have spoiled it now. As we have said, you weren't allowed to mention some names when you were at sea, but we were allowed to mention the name of the devil. The best part of the crew had nicknames (false names) and everyone used to use those names on board the boat'.

5. Mrs. SAGE KINVIG, Ronague, Arbory
(YCG/34(1953), HLSM/I: 376-77)

[Followed by the 'Moddey Dhoo'*]

/ve mi 't͡ʲit wus´ peːt d´en 'end´ə, ve mi t´et as 'ren´ mi gedən dus ko'n´eːl´ 'soloman as va 'iː 'boːiax oːn as ə 'n´iːs sal's´eːdn as 'ren´ mi t͡ʲit 'eːr as ren´ mi klas´tən rud in 'kuːl´ iməs. ren´ mi d´idn haris´ mə 'geːl´ən as, oː va 'maːdə 'duː t´et os vi t͡ʲit as t´et as va mi 'kreːl də 'rau i 'gol dus ən 'toːi erə'reːd əs 'oː d⁻enu.., as vi t͡ʲit 'eːr əs t͡ʲit ən 'kuːl´əm il´u ən 'reːd. əs va mi gidn 'aːglax as 'ren´ me 'skjau ən umbə'reləve 'em əs vi t͡ʲit 'eːr əs ren mi gidən dəs aun ə'korən dus van 'moːdə t͡ʲit kuːl´em 'il´u ən 'reːd. as van gonis´ 'riː d⁻im, oː va mi gidən 'beːrən 'hiːn də bo'geːdn wus´ kaːs´t´al poːtnə 'hins´ə t͡ʲit 'meːrəm ul´un 'reːd ve mi 'kraːl. aːs ve mi t͡ʲit 'eːr as 'ren´ mi gedn dəs 'taːiən dəhoːs´t´ərən kroŋk. aːs veː toːiən o's´en as van 'moːdə, vina fo 'reːd 'g´aunstə as g´aunstə as g´aunstə, as ven 'moːdəegə'toːi; s´en ən bə'weːn va 'mis´ kl´aːxt´ə 'faːgin´, as vi 'g´aunstə. ren´ mi go 's´iːd´əs aun´ as 'peːt´s´ 'el´əas gol 'soːs erə 'kroŋk, əs vi 'g´aunstəil´u 'reːd əs 's´en ən d´erə. ve mi 'aːglit 'aːs, və mi 'aːglit 'aːs/

Va mee cheet woish Purt ny Hinshey, va mee cheet as ren mee geddyn dys Corneil Solomon, as va oie bwaagh ayn as yn eayst soilshean. As ren mee cheet er as ren mee clashtyn red yn cooyl aym's. Ren mee jeeaghyn harrish my geaylin as, oh, va moddey dhoo cheet as v'eh cheet as v'eh cheet as cheet as va mee credjal dy row eh goll dys yn thie er y raad as, oh, jannoo.., as v'eh cheet er as cheet yn cooyl aym ooilley yn raad. As va mee geddyn agglagh as agglagh as ren mee skeouw yn *umbrella* va aym, as v'eh cheet er as ren mee geddyn dys Awin y Corran dys va'n moddey cheet cooyl aym ooilley yn raad. As va'n gollish roie jeem, ah, va mee geddyn baaryn hene dy buggane woish Cashtal Purt ny Hinshey cheet mârym ooilley yn raad, va mee credjal. As va mee cheet er as ren mee geddyn dys thieyn ta heose er yn cronk, as va thieyn aynshen as va'n moddey, v'eh fo raad gounstyr as gounstyr as gounstyr, as va'n moddey ec y thie; shen yn bwaane va mish cliaghtey fakin, as v'eh gounstyr. Ren mee goll sheese dys yn awin ayns paart elley as goll seose er y cronk, as v'eh gounstyr ooilley y raad as shen yn jerrey. Va mee agglit ass, va mee agglit ass.

'I was coming from Peel, I was coming and I got to Solomon's Corner, and it was a beautiful night and the moon was shining. And I proceeded on and I heard something behind me, I looked over my shoulder and, oh, there was a black dog coming, and it kept on coming and I was believing it was going to the house along the road, and oh, (it was) carrying on.., and it was coming on following me all the way. And I was becoming quite afraid and I cut air with the umbrella I had, but it kept coming, and I got to Awin y Corran and the dog was following mee all the way. And the sweat was running off me, ah, I was getting ? the company of a buggane (sprite) from Peel Castle as it came with me all the way, I belioeved. And I came on and I got to houses that are up on the hill. There were houses there and the dog, it started barking and kept on barking, and (then) the dog was at the house; that was the cottage I was used to seeing. It was barking. I went down to the river in another part and up on to the hill, and it was barking all the way, and that's the end. I was frightened out of my wits, I really was'.

* For details of the *Moddey Dhoo* in Manx folklore, cf. Killip (1975: 150-51).

6. NED MADDRELL, Glenchass, Rushen
(YCG/13(1953), HLSM/I: 358-60)

[Falling down the stairs]

/va mi 'rugit˅ usə kə'vaːl˅ə as 'treː va mi mus˅ 'b˅l˅en də 'eːs˅ va mi kurt l˅es˅ dəs kre'neːs˅, as oːn 'leː 'treː va mi mus˅ 'triː v˅l˅intən də 'eːs˅ va mi kər l˅es˅ 'meːris˅ mə 'vumig son də ku 's˅il˅e e t˅s˅en 'nunt d˅emə 'vumig˅, as 'va mi..., e'l˅am də 'rau mi fiːə miˈt˅s˅uːrax, as 'va mi 'gol maˈgit asa 'sem kirəd va mi d˅inu 'il˅u, as 'snau mi 'seis ne 'griːsən. treː va mi eːgə 'vulax nə 'griːsən va mi 'laːl˅ ˅foːslə ən 'dores˅ d˅e 'neːn d˅e nə 's˅imərən, as 'ren˅ mi 'koːl mə 'holt as tut mi 'siːs nə 'griːsən. van 't˅s˅en 'vedn sei egə 'budn nə 'griːsən eːr 'stoːl as 'ren˅ i klaːs˅t˅ən ən s˅idn as 'rei i gəs nə griːsən as 'kum i 'maːx e 'vrat as 'ren˅ mi tud˅əm 'oːn. as 'ren˅ i kuə l˅es˅ mi gəs mə 'vumig˅ as 'dut i, - s˅ox 'gau a. lug s˅en va mi ku 'les˅ l˅es˅ mə 'straidn˅ asə 'fuil˅ rei 'aːs gəs 'vedn 'il˅ə va d˅inu 'oːləs son də 'freːl˅ in 'ul, asa 'sem, ha nel 'kuːn˅axtən em kirəd˅ ren˅ 'taːgət 'lug s˅en, ox 'vix slei 'braiax d˅im - kirəd˅ ren˅ anti 'pai greː, as 'jinin˅ greː - s˅ox 'gau a. as ta 's˅edn in k˅ed 'kuːn˅axtin tə 'ems d˅e 'gilg, as 'ren˅ a 'taːgət uns kre'neːs˅ treː va mi mus˅ triː v˅l˅intən də 'eːs˅/

Va mee ruggit ayns y Corvalley, as tra va mee mysh blein dy eash va mee curt lesh dys Creneash, as un laa tra va mee mysh tree vleeantyn dy eash va mee curt lesh mârish my vummig son dy cur shilley er chenn naunt jeh my vummig, as va mee..., er-lhiam dy row mee feer mitchooragh, as va mee goll mygeayrt as cha 's aym c'red va mee jannoo ooilley, as snaue mee seose ny greeishyn. Tra va mee ec y vullagh ny greeishyn va mee laccal fosley yn dorrysh jeh nane jeh ny shamyryn, agh ren mee coayl my holt as tuitt mee sheese ny greeishyn. Va'n chenn ven soie ec y bun ny greeishyn er stoyll as ren ee clashtyn yn sheean as roie ee gys ny greeishyn as cum ee magh e vrat as ren mee tuittym ayn. As ren ee cur lesh mee gys my vummig as dooyrt ee, - Shoh gow eh! Lurg shen va mee curt lesh lesh my stroin as y fuill roie ass gys ven elley va jannoo oalys son dy freayll yn uill, agh cha 's aym, cha nel cooinaghtyn aym c'red ren taghyrt lurg shen, agh veagh sleih briaght jeem, - C'red ren Auntie Paaie gra? As yinnin gra, - Shoh gow eh! As ta shen yn chied cooinaghtyn t'aym's jeh Gaelg, as ren eh taghyrt ayns Creneash tra va mee mysh tree vleeantyn dy eash.

'I was born at the Corvalley, and when I was about a year old I was brought to Cregneash, and one day when I was about three years old I was taken by my mother for to visit an old aunt of my mother's. And I was..., I think I was very mischievous, and I was going around and I don't know all of what I was doing, but I crawled up the stairs. When I was at the top of the stairs I was wanting to open the door of one of the rooms, but I lost my grip and fell down the stairs. The old woman was sitting at the bottom of the stairs on a stool and she heard the noise, and she ran to the stairs and held out her apron and I fell into it. And she brought me to my mother and said, - Here, take him! After that I was taken with my nose bleeding to another woman who was making a charm for to stop the blood, but I don't know, I don't remember what happened after that, but people would ask me, - What did Auntie Paaie say? And I would say, *Shoh gow eh!* And that's the first memory I have of Manx, and that happened in Cregneash when I was about three years old'.

Index

The following idexes take their material from all five sections, with the exception of the Gaelic indexes which include material also from Marstrander's diary (Appendix A). In the sentence examples of Section 4, only the salient items relevant to the examples are included. The following parish abbreviations are used in the following indexes:

AN - Andreas, AR - Arbory, BA - Ballaugh, BN - Braddan, BR - Bride, GE - German, JU - Jurby, LE - Lezayre, LO - Lonan, MA - Maughold, MI - Michael, ML - Malew, MR - Marown, ON - Onchan, PA - Patrick, RU - Rushen, SA - Santan.

1. Language Index

Abresh Albanian 2.
Afro-Asiatic languages 1.
Alsatian 2.
Arbanassi Albanian 2.
Aromân / Vlašk 2.
Aromân / Koutsovlahiká 2.
Arvanítika Albanian 2-4, 7, 169.
Breton 2, 4, 46, 77, 79, 95, 106, 168.
Breton: Buhulien dialect of 78.
Britannic Celtic 71. See also Brittonic.
British 13.
Brittonic 77. See also Britannic Celtic.
Cacaopera 1.
Cape Breton Scottish Gaelic 1.
Chengey ny Mayrey Ellan Vannin 187.
Chiapanec 1.
Chicomuceltec 1.
Chilquimulilla Xinca 1.
Classical Manx; see under Manx.
Common Gaelic 49, 73.
Continental Celtic 1.
Cornish 4, 40, 77.
Cupeño 1.
Dibrë / Dibra Albanian 2.
Dyirbal 2, 3.
Early Manx; see under Manx.
Early Modern Irish 14.
East Sutherland Gaelic 3-5, 7, 79, 102, 116, 118, 126, 128, 130, 163, 169.

Eastern Gaelic 73.
English 5, 6, 8, 15, 16, 18-23, 25, 29, 30, 32, 34, 36, 38-41, 45, 46, 56, 57, 69, 71, 143, 144, 158, 159, 162-64, 166, 167, 170, 181.
Etruscan 1.
Gaeilg 34.
Gaelic (in Man) 50, 51, 176.
Gaelic 13, 14, 18, 19, 25, 35, 45, 71, 91.
Goidelic 3, 13, 77, 91.
Gothic 1.
Greek 18.
Gros Ventre (Montana) 1.
Guazacapan 1.
Gusi Albanian 2.
Hebrew 9.
Hittite 1.
Honduran Lenca 1.
Iberian 1.
Insular Celtic 4.
Insular Celtic languages 50, 54, 90.
Irish 2, 18, 45, 46, 48, 50, 53, 77, 91.
Italo-Albanian 3.
Ivrith 9.
Jicaque Yoro 1.
Jumaytepeque Xinca 1.
Kansas German 1.
Late Manx; see under Manx.
Latin 1, 13, 18.
Liverpool dialects (of English) 159.
Malinche-region Mexicano 1.
Màndres Albanian 2.

2. Manx Gaelic

3. Old and Middle Irish

4. Modern Irish and Scottish Gaelic

5. Welsh

6. English

7. Manx English

8. German

9. Index of Books, Journals, Newspapers

10. Subject Index

11. Index of Place-Names

12. Index of Persons, Societies, and Institutions